DAM PREIS FÜR
ARCHITEKTUR
IN DEUTSCHLAND

DAM AWARD
FOR ARCHITECTURE
IN GERMANY

2014|15

MICHAELA BUSENKELL

Innerhalb des städtebaulichen Entwicklungsgebiets der Zentralen Bahnflächen München mit vielerorts gesichtsloser Bauträgerarchitektur prägt die zweigeschossige Grundschule einen identitätsstiftenden Ort aus.

Within the context of Munich's 'Zentrale Bahnfläche' ('central railway facilities') urban development area, with its many examples of faceless property development architecture, the two-storey primary school shapes the location's sense of identity.

An der Nordfassade leuchtet kiwigrün die überdachte Laufbahn. | The covered running track on the northern façade is illuminated in kiwi green.

Es ist ein Privileg, für Kinder bauen zu dürfen. Erst wenn ein pädagogisches Konzept in inspirierende Architektur umgesetzt wird, entsteht „Schulbaukultur". Die Grundschule am Arnulfpark zeigt uns, wie kraftvoller Städtebau, eine klare Gebäudefigur und schöne Formensprache einen besonderen Ort mit hohem Wiedererkennungswert herstellen.

It is a privilege to be able to build something for children. Only when an educational concept is translated into inspiring architecture does a 'school building culture' come into being. The Grundschule am Arnulfpark (Arnulfpark primary school) shows us how strong urban design, a clear building outline and a beautiful formal language can produce a unique location with high recognition value.

Der leicht abgeknickte Haupteingang | The slightly angled main entrance

Die Südfassade ist mit rosafarbenen Holzlamellen eingehüllt. | The southern façade is clad in pink wooden panels.

DOMINIQUE GAUZIN-MÜLLER

Das Raumgefühl und damit die Beziehung zur Architektur entwickeln sich zwischen dem vierten und siebten Lebensjahr. Daher gehören Grundschulen zu den wichtigsten Bauaufgaben. An die Schule am Arnulfpark mit ihrem kleingliedrigen Maßstab werden sich die Kinder, die in diesen Lernhäusern Geborgenheit gefunden haben, sicherlich gerne erinnern.

Between the ages of three and six, human beings develop a sense of space, and with it, a relationship to architecture. This is why primary schools are among the most important architectural tasks. The school at Arnulfpark, with its small units, will surely be a cherished memory for the children who have found warmth and security in these 'houses of learning'.

Blick vom Wandelgang auf die Laufbahn | View of the track from the covered walkway

Wettrennen auf der Laufbahn | Racing on the track

PETER CACHOLA SCHMAL

Ein innovatives räumlich-organisatorisches Konzept, ausgeführt in frischer Materialität von jungen Architekten für eine der wichtigsten sozialen Bauaufgaben der Zukunft – was mehr kann man sich da wünschen?

An innovative spatial and organizational concept, realized in a fresh material form by young architects, for one of the most socially important architectural tasks of the future – what more can one wish for?

Eine der Dachterrassen zwischen den Lernhäusern | One of the roof terraces between the 'Lernhäuser'

Laubengang an der Südseite im Obergeschoss | Arcade on the upper floor of the south side

BARBARA ETTINGER-BRINCKMANN

Diese Schule, eine Grundschule, ist robust und herzerwärmend zugleich. Sie drückt Respekt und Wertschätzung aus – und ist es nicht das, was unsere Gesellschaft Kindern und Lehrern immer entgegenbringen sollte?

This school, a primary school, is robust and heart-warming at the same time. It communicates respect and appreciation – and aren't those the emotions that our society should always express toward children and their teachers?

Gang vor den Klassenzimmern; an der Wand eines der vier symbolhaften Kunstwerke, die logoartig in den Treppenhäusern und an der Außenwand der Nordfassade auftauchen. | Corridor outside the classrooms; on the wall is one of the four emblem-like works of art that appear as a motif in the staircases and on the outer wall of the northern façade.

Die Turnhalle liegt abgesenkt zwischen Wandelgang und Südfassade. | The sunken gymnasium lies between the covered walkway and the southern façade.

ULRICH MÜLLER

Neben der funktionalen Konzeption überzeugt besonders die Materialität. Sie zeigt, wie der gute alte Sichtbeton eine positive ästhetische Erfahrungswelt herstellen kann; rätselhaft konterkariert durch die rosarot lasierten Holzbalken-Lamellen an der Straßenseite.

In addition to the functional concept, the material texture is especially convincing. It demonstrates how simple exposed concrete can create a positive aesthetic realm of experience – curiously contradicted by the pink, varnished timber slats on the street side.

HESS TALHOF KUSMIERZ

GEBÄUDE | BUILDING

GRUNDSCHULE AM ARNULFPARK
MÜNCHEN

TEXT PETER CACHOLA SCHMAL

01

ARCHITEKTEN | ARCHITECTS

Leistungsphasen 1–5,
baukünstlerische Oberleitung
work phases 1–5, senior architectural
management:
Hess Talhof Kusmierz
Architekten und Stadtplaner
Thomas Hess, Johannes Talhof,
Fedor Kusmierz
Wagmüller Straße 19
80538 München | Munich
www.hot-architekten.de

Ausführung | execution
Assmann Beraten und Planen
GmbH, München | Munich

MITARBEITER | TEAM

Sarah Michels
(Projektleitung | project architect),
Veronika Seitz, Bettina Schneck,
Stephan Zirngibl

BAUHERR | CLIENT

Landeshauptstadt München,
Baureferat und Referat für Bildung
und Sport

LANDSCHAFTSARCHITEKTUR
LANDSCAPE ARCHITECTURE

OK Landschaft Andreas Kicherer
Büro für Landschaftsarchitektur,
München | Munich

TRAGWERK | STRUCTURE

Christoph Ackermann Beratendes
Ingenieurbüro für Bauwesen,
München | Munich

BAULEITUNG
SITE MANAGEMENT

Hess Talhof Kusmierz
Architekten und Stadtplaner
Assmann Beraten und
Planen GmbH

PROJEKTSTEUERUNG
PROJECT MANAGEMENT

DU Diederichs & Partner GmbH,
Puchheim

BRANDSCHUTZ
FIRE PREVENTION

Osterrieder Sobotta Schmidbauer
Ingenieurbüro für das Bauwesen,
Penzberg

HAUSTECHNIK | M & E ENGINEERS

Allwärme GmbH Beratende
Ingenieure,
München | Munich

BAUPHYSIK + AKUSTIK
BUILDING PHYSICS + ACOUSTICS

PMI P. Mutard
Ingenieurgesellschaft für
Technische Akustik,
Schall- und Wärmeschutz mbH,
Unterhaching

ELEKTROPLANUNG
ELECTRICAL SERVICES ENGINEER

Schuster Buchner Schmid
GmbH & Co. KG Ingenieurbüro
für elektrotechnische
Gebäudeplanung,
Hohenlinden

KUNST AM BAU | ART

Martin Wöhrl, München | Munich

FERTIGSTELLUNG | COMPLETION

September 2012

STANDORT | LOCATION

Helmholtzstraße 6
80636 München | Munich

FOTOS | PHOTOS

Florian Holzherr,
München | Munich
Markus Lanz, Sebastian Scheels,
Simon Scheels, The Pk.Odessa Co.
München | Munich

Lageplan | Site plan

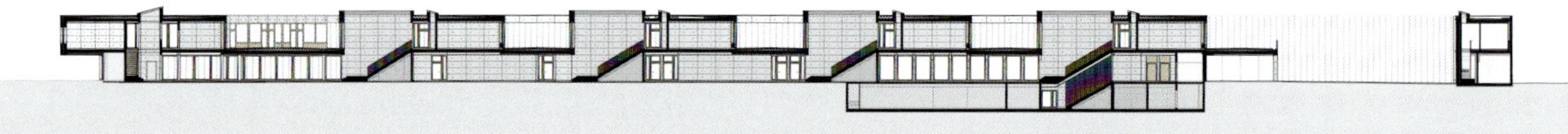

Längsschnitt | Longitudinal section

Teil der Nordfassade mit logohaftem Ausschnitt in der Wand | Detail of the northern façade with emblem-like cutout in the wall

„Das Münchner Lernhauskonzept wird derzeit an vielen Bildungs-einrichtungen und in der Öffentlichkeit diskutiert und an einigen Schulen bereits umgesetzt... Vor dem Hintergrund heterogener Lerngruppen, großer Klassen und beengter Raumverhältnisse kommt der Architektur eine besondere Bedeutung zu, um sowohl Lernenden als auch Lehrenden ein bewegtes, schülerzentriertes und handlungsorientiertes Lernen und Agieren zu ermöglichen. Ein Lernhaus versteht sich räumlich wie auch organisatorisch als eine ‚kleine Schule' innerhalb der großen Schulgemeinschaft, in der mehrere Jahrgangsstufen zusammengefasst werden."
Landeshauptstadt München, Referat für Bildung und Sport, 2014

Da entdecken die Architekten eines jungen und kaum bekannten lokalen Architekturbüros ein neues räumlich-pädagogisches Schweizer Konzept für Schulen mit einzelnen gebündelten „Gruppenhäusern" statt der üblichen Reihung von Klassen beidseits eines Ganges. Sie setzen das Konzept geschickt in einem Wettbewerb für eine neue Grundschule ein. Dank des ungewöhnlichen Ansatzes fällt der Beitrag deutlich aus dem Rahmen. Die Architekten Hess Talhof Kusmierz gewinnen 2008 den Wettbewerb und dürfen die Schule planen. Leider werden die Architekten nur bis zur Werkplanung und mit der künstlerischen Oberbauleitung beauftragt. Andere Architekten werden mittels eines VOF-Verfahrens mit der eigentlichen Ausschreibung und Realisierung betraut, ein in München übliches Verfahren. Aber die jungen Planer verteidigen ihre Ideen hartnäckig in unzähligen Bausitzungen, wenn auch ohne Bezahlung. Vier Jahre später ist die Schule fertig und entwickelt sich zu einem Erfolg. Denn inzwischen hat sich das Münchner Schulamt dieses neuartigen Schultyps angenommen und ihn räumlich deutlich ausgeweitet. Das sogenannte „Münchner Lernhauskonzept" dient künftig als Grundlage für alle neuen Schulbauten und wird sicher noch weiter von sich reden machen.

'The "Munich house-of-learning concept" is currently being discussed in many educational institutions and in public, and has already been implemented in several schools... Against the background of heterogeneous learning groups, large classes and cramped conditions, the architecture is an especially important factor in making an animated, pupil-centred and action-oriented form of learning and operating possible for both pupils and teachers. Both spatially and organizationally, a "house of learning" ("Lernhaus") can be understood as a "mini school" within the larger school community, in which several grade levels are combined.´
City of Munich, Department of Education and Sport, 2014

Here, the architects from a young and little-known architectural firm discovered a new Swiss spatial and educational concept for schools consisting of indi-vidual, compact 'group houses' instead of the usual row of classrooms along each side of a corridor. They skilfully applied this concept in a design competition for a new primary school. Thanks to their unusual approach, the entry stood out significantly from the crowd. In 2008, the architects Hess Talhof Kusmierz won the competition and were allowed to design the school. Unfortunately, the architects were only com-missioned for the artistic project management, and only as far as the construction design phase. Other architects were entrusted with the actual tendering and realization of the project via a VOF (award of professional services) procedure – a process that is common in Munich. However, the young planners stubbornly defended their ideas in countless building

„Eine besondere Bedeutung kommt im Idealfall der gemeinsamen Mitte zu. Ursprünglich ein konventioneller Flur, ist dieses Zentrum eines Lernhauses mehr als nur ein ausgeweiteter Verkehrsweg. Diese gemeinsame Mitte bietet zahlreiche Optionen für eine zeitgemäße Lernkultur. Der Marktplatz steht als erweiterte Fläche des Klassenzimmers zur Verfügung und kann für Differenzierung, Individualisierung, Gruppenarbeiten, Präsentationen oder einfach für Pausen und Entspannung genutzt werden." In der räumlichen Definition und Abgrenzung von Lernhaus und Mitte ist der wesentliche Unterschied zwischen dem neuen städtischen und dem realisierten Konzept zu sehen: Hess Talhof Kusmierz ordneten auf dem fast dreieckigen Grundstück im neuen Wohngebiet „Arnulfpark" auf dem Areal des ehemaligen Güterbahnhofs ihre vier Lernhäuser an der südlichen Grundstücksgrenze an. Somit blieb Platz für die Freiraumbereiche im Inneren des Grundstücks. Ein zweigeschossiger, geknickter Baukörper dient als Eingang von Osten. In ihm befinden sich oben die Verwaltung sowie die Lehrerzimmer und unten die Pausenhalle. Das gesamte Erdgeschoss dient den übergeordneten Funktionen wie Mehrzweckraum, Küche, Musik- und Werkräume. Außerdem liegt hier eine eingegrabene Sporthalle, die von der Straße und von einem inneren Wandelgang aus einsehbar ist. Dieser Wandelgang ist die eigentliche Mitte, und zwar der gesamten Schule und nicht eines einzelnen Lernhauses, wie im Münchener Konzept formuliert, das eine viel stärkere Abschottung der Lernhäuser vorsieht. Bei der Schule am Arnulfpark genügen sich die Lernhäuser nicht selbst, sondern sind stark in die Gemeinschaft eingebunden.

Vom Wandelgang geht der Blick hinaus auf die parallel laufende knallgrüne Tartanbahn mit der ebenso knallgrün gestrichenen Decke. Diese 50-Meter-Laufbahn wird vom Obergeschoss komplett überdacht und erlaubt somit eine Nutzung auch an nassen Tagen. Der originell gestaltete Ort ist vielleicht gerade wegen seines geschützten Charakters und der ungewöhnlichen Färbung der Lieblingsaufenthaltsort vieler Schüler.

meetings, even without remuneration. Four years later, the school was finished and it has proved to be a success. By this time, the Munich education authority had accepted this innovative school form and greatly expanded it in terms of space. The so-called 'Munich house-of-learning concept' will now serve as the basis for all new school construction and will no doubt continue to make a name for itself.

'Ideally, the shared centre space takes on a special importance. Originally a conventional corridor, in a 'Lernhaus', this centre is more than an expanded communications area. This shared centre space offers many options for a modern type of learning culture. The marketplace is available as an extended area of the classroom, and may be used for differentiation, individualized activity, group work, presentations, or simply for breaks and relaxation.'

The major difference between the new municipal concept and the one that was realized can be seen in the spatial definition between the 'Lernhaus' and the centre space: on the nearly triangular property in the new Arnulfpark residential district, on the site of an old freight terminal, Hess Talhof Kusmierz arranged their four 'houses of learning' on the southern edge of the plot, thereby leaving room for an open space in the inner section. An angled two-storey structure serves as the entrance on the east side; it contains the school office and the staff room on the upper floor, with the break hall underneath. The entire ground floor is devoted to the more important functions, such as the multi-purpose room, kitchen, music room and workshop. It also contains a sunken sports hall which is visible from the street and from a covered inner walkway. This walkway is the actual centre – not just of a single 'Lernhaus', as formulated in the Munich concept, in which the different houses are much more clearly separated – but of the entire school. At the school in Arnulfpark, the houses are not sufficient unto themselves, but strongly integrated into the whole.

From the covered walkway, the view leads outward onto the bright green Tartan running track that runs parallel to it, with its ceiling painted in an equally bright green. This 50-metre track is completely covered by the upper storey, allowing it to be used even on rainy days. Perhaps because of its sheltered character and unusual colour scheme, this creatively designed space is a favourite meeting place for many of the children.

Also branching off from the walkway are two open stairways, brightly illuminated with zenith lighting, leading up to each 'Lernhaus'. Each upper storey contains three classrooms along with two rooms for afternoon supervision, and toilets. The glass-panelled rooms open on to terraces on both sides: the classrooms toward the west, the afternoon rooms to the east. From each terrace, a prominent outdoor stairway leads directly down to the large open area, thereby serving as both a first and a second emergency escape route. This left the architects without cons-

Kunst am Bau: Jedes Lernhaus erhält ein „Logo". | Art in architecture: each 'Lernhaus' has its own 'emblem'.

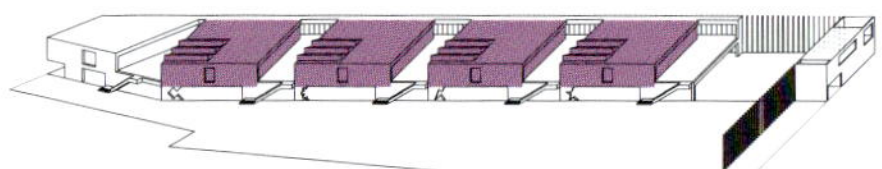

Axonometrie Lernhäuser
Axonometric drawing of the 'Lernhäuser'

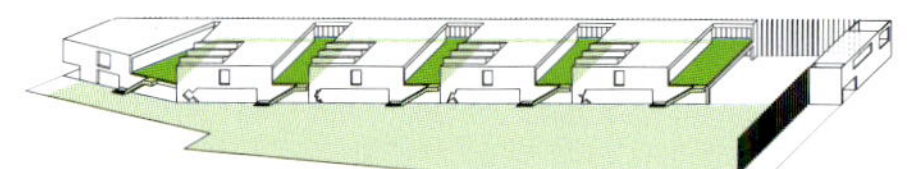

Axonometrie Terrassen
Axonometric drawing of the terraces

Grundriss Erdgeschosss | Plan of ground floor

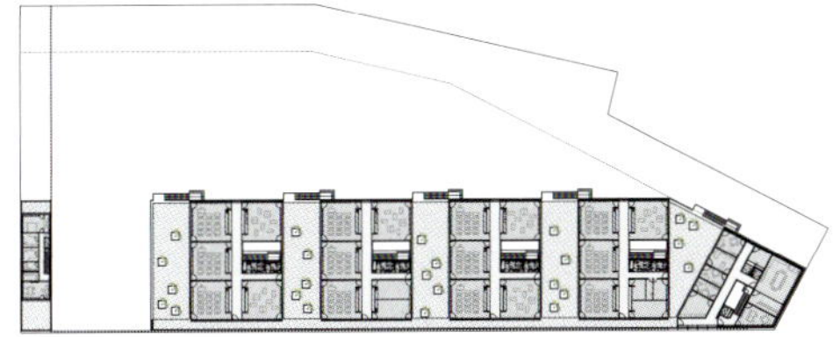

Grundriss Obergeschoss | Plan of 1st floor

Von dem Wandelgang zweigen auch die offenen und von Zenitlicht hell erleuchteten Treppenaufgänge zu den Lernhäusern ab. Im Obergeschoss befinden sich jeweils drei Klassenzimmer sowie zwei Zimmer für die Nachmittagsbetreuung und WCs. Auf beiden Seiten öffnen sich die vollverglasten Zimmer zu Terrassen; nach Westen die Schulklassen, nach Osten die Nachmittagsräume. Diese Terrassen führen über eine prägnante außen liegende Treppe direkt auf die große Freifläche und dienen somit sowohl als erster als auch als zweiter Fluchtweg. Daher konnten die Architekten den inneren Wandelgang ohne Zwänge frei gestalten. Zur Straße hin wird der lineare Bau von einem über die ganze Länge laufenden Spalier rosaroter Holzbalken begrenzt, das in deutlichem Kontrast zum leuchtenden Grün, hier als Deckenuntersicht, steht. Das westliche Ende, hinter einem offenen Ballsportplatz, wird von einem kleinen Bauwerk definiert, das nicht nur Sportgeräte sowie einen Parkplatz beherbergt, sondern im Obergeschoss auch die Hausmeisterwohnung: „4-Zi-Whg, 100 qm, Küche, Bad, 2 Terrassen, Garage, zentrale Lage, günstig". Wo findet man das schon in München?

Die Übersichtlichkeit der vier Hauseinheiten sollte ursprünglich auf die vier Grundschulklassen übertragen werden. Die Schüler wären Jahr für Jahr ein Haus weiter gezogen, daher hießen die Lernhäuser anfangs noch Jahrgangshäuser. Doch inzwischen hat sich das pädagogische Konzept verändert. Nun wird altersmäßig etwas mehr gemischt, und die Schüler wechseln nur einmal ihr Lernhaus.

Die materielle Ausführung der Architektur ist sehr reduziert und erstaunlich für Schulen, besonders für Münchner Schulen: Sichtbeton, Holz und Glas. Holzwolle-Leichtbauplatten an den Decken, Sichtbeton an den Wänden, geschliffener Estrich auf den Böden und Holz auf den Treppen. Oben in den Lernhäusern dominieren warme Materialien, wie holzverkleidete Wände und Industrieparkett. So stellen sich die Architekten eine Schule zum Aneignen durch die Schüler vor.

Vor zehn Jahren gründeten Thomas Hess (*1970) und Johannes Talhof (*1974) ihr Architekturbüro, nachdem sie beide bei Allmann Sattler Wappner gearbeitet hatten. Vier Jahre später kam Fedor Kusmierz (*1972) hinzu. Zwei weitere Bauten konnten sie bislang neben der Münchener Grundschule realisieren: den ersten Bauabschnitt eines komplexen Projekts in Marburg, bestehend aus einer ebenfalls grün leuchtenden Schulerweiterung und einer sich derzeit in der Werkplanung befindlichen Stadthalle, sowie einen strahlend orangefarbenen Wertstoffhof in München. Zahllose Wettbewerbe haben sie bereits bearbeitet. Beim Wettbewerb für das Kunstmuseum Ravensburg, dem DAM-Preisträger des Vorjahres, erhielten sie damals den 3. Preis.

Die Jury des DAM Preises unter der Leitung der letztjährigen Preisträgerin, Jórunn Ragnarsdóttir von LRO Lederer Ragnarsdóttir Oei Architekten aus Stuttgart, votierte einstimmig für die Münchener Grundschule am Arnulfpark von Hess Talhof Kusmierz als Gewinner des diesjährigen DAM Preises für Architektur in Deutschland.

traints in designing the inner walkway. On the street side, the entire length of the linear building is lined by a cordon of pink wooden columns which contrast strikingly with the bright green of the soffit. The western end of the site, behind an open field for ball games, is defined by a small structure which not only contains a space for sports equipment and a parking place, but also houses the caretaker's flat on the upper floor: '4-room flat, 100 m², kitchen, bath, 2 terraces, garage, central location, reasonably priced'. Where else can you find something like this in Munich?

The clarity of the four house units was originally intended to apply to the four primary school classes as well. Each year, the pupils would move one house along – thus, in the beginning, the houses were called 'Jahrgangshäuser' ('grade level houses'). In the meantime, however, the educational concept has changed. Classes now consist of children of a greater range of ages, and the pupils change houses only once.

The material execution of the architecture is very scaled back and remarkable for a school – particularly for a school in Munich: exposed concrete, wood and glass. There are wood-wool building slabs on the ceilings, exposed concrete on the walls, polished cement floors and wood on the staircases. Upstairs in the houses, warm materials are dominant – such as wood-panelled walls and industrial parquet flooring. This is how the architects envision a school that the pupils can embrace as their own.

Thomas Hess (b. 1970) and Johannes Talhof (b. 1974) founded their architectural firm ten years ago, after both of them had worked at Allmann Sattler Wappner. Fedor Kusmierz (b. 1972) joined the company four years later. Up to now, in addition to the Munich primary school, they have completed two other buildings: the first stage of a complex project in Marburg, consisting of another bright-green school extension and a community hall that is currently in the construction design phase; as well as a bright-orange recycling depot in Munich. They have already designed numerous competition entries. In the competition for the Kunstmuseum Ravensburg (Ravensburg Art Museum), the winner of last year's DAM Award, they came third.

The jury of the DAM Prize, chaired by last year's prizewinner, Jórunn Ragnarsdóttir of LRO Lederer Ragnarsdóttir Oei Architekten in Stuttgart, voted unanimously for the 'Grundschule am Arnulfpark' in Munich, designed by Hess Talhof Kusmierz, as the winner of this year's DAM Award for Architecture in Germany.

GRUNDSCHULE AM ARNULFPARK AUS DER SICHT DES BAUHERRN

Im neuen Stadtquartier Arnulfpark, einem Teil des städtebauli-
chen Entwicklungsgebiets „Zentrale Bahnflächen München", ist
die Schule das einzige öffentliche Gebäude. Mit seiner Lage an
der Quartierachse Marlene-Dietrich-Straße und seiner besonderen Gestaltung ist der Bau nicht nur für die Schüler des
Viertels und deren Eltern ein besonderer und wichtiger Ort.
Für das Bauvorhaben war ein Architektenwettbewerb ausgelobt
worden. Der Entwurf des Münchner Architekturbüros Hess
Talhof Kusmierz Architekten und Stadtplaner BDA wurde mit
dem ersten Preis ausgezeichnet. Das beispielhafte pädagogische
Konzept des prämierten Entwurfs wurde vom Preisgericht besonders hervorgehoben. Mit seinen vier Klassenhäusern nimmt
dieses Konzept bereits wesentliche Aspekte der sogenannten
„Lernwelten" des aktuellen pädagogischen Konzepts Münchens
vorweg. Mit der Entwurfsüberarbeitung nach dem Wettbewerb
wurde diese besondere Qualität der Planung noch weiterentwickelt, aber auch eine wirtschaftliche Optimierung erzielt.
Eine weitere Besonderheit neben den Klassenhäusern mit
ihren zugeordneten Dachterrassen ist die Anordnung der Lauf-
bahn unter den auskragenden Bereichen des Obergeschosses.
Eine ungewöhnliche, aber sehr funktionelle Lösung mit hoher
Aufenthaltsqualität. Das Zusammenspiel der Materialien
Beton und Holz prägt das Erscheinungsbild innen wie außen.
Buchenparkett und Lärchenholzfenster ergänzen mit ihren
warmen Farbtönen den Sichtbeton der Wände. Für farbige
Akzente sorgen grüne Deckenplatten und Fliesen.
Das Kunst-am-Bau-Projekt von Martin Wöhrl reagiert auf
die bestimmende architektonische Gliederung und stattet die
Treppenaufgänge der vier Klassenhäuser mit unterschiedli-
chen „Wahrzeichen" aus. Die Elemente Wasser – Erde – Luft
– Feuer finden darüber hinaus noch eine Erweiterung in der
skulpturhaften Formung der großen, tragenden Betonstützen
der Außenwand zum Pausenhof.

Johannes Gleissner, Projektleiter des Bauherrn
Landeshauptstadt München | Referat für Bildung und Sport, Baureferat

ARNULFPARK PRIMARY SCHOOL FROM THE CLIENT'S PERSPECTIVE

In the new Arnulfpark residential district, part of the
'Zentrale Bahnflächen München' ('Munich Central
Railway Facilities') urban development area, the
school is the only public building. With its location
on the district's central axis, Marlene-Dietrich-
Strasse, and its unique design, the building is an
important and special place, and not only for the
children of the district and their parents.
An architectural competition was held for the building
project, and the design by the Munich architectural
office of Hess Talhof Kusmierz Architekten und
Stadtplaner BDA was awarded first prize. The jury
particularly emphasized the exemplary educational
concept behind the winning design. With its four
classroom houses, this concept already anticipates
significant aspects of the 'Lernwelten' ('learning
worlds') that are part of Munich's current educational
concept. The design revision process that followed
the competition developed this particular quality
of the planning still further, while at the same time
achieving economic optimization.
In addition to the classroom houses with their roof
terraces, an another special feature of the school
is the position of the running track underneath the
overhanging sections of the upper storey. This is an
unusual but highly functional solution which creates
a high-quality space for children to spend their time.
The material interplay of concrete and wood charac-
terizes the school's appearance both inside and out.
With their warm colours, the beech parquet floors
and larchwood windows complement the exposed
concrete walls. Green ceiling panels and tiling
provide colourful accents.
Martin Wöhrl's Kunst am Bau (art in architecture)
project picks up on the defining architectural
structure, endowing each of the staircases leading
to the four classroom houses with a different
'emblem'. The element motifs of water–earth–air–
fire are carried over further in the sculptural forms
of the large concrete supporting columns on the
outside wall facing the schoolyard.

Johannes Gleissner, Client project manager
Munich City Council | Department of Education and Sports,
Building Authority

**Im Wandelgang auf Augenhöhe mit
der Lehrerin |** At eye level with the
teacher in the covered walkway

DEUTSCHES ARCHITEKTUR JAHRBUCH

GERMAN ARCHITECTURE ANNUAL

2014|15

DEUTSCHES ARCHITEKTURMUSEUM FRANKFURT AM MAIN

PRESTEL VERLAG MÜNCHEN | LONDON | NEW YORK

VORWORT | FOREWORD

YORCK FÖRSTER, CHRISTINA GRÄWE, PETER CACHOLA SCHMAL

Das Interesse des Lesepublikums am Deutschen Architektur Jahrbuch reißt nicht ab. Die Attraktivität dieses nun bereits zum 32. Mal erschienenen Buchs liegt wohl darin begründet, dass es jährlich aufs Neue einen sorgfältig recherchierten und ausgesuchten Querschnitt hochwertiger Bauten in Deutschland vorstellt. Diese Konstante eint die wechselnden Herausgeber der Publikation. Optisch hat sich das Deutsche Architektur Jahrbuch im Lauf der Jahrzehnte immer wieder gewandelt. Inhaltlich wurde es seit 2007 stark erweitert und die gesamte Auswahl der Bauten durch den neu geschaffenen DAM Preis für Architektur in Deutschland untermauert. „Die besten Bauten in/aus Deutschland", so der Titel der begleitenden Ausstellung, unterstreicht diesen selbstgestellten Anspruch und beinhaltet wie auch das Buch eine kleine, feine Auswahl von Bauten deutscher Architekten im Ausland. Der Preis ist undotiert, aber Preisträger wie Diener & Diener (2011) oder Lederer Ragnarsdóttir Oei (2013) betonen seine Wichtigkeit und die Ehre, die es für sie bedeute, diese Auszeichnung erhalten zu haben. Wie die Auswahl der nominierten Gebäude eines Jahrgangs, erfolgt auch die Wahl des jeweiligen Preisträgers mit Bedacht: Über beides entscheidet eine Jury aus berufenen Experten. Die Gebäude, die dieses Gremium auswählt, werden schließlich von unabhängigen, professionellen Autoren aufgesucht und für das Buch besprochen – darin sehen wir einen weiteren Grund für die Qualität dieses alljährlichen Architektur-Überblicks.

So geschehen auch im hier vorliegenden Buch, das wie üblich mit einem Beitrag über den Gewinner des DAM Preises für Architektur in Deutschland eingeleitet wird. In den letzten Jahren waren auffallend viele Museumsbauten unter den ausgezeichneten Gebäuden. 2014 hat sich die Jury einhellig für die Grundschule am Arnulfpark in München von den ortsansässigen Architekten Hess/Talhof/Kusmierz begeistert. Die Schule bereichert ein neu entstehendes Wohngebiet auf einem ehemaligen Bahngelände. Sie ist ein herausragendes Beispiel für die Umsetzung neuer lernpädagogischer Konzepte in Architektur, denn hier werden nicht einfach Klassen- und Fachräume aneinandergereiht, sondern eigenständige „Lernhäuser" zu einem Komplex zusammengefasst und von attraktiven Freiräumen gerahmt. Das schafft eine hohe räumliche und durch die klare und zugleich liebevolle Ausstattung auch eine atmosphärische Qualität.

The reading public's interest in the German Architecture Annual never wanes. The attractiveness of this book, which is now being published for the 32nd time, may perhaps lie in the fact that every year, it once again presents a carefully researched and selected cross-section of high-quality building projects in Germany. It is this constant that unites the changing editors of the publication. Over the years, the look of the German Architecture Annual has changed again and again. Since 2007, its content has been greatly expanded, and the complete selection of buildings has been reinforced by the newly-created DAM Award for Architecture in Germany. 'The Best Buildings in/from Germany' is the title of the accompanying exhibition, which underscores this self-imposed standard and, like the book, includes a small but exquisite selection of buildings created by German architects outside the country's borders. The prize carries no monetary reward; nevertheless, recipients such as Diener & Diener (2011) or Lederer Ragnarsdóttir Oei (2013) have emphasized its importance and the honour that it signifies for them to have received it. Like the selection of each year's nominated buildings, the choice of that year's winner is carefully considered: both are decided by a jury of qualified experts. Finally, the buildings that they select are visited and reviewed for the book by independent professional authors: this, we believe, is a further explanation for the high quality of this annual architecture review. This was also the case in the current book, which, as usual, begins with a report on the winner of the DAM Award for Architecture in Germany. In recent years, the award-winning selections have included a conspicuously large number of museum buildings. In 2014, the jury was unanimously impressed by the Grundschule am Arnulfpark (Arnulfpark Primary School) in Munich, designed by the local architects Hess/Talhof/Kusmierz. The school is a rich addition to a new residential district located on a former railway yard. It is an outstanding example of the application of a new educational concept in architectural form: here, classrooms and subject rooms are not simply lined up side by side. Instead, independent 'Lernhäuser' ('houses of learning') are combined into a single complex and framed by attractive outdoor spaces. Combined with the clear yet lovingly designed furnishings, the result is an excellent spatial and atmospheric quality.

ESSAYS AND ARCHITECTURAL EXPORTS

The Annual compiles examples of sophisticated construction. One method for ensuring that such examples actually come into being is to

ESSAYS UND ARCHITEKTUREXPORT

Das Jahrbuch versammelt Beispiele anspruchsvollen Bauens.
Ein Instrument dafür, dass sie überhaupt entstehen, sind
Wettbewerbe. Wenn auch über das Wettbewerbswesen viel
gestritten und transparentere Verfahren gefordert werden und
man sich bei den Entscheidungen mehr Mut zu jungen, unbe-
kannteren Büros neben den „üblichen Verdächtigen" wünscht:
Manche Länder beneiden Deutschland um das relativ ausge-
prägte Wettbewerbswesen. Einer der es klug und erfolgreich
in der Rolle der öffentlichen Hand einsetzt, ist Bürgermeister
Alexander Wetzig, der im Ulmer Rathaus den Fachbereich
„Stadtentwicklung, Bau und Umwelt" leitet. Er beschreibt im
inlandsbezogenen Essay Verfahren und Ergebnisse.
In den auslandsbezogenen Essays der letzten Jahre haben die
Autoren häufig den Blick nach Osten gerichtet, darunter nach
China, Vietnam und Georgien. Dieses Mal hat der Münchner
Architekturjournalist und langjährige Chefredakteur des
„Baumeister", Wolfgang Bachmann, nach Westen geschaut
und sich mit Stefan Behnisch über dessen äußerst erfolgreiche
Arbeit in den USA unterhalten. Den Anlass dazu bot das
jüngste Projekt des Büros, das John and Frances Angelos Law
Center in Baltimore, das ebenfalls im Buch vorgestellt wird. Bei
der Arbeit deutscher Architekten im Ausland bleibt die Auseinandersetzung, ob es ein „gutes Bauen" in demokratischen
Ländern und ein „böses Bauen" in etlichen anderen Staaten
gibt, nicht aus. Deshalb haben wir ergänzend Eckhard Gerber,
den Gründer des international operierenden Büros Gerber
Architekten und in der Auswahl mit der King Fahad Nationalbibliothek in Riad vertreten, gebeten, seine Haltung dazu und
seine Erfahrungen zu schildern.
Vorweggenommen sei an dieser Stelle noch das dritte
Auslandsprojekt in diesem Jahrbuch genannt: Aus China ist
diesmal von keinem Großprojekt, sondern von einem intimen
Ensemble zu berichten. In einem Künstlerdorf nahe Beijing hat
Erhard An-He Kinzelbach zwei Atelierhäuser als Symbiose aus
traditionellem und modernem Bauen entworfen.

DIE JURY DES JAHRBUCHS

Ende Januar 2014 traf sich die bereits erwähnte Jury im Deutschen Architekturmuseum in Frankfurt am Main, um aus rund
hold competitions. Even though there is a great deal of debate about
the concept of competitions, and more transparent practices are called
for – and although one could wish that decision-makers would take
more risks with young, lesser-known firms in addition to the 'usual
suspects' – many countries are envious of Germany for its relatively
widespread use of competitions. One person who has cleverly and successfully applied it in the role of a public authority is Alexander Wetzig,
who heads the department of Urban Development, Construction and
Environment in Ulm. He describes competition methods and results in
his essay on domestic architectural trends.
In recent years, the essays on international architecture have frequently turned their attention toward the east – for example, toward China,
Vietnam and Georgia. This time, the Munich architectural journalist
and long-time editor-in-chief of the journal 'Baumeister', Wolfgang
Bachmann, looked toward the west, speaking with Stefan Behnisch
about his highly successful work in the USA. The opportunity for this
came with the firm's most recent project, the John and Frances Angelos Law Center in Baltimore, which is also profiled in this book. In
the case of German architects working outside their own country, the
debate over whether there is such a thing as 'good construction' in
democratic countries and 'bad construction' in many other nations is
unavoidable. Therefore, we have also asked Eckhard Gerber, founder of
the internationally operating company Gerber Architekten – which is
also represented in our selection with the King Fahd National Library in
Riyadh – to share his opinion and experiences on this subject.
At this point, we must also mention the third international project featured in this Annual: coming from China, this time our report is not on
a large-scale project but on an intimate ensemble. In an artists' village
outside of Beijing, Erhard An-He Kinzelbach has designed two studio
houses as a symbiosis of traditional and modern building forms.

THE JURY OF THE
GERMAN ARCHITECTURE ANNUAL

In late January 2014, the aforementioned jury met at the Deutsches
Architekturmuseum in Frankfurt am Main in order to make their selection for the German Architecture Annual 2014/15 from approximately
100 nominated building projects. Chairing the jury was last year's
award winner, Jórunn Ragnarsdóttir from the Stuttgart office of Lederer
Ragnarsdóttir Oei. Other members of the jury were architect and
president of the Bundesarchitektenkammer (German Federal Chamber

100 nominierten Bauten die Auswahl für das Deutsche Architektur Jahrbuch 2014/15 zu treffen. Vorsitzende war die letztjährige Preisträgerin Jórunn Ragnarsdóttir aus dem Stuttgarter Büro Lederer Ragnarsdóttir Oei. Außerdem waren die Architektin und Präsidentin der Bundesarchitektenkammer, Barbara Ettinger-Brinckmann, die Münchner Fachjournalistin und Kuratorin Michaela Busenkell, die Chefradakteurin der französischen Architekturzeitschrift „écologiK", Dominique Gauzin-Müller aus Stuttgart und der Leiter der Architektur Galerie Berlin, Ulrich Müller, im Preisgericht vertreten. Aus dem DAM waren sein Direktor Peter Cachola Schmal sowie die Kuratoren Christina Budde und Oliver Elser beteiligt. Die Jury wurde von den Mitherausgebern des diesjährigen Deutschen Architektur Jahrbuchs, Yorck Förster und Christina Gräwe, vervollständigt. Während der zweitägigen Sitzung gab es intensive Gespräche, die mitunter in kontroversen Debatten mündeten, wie über das Landesarchiv NRW in Duisburg von Ortner&Ortner Baukunst und das Berliner Museum für Architekturzeichnung von SPEECH, Sergei Tchoban und Sergey Kusnetzov. Teilweise verlief die Entscheidungsfindung auch sehr übereinstimmend, wie im Fall des Preisträger-Gebäudes.

ARCHITEKTUR IN DEUTSCHLAND

Auffallend an der diesjährigen Auswahl ist eine größere Anzahl von Kleinoden, weshalb die Jury entschied, die Gesamtanzahl der besprochenen Gebäude auf 24 auszuweiten. Dazu gehören die Archäologische Vitrine, ein Hauch von einem Pavillon von kadawittfeldarchitektur in Aachen und ein Wirtschaftsgebäude mit dem bezeichnenden Namen „Hangar XS" von Ecker Architekten in Buchen. Außerdem das Werkhaus Schütze von Thomas Kröger, ein kombiniertes Werkstatt- und Wohngebäude in der Uckermark, das Teile einer alten LPG-Schlosserei intergiert, sowie ein schlankes, hölzernes Gemeinschaftshaus im oberfränkischen Selb von Beer Architektur Städtebau. Mit der auf einer Tiefgaragenrampe entstandenen Erweiterung des Clubs „Hotel Shanghai" in Essen ist in diesem Jahr ausnahmsweise eine reine Innenraumplanung Teil der Auswahl.

Auch die anderen Gebäude bilden ein breites Nutzungsspektrum ab. Von Staab Architekten ist das Kunstmuseum Ahrenshoop,

of Architects), Barbara Ettinger-Brinckmann; Munich-based architectural journalist and curator Michaela Busenkell; the editor-in-chief of the French architecture magazine 'écologiK', Dominique Gauzin-Müller from Stuttgart; and the director of the Architektur Galerie Berlin, Ulrich Müller. Representing the DAM were its director, Peter Cachola Schmal and curators Christina Budde and Oliver Elser. The co-editors of this year's German Architecture Annual, Yorck Förster and Christina Gräwe, completed the jury. The two-day session included intensive discussions, some of which evolved into heated debates – such as those concerning the North Rhine-Westphalia State Archive in Duisburg designed by Ortner&Ortner Baukunst and the Berlin Museum für Architekturzeichnung (Museum of Architectural Drawing) by SPEECH, Sergei Tchoban and Sergey Kusnetzov. In some cases, however, the decision-making process was quite unanimous, as in the case of the prize-winning building.

ARCHITECTURE IN GERMANY

This year's selection is notable for its larger number of little gems – which are the reason why the jury decided to expand the overall number of buildings profiled to 24. Among these are the Archaeological Vitrine, a soupçon of a pavilion, designed by kadawittfeldarchitektur in Aachen, and a service building with the descriptive name 'Hangar XS' by Ecker Architekten in Buchen. There is also the Werkhaus Schütze by Thomas Kröger, a combination workshop and house in the Uckermark region, which integrates sections of an old collective-farm locksmith's shop, as well as a lean wooden community centre in the Upper Franconian town of Selb, designed by Beer Architektur Städtebau. By way of exception, this year's selection also includes a pure interior design project with the extension of the 'Hotel Shanghai' club in Essen, which was built on top of a parking garage entrance ramp.

The other profiled buildings also represent a broad spectrum of uses. From Staab Architekten comes the Kunstmuseum (Art Museum) Ahrenshoop, an abstraction of the area's typical thatched-roof houses in the form of an integrated ensemble of five cuboids. Another museum, the half-buried Archäopark (Archaeological Park) in the Swabian Alb, designed by Ritter Jokisch Architekten on the site of an archaeological excavation site, contains the (probably) oldest-known works of art made by human beings. The subject of dwelling places is represented in very contemporary fashion by two Berlin building group houses: the 'Elf Freunde', a row of townhouses designed by AFF Architekten, and

eine Abstraktion des ortstypischen Reetdach-Hauses als zusammengewachsenes Ensemble aus fünf Kuben vertreten. Ein weiteres Museum, der halb eingegrabene Archäopark auf der schwäbischen Alb von Ritter Jokisch Architekten am Ort einer archäologischen Grabungsstelle, birgt die wohl ältesten Kunstwerke der Menschheit. Das Thema Wohnen wird sehr zeittypisch von zwei Berliner Baugruppen-Häusern vertreten: den „Elf Freunden", einer Aneinanderreihung von Stadthäusern von AFF Architekten und dem R50, einem Haus, bei dem die Bauherren den Gemeinschaftsgedanken in den Mittelpunkt der Planung gestellt haben. Entworfen und realisiert hat es die Planungsgemeinschaft ifau, Jesko Fezer und HEIDE & VON BECKERATH. Ein strahlend weißes, sorgfältig in die kleinteilige Stadtstruktur eingefügtes Doppelhaus namens „Duett" mit dauerhaft bewohnten und Ferienapartments ist in Warnemünde nach Plänen von Löser Lott Architekten entstanden. Auch zwei Forschungsgebäude sind diesmal dabei: Glass Kramer Löbbert haben zusammen mit Uta Graff für das Institut für Luft- und Raumfahrtmedizin des DLR auf deren Kölner Campus das :envihab entwickelt, ein Gebäude wie eine schwebende weiße Scheibe, in dem Extremsituationen für Astronauten simuliert werden. In Garching bei München wurde von Auer Weber das Hauptquartier der ESO, der Europäischen Südsternwarte, erweitert. Der Neubau reagiert mit seiner Kreisform auf das bereits 1980 vollendete Gebäude von Fehling Gogel.

In und bei Frankfurt am Main sind in jüngster Zeit gleich zwei Brücken entstanden, die die Jury überzeugt haben, nämlich die kleine elegant geschwungene Ölhafenbrücke von schneider+schumacher und die Doppelbrücke aus sanierter Honsellbrücke und neuer Osthafenbrücke von Ferdinand Heide. Dem bayerischen Wettstetten haben Bembé Dellinger eine neue Ortsmitte gegeben: Hier sind regionaltypisch und zeitgemäß zugleich ein Verwaltungs- und ein Gemeinschaftsbau sowie eine Tageseinrichtung für Kinder und Senioren entstanden. Die Kombination aus ortstypischen Elementen, eigener Handschrift und flexibler Nutzung ist Florian Nagler mit dem Kunst + Kongress Forum, einem lange schon benötigten Versammlungsort in Altötting, beeindruckend gelungen. Auch als Treffpunkt, hier im universitären Bereich, dient die

the R50, a house in which the clients made the idea of community the central focus of their planning. It was designed and realized by the ifau planning group, Jesko Fezer and HEIDE & VON BECKERATH. A brilliant white pair of semi-detached houses called 'Duett', containing permanently occupied flats as well as holiday apartments, was built in Warnemünde – and carefully integrated into the small-scale structure of the town – according to plans by Löser Lott Architekten. Two research facilities also appear in this year's selection: together with Uta Graff, Glass Kramer Löbbert developed the :envihab for the German Aerospace Center's Institute of Aerospace Medicine on its Cologne campus – a building that resembles a floating white disk, in which extreme situations are simulated for astronaut training. In Garching, near Munich, Auer Weber expanded the headquarters of the ESO, the European Southern Observatory. With its circular form, the new addition draws on the concept of the building completed by Fehling Gogel in 1980. In and around Frankfurt am Main, two bridges have recently been erected which won the jury over: namely, the small, elegantly curving Ölhafenbrücke (Oil Terminal Bridge) by schneider+schumacher and the bridge ensemble that includes the renovated Honsell Bridge and the new Osthafen Bridge, designed by Ferdinand Heide. Bembé Dellinger provided a new centre for the Bavarian town of Wettstetten, building an office block and a community centre as well as a children's and old people's day centre, all of which are contemporary in style while remaining consistent with the typical regional architecture. Florian Nagler's Kunst + Kongress Forum (Art and Conference Forum), a long-needed congress venue in Altötting, is a strikingly successful combination of typical regional elements, flexibility of usage and the architect's own signature. Serving as another meeting place – this time in a university context – is the addition to the student refectory in Kassel, where augustinundfrank consciously broke away from the stylistic mix of the neighbouring buildings with a steel grid framework.

For the DAM, 2014 marks the 30th anniversary of the house on Schaumainkai, which was inaugurated on 1 June 1984. In honour of the museum's founding director, the exhibition 'Mission: Postmodern. Heinrich Klotz und die Wunderkammer DAM' ('Heinrich Klotz and the DAM's Chamber of Wonders') was devoted to the origins of the museum's own collection. Many of the former protagonists were invited to speak at a conference on the actual anniversary. Tape recordings of Heinrich Klotz were published in an extensive special issue along with the architecture magazine Arch+.

Erweiterung der Mensa in Kassel, wo augustinundfrank sich
mit einer Stahl-Fachwerkkonstruktion bewusst vom Stilmix
der Nachbarbebauung absetzten.
Das Jahr 2014 markiert für das DAM den 30-jährigen Geburtstag des Hauses am Schaumainkai, das am 1. Juni 1984 eingeweiht wurde. Zu Ehren des Gründungsdirektors beschäftigte
sich die Ausstellung „Mission: Postmodern. Heinrich Klotz
und die Wunderkammer DAM" mit der Entstehung der eigenen
Sammlung und ließ in einer Tagung am eigentlichen Geburtstag
viele ehemalige Protagonisten zu Wort kommen. Die Tonband-
aufnahmen von Heinrich Klotz wurden in einer umfangreichen
Publikation, zusammen mit der Zeitschrift Arch+, veröffentlicht.
Dem Prestel Verlag (speziell Katharina Haderer und Anja
Besserer) sei erneut für sein großes Engagement gedankt,
ebenso Willfried Baatz für das Lektorat und Christian Brensing
für die Anzeigenakquise. Dank gilt auch dem gesamten Team
des DAM, besonders Constanze Becker, Jahrespraktikantin am
DAM, für ihre Assistenz bei der Jury sowie allen Architekten,
Fotografen und Autoren für die Mitwirkung bei Nominierung
und Auswahl, Publikation und Ausstellung.

Once again, we wish to express our thanks to the Prestel Verlag
(particularly Katharina Haderer und Anja Besserer) for its hard work
and commitment to this project, as well as Willfried Baatz for his
work as editor and Christian Brensing for finding advertisers. We also
thank the entire team at the German Architecture Museum, especially
Constanze Becker, one-year intern at the DAM, for her assistance to
the jury, as well as all the architects, photographers and authors for
their participation in the nomination and selection process and in the
publication and exhibition.

Das DAM zeigt seit 2008 alle Projekte des Deutschen Architektur Jahrbuchs in einer Ausstellung. Der Preisträger des DAM Preis für Architektur in Deutschland 2014, die Grundschule am Arnulfpark in München, wird wieder im „Haus im Haus" präsentiert werden.

Since 2008, the DAM has presented all the projects featured in the German Architecture Annual in an exhibition. The winner of the DAM Award for Architecture in Germany 2014, the primary school in Arnulfpark in Munich, will be displayed, like the previous winners, in the 'House within the House'.

QUO VADIS ARCHITEKTENWETTBEWERB?

QUO VADIS, ARCHITECTURAL COMPETITION?

ANMERKUNGEN ZUM NIEDERGANG EINER PLANUNGSKULTUR

NOTES ON THE DECLINE OF A PLANNING CULTURE

ALEXANDER WETZIG

E1

Das Ulmer Zentrum: die pyramidenförmige Bibliothek (G. Böhm); links Kunstsammlung Weishaupt (W. Wöhr); mittig Sparkasse;
rechts Kaufhaus Münstertor (beide S. Braunfels) | Ulm's city centre: the pyramid-shaped library (G. Böhm); left, the Kunstsammlung Weishaupt (W. Wöhr);
centre, Sparkasse; right, Kaufhaus Münstertor (both S. Braunfels)

Es wird hierzulande wieder viel von Baukultur geredet. Gut so, denn ohne eine breite Bewusstseinsbildung und die entsprechende mediale Aufmerksamkeit bewegt sich nichts auf diesem üblicherweise im Spannungsfeld zwischen ökonomischer Rationalität und architektonischem Hochglanz-Modejournalismus angesiedelten Thema. Freilich – die Zahl der Symposien, Tagungsbände, Memoranden und mahnender Appelle in den (fach-)politischen Schaufensterreden von Politikern und Funktionären sagt herzlich wenig aus über den tatsächlichen Zustand der Qualität des Planens und Bauens in unseren Städten und Gemeinden. So lobenswert (und wichtig) die administrativen Einrichtungen in obersten Landesbehörden und natürlich vorneweg die stiftungsrechtlich geadelte Bundeszentralinstanz in Sachen Baukultur in Berlin und Potsdam auch sind – Baukultur definiert sich über das Handeln und weniger über das Darüber-Reden. Hier ist weniger nach feuilletonistischen Höhenflügen in Hinblick auf architektonische Innovationen zu fragen als nach den originären Bedingungen des Bauens, denen dieser Bereich unserer gesellschaftlichen Wertschöpfung im materiellen wie immateriellen Sinne unterworfen ist. Damit begibt man sich freilich in die Niederungen des rechtlichen, ökonomischen, gesellschaftlichen und damit auch kulturellen Alltags jenseits des Feuilletons, der weitaus mehr Einfluss auf das Niveau der hier zur Debatte stehenden Kulturleistung hat, als alle baukulturellen Leuchtturmprojekte dieser Republik von der Elbphilharmonie bis zum Wiederaufbau des Berliner Stadtschlosses (!).

Baukultur hat zunächst einmal mit Planungskultur zu tun. Es bedarf darüber hinaus weiterer grundsätzlicher konstitutiver Bedingungen, nämlich einer Verantwortungskultur und einer Dialogkultur. Erst im Zusammenwirken dieser drei Faktoren kann sich das Bauen über die bloße Funktionsbefriedigung hinaus als Kulturleistung darstellen. Im Mittelpunkt steht immer die Planung des Bauwerks und gleichzeitig die Frage, wie die Qualität der Planung sichergestellt werden kann.

Seitdem diese Frage gestellt wird, lautet die Antwort darauf schlicht und einfach: über den Wettbewerb. Spätestens seit der Entfaltung des Individuums im Zeitalter der Renaissance und damit auch der Herausbildung des Architekten zu einem

Once again, there is a great deal of discussion going on about building culture in this country. This is a good thing, since without a widespread rise in awareness, and the corresponding media attention, nothing would change with regard to this subject, which is generally caught up in the tug-of-war between economic rationality and glossy architectural fashion journalism. Admittedly, the number of symposia, conference proceedings, memoranda and cautionary appeals in the (sector-specific) showcase policy speeches of politicians and functionaries says precious little about the actual state of planning and building quality in our cities and communities. As commendable (and important) as the administrative institutions of the highest state authorities are – and of course, the central federal agency dealing with architectural culture, now with the accolade of foundation ('Stiftung') status, based in Berlin and Potsdam – building culture is defined by action, and much less by talking about it. Here it is less a question of arts-page flights of fancy with regard to artistic innovation than it is of the original conditions of construction, to which this area of value creation in our society is subject – both in a material and an immaterial sense. With this, of course, we enter into the legal, economic, societal – and thus cultural – lowlands of everyday life beyond the arts pages, which have far more influence on the quality of the cultural achievements being debated here than all the architectural flagship projects in the country, from the Elbphilharmonie to the reconstruction of the Berlin City Palace (!).

First of all, building culture has to do with planning culture. Furthermore, it requires additional constitutive conditions: namely, a culture of responsibility and a culture of dialogue. Only with the interaction of these three factors can building be represented as a cultural achievement above and beyond mere functionality. The central focus is always on the planning of the structure and, at the same time, on the question of how the quality of that planning can be ensured.

Ever since this question was first posed, the answer has been quite simply: through a competition. Beginning at the latest with the unfolding of the individual in the Renaissance era – and hand in hand with this, the emergence of the architect as an independent artist – the idea of a planning competition has been established as an obvious method for obtaining the best possible solution. The history of architecture is brimming with fascinating stories of such competitions and of the wrangling for particular palms of victory.

Zentralbibliothek Ulm (Gottfried Böhm) | Central Library Ulm (Gottfried Böhm)

Rechts: Kaufhaus Münstertor, links Sparkasse (beide Stephan Braunfels)
Right: Kaufhaus Münstertor; left: Sparkasse (both Stephan Braunfels)

selbständigen Künstler hat sich der Planungswettbewerb als selbstverständliche Methode zur Erlangung der besten Lösung etabliert. Die Baugeschichte ist übervoll von spannenden Geschichten um solche Wettbewerbe und dem Ringen um die jeweilige Siegespalme.

An diesem Grundprinzip hat sich bis heute im Kern nichts geändert. Außer, dass das Prinzip „Wettbewerb" in schöne ausgefeilte Verfahrensregelwerke formatiert wurde, von den früheren „Grundsätzen und Richtlinien für Wettbewerbe (GRW)" bis hin zu den aktuellen „Richtlinien für Planungswettbewerbe (RPW)" des Bundesbauministers. Wo kämen wir auch ohne Regelwerke hin! Da könnte ja jeder machen was er wollte! Sei´s drum: Um die Kritik an diesem Verfahrenskorsett soll es hier nicht gehen, denn darüber haben Wettbewerbsakteure immer schon ebenso ausdauernd wie vergeblich gelästert. Es geht an dieser Stelle um das, was sich in den letzten Jahren von einer breiteren, davon aber erheblich betroffenen Öffentlichkeit ziemlich unbemerkt als Zwangsjacke über das Wettbewerbswesen gestülpt hat: das Vergaberecht. Und es geht um die damit einhergehende Krise des Wettbewerbswesens jenseits aller schönfärberischen Statistiken und Statements der Architektenkammern. Diese Krise ist nicht nur das Resultat jenes Vergaberechtsdrachens namens „Verdingungsordnung für freiberufliche Leistungen (VOF)", sondern sie ist zu einem Gutteil hausgemacht. Mit dem neuen Vergaberecht wurde das alte Wettbewerbsprinzip konterkariert und schlimmer noch: degradiert.

Das Postulat der Krise bedarf zunächst der näheren Erläuterung. Bei einer nüchternen Standortbestimmung nach jahrzehntelanger kommunaler Verwaltungspraxis destillieren sich eine ganze Reihe ursächlicher Faktoren heraus, die nicht erst heute Wirkung entfalten, aber in ihrem Zusammenspiel mit den aktuellen Rechtszwängen ein neues „Downgrading" des Planungswettbewerbs nach sich ziehen: An erster Stelle steht ein zunehmender Bedeutungsverlust des Planungswettbewerbs selbst. War früher der Architektenwettbewerb als ein selbstständiges Instrument zur Erlangung eines bestmöglichen Entwurfs und damit zur Auswahl des dahinterstehenden Planungsbüros die Königsdisziplin des Planungs- und Auftragsvergabeverfahrens, mutierte er im System der VOF zur unterstützenden Hilfsdisziplin. Wo früher nach einer Juryentscheidung ein öffentlicher

The core of this basic principle has not changed to this day – except that the concept of a 'competition' has been formatted into complex and elaborate rules of procedure, from the former 'Grundsätze und Richtlinien für Wettbewerbe (GRW)' (Principles and Guidelines for Competitions) to the present-day 'Richtlinien für Planungswettbewerbe (RPW)' (Guidelines for Planning Competitions) issued by the Federal Ministry for Building. Where would we be without codes of procedure? Then everyone could do whatever they wanted! Be that as it may: my point here is not to criticize this corset of procedural regulations. After all, competition participants have complained about this persistently and to no avail from the very beginning. The subject here is something which has been forced on to the competition procedure like a straitjacket in recent years, more or less unnoticed by the wider but nevertheless significantly affected public: government procurement law. We are talking about the accompanying crisis in the competition system that extends beyond all the euphemistic statistics and statements by the Chambers of Architects. This crisis is not only the result of that dragon of public procurement law called the 'Verdingungsordnung für freiberufliche Leistungen (VOF)' (Contracting Regulation for the Awarding of Contracts for Professional Services); rather, it is in large part self-inflicted. With the new public procurement law, the old principle of competition was thwarted, and worse still, degraded.

The postulate of a crisis first requires further clarification. In the matter-of-fact process of selecting a location after decades of local administrative experience, a long series of causal factors can be distilled out which not only show their effects immediately, but – in combination with current legal constraints – lead to a new 'downgrading' of the planning competition. First of all we see the increasing loss of importance of the planning competition itself. While in the past, the architectural competition – as an independent instrument for obtaining the best possible design and selecting the planning firm responsible for it – was the most prestigious discipline in the process of planning and of awarding contracts, under the VOF system it has mutated into a supporting auxiliary discipline. Whereas before, following a decision by the jury, public-sector clients would make a professionally based decision from among the winners on their own responsibility, today a bureaucratic negotiation process takes place, consisting of pseudo-objective haggling over percentage points based on predefined criteria. Within this context, the jury's decision still carries the greatest weight; however, other criteria such as remuneration,

Münsterplatz Ulm, unterhalb des Münsters das Stadthaus (Richard Meier) | Münsterplatz, Ulm: beneath the minster is the Stadthaus (Richard Meier).

Kundencenter Stadtwerke Ulm (Michelgroup) | Kundencenter Stadtwerke Ulm [public utilities service centre] (Michelgroup)

Auftraggeber unter den Preisträgern eine fachlich fundierte Entscheidung in eigener Verantwortung traf, tritt heute an diese Stelle in bürokratisch abgehandelten Verhandlungsverfahren ein pseudoobjektives Prozentpunktegeschacher um vordefinierte Beurteilungskriterien. Innerhalb dessen hat zwar die Juryentscheidung noch das größte Gewicht, aber andere Kriterien wie Honorarangebot, Büroerfahrung oder die „Performance" der Bewerber spielen durchaus eine große Rolle und können sich im Einzelfall durchsetzen. Wo früher das Abweichen eines Auftraggebers vom ersten Preis der Juryempfehlung argumentativ eine schwer zu bewältigende Herausforderung war, werden jetzt im anschließenden Verhandlungsverfahren die Vergabekarten neu gemischt und in einem Rechenexempel neu verteilt.

Damit einher geht eine steigende Dominanz des Verfahrensrechts und seiner Regelungen innerhalb der Auswahlentscheidungen zu Planung und Auftragsvergabe. Waren schon die früheren reinen Wettbewerbsregelwerke der GRW und der aktuellen RPW nicht gerade von biblischer Klarheit, so konnten sie dennoch von jeder halbwegs ordentlich aufgestellten Bauverwaltung selbst angewendet werden. Inzwischen bedarf es externer Verfahrensspezialisten, weil die komplexen Vorschriften der Verdingungsordnung weder überschaubar sind noch in ihrer Verrechtlichung sicher umgesetzt werden können. Die rechtssichere Abwicklung des Verfahrens drängt die inhaltliche Auseinandersetzung um die Lösung der gestellten Planungsaufgabe in den Hintergrund!

Die Wettbewerbsverfahren werden zunehmend komplizierter, und europäisches sowie deutsches Vergaberecht lassen wenig Spielraum. Was waren das noch für paradiesische Zeiten, als auf die Bedeutung der Planungsaufgabe hin maßgeschneiderte örtliche bis überregionale/bundesweite Zulassungsbereiche für Wettbewerbsteilnehmer definiert werden konnten! Heute ergeht pro forma eine EU-weite Einladung als vorausgeschaltetes Bewerberverfahren, um anschließend die Lostrommel für die Teilnehmerauswahl zu bemühen. Der örtliche Architekt, der sich dem Wettbewerb um die beste Lösung für seine Heimatstadt stellen möchte, hat da kaum eine Chance – es sei denn, es wird ein grundsätzlich offener Wettbewerb durchgeführt, was aus Aufwandsgründen seitens der Auslober immer seltener der

the office's experience, or the 'performance' of the candidates certainly play a large role, and in some individual cases may prevail. While in the past, a client's rejection of the jury's recommended prizewinner was a challenge that was hard to meet through argument, nowadays, a subsequent negotiation process takes place in which the prizewinning cards are reshuffled and re-dealt using simple arithmetic.

This is accompanied by a growing dominance of procedural law and its provisions within the selection decisions for planning and awarding contracts. While by themselves, the rules of procedure for competitions set by the GRW in the past and by the current RPW were not exactly clear as gospel truth, nevertheless, any half-decently organized building authority was capable of applying them. Nowadays, external specialists are required, because the complex regulations of the VOF are neither easily comprehensible, nor does their juridification permit them to be safely implemented. The legally secure handling of the process is pushing substantive discussions about the solution of the given planning task into the background.

Competition processes are becoming increasingly complicated, and European as well as German public procurement law leaves little room for manoeuvring. Wasn't it wonderful in the old days, when it was possible to define, tailor-made, the qualifications required for competition participants – from local to supra-regional or nationwide! Today, an EU-wide invitation is issued pro forma as an advance application method, prior to spinning the lottery wheel to select the participants. The local architect, who would like to present the competition with the best solution for his or her home city, has scarcely any chance – unless, of course, a completely open competition is held, which, owing to the effort and expense required on the part of the awarding authorities, is becoming increasingly rare. Certainly, competition organizers themselves are in large part to blame for this state of affairs: planning competitions degenerate into wars of attrition whose expense is completely out of proportion to the actual task at hand. Exuberant over-regulation on the part of the rule-makers – and organizers' unrealistic expectations regarding the scope of the services required – result in a workload for both the organizers and the participants which is not only unnecessary, but does nothing to contribute to the actual task. This begins with requests for tender that run to the length of a fair-sized book (not forgetting the lovingly sketched outline of the history city in question), and continues with the perfectionist graveyards of data from preliminary exami-

Links: Sparkasse (Stephan Braunfels), Mitte rechts Museumsgesellschaft Ulm (Schaudt, Rogg) | Left: Sparkasse (Stephan Braunfels); centre right, Museumsgesellschaft Ulm (Schaudt, Rogg)

Kunstsammlung Weishaupt (Wolfram Wöhr, WWA) | Kunstsammlung Weishaupt (Wolfram Wöhr, WWA)

Fall ist. Freilich sind die Wettbewerbsverantwortlichen zu einem guten Teil selber schuld an diesem Zustand: Planungswettbewerbe degenerieren zu Materialschlachten, deren Aufwand in keinem Verhältnis mehr zur eigentlichen Aufgabenstellung steht. Überbordende Regelungswut der Richtlinienurheber und überzogene Erwartungen der Auslober an den geforderten Leistungsumfang führen sowohl bei den Auslobern als auch den Teilnehmern zu einem unnötigen und die eigentliche Aufgabenstellung nicht erhellenden Arbeitsaufwand. Das beginnt mit Auslobungstexten im Buchformat, die auch einen Abriss der jeweiligen Stadtgeschichte liebevoll aufführen, und setzt sich mit den perfektionistischen Datenfriedhöfen der Vorprüfungsberichte fort, die ebenfalls weniger der Klärung des grundsätzlichen Informationsbedarfes der Jury als dem rechtfertigenden Honorarnachweis des Wettbewerbsbetreuers als externem Dienstleister dienen. Ohne den geht es sowieso nicht mehr, da die kommunalen Verwaltungen aus Haushaltsgründen teilweise drastisch abgebaut wurden und jetzt das nicht vorhandene Geld lieber in doppelter Höhe extern ausgegeben wird. Die Organisation der Wettbewerbsverfahren hat sich so zu einem aufgeblasenen „Klapperatismus" verselbständigt, der nicht mehr wirklich gesteuert wird.

Damit bestätigt sich das seit eh und je seitens der Bauherren latent vorhandene Vorurteil, dass ein Planungswettbewerb zu zeitraubend und zu teuer sei. Die Abwertung und Geringschätzung des Instruments Wettbewerb schreitet so munter voran. Als Resultat dieser Entwicklung werden angesichts des Gesamtbauvolumens im Lande erschreckend wenige Wettbewerbe durchgeführt, vor allem zu wenige klassisch-offene Verfahren. Das hat sehr viel mit einer vorauseilenden Überabsicherung bei den Auslobern, sprich Bauherren zu tun. Das Sicherheitsdenken im Hinblick auf die Abwicklung der Baumaßnahme – Kosten! Zeit! Referenzen! (schon mal eine Schule gebaut?) – im Verbund mit der Scheu vor Verantwortung führt zu ausgeprägten Hemmschwellen, sowohl gegenüber dem Wettbewerb als solchem wie auch der Gestaltung des Wettbewerbsverfahrens: Risikominimierung anstelle von Ideenmaximierung.

Die „heilige Kuh" des Diskriminierungsverbots im Europarecht mündet so auf unbeabsichtigte Weise in eine neue Diskriminierung, weil nämlich junge und kleine Büros in den Wettbewerbs-

nation reports, which likewise serve not so much to clarify the basic information requirements of the jury as to justify the fee of the competition supervisor as an external service provider. Without the latter, nothing can happen at all any more, since, for budgetary reasons, many local administrations are being drastically cut back, and it is now preferable to spend twice the amount of non-existent money on external services. The organization of the competition process has taken on such an overblown and complicated life of its own that it can no longer really be controlled.

This confirms the latent prejudice which has always existed among clients: that a planning competition is too time-consuming and expensive. Thus, disdain and disparagement for the competition as a tool continue as healthily as ever. As a result of this development, a distressingly small number of competitions are being held in relation to the overall volume of construction – and too few classic open competitions in particular. This is largely due to an overabundance of caution on the part of those holding the competition – that is, the clients. This safety-first mentality with regard to the execution of the building project – Costs! Time! References! (Have you ever built a school before?) – combined with a fear of taking responsibility leads to pronounced inhibitions vis-à-vis both the competition as such and the organization of the competition process: minimizing risk instead of maximizing creativity.

In this way, the sacred cow of non-discrimination in European law is unintentionally evolving into a new form of discrimination – since now it is the younger and smaller firms which are increasingly disadvantaged in the competition award process. In the predominantly closed public competition process, they easily slip through the net of too-strictly formulated qualification criteria; and in the event that they do win a prize, they are confronted during the negotiation process with additional award criteria which – owing to their comparatively small company structures – they are unable to fulfil. The result is a 'legal protectionism' that benefits the large, well-known and market-savvy firms who know how to 'sell' themselves.

The greatest – but largely unconsidered – problem with the competition concept, however, is its lack of openness. As intensively as our mainstream society has, for many years now (and not only since Stuttgart 21), been strengthening its fundamental development toward a citizen-participation society in particular with its demand for a voice in the planning of our environment – this demand has comple-

Kunstsammlung Weishaupt (Wolfram Wöhr, WWA) | Kunstsammlung Weishaupt (Wolfram Wöhr, WWA)

Synagoge am Weinhof (kister scheithauer gross) | Synagogue at the Weinhof (kister scheithauer gross)

vergabeverfahren zunehmend benachteiligt werden. Sie fallen in den überwiegend beschränkt öffentlichen Wettbewerbsverfahren leicht durch das zu eng formulierte Sieb an Zulassungskriterien und werden im Falle eines Preisgewinns im späteren Verhandlungsverfahren mit Zuschlagskriterien konfrontiert, die sie aufgrund ihrer vergleichsweise kleinen Bürostruktur nicht erfüllen können. Die Folge ist ein „legaler Protektionismus" der großen, bekannten und am Markt erfahrenen Büros, die wissen, wie sie sich „verkaufen" müssen.

Das allergrößte, doch weithin unreflektierte Problem des Wettbewerbswesens ist jedoch sein Öffentlichkeitsdefizit. So intensiv sich im Mainstream unserer Gesellschaft seit Jahren (und nicht erst seit Stuttgart 21) die grundlegende Entwicklung hin zur Bürgergesellschaft mit dem Anspruch auf Partizipation gerade in der räumlichen Gestaltung der Umwelt auch verstärkt – am Wettbewerb und erst recht im Vergaberecht geht dieser Anspruch komplett vorbei. Daran ändert auch die selbstverständlich praktizierte breite öffentliche Ergebnisvermarktung von nichtöffentlichen Juryentscheidungen in den Medien nichts. Das Grundprinzip des Wettbewerbs- und Vergabeverfahrens ist ja seine Nicht-Öffentlichkeit! Eine wachsende bürgerschaftliche Öffentlichkeit ist jedoch nicht mehr bereit, den von einer mehr oder weniger anonymen Jury getroffenen Auswahlentscheidungen zur beglückenden Bereicherung ihres Lebensraumes zu applaudieren. Im Gegenteil: die preisgekrönten Kaninchen aus dem schwarzen Hut der Wettbewerbsjury haben oftmals nur ein kurzes politisches Leben. Unter diesem Aspekt gesehen, begegnet eine betroffene Bürgerschaft dem Wettbewerbsverfahren von vornherein häufig mit Misstrauen, da sie sich in keiner Weise im Verfahren vertreten sieht.

Lässt sich diese problembeladene Entwicklung des Wettbewerbswesens überwinden? Dazu bedarf es der Besinnung auf die grundlegenden Ziele und Zwecke des Instruments Planungswettbewerb, die von inzwischen alltagspragmatischen Sekundärthemen zugeschüttet worden sind. An erster Stelle geht es um die Qualität der Planung und des Bauens bei der Gestaltung unserer Umwelt – also um Baukultur. Analog zur Vitruv´schen Trias von utilitas/venustas/firmitas geht es, im heutigen Sprachgebrauch formuliert, um Nachhaltigkeit, das Optimieren von Nutzungen, ein qualitätvolles Gestalten (Schönheit!) und um

tely bypassed architectural competitions, and certainly public procurement law. The self-evident widespread public marketing of the results of non-public jury selections in the media does nothing to change this. The basic principle of the competition and awards process is, after all, its non-public character. However, an increasingly open civil society is no longer prepared to applaud the decisions made by a more or less anonymous jury for the delightful enrichment of its living environment. On the contrary, the prize-winning rabbits pulled out of the hats of competition juries often have only a brief political lifespan. Seen from this angle, the affected citizenry often greet the competition process with mistrust from the very beginning, since they do not perceive themselves to be represented in the process in any way.

Is it possible to overcome this highly problematic development in the competition system? To do so would require reflexion on the fundamental aims and purposes of the planning competition approach, which by now have been buried under a deluge of mundane and pragmatic secondary issues. First and foremost, it is concerned with the quality of planning and building with regard to the design of our environment – that is, with building culture. In an analogy to Vitruvius's triad of utilitas/venustas/firmitas, formulated in our contemporary language, it is concerned with sustainability, optimization of usage, high-quality design (beauty!) and economic efficiency. On the way to achieving this, it is essential to provide the professional groups which are qualified to do so with the possibility of contributing their individual services under conditions of equal opportunity. Transparency, equal treatment and objectivity are the key terms associated with such an approach to awarding contracts – which, above all represent the expression of a mind-set. Such aims, then, are also concerned with the protection and qualification of the planning profession, the breadth and variety of their company structures, including fair entrance requirements for young, small and medium-sized firms in particular. It is also important to apply the principle of efficiency not only to the execution of the building project itself, but also to the competition process. Ultimately, these are self-evident requirements which no one would have reason to argue with, but which we have apparently lost sight of.

Where can we go from here? A new procedural culture is needed which can break through the rigid encrustations of public procurement and competition law. First of all, an attitude is required on the part of the parties involved which once again places the substantive goals

Stadthaus (Richard Meier) | Stadthaus (Richard Meier)

Sparkasse Ulm, im Bau (Lederer Ragnarsdóttir Oei) | Sparkasse Ulm, under construction (Lederer Ragnarsdóttir Oei)

ökonomische Effizienz. Auf dem Weg dorthin gilt es, den dafür qualifizierten Berufsgruppen unter Wahrung der Chancengleichheit die Möglichkeit zu eröffnen, ihre individuelle Leistung einzubringen. Transparenz, Gleichbehandlung und Objektivität sind die Schlüsselbegriffe einer solchen Methodik der Auftragsvergabe, die vor allem Ausdruck von Haltung ist. Mit solchen Zielen verbindet sich dann auch der Blick auf die Sicherung und Qualifizierung des Berufsstands der Planer, auf die Breite und Vielfalt ihrer Bürostrukturen mit fairen Zugangsbedingungen gerade für junge, kleine und mittlere Büros. Dazu gilt es, das Effizienzprinzip nicht nur auf die Abwicklung der Baumaßnahme selbst zu projizieren, sondern auch auf das Wettbewerbsverfahren. Es sind letztlich Selbstverständlichkeiten, denen niemand wirklich zu widersprechen vermag, die aber offensichtlich aus dem Blickfeld geraten sind.

Wie kann es weitergehen? Notwendig ist eine neue Verfahrenskultur, die die gewachsenen Verkrustungen des Vergabe- und Wettbewerbsrechts aufbricht. An erster Stelle bedarf es einer Haltung der beteiligten Akteure, welche die inhaltlichen Ziele wieder vor die fehlerfreie Anwendung des Vergaberegelwerks stellt. Es bedarf keiner neuen Instrumente und Regelungen, sondern lediglich anderer Gewichtungen und einer Ausnutzung aller Spielräume, die die rechtlichen Vorgaben und Richtlinien ja trotz allem ermöglichen:

– Das entscheidende Gewicht im Verfahren muss wieder auf dem Wettbewerbsergebnis selbst und damit der Juryentscheidung liegen! Es kann also nicht sein, dass im anschließenden Verhandlungsverfahren die weiteren Zuschlagskriterien die (nahezu) gleiche Bedeutung haben, wie so oft praktiziert. Es liegt am Auslober, dem Preiskriterium in den Ausschreibungsunterlagen beispielsweise 70 % der zu vergebenden Punkte zuzuordnen.
– Der offene Wettbewerb muss wieder häufiger praktiziert werden! Der Sorge um ausufernde Teilnehmerzahlen kann durch zweistufige Verfahren begegnet werden, die im ersten Schritt bewusst nur wesentliche Ideenkonzepte abfragen und im zweiten Schritt von einer beschränkten Teilnehmerzahl die sorgfältigere Ausarbeitung der Aufgabe verlangen. In beiden Phasen gilt der alte Grundsatz des „weniger ist mehr".

ahead of the precise application of public procurement regulations. We do not need any new instruments or regulations; we simply need different emphases, and we need to take advantage of all the room for manœuvre that the legal regulations and guidelines do in fact allow.

– The decisive influence in the process must once again lie with the competition results themselves, and thus, with the jury's decision. It must not be the case that in the subsequent negotiation process, the additional award criteria carry an (almost) equal weight, as so often occurs in practice. It is the awarding authority's responsibility to apply, for example, 70 % of the points available to the award criteria listed in the RFT.
– Open competitions must once again be conducted more frequently. Concerns that participant numbers will get out of hand can be dealt with through a two-stage process in which the first phase consciously calls only for basic concepts while in the second phase, a limited number of participants are asked to submit a more precisely elaborated design. The old principle of 'less is more' should be applied to both phases. In addition, this two-stage approach will raise the quality of the decision-making process.
– If competitions are held in which participation is restricted, the qualification criteria should then be scaled back in order to avoid excluding many firms from the very beginning. The appropriateness of competence credentials with regard to the difficulty and complexity of the planning task must be guaranteed.
– In the case of younger firms, a participant group should be determined specifically for this purpose and – just as importantly – if they win the contract, they should be expressly provided with the opportunity to enter into the negotiation process together with an experienced company of their own choosing.
– The principle of competition must also be followed below the threshold of the VOF: in the case of numerous smaller planning tasks, higher-quality planning can be achieved through a competition for ideas using informal processes such as multiple commissions. In this case, the organizers should make contact with local and regional groups within the Chambers of Architects and agree on appropriate guidelines.
– Local councils should take advantage of their powerful position as planning authorities, and in the context of their real estate policies, to require private clients to hold competitions as well. In this

Ulmer Wohnungs- u. Siedlungsgesellschaft (Braunger Wörtz)
Ulmer Wohnungs- u. Siedlungsgesellschaft [housing association] (Braunger Wörtz)

Münsterbasar (Bidlingmaier, Egenhofer, Dübbers) | Münsterbasar [Minster Bazaar]
(Bidlingmaier, Egenhofer, Dübbers)

Mit der Zweistufigkeit steigt im Übrigen auch die Qualität des Entscheidungsprozesses.

– Wenn schon beschränkt offene Wettbewerbe durchgeführt werden, dann jedoch mit reduzierten Zulassungskriterien, so dass viele Büros nicht schon von vorneherein ausgeschlossen werden. Die Angemessenheit des Qualifikationsnachweises in Bezug auf die Komplexität und Schwierigkeit der Planungsaufgabe muss gewahrt bleiben!

– Für junge Büros sollte eine eigens definierte Teilnehmergruppe festgelegt und – ebenso wichtig – ihnen ausdrücklich ermöglicht werden, im Preisfall zusammen mit einem erfahrenen Büro eigener Wahl ins Verhandlungsverfahren zu gehen!

– Das Wettbewerbsprinzip muss auch unterhalb der Schwellenwerte der VOF beherzigt werden: Mit formlosen Verfahren wie Mehrfachbeauftragungen kann bei vielen kleineren Planungsaufgaben durch eine Ideenkonkurrenz eine höhere Planungsqualität erzielt werden. Dazu sollte man den Kontakt zu den örtlichen und regionalen Gruppierungen der Architektenkammern suchen und eine entsprechende Regel-Vorgehensweise abstimmen!

– Städte und Gemeinden sollten ihre starke Stellung als Träger der Planungshoheit und im Rahmen ihrer Grundstückspolitik nutzen, um private Bauherren ebenfalls zum Wettbewerb zu verpflichten. Gerade hier bestünde ein hohes Potenzial an Qualitätsgewinn, das aber häufig ausgeblendet wird, da man ja keine Investoren verschrecken will.

– Last but not least: die Öffentlichkeit integrieren! Die Bürgerbeteiligung steht am Anfang, der Wettbewerb am Ende des Kommunikations- und Planungsprozesses. In zweistufigen Verfahren besteht die Möglichkeit, auch innerhalb des Wettbewerbsverfahrens die Bürgerschaft einzubinden und so eine erhöhte Akzeptanz und mehr Sicherheit für eine spätere Umsetzung zu erreichen.

Fazit: Wir brauchen eine neue Lust auf Wettbewerbe! Liefern wir uns dem Vergaberecht nicht aus. Gestalten wir Verfahren statt sie abzuwickeln, ohne Angst vor Kontrollverlusten und ohne das Ziel aus den Augen zu verlieren: um die beste Lösung für die Aufgabe zu finden! Mehr Baukultur heißt mehr Wettbewerbe – tun wir´s!

area in particular, there is great scope for improved quality which, unfortunately, is often forgotten in order to avoid scaring off any investors.

– Last but not least: involve the public! Citizen participation takes place at the beginning of the communication and planning process, the competition at the end. A two-stage process offers the possibility of involving the citizenry even within the competition process and thereby achieving a higher level of acceptance and security for the later execution of the project.

To sum up: we need to spark new enthusiasm for competitions! Let us not surrender to public procurement law. Let us design processes instead of merely carrying them out, without fear of losing control and without losing sight of our goal: to find the best solution for the task! More building culture means more competition – let's do it!

ARCHITEKTUR IN DEUTSCHLAND
ARCHITECTURE IN GERMANY

02 – 21

DEUTSCHLAND
GERMANY

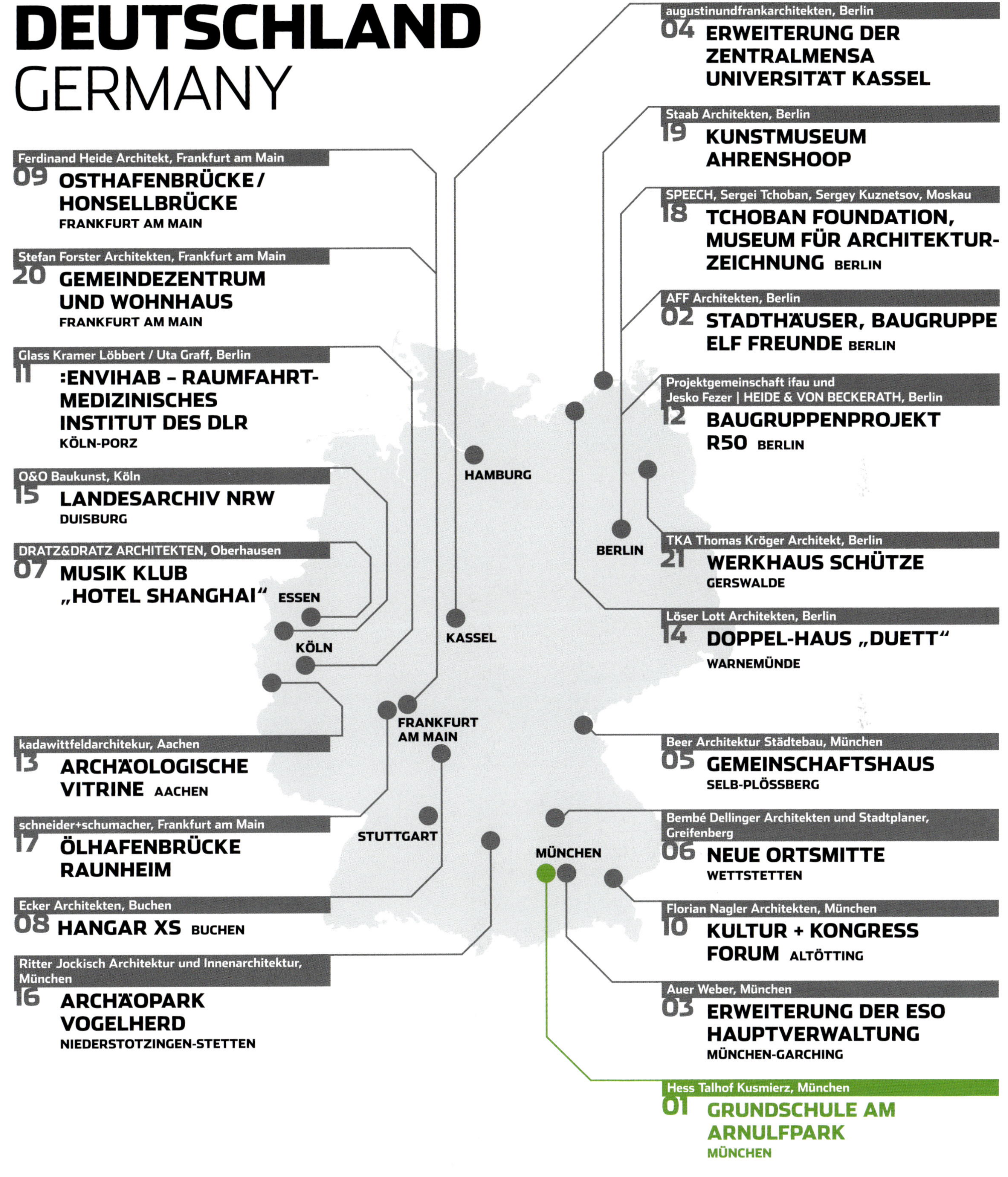

AFF ARCHITEKTEN

GEBÄUDE | BUILDING

STADTHÄUSER
BAUGRUPPE ELF FREUNDE
BERLIN

TEXT OLIVER G. HAMM

02

ARCHITEKTEN | ARCHITECTS

AFF architekten GmbH
Wedekindstraße 24
10243 Berlin
www.aff-architekten.com

MITARBEITER | TEAM

Martin Fröhlich, Thomas Weisheit,
Ulrike Dix

BAUHERR | CLIENT

Elf private Bauherren
Eleven private clients

AUSFÜHRUNGSPLANUNG
EXECUTION PLANNING

AFF architekten GmbH

**BAULEITUNG /
PROJEKTSTEUERUNG**
SITE MANAGEMENT /
PROJECT MANAGEMENT

Martin Fröhlich, Thomas Weisheit

**TRAGWERK UND
BRANDSCHUTZ | STRUCTURE**
AND FIRE PREVENTION

Ingenieurbüro bauArt, Berlin

HAUSTECHNIK | M & E ENGINEERS

Ingenieurbüro Claus Carnarius,
C&F Haustechnik, Strausberg

BAUPHYSIK + AKUSTIK
BUILDING PHYSICS + ACOUSTICS

GF Dipl.-Ing. Uwe Gronau,
Weimar

TÜRKLINKEN UND BESCHLÄGE
HANDLES AND FITTINGS

FSB, Brakel

FERTIGSTELLUNG | COMPLETION

Oktober | October 2012

STANDORT | LOCATION

Vicki-Baum-Straße,
Berlin

FOTOS | PHOTOS

AFF architekten, Berlin

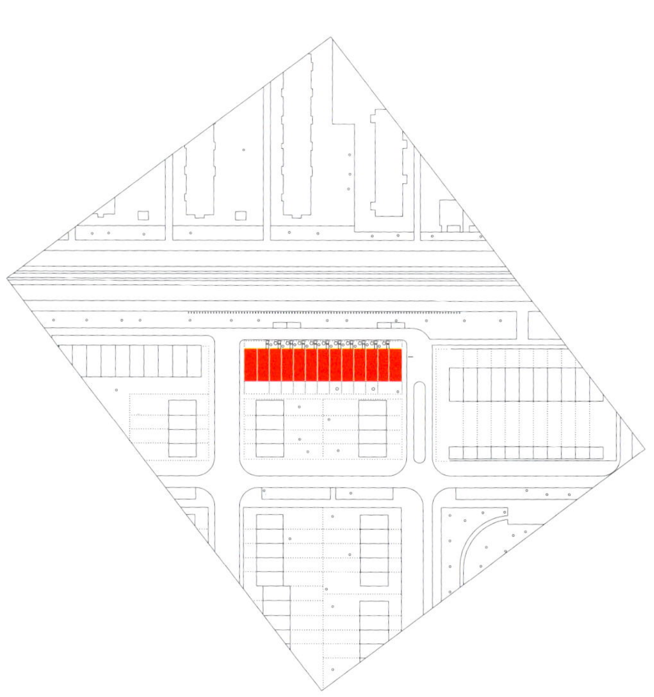

Lageplan | Site plan

Die Nordostfassade mit den „tanzenden" Fenstern. Der Reihenhauscharakter ist durch unterschiedliche Putzfarben rhythmisiert.
The northeastern façade with its 'dancing' windows. Different-coloured rendering adds rhythm to their townhouse character.

„Elf Freunde müsst ihr sein." Dieser viel zitierte Satz zierte bereits 1903 die „Viktoria", den Vorgänger-Pokal der heutigen Fußball-Meisterschale. Nun wählten auch Architekten diese Bezeichnung für ein kleines Baugruppenprojekt an der Rummelsburger Bucht, das in mehrfacher Hinsicht aus dem Rahmen des bislang Gebauten an der Grenze der Berliner Stadtbezirke Friedrichshain und Lichtenberg fällt.

Seit 1994 entsteht am Rummelsburger See mit der Halbinsel Stralau die „Wasserstadt". Das rund 130 Hektar große Areal hatte zuvor größtenteils eine industrielle Nutzung. Lange Zeit beherbergte es aber auch ein Waisenhaus und ein berüchtigtes Gefängnis. Rund 3000 Wohnungen sind bereits entstanden. Insgesamt bietet die Wasserstadt Platz für bis zu 4200 Wohnungen sowie Gewerbeflächen und Infrastruktur, wie eine Schule, Kindertagesstätten, Freizeiteinrichtungen und rund 16 Hektar Grünflächen.

Die ursprünglichen Pläne sahen eine höhere Bebauungsdichte sowie weitere Büro- und Gewerbeflächen vor. Doch nachdem ein großer Teil der Stralauer Halbinsel und des Nordufers der Rummelsburger Buch bebaut worden war, passte der Berliner

'Elf Freunde müsst ihr sein.' ('You've got to be eleven friends.') This oft-quoted dictum adorned the 'Viktoria' trophy – the predecessor of today's German Football Association championship cup – as early as 1903. Now architects have also chosen this title for a small building group project on the Rummelsburger Bucht which, in more ways than one, stands apart from what has been built up to now on the border between the Berlin districts of Friedrichshain and Lichtenberg.

Since 1994, the 'Wasserstadt' ('Water City') has been under construction on the Rummelsburg Lake with its Stralau peninsula. Previously, this 130-hectare area had primarily been an industrial site. However, it was also long home to an orphanage and a notorious prison. Altogether, the Wasserstadt includes space for up to 4200 dwellings, as well as commercial properties and infrastructure such as a school, day-nurseries, recreational facilities and around 16 hectares of green space.

Garten- und Straßenseite; an den Kopfenden befinden sich Garagen. | Garden and street side; garages are located on the front ends.

Senat die Entwicklungsziele für die angrenzenden Bereiche der mittlerweile stark veränderten Nachfrage nach anderen Wohnmodellen an. Seitdem prägen nicht mehr bis zu zwölfgeschossige Wohnblocks, wie noch im ersten Bauabschnitt, sondern vor allem viergeschossige Reihenhaustypen von Baugemeinschaften die räumliche Struktur am Nordufer der Rummelsburger Bucht.

Auch die „Elf Freunde" – fast alle wohnten zuvor am Prenzlauer Berg, und einige sind als Architekten tätig – fanden sich zu einer Baugemeinschaft zusammen. Sie einigten sich auf das Grundmodul einer Zeile aus elf schmalen, viergeschossigen Stadthäusern mit jeweils eigenem Eingang, deren innere Struktur sich nach den individuellen Wünschen richtete. Lediglich die Lage der internen Treppen an einer Wohnungstrennwand war verbindlich vorgegeben, ob als Kaskade oder mit einzelnen Treppenläufen.

Die Varianz der individuellen Aufteilung des immer gleichen Raumvolumens spiegelt die Vielfalt städtischen Wohnens wider: Sie reicht von der konventionellen Kleinräumigkeit mehrerer Zimmer pro Etage über die gesamte Tiefe der Geschosse

The original plans provided for greater building density and additional office and commercial buildings. However, once a large portion of the Stralau peninsula and the north shore of the Rummelsburger Bucht had been developed, Berlin city council adapted the development goals for the adjacent areas to accommodate demands for other residential models, which by that time had changed significantly. As a result, the spatial structure on the northern shore of the Rummelsburger Bucht is no longer dominated by twelve-storey apartment blocks as it was in the first stage of construction, but rather by four-storey townhouse-style residences constructed by joint building ventures.

The 'Eleven Friends' – almost all of them had previously lived in Prenzlauer Berg, and several of them work as architects – also came together as a joint building venture. As their basic model, they agreed on a row of narrow, four-storey townhouses, each with a separate entrance, whose interior structures

einnehmende „fließende Räume" bis zu geschossübergrei-
fenden Räumen. Je nach Bedarf wurden Lufträume, Wohnhöfe und Dachterrassen eingeschnitten. Trotz der mit knapp
über fünf Metern äußerst schmalen Parzellenbreiten waren
dem individuellen Bedürfnis, sich „gefühlt" mehr Raum zu
verschaffen, praktisch keine Grenzen gesetzt.
Ebenso wie die Treppen sind die Decken und Wände aus Beton
gefertigt. Einigen Eigentümern war diese „Rohbauästhetik"
aber wohl nicht geheuer: Sie ließen die großen Flächen ver-
putzen. Passend zu den übrigen raumumschließenden Flächen
entschieden sich einige der Freunde für Zementestrich-, andere
für Holzböden. Im Eingangsbereich war ein Fußboden-Niveau-
sprung unabdingbar, weil hier ein Revisionsschacht für die
Fernwärmeleitung frei gehalten werden musste. Wie die Architekten mit dieser Einschränkung – und auch mit anderen räumlichen sowie ökonomischen Zwängen – umgegangen sind, ist
besonders bemerkenswert: Das Podium über dem Revisionsschacht wird teilweise als Stauraum genutzt, die Räume unter
den Treppen dienen als Gästebad oder Abstellraum. Mancher-
orts wurden alte Holztüren, die aus Abbruchhäusern geborgen
wurden, in die Holzverkleidungen unter den Treppenläufen

would conform to the individual wishes of the residents. The only bindingly prescribed element was
the location of the internal stairs on a dividing wall
between the houses, either in the form of a casca-
ding staircase or individual flights of stairs.
The variations found in the partitioning of identical
volumes mirror the diversity of urban living: they
range from the conventional small-space model
of several rooms per floor, to 'flowing rooms' that
occupy the entire depth of the storey, to rooms that
extend across more than one level. Air spaces, atria
and roof terraces were added as necessary. Despite
the extremely narrow plot width of just over five
metres, there were practically no limits placed on
individuals' desires for creating a sense of more
space.
Like the stairs, the ceilings and walls are made of
concrete. Evidently, however, some of the owners
were uneasy with this 'unfinished' aesthetic, and
they had the large surfaces plastered. Consistent
with the other space-enclosing surfaces, some of
the Friends chose cement screed floors; others
chose wooden flooring. An elevated floor was an
indispensable feature in the entrance areas, since an
inspection shaft needed to be kept free here for the
heating pipelines. The way in which the architects
handled this limitation – as well as other spatial and
economic constraints – is especially remarkable:
in some cases, the podium above the inspection
shaft is used as a storage space; the spaces under
the stairs serve as guest bathrooms or storerooms.
In some places, old wooden doors salvaged from
demolished buildings were integrated into the wood
panelling underneath the flights of stairs, or old
washbasins were given new life.
In places where rooms were extended through the
entire depth of the storeys – such as, for example
in the open kitchen/living rooms on the ground

Ausschnitt der Straßenfassade
Detail of the street-side façade

eingefügt oder alte Waschbecken zu neuem Leben erweckt. Wo Räume durch die gesamte Tiefe der Geschosse „durchgesteckt" wurden – etwa in den offenen Wohnküchen im Erdgeschoss, für die sich die meisten Bauherren entschieden –, kommen die großen Fensterelemente aus mit Bronze eloxiertem Aluminium besonders gut zur Geltung. Auf der Eingangsfassade „tanzen" die immer gleich großen (nur im Erdgeschoss nicht unterteilten) Fenster nach dem „Takt" des unterschiedlich gekörnten Außenputzes. Auf der nach Süden gerichteten Gartenseite werden die geschosshohen Fenster wahlweise durch Schiebeelemente oder Öffnungsflügel mit aufgedrucktem Bildraster ergänzt. Diese „lebendigen" Ansichten heben sich wohltuend von den Nachbarbauten mit ihren meist gleichförmigen Ziegel- oder hellen Putzfassaden ab.

Aus der Platznot machten die elf Freunde auch im Außenbereich eine Tugend: Autostellplätze wurden in offenen Garagen an den Stirnseiten des Gebäudes untergebracht. Dadurch blieb auf der Eingangsseite ein kleiner Vorgarten übrig, der als Spiel- und Begegnungszone genutzt werden kann. Nur die allzu klein geratenen Gärten auf der Südseite können nicht so recht überzeugen. Doch dafür lockt der Blick von der Dachterrasse über ein paar Schrebergärten bis auf die sogenannten Knabenhäuser, Relikte des Waisenhauses als ältester baulicher Hinterlassenschaft an der Rummelsburger Bucht.

floor, which most of the clients chose – the large window units made of bronze-anodized aluminium are especially effective. On the entrance façade, the uniformly-sized windows (subdivided except on the ground level) 'dance' to the 'beat' of the variously-grained exterior rendering. On the south-facing garden side, owners have the option of supplementing the floor-to-ceiling windows with sliding elements or opening casements with embossed optical grids. These 'lively' views provide a pleasant contrast to the neighbouring buildings, with their mostly identical brick or light-coloured plaster façades. In the outdoor area, the Eleven Friends made a virtue out of the lack of space: parking places were located in open garages at the front end of the buildings. This left room for a small front garden on the entrance side, which can be used as a play or socializing area. The only not really convincing feature is the much-too-small garden on the entrance side. Instead, one can enjoy a wonderful view from the roof terrace, across a few allotment gardens to the so-called 'Knabenhäuser' ('boys' homes') – relics of the orphanage, the oldest remaining building on the Rummelsburger Bucht.

Wohnraum im Erdgeschoss mit zurückhaltender Farb- und Materialpalette
Ground floor living area with restrained colour and material pallette

Ausschnitt der Gartenfassade
Detail of the garden side façade

Jede Nische wird ausgenutzt: Sitzecke unter der Treppe | Every niche is put to use: seating corner underneath the stairs

Grundriss 1. Obergeschoss | Plan of 1st floor

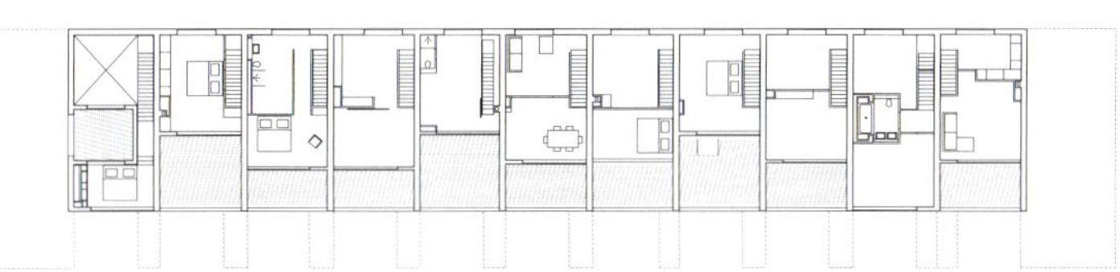

Grundriss 3. Obergeschoss | Plan of 3rd floor

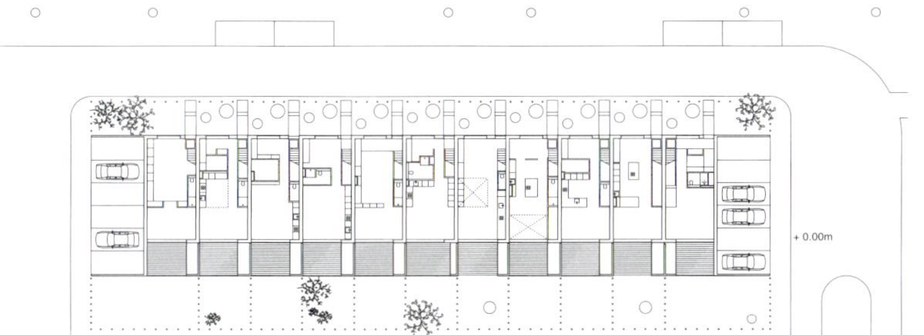

Grundriss Erdgeschoss | Plan of ground floor

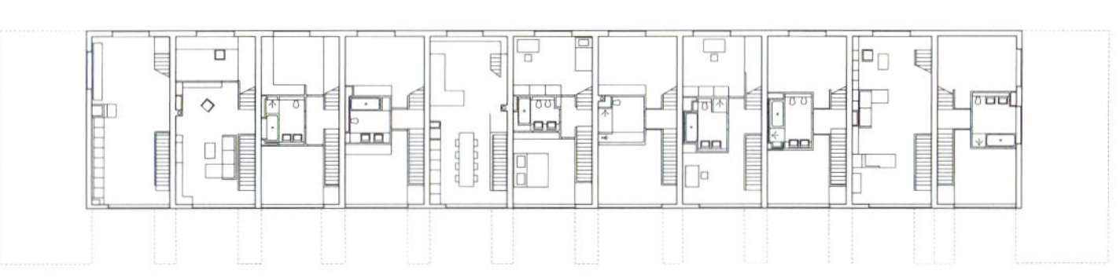

Grundriss 2. Obergeschoss | Plan of 2nd floor

AUER WEBER

ERWEITERUNG DER ESO HAUPTVERWALTUNG
MÜNCHEN-GARCHING

TEXT CHRISTIAN BRENSING

03

ARCHITEKTEN | ARCHITECTS

**Auer Weber Architekten BDA
Sandstraße 33
80335 München** | Munich
www.auer-weber.de

MITARBEITER | TEAM

**Philipp Auer (verantwortlicher
Partner** | managing partner**),
Martin Klemp (assoziierter
Projektleiter** | project
manager associate**),
Christian Richardt (stellv.
Projektleiter**
deputy project manager**),
Heinz Wendl**
(**Bauleiter** | construction manager**),
Dominic Horn (assist. Bauleiter**
deputy construction manager**),
Birte Böttger, Sascha Dehnst,
Joachim Esser, Stefanie Kahle,
Jakob Plötz, Ingo Pucci**

BAUHERR | CLIENT

**Die Europäische
Südsternwarte (ESO),
Garching**

AUSFÜHRUNGSPLANUNG
EXECUTION PLANNING

Generalplaner | general planner:
**Auer Weber Architekten BDA,
München** | Munich
**Kostenplanung und
Ausschreibung** | cost calculation
and call for tenders**:
Wenzel + Wenzel
Freie Architekten Dipl. Ing.
Partnerschaft,
München** | Munich

LANDSCHAFTSARCHITEKTEN
LANDSCAPE ARCHITECTS

**Gesswein Landschaftsarchitekten,
Ostfildern,
naturaplan, Gauting**

TRAGWERK | STRUCTURE

**Mayr I Ludescher I Partner
Beratende Ingenieure,
München** | Munich

BRANDSCHUTZ
FIRE PREVENTION

**hhpberlin Ingenieure
für Brandschutz,
Niederlassung München** | Munich

**HAUSTECHNIK, ENERGIE-
UND FASSADENPLANUNG,
BAUPHYSIK** | M & E ENGINEERS,
ENERGY AND FAÇADE
PLANNING, BUILDING PHYSICS

**DS Plan Ingenieurgesellschaft,
Stuttgart**

AKUSTIK | ACOUSTICS

Müller-BBM, Planegg

ELEKTROSCHALTER
ELECTRICAL SWITCHES

**Albrecht Jung GmbH & Co. KG,
Schalksmühle**

FERTIGSTELLUNG | COMPLETION

Dezember | December **2013**

STANDORT | LOCATION

**Karl-Schwarzschild-Straße 2
85748 Garching bei München
www.eso.org**

FOTOS | PHOTOS

**Roland Halbe,
Stuttgart**

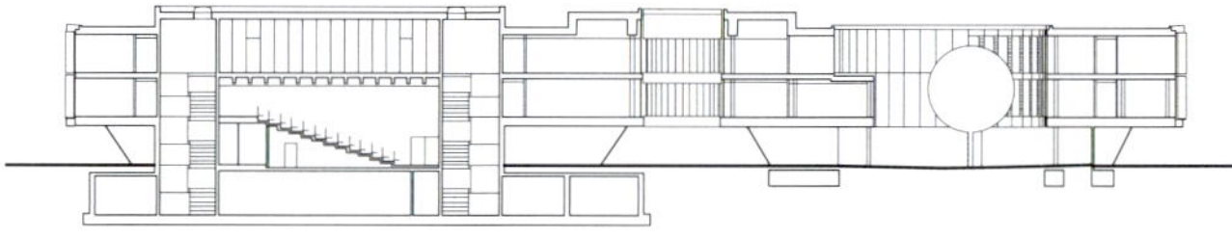

Schnitt | Section

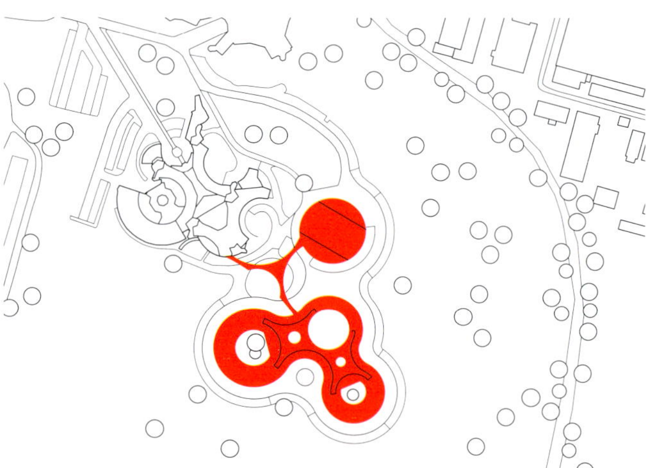

Lageplan | Site plan

Die dreiarmige Brücke führt vom Altbau sowohl zum Technikgebäude (links) als auch zum Büro- und Konferenzgebäude (rechts).
From the old structure, the three-armed bridge leads to both the technical building (left) and the office and conference building (right).

Die Spiralgalaxie NGC 7424 ist rund 40 Millionen Lichtjahre von der Erde entfernt. Auf sie und viele andere Himmelskörper richten sich in bis zu 5000 Metern Höhe in der chilenischen Atacama-Wüste die Teleskope der ESO (European Southern Observatory / Europäische Südsternwarte). Die ESO ist eine multinationale europäische Forschungseinrichtung für Astronomen und Astrophysiker. Sie ermöglicht astronomische Spitzenforschung, indem sie leistungsfähige bodengebundene Teleskope entwirft, baut und betreibt. Alle von den Teleskopen eingefangenen Daten kommen zur Auswertung auf den Forschungscampus in Garching vor den Toren Münchens. Dort befindet sich seit 1980 die ESO Hauptverwaltung, wo über 600 Forscher aus vielen europäischen Ländern unser Universum bis in seine hintersten Winkel erkunden.
Die zwischen 1976 und 1980 von den Architekten Fehling Gogel errichtete Hauptverwaltung basiert in ihrem Entwurf auf unterschiedlichen Kreiskonstellationen. Die als offene Kreissegmente ausgebildeten Bauteile liegen entlang einer Mittelachse und stellen dem Grundriss nach ein eigenes architektonisches Universum dar. Dieses gestalterische Konzept enthält eine Vielzahl von potenziellen baulichen Erweiterungsmöglichkeiten. Daran knüpft der Entwurf für die Erweiterung der ESO Hauptverwaltung an, mit dem sich Auer Weber 2007 in einem internationalen Architektenwettbewerb durchsetzen konnten.
Vom Stammhaus geht man über eine Brückenverbindung im 1. Obergeschoss zu den beiden neuen Baukörpern: ein im Erdgeschoss aufgeständertes zweigeschossiges circa 14 000 Quadratmeter umfassendes Büro- und Konferenzgebäude sowie ein

Spiral galaxy NGC 7424 is located approximately 40 million light years away from the Earth. In Chile's Atacama Desert, telescopes operated by the ESO (European Southern Observatory) at heights of up to 5000 metres are directed at these and other celestial bodies. The ESO is a multinational European research organisation for astronomers and astrophysicists. It facilitates state-of-the-art astronomical research by designing, building and operating powerful ground-based telescopes. All of the data collected by the telescopes is transmitted to the research campus in Garching, on the outskirts of Munich, for evaluation. Since 1980 this has been the site of ESO headquarters, where over 600 researchers from numerous European countries study every distant corner of our universe.
The design for the headquarters, which was built between 1976 and 1980 by the architects Fehling Gogel, was based on a variety of circular configurations. The structural elements, shaped like open segments of a circle, lie along a central axis, with the building's floor plan constituting an architectural universe. This design concept provides a wide variety of structural possibilities for expansion. The design for the extension of the ESO headquarters, with which Auer Weber won an international architectural competition in 2007, draws upon these possibilities.

zweigeschossiges 4500 Quadratmeter großes Technikbauwerk inklusive Montagehalle. Die vollverglaste Brücke fungiert als eine Art Nabelschnur zu den neuen kreisrunden Satelliten, die der alten Hauptverwaltung in südöstlicher Richtung vorgelagert sind. Schon die Wegeführung der dreiarmigen Brücke beschreibt Kreissegmente, was eine direkte Zuwegung verhindert. Man wähnt sich auf einer neuen Umlaufbahn, die einen schließlich in die neuen Forschungstrakte führt. Der Eintritt in die beiden Satelliten ist ebenfalls im 1. Obergeschoss, und deren Anziehungskraft beginnt sogleich zu wirken. Besonders in dem aus drei Kreisen konfigurierten Büro- und Konferenzgebäude wird man auf den Bahnen der runden Korridore förmlich durch das Gebäude gezogen. Schwungvoll umrundet man die Zylinder zweier Lichthöfe, das Auditorium mit darüber liegendem „Council Room" und bewegt sich entlang der geschwungenen konvex-konkaven Außenfassade mit ihrem durchgängigen Band von Büros. Die gesamte Auslegung des dreigliedrigen Büro- und Konferenzbaus ist vollkommen auf die speziellen Arbeitsweisen und Anforderungen der Forscher ausgerichtet. So gibt es keinerlei Kombi- oder Großraumbüros, nur 257 einzelne Zellenbüros, denen an den beiden Innenhöfen je zwei Besprechungsräume und vor dem Auditorium eine Cafeteria angegliedert sind. Sie bilden kommunikative Inseln in einem ansonsten individuell hochkonzentrierten Forscheralltag. Allseits ist der Fokus auf die wissenschaftliche Arbeit gerichtet. Dem kommt die sachlich rationale Atmosphäre der schwungvollen, aber stringenten Architektur entgegen. Dies lässt sich auch an zwei konstruktiven Details ablesen: So musste zum einen das aufgeständerte Erdgeschoss einschließlich seiner umlaufenden Auskragung von fünf Metern auf eine äußere Stützenreihe verzichten.

From the existing building, a connecting bridge on the first floor leads to the two new structures: an approximately 14,000-square metre, two-storey office and conference building with an elevated ground floor, and a two-storey technical building including an assembly hall, with a total area of 4500 square metres. The fully glazed bridge serves as a kind of umbilical cord connecting to the new circular satellites, which are located on the southeast side of the old headquarters. Even the paths of the three-armed bridge describe circular segments, preventing direct access. One feels as if one is on a new orbital path, which ultimately leads to the new research wings. The entrance to the two satellites is also on the first floor, and their attractive force begins to work immediately. Particularly in the office and conference building, which consists of three circles, one is literally drawn through the building along the pathways of the round corridors. One follows a sweeping circle around the cylinders of two atria and the auditorium with the Council Room above, and moves along the convex-concave curvature of the outer façade with its continuous row of offices.

The entire design of the three-part office and conference building is oriented toward the researchers' specific working methods and requirements. Thus, there are no open-plan offices – only 257 individual offices connected to two meeting rooms on each of the two courtyards and to a cafeteria in front of

Einer der Innenhöfe des Büro- und Konferenzgebäudes | One of the courtyards in the office and conference building

Untersicht der dreiarmigen Brücke und Blick auf das kreisförmige Technikgebäude | Underside of the three-armed bridge and view of the circular-shaped technical building

Blick vom Foyer in die Büroetagen | View from the foyer to the office floors

Foyer des Büro- und Konferenzgebäudes | Foyer of the office and conference building

Statisch anspruchsvolle Brückenträger auf den Dächern der drei runden Bauteile im Verbund mit Hängestützen im 1. Obergeschoss und Schottwänden in jeder 4. Achse im 2. Obergeschoss ermöglichen diesen Eindruck des scheinbar von der Erde losgelösten Bauwerks. Das zweite auffällige technische Detail ist die geschuppte Fassade aus geschosshohen und vollverglasten Kastenfenstern. Sie ist in zwei übereinanderliegenden Fassadenbändern angeordnet und gibt dem Bauwerk seine charakteristische Erscheinung einer flachen, schwebenden Scheibe, deren konvex-konkav-gekurvten Ränder eine schwingende Elastizität verkörpern. Eine dreifache Isolierverglasung, manuell zu öffnende Klappen für eine natürliche Lüftung, Fernwärme aus dem benachbarten Geothermiekraftwerk und eine Betonkernheizung und -kühlung mittels Grundwassernutzung übertreffen die geltenden energetischen Standards.

In der farblich sachlich-nüchternen Atmosphäre des Bauwerks – dunkle Aluminiumfassade, weiße Innenwände und Bodenbeläge in Anthrazit – verweist nur die terrakottafarbene Brüstung des zentralen Treppenaufgangs vor dem Auditorium dezent auf die 12 000 Kilometer entfernte Atacama-Wüste. Denn neben den Teleskopen existiert dort noch ein weiterer baulicher wie farblicher Bezug: Das gleichfarbige ESO Hotel (siehe DAM Jahrbuch 2002), entworfen von Auer Weber.

the auditorium. These form communicative islands in the otherwise individual and highly concentrated daily lives of the researchers. In every respect, the focus is directed toward scientific work. The rational and matter-of-fact atmosphere of the dynamic yet austere architecture also accommodates this focus, as illustrated in two structural details: first, the elevated ground floor with its surrounding five-metre-wide overhang was built without an outer row of supports. Structurally sophisticated bridge girders located on the roofs of the three round buildings, combined with suspension columns on the first floor and partition panels at every fourth axis on the second floor, create the appearance of a building that seems to be detached from the ground. The second striking technical detail is the façade made up of floor-to-ceiling, all-glass angled box-type windows. These are arranged in two rows, one above the other, giving the building its characteristic appearance of a shallow, floating disc whose curving, convex-concave edges epitomize an oscillating elasticity. With triple-glazing throughout, window flaps that can be opened manually for natural ventilation, district heating provided by the nearby geothermal power plant, and concrete core heating and cooling using groundwater, the building surpasses current energy standards.

Amidst the sober colours of the building – dark aluminium façades, white interior walls and anthracite flooring – only the terracotta-toned balustrade of the central stairway in front of the auditorium makes a subtle reference to the Atacama Desert, 12,000 kilometres away. There, one can find an additional reference in terms of structure and colour: the identically-hued ESO Hotel (see the 2002 DAM German Architecture Annual), designed by Auer Weber.

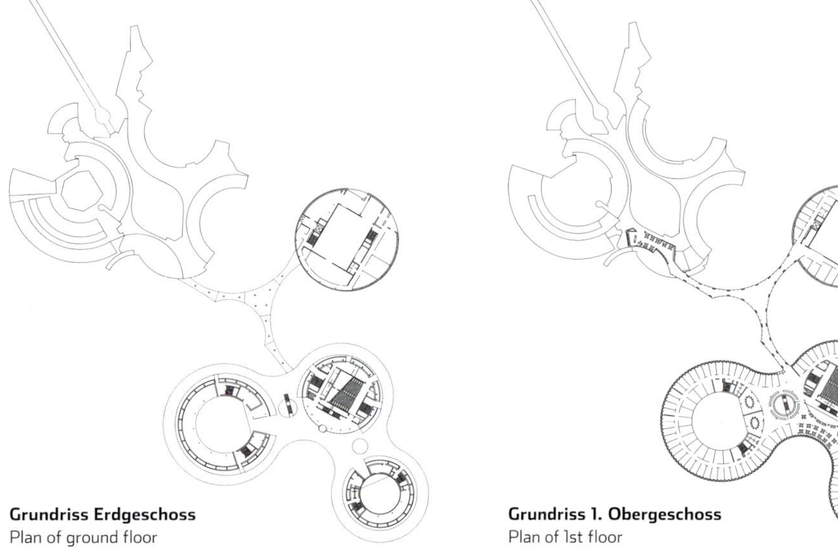

Grundriss Erdgeschoss
Plan of ground floor

Grundriss 1. Obergeschoss
Plan of 1st floor

Der Eingangsbereich des Büro- und Konferenzgebäudes | Entrance area of the office and conference building

AUGUSTINUNDFRANK-ARCHITEKTEN

ERWEITERUNG DER ZENTRALMENSA
UNIVERSITÄT KASSEL

TEXT GERWIN ZOHLEN

04

ARCHITEKTEN | ARCHITECTS

augustinundfrankarchitekten
Schlesische Straße 29–30
10997 Berlin
www.augustinundfrank.de

MITARBEITER | TEAM

Monika Losos
(Projektleitung | project architect),
Alexander Ammon, Enisa Vatres,
Julia Lorenz, André Debus

BAUHERR | CLIENT

Land Hessen, vertreten durch das
Hessische Ministerium für Wissenschaft und Kunst, vertreten durch
das Hessische Baumanagement,
Regionalniederlassung Nord

AUSFÜHRUNGSPLANUNG
EXECUTION PLANNING

augustinundfrankarchitekten

BAULEITUNG | SITE MANAGEMENT

Penkhues Architekten,
Kassel

TRAGWERK UND BRANDSCHUTZ
STRUCTURE AND FIRE PREVENTION

Leonhardt Andrä und Partner,
Berlin

HAUSTECHNIK | M & E ENGINEERS

Winter Ingenieure, Berlin

BAUPHYSIK | BUILDING PHYSICS

Müller-BBM, Berlin

AKUSTIK | ACOUSTICS

Ingenieurbüro Moll, Berlin

KÜCHENPLANER
KITCHEN PLANNING

Ingenieurbüro Geisel,
Reutlingen

AUFZUGPLANER | LIFT PLANNING

Winter Ingenieure, Berlin

LEUCHTEN | LUMINAIRES

Zumtobel, Dornbirn

FERTIGSTELLUNG | COMPLETION

März | March 2013

STANDORT | LOCATION

Moritzstraße 10
34119 Kassel

FOTOS | PHOTOS

Werner Huthmacher, Berlin

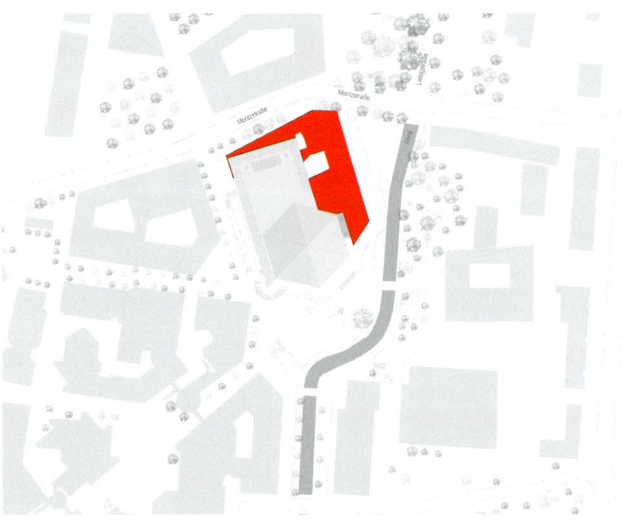

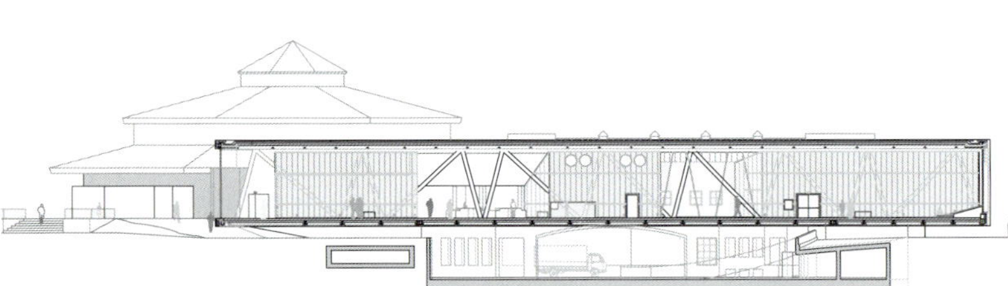

Längsschnitt | Longitudinal section

Lageplan | Site plan

Die Erweiterung der Mensa dockt an den Altbau an, setzt sich aber optisch deutlich ab. | The addition to the refectory is connected to the old structure, but strikingly different in appearance.

Die Universität Kassel zeigt sich der Innenstadt am Campus Holländischer Platz mit einem kühlen, strikten, verschlossenen Gebäuderiegel aus Glas, Stahl und Aluminium. Wehrhaft schirmt er den Verkehr einer Durchgangsstraße ab. Sinnigerweise ist darin das Institut für Ingenieurswissenschaften untergebracht; nichts anderes erwartet oder vermutet der Besucher. Doch wie durch ein Nadelöhr wird er zwischen diesem Trumm und einem schräg gegenüberliegenden kleineren Gebäude auf eine Diagonale gezogen, die ins Innere des Campus führt. Sie dient als Rückgrat der Erschließung dieser Wissenschafts- und Bildungsinsel am Nordrand der Kasseler Innenstadt. Eingefasst und räumlich profiliert wird sie durch Backsteinbauten. Deren Stilmischung setzt sich aus Gebäuden der „guten alten Zeit" des Industriebaus um 1900 der vormaligen Henschel-Fabrik und postmodernen Bauten der 1980er-Jahre zusammen, in denen sich diese Reformhochschule aus der Ära Willy Brandts langsam durch An- und Zubauten zur Universität mauserte. Der einst als Fortschrittssignal und Ehrentitel genutzte Begriff der „Gesamthochschule" verlor sich im Lauf der Jahre. Zuspruch und Erfolg der Universität mit einem entsprechenden Andrang der Studenten machten eine Erweiterung und räumliche Konzentration nötig, da sich einzelne Institute noch über das Kasseler Stadtgebiet verteilten. Seit 2003 sind die Arbeiten an der Nachverdichtung des Campus Holländischer Platz im Gang. Und natürlich brauchte in diesem Zug auch die Zentralmensa eine Erweiterung ihrer Kapazität. Sie erhielt sie 2013 durch die Berliner Architekten Georg Augustin und Ute Frank.
Folgt man der mit Katzenköpfen gepflasterten Diagonale durch und über die bewegte Topographie des Geländes, ist die Blaupause „Stadt" des Grundentwurfs jederzeit greif- und spürbar. Vielleicht sollte man korrekterweise sagen, dass es sich eher um

At its campus on Holländischer Platz, the University of Kassel presents itself to the city centre as a cool, austere and reserved block made of glass, steel and aluminium, defensively shielding off the traffic on a main road. Appropriately enough, the Institute for Engineering Sciences is housed here; visitors do not expect or suspect anything else. Yet, as if passing through the eye of a needle, one is drawn between this hulk of a building and a smaller structure diagonally opposite, along a path that leads into the inner part of the campus. It serves as the backbone for accessing this island of science and education on the northern edge of Kassel's city centre. The area is framed and spatially distinguished by its brick buildings. Their mixture of styles is a combination of buildings from the 'good old days' of industrial construction at the former Henschel factory around the turn of the twentieth century and the postmodern structures of the 1980s, out of which this Reformhochschule ('reform college') from the Willy Brandt era gradually evolved – through additions and extensions – into a university. The term 'Gesamthochschule' ('comprehensive university'), once seen as a symbol of progress and a badge of honour, disappeared over the years. The university's acclaim and success, and the accompanying rush of students, made expansion and spatial concentration necessary, since the individual institutes were still spread out across Kassel. Work on the densification of the Holländischer Platz campus has been under way since 2003. And in connection with this, of course,

Im Inneren der Mensa herrscht eine technisch-freundliche Atmosphäre. | Inside the cafeteria, a technical but friendly atmosphere prevails.

Das Gegenüber aus Alt und Neu | A contrast between old and new

einen kleinstädtisch-dörflichen Charakter handelt als um Stadt
im veritablen Sinne. Kantig verwinkelte Pavillons, tief gezogene
Traufen, weiße Sprossenfenster in meist roten Backsteinfas-
saden; das menschelnd Anheimelnde, das niedlich Vertraute
prägt die Atmosphäre. Mit allen Sinnen zu erfassen ist diese
am zentralen Platz des Campus mit der Hauptmensa. Hier fühlt
man sich unversehens nach Spiekeroog oder Langeoog versetzt.
Die Mensa ist ein sechseckiger Zentralbau mit Erkern, umlau-
fender Terrasse und weißen Holzstützen. Mit den Jahren sind
die Glyzinen an den Fassaden kräftig gewachsen und werden
die Häuser sommerlich-heiter mit Blüten überziehen: Studium
als Kur-Aufenthalt oder Stadt-Therapie in der Nordsee-Gischt.
Auch innen glaubt man sich wegen der obenauf thronenden
Laterne in den Speisesaal eines Ferienheims versetzt. Die mächtigen Holzstützen erinnern an anthroposophische Architektur.
Da Georg Frank selbst an der Universität Kassel architektonischen Entwurf lehrt, mag man sich neben seiner Vertrautheit
mit dem Ort auch lebhaft sein Befremden mit dem vorgefun-
denen räumlichen Charakter vorstellen. Augustinundfrank
haben ihre Aufgabe mit einer bewussten Kontrastbildung
gelöst. Ein wuchtiges, dunkel anthrazitfarbenes, von außen fast
düsteres Stahltragwerk, das aus dem Polygon des Bestandsbaus im Nordosten scherengitterartig herausgezogen ist, kenn-
zeichnet den Neubau. Konstruktiv handelt es sich in Wirklichkeit um den Fachwerkträger einer Brückenkonstruktion. Der
60 Meter lange neue Speisesaal überspannt den in einer Senke
gelegenen Wirtschaftshof der Mensa. Durch die vom Bestand
zunächst unabhängige Brückenkonstruktion war es möglich,
die Mensa auf fast das Doppelte ihrer Kapazität zu erweitern.

the central refectory also needed to expand its
capacity. This was done in 2013 by Berlin architects
Georg Augustin und Ute Frank.
If one follows the cobbled diagonal path over and
through the varied topography of the grounds, the
'city' blueprint of the basic design is palpable and
tangible at all times. Perhaps one should more
correctly say that the campus has a 'village' character rather than that of a town in the true sense.
Winding alleys of pavilions, low-hanging eaves,
white latticed windows in mostly red brick façades:
something cosily human and familiar permeates
the atmosphere. You can experience this with all of
your senses on the central square of the campus,
with its refectory. It is as if you have suddenly been
transported to the North Sea islands of Spiekeroog
or Langeoog. The refectory is a hexagonal structure with bay windows, an all-around terrace and
white timber buttresses. Over the years, the wisteria
on the façades has grown abundantly, covering the
buildings in cheerful, summery blossoms: university
studies take on the character of a health spa stay –
or city therapy amid the spray of the North Sea.
In the interior, as well, the lantern enthroned at the
top gives one the feeling of being transported to the
dining hall of a holiday home. The heavy timber supports are reminiscent of anthroposophic architecture.
Since Georg Frank himself teaches architectural
design at the University of Kassel, one can vividly

Die Straßenfassade nach Norden | The street-side façade facing north

Die neue Mensa „schwebt" über dem Boden ... | The new refectory 'floats' above the ground ...

... und spannt sich stellenweise wie eine Brücke über den tiefer liegenden Wirtschaftshof. | ...and extends in some places like a bridge across the recessed courtyard.

Folgerichtig prägt die Konstruktion nun die Gestalt der Mensaerweiterung. Die Baumaßnahmen mussten weitgehend bei „laufendem Betrieb" vorgenommen werden.

Innen ist der Neubau überraschend licht und hell und zeigt eine verhalten elegante Sachlichkeit. Dazu tragen die reduzierte Farbskala und der karge Materialmix gewiss bei. Hellgrau ist der geschliffene Zementestrich, auf dem weiße Tische chromstahlblitzend stehen. Grasgrüne und schwarze Stahlrohrstühle wechseln sich in den Reihen ab. Die technische Infrastruktur ist robust und sichtbar, weiße Akustikpaneele kleben unter dem schwarzen Stahldach, und die Lüftungsrohre aus Nirostastahl glänzen noch unverbraucht silbern und blank. Weiße, transluzente Plastikverkleidungen vor den Wänden des Bestandsbaus markieren mit einer „Freeflow-Zone" den Übergang zur Erweiterung. Erstaunlich ist, dass die wuchtigen, mit Glas ausgefachten Scherengitterträger den Blick in die heterogene Umgebung gar nicht stören, sondern im Gegenteil das Bild fast schon freundlich rahmen. Klar ist aber auch hier, dass augustinundfrankarchitekten die kühle, sachlich distanzierte Haltung jedweder Gemütlichkeit vorziehen, die sie im Bestand vorfanden. Zu Recht, denn ein Studium ist heutzutage wahrlich kein Ferienaufenthalt.

imagine his intimate knowledge of the location as well as his irritation with the existing spatial character.

In carrying out their assignment, augustinundfrank consciously created contrasts. The new construction stands out as a massive, dark-anthracite steel support structure with an almost gloomy exterior, extending out from the polygon of the existing building on the northeast side like a folding grille. The structural element is, in fact a trussed girder as used in the construction of a bridge. The new, 60-metre-long dining hall stretches across the sunken utility courtyard of the refectory. Thanks to the initially independent bridge construction, it was possible to expand the refectory to almost twice its former capacity. As a consequence, this structural element strongly shapes the appearance of the extension. Most of the construction work had to take place while the facility was in operation.

On the inside, the new addition is surprisingly light and bright, with a practical appearance of restrained elegance. The reduced colour range and the sparse combination of materials certainly contribute to this. The gleaming white tables with their chrome steel fittings stand on a smooth, light-grey cement screed, along with alternating rows of grass-green and black tubular steel chairs. The technical infrastructure is sturdy and visible: white acoustic panels are attached beneath the black steel roof; the silver stainless-steel ventilation pipes still shine like new. White, translucent plastic cladding on the walls of the existing structure marks the 'freeflow zone' that leads to the new addition. Astonishingly enough, the massive, glass-fitted folding-grille girders do not disturb the view into the heterogeneous surroundings in the least. On the contrary – they frame the scene in an almost friendly manner. It is also clear, however, that augustinundfrankarchitekten have favoured a cool, sober detachment over any type of cosiness that they found in the existing buildings. And rightly so: because university studies today are truly no holiday.

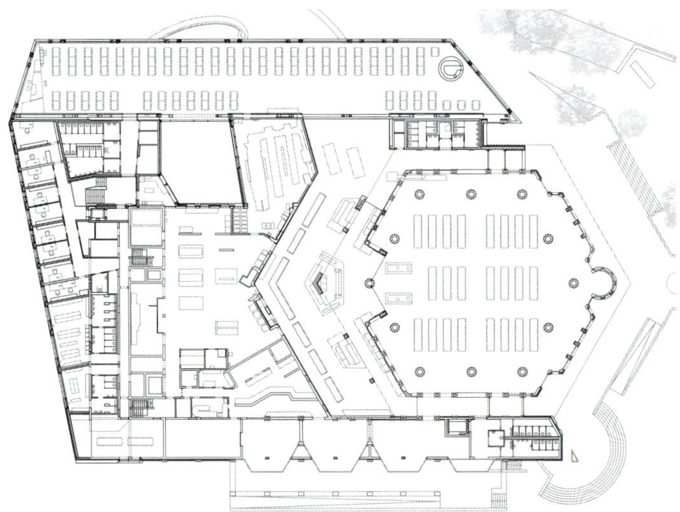

Grundriss Erdgeschoss | Plan of ground floor

Das Stahlfachwerk der Ostfassade gibt der Mensaerweiterung ihren Charakter. | The steel framework of the eastern façade gives the refectory addition its distinctive character.

ARCHITEKT | ARCHITECT

BEER ARCHITEKTUR STÄDTEBAU

GEBÄUDE | BUILDING

GEMEINSCHAFTSHAUS SELB-PLÖSSBERG

TEXT CHRISTINA GRÄWE

05

ARCHITEKTEN | ARCHITECTS

Beer Architektur Städtebau,
Prof. Anne Beer
Leopoldstraße 76
80802 München | Munich
www.beerarchitektur.de

MITARBEITER | TEAM

G. Wohlrab, D. Vesenberg

BAUHERR | CLIENT

Stadt Selb

AUSFÜHRUNGSPLANUNG
EXECUTION PLANNING

Beer Architektur Städtebau

BAULEITUNG / PROJEKTSTEUERUNG
SITE MANAGEMENT / PROJECT MANAGEMENT

Beer Architektur Städtebau

TRAGWERK UND BRANDSCHUTZ
STRUCTURE AND FIRE PREVENTION

Merz Kley & Partner, Dornbirn

HAUSTECHNIK | M & E ENGINEERS

IB Peter Möller, Hof,
Rennert Consulting, Hof

BAUPHYSIK + AKUSTIK
BUILDING PHYSICS AND ACOUSTICS

IBAS, Bayreuth

FERTIGSTELLUNG | COMPLETION

Ende | end of 2012

STANDORT | LOCATION

Jakob-Zeidler-Straße 5
95100 Selb-Plößberg
www.jochen-klepperhaus.de

FOTOS | PHOTOS

Fernando Alda, Sevilla

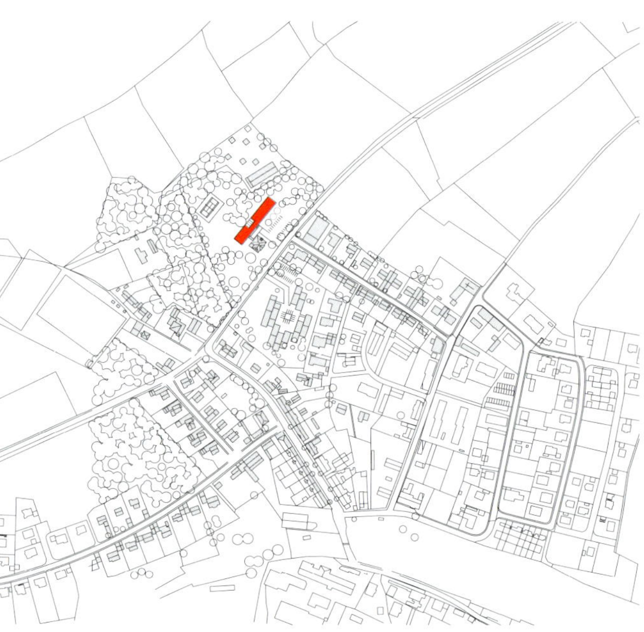

Lageplan | Site plan

Die Nordostfassade mit dem als schwarze Kiste eingeschobenen Haupteingang, links die historische Villa.
The northeastern façade with its main entrance inserted as a black box; on the left is the historic mansion.

Eigentlich dürfte es dieses Haus gar nicht geben. Wenn man die Rahmenbedingungen betrachtet, sprach weit mehr gegen einen solchen Bau als dafür: eine schrumpfende Stadt – das oberfränkische Städtchen Selb hat seit den 1970er-Jahren ein Drittel seiner Einwohner verloren –, eine seit dem Niedergang der Porzellanindustrie wirtschaftlich nicht gerade prosperierende Gegend sowie eine im Grunde leere Stadtkasse. Aber ein findiger Bauamtsleiter setzt hier auf architektonische Qualität als Gegenbewegung zur Stagnation. Innerhalb des Programms „Soziale Stadt" entstehen Bausteine zur gezielten Aufwertung des Ortes. Der aktuellste ist der lang gestreckte Neubau auf dem Grundstück des Jochen-Klepper-Hauses in Selb-Plößberg. Die Evangelische Kirche betreibt dort in einer ehemaligen Fabrikantenvilla eine Tagungs- und Erlebnisstätte für Jugendliche, Erwachsene und Familien. Auf dem parkartigen Anwesen ist zudem ausreichend Raum für einen Zeltplatz und sportliche Aktivitäten. Dem noblen Potenzial entgegen stand indessen die Situation im Ortsteil Plößberg. Die Schule ist aufgegeben, Gastronomie und Läden sind geschlossen. Dennoch oder gerade deshalb gibt es ein großes Bedürfnis der Bewohner nach einer Einrichtung, in der sie sich treffen und verschiedenen Aktivitäten

Actually, this house should not even exist. When we look at the circumstances, there were many more arguments against such a building project than there were in favour: a shrinking town (the little Upper Franconian town of Selb has lost one third of its population since the 1970s), a region that has not been particularly prosperous since the decline of the porcelain industry, and municipal coffers that were basically empty. However, in this case, a resourceful head of the buildings department is placing his bets on architectural quality as a counterforce against stagnation. In the context of the programme 'Soziale Stadt' ('socially-minded town'), the groundwork is being laid for a targeted upgrading of the place. The most recent project is this elongated new building on the grounds of the Jochen-Klepper-Haus in Selb's Plössberg district. Here, in the mansion of a former factory owner, the Protestant church runs an event and recreational centre for young people, adults and families. The park-like grounds also include ample space for a camping area and athletic activities.

nachgehen können. Dieser Bedarf wurde an das bestehende **Jugendprogramm gekoppelt. Die Stadt erklärte sich bereit, das Grundstück in Erbpacht für 25 Jahre zu übernehmen und einen Ergänzungsbau als Gemeinschaftshaus zu finanzieren. Das Dekanat kommt für den Unterhalt auf. Zehn regionale und überregionale Büros wurden 2009 eingeladen, Vorschläge für einen Neubau zu liefern, der die alten, energetisch völlig unzulänglichen Räume, die vorher hier standen, ersetzt. Das Münchner Architekturbüro von Anne Beer ging als Sieger aus dem Wettbewerb hervor. Die Idee war, ein unaufdringliches Haus zu bauen, das die historische Backsteinvilla nicht dominiert. Es streckt sich – durch einen kleinen Schnorchel mit dem Altbau verbunden –**

Standing in the way of this noble goal, however, was the Plössberg district itself. The school has been abandoned; restaurants and shops are closed. Nevertheless – or perhaps for this very reason – the residents have a strong need for a facility where people can meet and pursue various activities together. This demand was coupled with the community's existing youth programme. The city agreed to take over the long-term lease for a period of 25 years and to finance the building of a new extension to serve as a community centre. The deanery is responsible for the maintenance. In 2009, ten regional and national offices were invited to submit proposals for a new addition that would replace the old rooms that stood here previously and were totally inadequate from an energy point of view. Anne Beer's Munich-based architectural firm emerged as the winner of the competition.

The idea was to build an unobtrusive house that would not dominate the historic brick mansion. Connected to the old building by a small passageway, the low, clearly-formed addition extends into

Die Loggia nach Südwesten
The southwest-facing loggia

Die Südostfassade zum Garten mit der eingeschnittenen Terrasse | The southeastern façade facing the garden, with its recessed terrace

flach und als klare Form rechtwinklig hinter der Villa in den Garten. Ein Wegducken ist dies allerdings nicht. Das Gebäude behält durch seine beinahe durchgängig und regelmäßig mit Lamellen aus Lärchenholz rhythmisierte Fassade bei aller Zurückhaltung einen eigenständigen Charakter. Die Konstruktion des Holzskelettbaus – die Kastenträger und Wandelemente wurden im Werk vorgefertigt – legte Anne Beer bewusst so aus, dass auch kleinere Zimmereibetriebe die Aufgabe bewältigen konnten. Denn es ging auch darum, die regionale Entwicklung zu fördern, was die Architektin mit einer „Wertschöpfung des Handwerks" erreichen wollte. Letztlich erhielt aber mangels regionaler Angebote eine Firma aus Oberbayern den Zuschlag. Gegenüber des ungefähr mittig gelegenen Haupteingangs befindet sich eine Terrasse, am südwestlichen Ende des Baues eine tief eingeschnittene Loggia. Beide Flächen ergeben schöne Außenräume. Geländer, wie man sie von Schwimmbecken her kennt, gaukeln einem vor, von hier aus direkt ins Wasser springen zu können.

Innen erkennt man die Durchlässigkeit des Hauses zu seiner Umgebung. Die Holzlamellen haben zwar ein recht breites Profil und lassen zwischen sich keine großen Abstände frei. Dennoch hat man den Eindruck von Großzügigkeit und Weitsicht, was

the garden behind the villa at a right angle. Nevertheless, the new building does not duck out of sight. For all of its restraint, it maintains a character of its own thanks to its nearly continuous, rhythmically-structured façade of regularly spaced larch wood lamellae. Anne Beer consciously planned the construction of the timber frame in such a way that even small carpentry workshops would be capable of handling the task. (The box girders and wall elements were preassembled in the factory.) After all, an additional aim of the project was to promote regional development, which the architect hoped to achieve by 'value creation through the craft trades'. In the end, however, owing to a lack of tenders from the region, a company from Upper Bavaria was awarded the contract.

A terrace is located across from the more or less central main entrance; at the southwest end of the building is a deeply recessed loggia. Both of these spaces provide pleasant outdoor areas. Railings resembling those found at swimming pools give the impression that from here one could leap directly into the water.

Der leicht abfallende Gang zum Mehrzweckraum | The gently sloping corridor to the multi-purpose hall

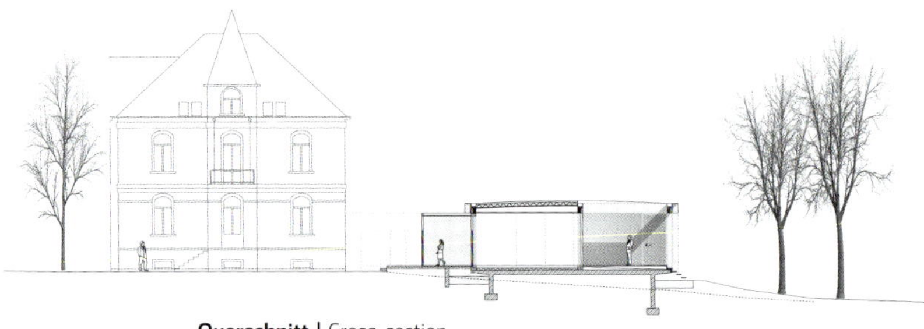

Das Panoramafenster des Mehrzweckraums mit Außentreppe in den Garten | The picture window in the multi-purpose hall; an exterior staircase leads to the garden

durch ein so einfaches wie wirkungsvolles Mittel unterstützt wird: In den kurzen Gebäudeseiten sitzen Panoramafenster, und trotz der Teeküche sowie der Seminar- und Büroräume bleibt eine Passage frei, und man kann das Haus über seine gesamte Länge mit Blicken durchmessen. Der Bau ist zudem der Topografie angepasst und fällt nach Nordosten leicht ab. An diesem Ende liegt ein großer und dabei doch behaglicher, quadratisch geschnittener und akustisch wunderbar funktionierender Mehrzwecksaal mit Schwingboden, in dem gerne die örtliche Musikgruppe probt und auch Konzerte stattfinden. Der Weg dorthin

In the interior, the building's permeability with its surroundings is apparent. The wooden lamellae have quite a broad profile, and the spaces in between them are not large; nevertheless, one has the impression of spaciousness and wide visibility, which is bolstered by an element as simple as it is effective: the short sides of the building contain picture windows, and despite the existence of a small kitchen, seminar rooms and offices, one passage remains free, enabling the view to traverse the entire length of the house. In addition, the building has been tailored to the topography, descending slightly toward the northeast. Located on this end is a large, but nevertheless comfortable, square multipurpose hall with a sprung floor and wonderfully functioning acoustics. It is a popular rehearsal location for the local music group, and concerts are held here as well. The path into this space, via a gently sloping ramp, is almost poetic in its staging when the sun casts the pattern of the lamellae as a shadow onto the grey wall.

Querschnitt | Cross-section

Der Mehrzweckraum von innen mit Blick in den Garten | Interior of the multi-purpose hall with a view into the garden

über die leicht abschüssige Rampe ist beinahe poetisch inszeniert, wenn die Sonne das Lamellenraster der Fassade als Schatten auf die graue Wand wirft.

Das Innere und die Einbaumöbel sind im Gegensatz zum (noch) hellen Holz außen vornehm anthrazitfarben gestrichen. Nischen für die Garderobe oder eine große Pinnwand sind mit grauem Filz ausgeschlagen. Ein heller Linoleumboden ergänzt die sparsame Farbpalette, die den bunt zusammengewürfelten Utensilien der Nutzer einen ruhigen Hintergrund verschafft.

Das Gebäude stand auch während der Bauphase noch auf der Kippe. In letzter Minute wurde der Baukrimi aus Insolvenz, Bauverzögerungen und unzähligen zurückgelegten Kilometern zwischen München und Selb aufgelöst, und nun kann sich der Ortsteil Plößberg glücklich schätzen, einen hochwertigen Vielzweckbau zu besitzen, der von unterschiedlichsten Nutzern mit Elan angenommen wird.

In contrast to the (still) light-coloured wood of the exterior, the interior and its built-in furniture are painted an elegant anthracite colour. Alcoves for coats or a large pinboard are lined with grey felt. A light-coloured linoleum floor complements the sparse palette, which provides a tranquil background for the colourful mishmash of the users' equipment. Even during the construction phase, the building's fate still hung in the balance. At the last minute, a story of insolvency, construction delays and countless kilometres of travel between Munich and Selb was finally brought to resolution. Now the Plössberg district can count itself lucky to be in possession of a high-quality multi-purpose building which has been greeted with great enthusiasm by a wide variety of users.

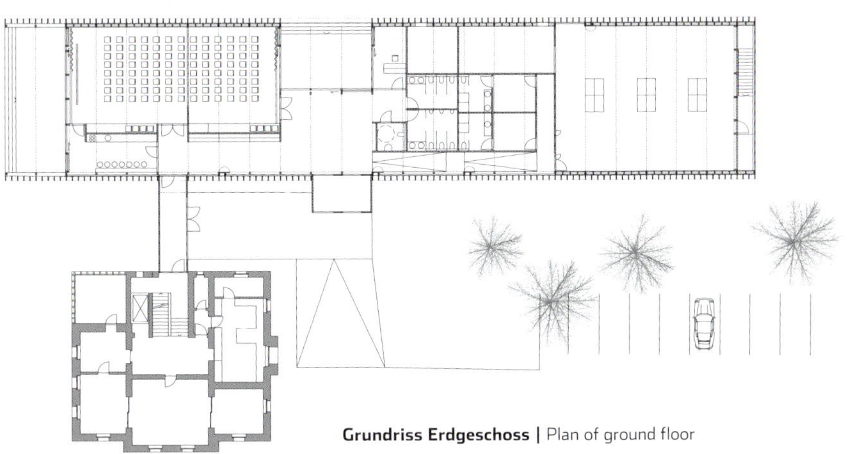

Grundriss Erdgeschoss | Plan of ground floor

BEMBÉ DELLINGER ARCHITEKTEN UND STADTPLANER

NEUE ORTSMITTE
WETTSTETTEN

TEXT DOMINIQUE GAUZIN-MÜLLER

06

ARCHITEKTEN | ARCHITECTS

Bembé Dellinger
Architekten und Stadtplaner
Im Schloß
86926 Greifenberg
www.bembe-dellinger.de

MITARBEITER | TEAM

Viktor Filimonow, Asja Boese

BAUHERR | CLIENT

Gemeinde Wettstetten,
vertreten durch Bürgermeister
Hans Mödl

AUSFÜHRUNGSPLANUNG
EXECUTION PLANNING

Bembé Dellinger
Architekten und Stadtplaner

**BAULEITUNG /
PROJEKTSTEUERUNG**
SITE MANAGEMENT /
PROJECT MANAGEMENT

Bembé Dellinger
Architekten und Stadtplaner

TRAGWERK UND BRANDSCHUTZ
STRUCTURE AND FIRE PREVENTION

Grad Ingenieurplanungen
Büro für Baustatik und
Konstruktion GmbH,
Ingolstadt

HAUSTECHNIK | M & E ENGINEERS

Ingenieurbüro Scholl,
Stammham Arzenheimer
Elektrotechnik GmbH & Co. KG,
Eichstätt

BAUPHYSIK + AKUSTIK
BUILDING PHYSICS + ACOUSTICS

IBN Bauphysik Consult,
Ingolstadt

ELEKTROSCHALTER
ELECTRICAL SWITCHES

Albrecht Jung GmbH & Co. KG,
Schalksmühle

LEUCHTEN | LUMINAIRES

Zumtobel, Dornbirn

FREIANLAGEN
OUTDOOR GROUNDS

Eberhard von Angerer,
München | Munich

FERTIGSTELLUNG | COMPLETION

Juni | June 2013

STANDORT | LOCATION

Kirchplatz 72
85139 Wettstetten

FOTOS | PHOTOS

Stefan Müller-Naumann,
München | Munich

Lageplan | Site plan

Die Neue Ortsmitte: links das administrative Rathaus, mittig das repräsentative mit Bürgersaal, Trau- und Sitzungsraum, rechts die Tagespflege
The new town centre: left, the administrative city hall; centre, the ceremonial building with community hall, wedding hall and meeting room; right, the care centre

Mit seiner selbstbewussten Bescheidenheit ist der neue Ortskern von Wettstetten ein glänzendes Beispiel für jene „kontextuelle Architektur", die immer mehr Anhänger findet. Das Bauerndorf zwischen Ingolstadt und Eichstätt hat sich in 60 Jahren von 900 auf 5000 Einwohner vergrößert und brauchte mehrere öffentliche Einrichtungen. Die kleinteilige Landwirtschaft mit der früheren Umtriebigkeit ist längst vorbei; das alte Schulhaus, das auch als Rathaus diente, konnte die Ansprüche einer modernen Verwaltung nicht mehr erfüllen. Die vernünftige Gemeinde lehnte jedoch jeden protzigen Klotz ab und unterstützte den Vorschlag für eine kleine Gebäudegruppe, mit dem sich das Büro Bembé Dellinger Architekten aus Greifenberg am Ammersee im Wettbewerb durchsetzen konnte. Seit dem Sommer 2013 beleben drei zweigeschossige, freistehende Baukörper die kleine Stadt. Der administrative Bau versammelt alle Büros der Verwaltung; der repräsentative vereint Bürgersaal, Trauungs- und Sitzungsraum, der soziale stapelt einen Hort für ein Dutzend Kinder über einer Tagespflege mit kleinem Garten für zwölf Demenzkranke. Jung und Alt unter einem Dach – mitten im Ort … und es klappt!

In its self-confident simplicity, Wettstetten's new town centre is a shining example of the type of 'contextual architecture' that is steadily gaining more followers. Over the course of 60 years, this farming village between Ingolstadt and Eichstätt has grown in population from 900 to 5000 residents and has required more and more public facilities. Small-scale agriculture and its accompanying activities are long a thing of the past; the old schoolhouse that had doubled as a town hall could no longer meet the demands of a modern administration. Nevertheless, the sensible town council rejected every proposal for a pretentious lump of a structure, and instead supported the idea of a small group of buildings with which the firm of Bembé Dellinger Architekten based in Greifenberg am Ammersee successfully emerged from the competition. Since the summer of 2013, three two-storey freestanding buildings now brighten up the little town. The administrative building contains all of the community's manage-

Das Foyer des Rathauses | The city hall foyer

Die Inneneinrichtung ist so zurückhaltend wie das Äußere der Gebäude.
The interior decoration is as restrained as the building's exterior.

Die drei Baukörper wurden im Maßstab ihrer Umgebung feinfühlig in den organisch gewachsenen Stadtgrundriss eingefügt. Die Fassaden übernehmen die Flucht bestehender Gassen, bilden einen größeren Platz vor der Kirche und einen kleineren mit familiärer Atmosphäre zwischen den Foyers der Neubauten. Großzügige Einschnitte im Erdgeschoss verbinden visuell die drei Einrichtungen, erleichtern die Beziehungen zwischen den Nutzern und fördern somit die Gemeinsamkeit. Das Innere findet Anklang durch gut proportionierte Räume, fein detaillierte, von den Architekten entworfene Einbaumöbel aus Holz und elegante Beleuchtungskörper. Natürliches Licht fällt durch schräge Dacheinschnitte in die Häuser. Der Bürgermeister Hans Mödl, der seit 24 Jahren im Amt ist, hat das Projekt stets getragen. Er ist stolz, dass es aus eigener Kraft der Gemeinde schuldenfrei finanziert wurde.

ment offices; the 'ceremonial' building combines a community assembly hall, wedding hall and meeting room; in the social services building, a day-care centre for a dozen children is situated above a care facility for twelve dementia patients. Young and old under one roof, in the centre of town... and it works! The three structures have been sensitively integrated into the organically developed layout of the town, maintaining the scale of their surroundings. The façades have adopted the alignment of the existing streets, forming a large square in front of the church and a smaller one with a more intimate atmosphere between the foyers of the new buildings. Generous recesses in the ground floors connect the three facilities visually, simplifying interactions between the users, and thereby contribute to the feeling of community. Well-proportioned rooms, finely detailed fitted wooden furniture designed by the architects, and elegant light fixtures all contribute to the appeal of the interiors. Diagonal incisions in the roofs allow natural light to enter the buildings. Mayor Hans Mödl, who has held the office for 24 years, has consistently supported the project. He takes pride in the fact that it was financed debt-free from the community's own resources.

Following in the footsteps of Alvar Aalto or Álvaro Siza Vieira, Felix Bembé and Sebastian Dellinger are among the German representatives of 'critical regionalism.' They aim for 'the rural impression of the group of buildings and their local rootedness.' The form of the seventeenth- and eighteenth-century Altmühltal-style 'Jura houses', which can still be seen in the town, has been developed further here while accommodating contemporary expectations for tech-

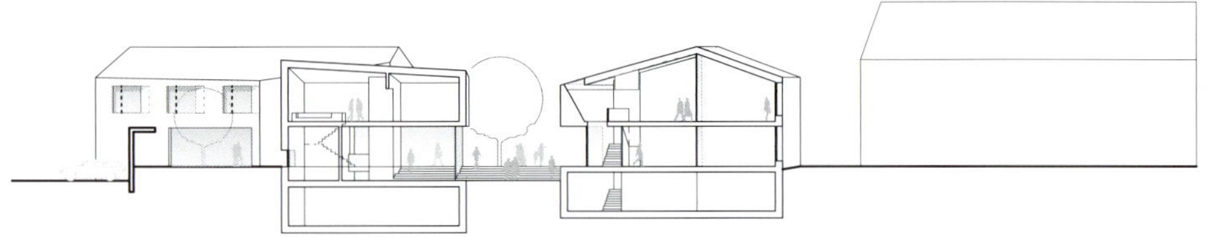

Schnitt durch Rat- und Gemeindehaus | Section through city hall and community centre

Der Blick auf das administrative Rathaus | View of the administrative city hall

BÜRGERSAAL

Der Durchgang zwischen administrativem und repräsentativem Rathaus | The passageway between the administrative and the ceremonial city halls

Die Einbettung des Ensembles in den Ort | The integration of the ensemble into the town

Auf den Spuren von Alvar Aalto oder Álvaro Siza Vieira gehören Felix Bembé und Sebastian Dellinger zu den deutschen Vertretern eines „kritischen Regionalismus". Sie streben „die ländliche Wirkung der Gebäudegruppe und ihre lokale Verwurzelung" an. Die Form der Altmühltal-Jurahäuser aus dem 17. und 18. Jahrhundert, die im Dorf noch zu sehen sind, findet hier eine den zeitgenössischen Techniken und Komforterwartungen angepasste Weiterentwicklung. Die flach geneigten Dächer sind entsprechend nicht mehr mit Steinen, sondern mit Betonziegeln gedeckt, behalten jedoch ihren sehr geringen Dachüberstand. Die Trägheit des doppelschaligen, im Kern isolierten Mauerwerks kommt dem Wohnkomfort zugute. Die Außenseite aus gelben Ziegeln voller Schattierungen wurde geschlämmt. Diese Oberfläche vermittelt ein sehr lebendiges Erscheinungsbild, und der mineralische Kalkputz nimmt außerdem Feuchtigkeit auf. Die schräg eingeschnittenen Laibungen der Fenster bringen Plastizität in die zurückhaltende helle Lochfassade.

Immer mehr Architekten sind auf der Suche nach der goldenen Mitte zwischen den vertrauten Formen der Tradition und den klaren Linien der Moderne, zwischen Low-Tech und High-Tech. Sie stützen sich dabei auch auf eine Vertiefung des Nachhaltigkeitsgedankens. Sie versuchen zwar, viel Energie zu sparen, jedoch nicht um jeden ästhetischen Preis, und entwickeln ihre Bauten nach einem ganzheitlichen Konzept. Die Isolierungsschicht ist dick, die Fenster sind luftdicht, die kontrollierte Be- und Entlüftungsanlage ist ausgeklügelt, und geheizt wird mit

nology and comfort. Thus, the shallow-pitched roofs are no longer covered with stones but with concrete tiles; yet they still retain a very minimal roof overhang. The robustness of the double-layer, core-insulated masonry walls contributes to the comfort of the buildings. The exteriors, covered in highly-nuanced yellow tiles, have been whitewashed in such a way the colour shows through. This surface creates a very lively appearance, and the mineral lime plaster also absorbs moisture. The bevelled window openings add plasticity to the restrained, pale façades.

More and more architects are searching for the golden mean between familiar, traditional forms and the clear lines of modernism, between low-tech and high-tech. In doing so, they look to a more profound interpretation of the concept of sustainability. They try to conserve a great deal of energy, but not at any aesthetic price; and they develop their building designs according to holistic concepts. The layers of insulation are thick, the windows are airtight, the controlled ventilation system is ingenious, and buildings are warmed with district heating from a wood-fired power plant. However, along with economy and ecology, the social and regional cultures play a decisive role. The Jura stone used in the ensemble in Wettstetten came from a quarry just 20 kilometres away. And while the oak for the parquet floors,

Fernwärme aus einem Holzkraftwerk. Neben Ökonomie und Ökologie spielen jedoch das Soziale und die regionale Kultur eine entscheidende Rolle. Der Jurastein für das Ensemble in Wettstetten kam aus einem 20 Kilometer entfernten Steinbruch; die Eiche für Parkett, Fenster und Türen wuchs zwar nicht in Oberbayern, aber im benachbarten Spessart. Ein örtlicher Schreiner hat die Fenster gefertigt, auch alle anderen Betriebe kamen aus Bayern. Die Wahl von Firmen mit höchster handwerklicher Qualität aus der näheren Umgebung fördert die regionale Wirtschaft. Die Verwendung heimischer Baumaterialien reduziert die graue Energie, dient jedoch auch der Identifikation der Bevölkerung mit den Neubauten.

Heute ist der Ortskern von Wettstetten aus seinem langen Schlaf erwacht. Bewegung und Begegnungen beleben den Stadtraum. Der Bürgermeister springt vom Rathaus zum Gemeindesaal und zurück, die Hochzeitsgäste bewundern den Trauungssaal, eine Betreuerin hilft zwei Alten im Garten, die Krippenkinder kommen in ihrem Leiterwagerl von einer kleinen Entdeckungsreise ... Die Bürger haben sich angefreundet mit diesen drei „brüderlichen" Bauten, die mit Empathie zum Ort und dessen Bewohnern gestaltet wurden.

window-frames and doors did not grow in Upper Bavaria, it did come from the nearby Spessart. A local carpenter built the windows; all the other companies came from Bavaria as well. The selection of firms providing top-of-the-line craftsmanship from the local vicinity supports the regional economy. The use of local building materials not only reduces grey energy use, but also fosters public identification with the new structures.

Today, Wettstetten's town centre has been awakened from a long sleep. Movement and human encounters enliven the public space. The mayor hops from the town hall to the community centre and back; wedding guests admire the marriage hall; a carer helps two old people through the garden; the children from the day nursery return from a short excursion in their little handcart... The citizens have made friends with these three 'brotherly' buildings, which were created with empathy for the town and its inhabitants.

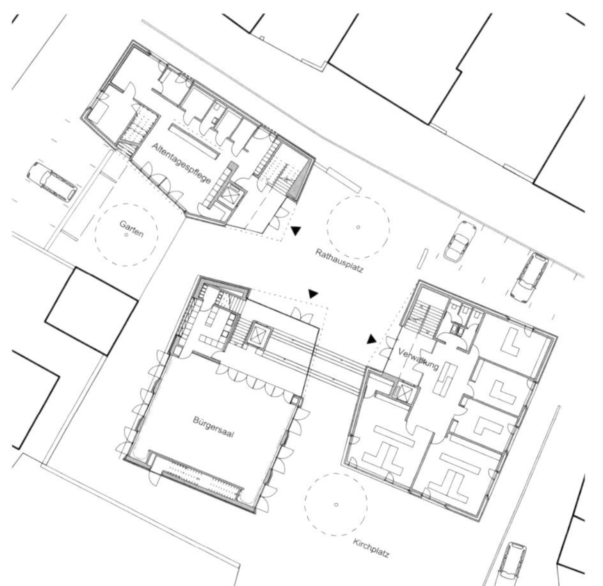

Grundriss Erdgeschoss | Plan of ground floor

Grundriss 1. Obergeschoss | Plan of 1st floor

DRATZ&DRATZ ARCHITEKTEN

MUSIK KLUB „HOTEL SHANGHAI"
ESSEN

TEXT OLIVER ELSER

07

ARCHITEKTEN | ARCHITECTS

DRATZ&DRATZ ARCHITEKTEN
Paul-Reusch-Straße 56
46045 Oberhausen
www.dratz-architekten.de

MITARBEITER | TEAM

Ivo Hartmann

BAUHERR | CLIENT

elektronik musik klub
„Hotel Shanghai" e. K.
Kay „Shanghai" Löber

AUSFÜHRUNGSPLANUNG
EXECUTION PLANNING

DRATZ&DRATZ ARCHITEKTEN

**BAULEITUNG /
PROJEKTSTEUERUNG**
SITE MANAGEMENT / PROJECT
MANAGEMENT

DRATZ&DRATZ ARCHITEKTEN

BRANDSCHUTZ
FIRE PREVENTION

IB Röhmling, Essen

HAUSTECHNIK | M & E ENGINEERS

Walter Brüll Maschinentechnik,
Essen

AKUSTIK | ACOUSTICS

Der Gute Ton
Veranstaltungstechnik, Neuss

BAUDURCHFÜHRUNG
CONSTRUCTION EXECUTION

Münter Design, Essen

FERTIGSTELLUNG | COMPLETION

Ende | end of 2012

STANDORT | LOCATION

Hotel Shanghai
Steeler Straße 33
45127 Essen
www.hotelshanghai.de

FOTOS | PHOTOS

Tomas Riehle, Bergisch-Gladbach
Oliver Elser, Frankfurt am Main

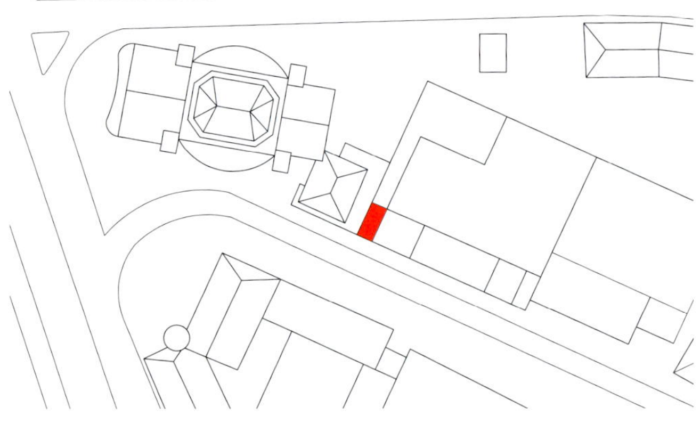

Lageplan | Site plan

Schnittmodell | Section model

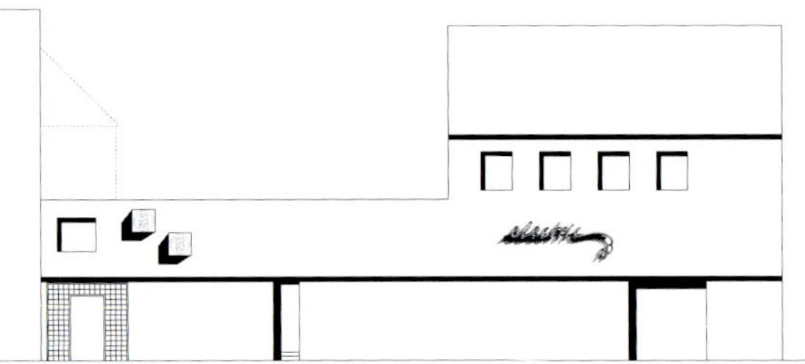

Straßenfassade | Street façade

Blick nach unten: Aus der ehemaligen Rampe zu einer Tiefgarage ist die Sitzlandschaft eines Clubs geworden.
View looking down: the former parking garage ramp has been converted into a dance club seating area.

Essen, Innenstadt, kurz vor Mitternacht. Wo tagsüber Einkaufstüten abgefüllt werden, ist nun niemand mehr. Doch die Stadt schläft nicht, im Gegenteil. Aus einer Seitenstraße leuchtet eine blaue, schwungvoll die optimistischen Kurven der 1950er-Jahre beschwörende Neonschrift hervor: „electric" steht auf einer irritierend fensterlosen Fassade. Kay, das ist der Besitzer, Wirt und gute Geist des „Hotel Shanghai", den alle hier nur den Kay nennen, hat sie angebracht. Er bastelt gerne. Seinen Tanzclub für die eher unter als über 30-jährigen Essener Nachtaktiven hat er innen in eine dunkle Höhle verwandelt. Es gibt Wände, die von gesplitterten Felsen bedeckt zu sein scheinen, jedoch aus Styropor bestehen. Man kann sich in eine bunt beleuchtete Glasnische setzen, deren zackige Form so aussieht, als habe Wilhelm Reich einen Orgonakkumulator bei Bruno Taut bestellt, aber eine Jugendsünde von Hans Scharoun geliefert bekommen. Dazu gibt es Schnitzwerk aus einem abgerissenen China-Restaurant, und von der Decke baumeln Hunderte, wenn nicht sogar Tausende von Origami-Kranichen, fein aus schwer entflammbarem Papier gefaltet. Diesem fröhlich-anarchischen Durcheinander haben die Brüder Ben und Daniel Dratz einen Raum hinzugefügt. Der Auftrag an die jungen Essener Architekten lautete: Kay braucht einen Raucherbereich.

Essen city centre, shortly before midnight: where during the day, the shopping bags are being filled, now there is no one around. But the city is not sleeping – quite the contrary. From out of a side street, blue fluorescent lettering shines forth from the darkness in optimistic curves that invoke the 1950s: the word 'electric' (in English) adorns a confusingly windowless façade. Kay – the owner, host and good spirit of the 'Hotel Shanghai,' whom everyone here knows only by his first name – installed the sign himself. He likes to make things. He transformed his dance club, which caters more to the under-30 crowd of Essen night owls, into a dark cave. There are walls that seem to be covered with splintered rock, although in fact they are made of Styrofoam. You can sit down in a colourfully-lit glass alcove whose jagged form looks as if Wilhelm Reich had ordered an orgone energy accumulator from Bruno Taut, but received an early mistake by Hans Scharoun instead. In addition, there are carvings from a demolished Chinese restaurant; and hundreds – if not thousands – of origami cranes dangle from the ceiling, delicately folded out of flame-resistant

Dafür wurde ein Stück Außenraum umgewidmet und dem Elektroclub einverleibt. Die Diskothek war einst vor einem Parkhaus errichtet worden. Eine der Zufahrtsrampen führte von der Straße durch das Gebäude hindurch steil nach unten. Da sie schon seit Jahren nicht mehr notwendig war, konnte die Durchfahrt verschlossen und zur Raucherzone umgenutzt werden. Sind für Aufgaben dieser Größenordnung Architekten überhaupt notwendig? Wer die anderen Räume der Diskothek hinter sich gelassen hat und nun zwischen rohen Betonwänden an einer kleiner Bar steht, der spürt: Ja, es gibt ihn, den Unterschied zwischen räumlichem Entwerfen und Raumausstattung. Zunächst wurden die Wände von Farbe befreit – es trat ein Betonschalungsmuster hervor. Das Gefälle der Rampe wurde mit einer Sitztreppe aus dunkelbraunen Phenolharzplatten überbaut. Dazu noch ein gebogener Edelstahlstab als Handlauf – und das war's an Gestaltung. Nicht zu vergessen natürlich die schwarz gestrichene Bar am Ende der Treppe und darüber ein quer verlaufender Betonsturz, der für Projektionen verwendet wird. Was diese so selbstverständliche Raumaufteilung tatsächlich bewirkt, das erschließt sich ab etwa 2 Uhr, wenn der Club gut gefüllt ist. Unten nämlich, an der Bar, hat man den perfekten Überblick, wer gerade nicht zu Indie-Elektro-Pop tanzen, sondern auf den Stufen herumsitzen will. Die horizontale Orientierung eines Clubs (man steht herum und sieht im Gedränge immer nur die nächsten Nachbarn) wird hier zu einer Art ad-hoc-Gemeinschaft umgepolt: Was ist heute auf der Treppe los? Geraucht wird dort zwar auch ein bisschen, aber

paper. Brothers Ben and Daniel Dratz have added another room to this festive and anarchic jumble. The instructions for the young Essen-based architects were these: Kay needs a smoking area. To this end, they converted a section of the exterior space and incorporated it into the electro club. At one time, the discotheque stood in front of a multi-storey car park. One of the access ramps led downward from the street on a steep incline directly through the building. Since for some years this ramp had no longer been needed, it was possible to close off the passageway and convert it into a smoking room. Are architects really necessary for a project of this scale? Anyone who has left the other rooms of the discotheque and is now standing at a small bar between raw concrete walls will feel it: yes, there is a difference between spatial design and interior decoration. First, the paint was removed from the walls – and a concrete formwork pattern was revealed. The slope of the ramp was built over with seating steps made of dark brown phenolic resin plates. This was combined with a curved stainless steel rod to serve as a handrail – and the design was finished. Of course, one mustn't forget the painted black bar at the end of the stairway; above it is a transverse concrete lintel used for projections. The effect of

Blick von unten nach oben | The view looking up from below

„Hotel Shanghai" von außen | Exterior of the 'Hotel Shanghai'

Der Neonschriftzug an der Fassade | The neon script on the façade

eine neue Gaststättenverordnung sieht mittlerweile vor, ganz ins Freie gehen zu müssen. So steht nun auf dem Gehweg, dem Raucher-Sitztreppen-Durchfahrtraum vorgelagert, wiederum ein Werk von Kay persönlich: Mit ein paar Baustellenabsperrgittern und grünen Plastikplanen hat er einen gar nicht mal hässlichen Kubus erzeugt, in dem nun offiziell geraucht werden darf. Den Übergang von Innen und Außen markiert eine Glasbausteinwand, die original aus den 1970ern zu stammen scheint, aber erst im Zuge des Umbaus durch Ben und Daniel Dratz hinzugefügt wurde. Auf ausdrücklichen Wunsch von Kay, der die Ornamentsteine bei ebay ersteigert und mit einer recht kostspieligen Taxifahrt nach Essen geholt hat.

Der Raucherraum im „Hotel Shanghai", dessen Name übrigens irgendwie mit Kays Jugend in Shanghai zu tun hat, dieser Raucherraum also dürfte die kleinste Baumaßnahme sein, die je in einem Jahrbuch des DAM veröffentlicht wurde. Architektur, das ist nicht, was man sich erst leistet, wenn zu viel Geld vorhanden ist. Architektur kann auch nahezu unsichtbar sein und auf jede Achtung-hier-kommt's!-Geste verzichten. Die Architektur auf den zweiten Blick, das auf Ausstellungen wie der Biennale in Venedig gefeierte „Reduce, Reuse, Recycling": Das gibt es, am Rande der Wahrnehmungsschwelle, nun immer häufiger zu entdecken, zum Beispiel mitten in der Nacht, mitten in Essen.

this quite self-evident floor plan becomes apparent beginning around 2 a.m., when the club is well filled. Down below, at the bar, you have a perfect view of those who don't feel like dancing to indie-electro-pop right at the moment, but might be chilling out on the steps instead. Here, the horizontal orientation of a club (people stand around and see only those closest to them in the crowd) is redirected into a kind of ad-hoc community: what's going on over on the stairs? People do still smoke there a little, but new restaurant regulations now stipulate that smokers must go all the way outdoors. Therefore, one of Kay's own creations now stands on the walkway in front of the smokers' seating step passageway: using a few construction-site barrier fences and green plastic sheeting, he built a cube where people are officially allowed to smoke – and it is not even very ugly. The passageway from the indoor to the outdoor space is marked by a glass brick wall, which appears to be an original relic from the 1970s – although it was only added by Ben and Daniel Dratz during the construction process. This, too, was at the express request of Kay, who purchased the decorative stones on eBay and transported them to Essen in a very expensive taxi ride. The smoking room at the 'Hotel Shanghai' – whose name, by the way, is a reference to Kay's youthful years in the Chinese city – may be the smallest building project ever profiled in a DAM Architecture Annual. Architecture is not something you can only afford when you have money to spare. Architecture can be nearly invisible, and it can exist without any 'wait for it!' gestures. The 'architecture at second glance' that is celebrated in exhibitions like 'Reduce, Reuse, Recycle' at the Biennale in Venice really exists: it exists at the edge of our perception threshold, and we can now discover it more and more often – for example, in the middle of the night in the centre of Essen.

Nach dem Entfernen der Wandfarbe wurde der raue Charakter des Betons belassen. | After removal of the paint, the concrete formwork of the walls was left exposed.

Grundriss | Plan

ECKER ARCHITEKTEN

HANGAR XS
BUCHEN

TEXT ARNE WINKELMANN

08

ARCHITEKTEN | ARCHITECTS

Ecker Architekten,
Dea Ecker + Robert Piotrowski
Römerstraße 29
69115 Heidelberg
www.ecker-architekten.de

MITARBEITER | TEAM

Joachim Schuhmacher,
Peter Borek, Mitja Sesko

BAUHERR | CLIENT

Sonnengarten-Stiftung,
Tannhausen/Buchen

**AUSFÜHRUNGSPLANUNG
EXECUTION PLANNING**

Ecker Architekten

**BAULEITUNG
SITE MANAGEMENT**

Ecker Architekten

TRAGWERK | STRUCTURE

Ingenieurbüro Kist+Theilig,
Mosbach

HAUSTECHNIK | M & E ENGINEERS

Ingenieurbüro Metzger,
Weikersheim
Ingenieurbüro Willhaug,
Mosbach

FERTIGSTELLUNG | COMPLETION

Dezember | December 2013

STANDORT | LOCATION

Hettingerstraße 3
74722 Buchen

FOTOS | PHOTOS

Brigida González, Stuttgart

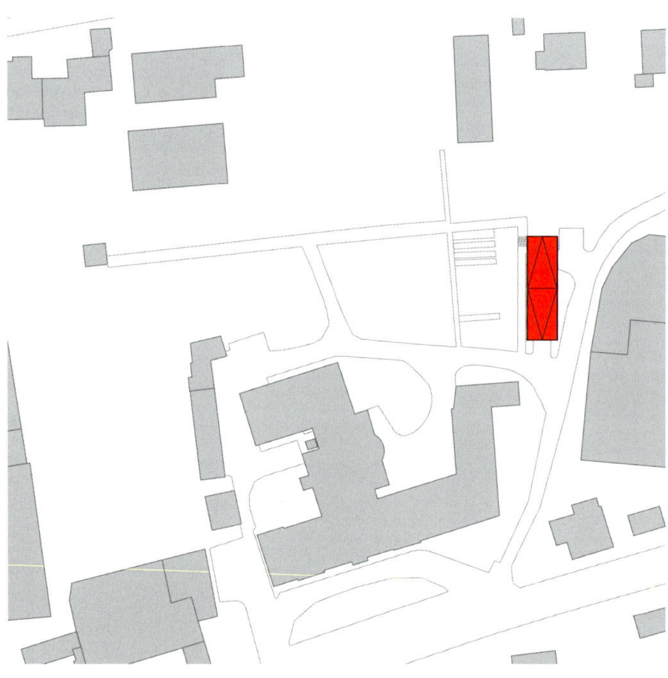

Lageplan | Site plan

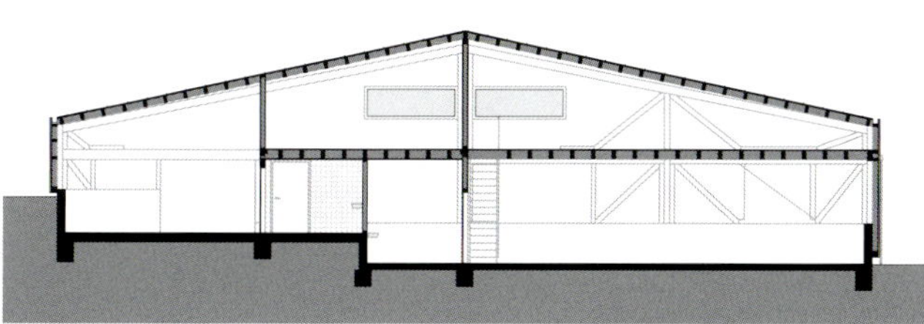

Die Westfassade | Western façade

In der Kleinstadt Buchen im Odenwald entstand für die Sonnen-garten-Stiftung für Wohnen und Pflege ein kleines Wirtschafts-gebäude, das sich doch sehen lassen kann. Als aufgeregt kann man das bauliche Umfeld kaum bezeichnen, und doch wirkt der monolithische Hangar XS irgendwie beruhigend und klärend. Das Gebäude steht hinter dem Seniorenheim zwischen dessen Nutzgarten und benachbarten Kuhställen und kontrastiert durch seine einfache Geometrie und seine graugrüne Farbe. Zwar nimmt der Bau, der eine Fahrzeughalle, eine Werkstatt und einen Müllraum beherbergt, die Formen der landwirtschaft-

In the small town of Buchen in the Odenwald, a small service building was built for the Sonnen-garten-Stiftung für Wohnen und Pflege (Sonnen-garten Residence and Care Foundation) that is truly something to see. The architectural environment can hardly be described as interesting, and yet, the monolithic Hangar XS somehow has a calming and clarifying effect on the viewer. The building is located behind the retirement home, between its kitchen garden and the neighbouring cowsheds, and stands out thanks to its simple geometry and grey-green colour. Even though the structure – which houses a vehicle shed, a workshop and a waste storage room – adopts the shapes of the neighbouring farm buildings, it varies this pattern through the use of an almost archetypal form: the roof of the elongated cuboid was 'cut' so as to produce four gable ends. As a result, the long façade appears squatter, vaguely recalling the comparable post-modern irritation of the Vanna Venturi House. The fact that this archetypal form is able to achieve

Schnitt | Section

Das geöffnete Schiebetor und der Blick ins Innere
View into the interior with the gate open

Blick von Südwesten; in der schmalen Südfassade sitzt ein großes Schiebetor für Nutzfahrzeuge.
View from the southwest: the narrow southern façade contains a large sliding gate for service vehicles.

lichen Gebäude der Nachbarschaft auf, variiert sie aber durch eine fast genial archetypische Form: Das Dach des länglichen Quaders wurde derart „beschnitten", dass vier Giebelseiten entstanden. Die längliche Fassade wirkt dadurch untersetzt und erinnert entfernt an die vergleichbare postmoderne Irritation des Vanna Venturi House. Dass diese archetypische Form so klar und kristallin wirken kann, verdankt der Bau seiner einheitlichen Verkleidung aus Titanzink. Es ist das einzige Material, das außen Verwendung findet und bedeckt nicht nur die Wände und Dachflächen – konsequent wurden die stehenden Falzkanten in exakter Ausrichtung auch über die Dachschrägen gezogen –, sondern aus ihm wurden auch sämtliche Details wie Türen, Tore und deren Führungsschienen gefertigt. Besonders die eingelassenen Regenrinnen und Fallrohre an den schmalen Seiten wurden sehr anspruchsvoll konstruiert. Die Metallverkleidung demonstriert, wie gewinnbringend eine frühe Einbindung der ausführenden Firma in die Planung sein kann.

Die Fassaden zeigen die unterschiedlichen Nutzungen: In der schmalen Südfassade sitzt ein Schiebetor für die Garage der Nutzfahrzeuge und erinnert zumindest typologisch an eine Scheune. Sie stellt quasi das Gesicht des Gebäudes dar, das man auch von der Hauptstraße aus sieht. Die Ostfassade ist

such a clear and crystalline appearance is thanks to the building's uniform titanium-zinc panelling. It is the only material used on the exterior of the structure, and it not only covers the surfaces of the walls and roof – the vertical seams were consistently extended in exact alignment over the slopes of the roof – but was also used in the construction of all the details, such as doors, gates and their corresponding guide rails. The design of the recessed rain gutters and downpipes is particularly sophisticated. The metal panelling is a good example of how beneficial it can be to involve the contracting company in the planning at an early stage.

The building's façades reveal its various uses: the narrow south façade contains a sliding gate for the service-vehicle garage and is reminiscent – at least typologically – of a barn. It more or less represents the 'face' of the building, which one can also see from the main road. The east façade is flanked by a well-used service road and opens into the building with both a door and a sliding gate leading to the waste storage room. A narrow window element

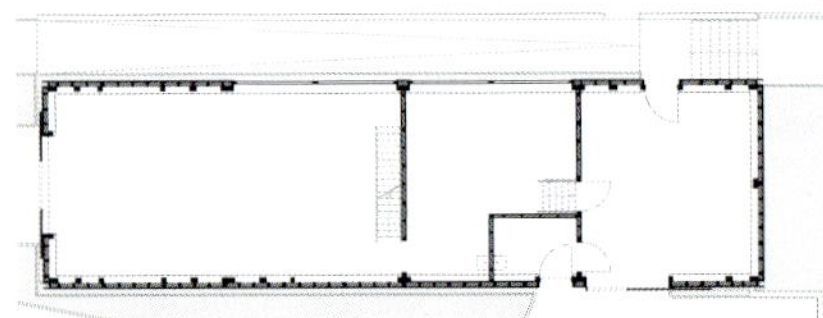

Grundriss Erdgeschoss | Plan of ground floor

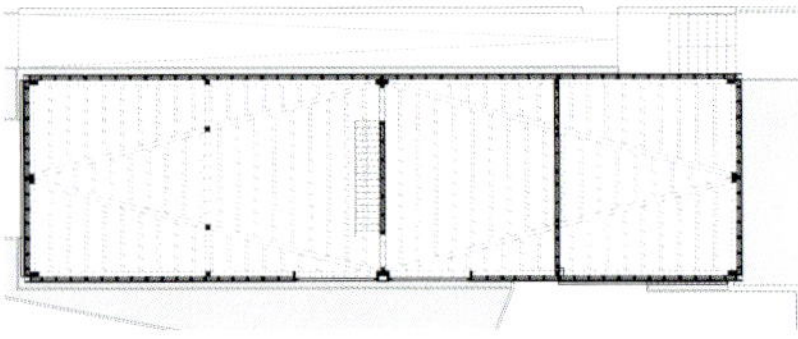

Grundriss Obergeschoss | Plan of 1st floor

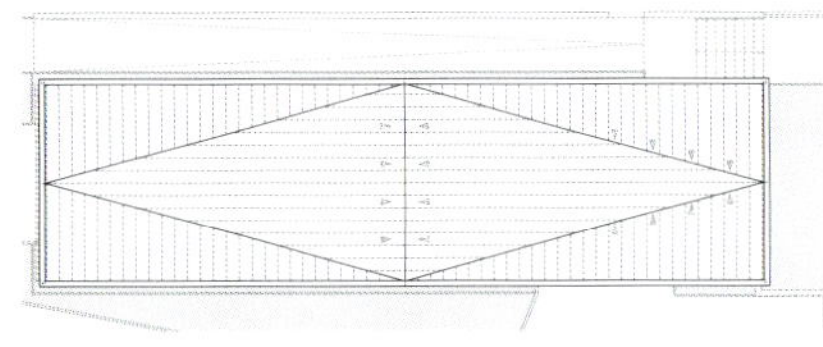

Dachaufsicht | View of the roof

Die Ostfassade am Wirtschaftsweg mit Tür und Schiebetor | The eastern façade on the service road with a door and sliding gate

Die Ansicht von Westen erinnert entfernt an das Vanna Venturi House. | The view from the west is vaguely reminiscent of the Vanna Venturi House.

von einem stark befahrenen Wirtschaftsweg flankiert und öffnet den Bau mit einer Tür und einem Schiebetor, hinter dem der Müllraum liegt. Ein schmales Fensterband darüber lässt erkennen, dass im Innern dieses niedrigen Gebäudes sogar noch ein zweites Geschoss untergebracht ist. Es belichtet die gesamte Lagerfläche der oberen Ebene. Die Westfassade, vor der ein schmaler Weg entlangläuft, gibt mit einem langen Fensterband Einblick in die Hausmeisterwerkstatt und die Fahrzeughalle.

Im Gegensatz zur Metallfassade außen wirkt der Innenraum durch die Exposition seiner Holzständerkonstruktion und den Ausbau mit Grobspanplatten warm und fast gemütlich. Bis auf den Betonsockel sind hier alle Wände und Decken in Holz gehalten. Auch die Innenräume bestechen durch die konsequent funktionale, aber ästhetisch ansprechende Detaillierung, angefangen von einer filigranen Schiffstreppe über Fugen und Rücksprünge bis hin zu der „ehrlichen" Elektroinstallation.

Der Hangar XS überzeugt durch seinen hohen entwerferischen Aufwand für eine vergleichsweise profane Bauaufgabe. Die handwerkliche Durchdringung seiner Konstruktion und der Details unterstreicht die markante Form und zeigt einmal mehr, dass keine Bauaufgabe zu gering für Qualität sein kann.

above reveals that the interior of this low building even includes a second storey. It illuminates the entire storage area on the upper level. The west façade, which is bordered by a narrow footway, contains a long row of windows that provide a view into the caretaker's workshop and the vehicle shed. In contrast to the exterior metal façade, the interior, with its exposed post-and-beam structure and coarse hardboard finish, has a warm and almost cosy feeling. With the exception of the concrete base, all of the walls and ceilings have been left in exposed wood. The interior spaces provide consistently functional, but aesthetically appealing details – from a delicate ship's companionway staircase, via joins and recesses, all the way to its 'straightforward' electrical installations.

Hangar XS is impressive on account of the high level of design effort expended on a relatively mundane building project. The craftsmanship that permeates its construction and details underscores its striking form and proves once again that no building project can be too small to merit high quality.

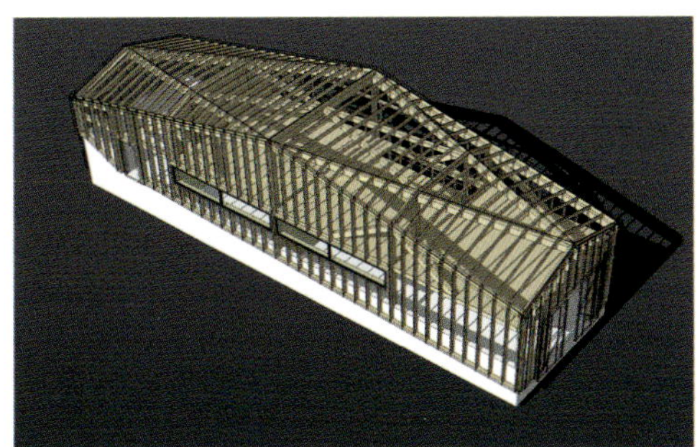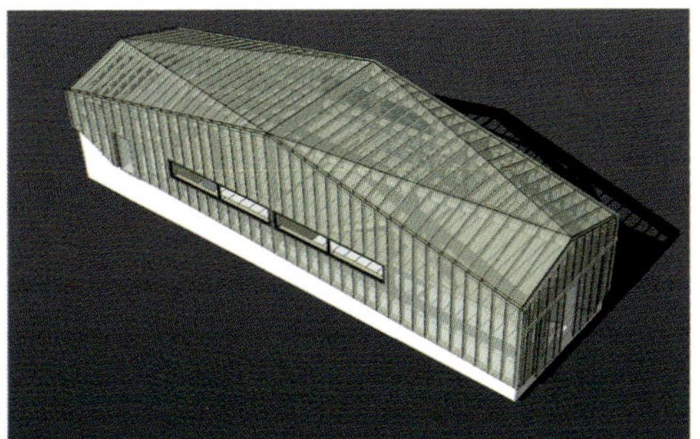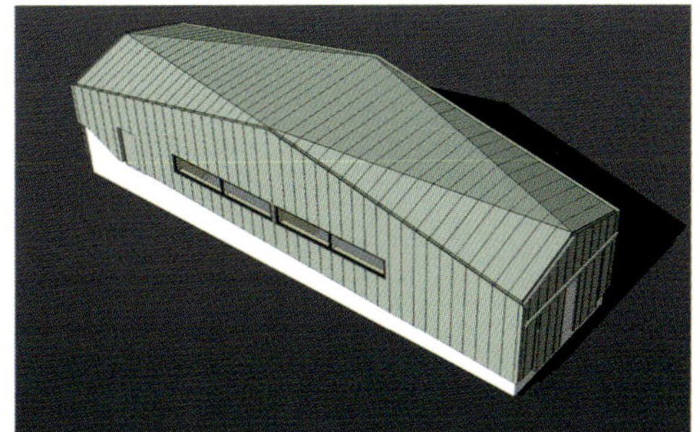

Konstruktion, Dachgeometrie und Verkleidung des Hangar XS | Construction, roof geometry and panelling of Hangar XS

FERDINAND HEIDE ARCHITEKT

GEBÄUDE | BUILDING

OSTHAFENBRÜCKE / HONSELLBRÜCKE
FRANKFURT AM MAIN

TEXT CHRISTIAN THOMAS

ARCHITEKTEN | ARCHITECTS

ARGE Ferdinand Heide Architekt –
Grontmij GmbH,
Osthafenbrücke
ARGE Ferdinand Heide Architekt –
König und Heunisch,
Honsellbrücke

Ferdinand Heide Architekt
Leinwebergasse 4
60386 Frankfurt am Main
www.ferdinand-heide.de

MITARBEITER | TEAM

Frank Heinen (Projektleitung |
project architect),
Sebastian Schultheis,
Herbert Duda

BAUHERR | CLIENT

Stadt Frankfurt am Main

AUSFÜHRUNGSPLANUNG
EXECUTION PLANNING

ARGE Ferdinand Heide Architekt –
Grontmij GmbH,
Osthafenbrücke
ARGE Ferdinand Heide Architekt –
König und Heunisch,
Honsellbrücke

**BAULEITUNG /
PROJEKTSTEUERUNG**
SITE MANAGEMENT /
PROJECT MANAGEMENT

Bauüberwachung
construction supervision:
TÜV Rheinland Grebner Ruchay
Consulting GmbH, Honsellbrücke
ZERNA Baumanagement GmbH,
Osthafenbrücke

Prüfingenieur | inspection engineer:
Weihermüller & Vogel GmbH,
Osthafenbrücke
Prüfingenieur für Baustatik
Dr. Ing. Joachim Hahn,
Honsellbrücke

Bauunternehmen bzw. Stahlbau
construction company and
steel construction:
Max Bögl Bauunternehmung
GmbH & Co. KG, Osthafenbrücke
ARGE Adam Hörnig
Baugesellschaft mbH & Co. KG
und Donges Steeltec GmbH,
Honsellbrücke

Projektsteuerung
project management:
Schüßler-Plan
Ingenieurgesellschaft mbH

FERTIGSTELLUNG | COMPLETION
Dezember | December **2013**

STANDORT | LOCATION
Frankfurt am Main
www.neue-mainbruecke-frankfurt.de

FOTOS | PHOTOS
Frank Heinen, CFH-Photography,
Frankfurt am Main
Michael Wolff,
Frankfurt am Main / Bochum
Yorck Förster, Frankfurt am Main

Lageplan | Site plan

Blick von der sanierten Honsellbrücke auf die neue Osthafenbrücke. Die alte Konstruktion ist durch aufgelegte Stahlbögen stabilisiert.
View of the new Osthafen Bridge from the renovated Honsell Bridge. Steel arches have been added to stabilise the old structure.

Bereits vor annähernd einhundert Jahren, als Frankfurts großer Stadtentwicklungsbeobachter, Siegfried Kracauer, den Osthafen seiner Stadt durchforschte, bemerkte er ausdrücklich eine nicht allein den Banken vorbehaltene „Bautätigkeit". Auch über die Kernstadt hinaus konnte er einem „wirtschaftlichen Ausdehnungsdrang" zusehen. Ebenfalls ein Ausdehnungsbedürfnis im Osten, mit einem besonderen Blick auf die Banken, hat sich die Stadt zuletzt mit einem Brückenschlag über den Main gestattet. Dazu zählte neben dem Neubau einer Osthafenbrücke die Sanierung der historischen Honsellbrücke. Wenn beide Brücken einen „Baustein" bilden, dann ist das eine sehr bescheidene Formulierung Ferdinand Heides. Ebenso sachlich spricht der Architekt von einem „stadträumlichen Bindeglied".
Nun, bereits mit dem Baustein hat Heide vielerlei angestellt. Angefangen damit, dass er jetzt eine Bogenbrücke fertiggestellt hat, die, mit einem eleganten (gar nicht bauchigen) Schwung, ohne einen Pfeiler im Wasser, auf einer Länge von

Nearly one hundred years ago, when Frankfurt's great observer of urban development, Siegfried Kracauer, was exploring his city's Osthafen (eastern harbour), he already specifically made note of 'building activity' which was not limited only to the banks. Even outside of the inner city, he observed an 'urge for economic expansion'. Recently, the city has granted itself just such a desire for expansion in its eastern section – particularly in view of the banks – in the form of a bridge across the River Main. In addition to the construction of the new Osthafen Bridge, this also includes the restoration of the historic Honsell Bridge. If the two bridges make up one 'building block', then this is very modest wording on the part of Ferdinand Heide. In an equally matter-of-fact fashion, the architect speaks of a 'city connective link'.

Die neue Osthafenbrücke; rechts der Neubau der Europäischen Zentralbank kurz vor der Fertigstellung | The new Osthafen Bridge; on the right is the new European Central Bank building shortly before completion.

173 Metern den Fluss überspannt. Auf der Brücke selbst, mit ihren Fußgänger- und Fahrradwegen, die die Straße säumen, zeigt sich der Baustein als ein Gebilde aus dunkelgrauem Stahl. Viermal werden die Doppelbögen zusammengeführt, bilden Öffnungen, und die gestreckten, abgeflachten Ovale sind ebenso etwas für das Auge wie deren leicht nach innen geneigte Krümmungen. Wenn der Laie bei den zwischen Fahrbahn und Bögen schräg verspannten Stahlseilen über das filigrane Geflecht staunt, identifiziert der Fachmann die an gekreuzten Hängerseilen abgehängte Konstruktion als eine „Nielsen-Brücke", als eine Netzwerkbogenbrücke.

Um 30 Meter wurden die Widerlager am Südufer zurückversetzt, um die Uferpromenade nicht zu beeinträchtigen und um zudem mit der breiten Freitreppe die Wirkung von Uferterrassen zu erreichen. Dass sie aus rotem Main-Sandstein sind, berücksichtigt die regionale Bautradition. Wenn auf der Nordseite, unterhalb der Honsellbrücke, sowohl deren rund 100 Jahre alte Konstruktion der Widerlager des Brückenbogens ebenso wie darüber die des neuen Stahlüberbaus offen zu sehen sind, und mit ihnen das Ornamentale und das Nüchterne als Nebeneinander, dann liefert der Kontrast einen Schauwert. Es ist nicht der einzige, denn mit Eintritt der Dunkelheit wird die Osthafenbrücke beleuchtet, gesittet illuminiert. Dann schwebt überm Fluss ein Gespinst.

In fact, even with this building block, Heide has been very innovative – beginning with the fact that he has now completed an arch bridge which spans the river across a length of 173 metres in an elegant sweeping shape that is not the least bit bulbous, and without a single pier in the water. On the bridge itself, with its pedestrian and bicycle paths lining the carriageway, the 'building block' appears as a structure made of dark grey steel. The double arches are brought together four times; they form openings, and these elongated, flattened ovals are as much a treat for the eyes as are their slightly inward-leaning curves. While a layperson may marvel at the steel cables stretched between the roadway and the arches over the filigree meshwork, the expert identifies the structure hanging from the crossed suspension cables as a 'Nielsen Bridge' – that is, a network arch bridge.

The abutments on the south bank were moved back 30 metres so as not to infringe on the embankment promenade and to create the sense of riverside terraces with the wide open stairway. The fact that they are made out of red Main sandstone is a nod to regional building tradition. If, on the north side,

Die Auffahrtsrampe zur Osthafenbrücke am südlichen Mainufer im regionaltypischen roten Sandstein
The access ramp to the Osthafen Bridge on the south bank of the Main, built from the region's typical red sandstone

Die illuminierte Osthafenbrücke abends, dahinter die Frankfurter Skyline | The illuminated Osthafen Bridge against Frankfurt's evening skyline

In die Bögen am Fuß der Honsellbrücke ziehen Kultur und Gastronomie ein. | The archways at the foot of the Honsell Bridge house restaurants and cultural venues.

Ferdinand Heide hat zusammen mit der Grontmij Ingenieursgesellschaft einen feingliedrigen Baukörper über den Main gespannt. Dazu gehört auch, dass zwischen den Fahrbahnen Lichtfugen eingezogen sind: So ist für Schiffer, Ruderer oder Promenadennutzer das Fachwerk der Unterkonstruktion auszumachen. Aufschauen, ja, für welche Brücke gilt das nicht, die mehr als nur eine simple Verbindung von A nach B ist, und das war bereits die historische Honsellbrücke. Das Denkmal fand in dem sanierungswilligen Architekten so etwas wie eine Stütze. Mit zwei gekrümmten Schienen oberhalb der alten Bögen wird das wackelig gewordene Erbe versteift. Gerahmt wurde das verbliebene Jugendstilgeländer. Überdies wurde auf der Vorlandbrücke der Basaltlavastein wiederverwendet. All das sind Gründe, um in der Brücke nicht nur eine Verkehrsverbindung zu sehen. Die eine wie die andere Brücke sind zusammen ein Aufenthaltsraum. Ein sinnfälliges Ensemble obendrein.
Die ersten Pläne für einen doppelten Brückenschlag über den Main sind über einhundert Jahre alt. Damals bereits wurde an ein „stadträumliches Bindeglied" gedacht, und weil sich Pläne gelegentlich nicht nur wiederholen, sondern verdichten, zumal in der Stadt, wurde das Ensemble zu einem Baustein im neuen Generalverkehrsplan. Denn deutlich ist die Nachbarschaft des Brückenensembles zu den Zwillingstürmen der Europäischen Zentralbank.

underneath the Honsell Bridge, both the nearly 100-year-old abutment structures of its arch as well as those of the new steel superstructure above it are exposed to public view – and with them, the ornamental and the plain placed side by side – then this contrast provides a visual spectacle. It is not the only one – because as darkness falls, the Osthafen Bridge is bathed in light, tastefully illuminated. Then a gossamer web hovers over the river.
Together with the Grontmij engineering company, Ferdinand Heide has extended a graceful structure across the Main. This also includes the threading of lighting seams between the traffic lanes, allowing those on boats or pedestrians on the promenade to make out the framework of the substructure. Is it worth looking up? Of course – this is true of any bridge which is more than a simple connection between A and B – as was already the case with the historic Honsell Bridge. With his willingness to restore this monument, the architect provided it with something like a buttress. This piece of cultural heritage, now grown rickety, was reinforced with two curved rails placed above the old arches.

**Weniger offensichtlich ist, wie Heides Osthafenbrücke über-
dies exakt in der Verlängerung des Goetheturms, der aus den
Wipfeln des Stadtwalds ragt, über den Main gespannt wurde.
So steht die Osthafenbrücke in einem besonderen Geflecht
aus Türmen – und ist darin tatsächlich zu einer Landmarke
geworden, was damit zu tun hat, dass von kaum einem anderen
Punkt Frankfurts aus die Skyline so zu sehen ist: zusammen-
gepresst einerseits in ein kompaktes Bild, zugleich aufgefä-
chert zur aufgelockerten Hochhausansammlung, mal als aufge-
spannter Fassadenprospekt, mal als dreidimensionale Skulptur.
Welch ein Frankfurtbild von hier aus: von den beiden Mainufern
gerahmt. Mainhattan mag unter verschiedenen Aspekten ein
Klischee sein. Von der Osthafenbrücke aus ist es ein Stillleben
der ganz seltenen Art.**

A frame was built around the remaining Art Nouveau
balustrade. In addition, the basalt lava stone on
the foreland bridge was reused. All of these are
reasons why the bridge should not only be seen as a
traffic connection. Together, the two bridges form a
common space to linger – and an obvious ensemble
at the same time.

The earliest plans for a double bridging of the Main
date from more than one hundred years ago. The
idea of a 'city connective link' existed even then:
and since plans sometimes not only repeat themselves but become condensed, especially in the
city, the ensemble became a building block in the
new general transport plan. The proximity of the
bridge ensemble to the twin towers of the European
Central Bank is very clear.

Less obvious is how, on top of all this, Heide's
Osthafen Bridge was stretched across the Main
in an exact extension of the Goethe Tower, which
stands out above the treetops of the city forest.
Thus, the Osthafen Bridge stands amid a unique
network of towers – and has actually become a
landmark among them. This is partly because from
here, Frankfurt's skyline can be viewed in a way
hardly possible from any other point: on the one
hand, pressed together into a compact picture, and
at the same time fanned out in a loose collection
of skyscrapers; sometimes as an open prospect of
façades; sometimes as a three-dimensional sculpture.

What an image one can see of Frankfurt from this
vantage point: framed by the two banks of the
Main. 'Mainhattan' might represent a cliché in many
respects; but viewed from the Osthafen Bridge, it is
a very special kind of still-life.

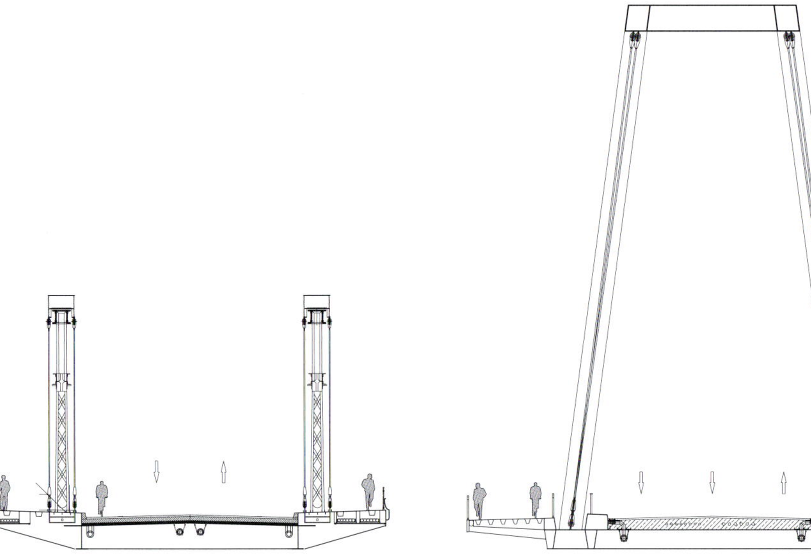

Schnitt Honsellbrücke | Section Honsell Bridge   **Schnitt Osthafenbrücke |** Section Osthafen Bridge

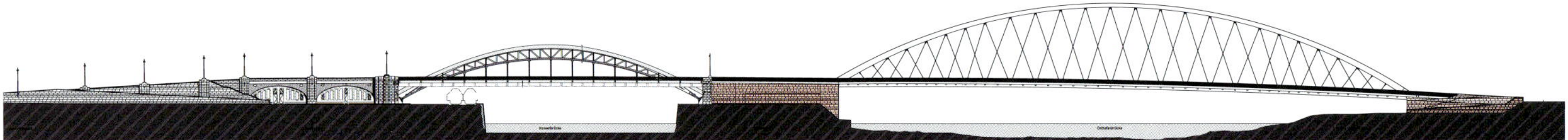

Ansicht von Westen gesehen: links die Honsell-, rechts die neue Osthafenbrücke | View from the west: left, the Honsell Bridge; right the new Osthafen Bridge

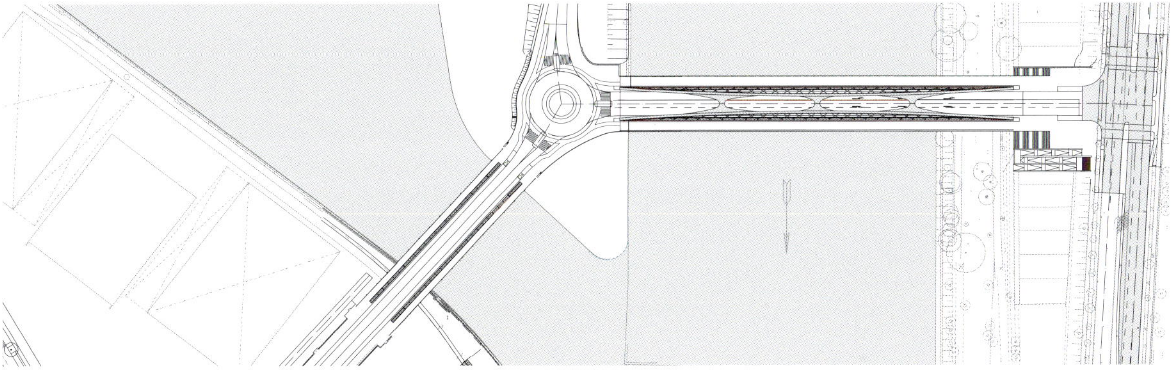

Blick von der Osthafenbrücke mit den eleganten Bogenovalen und zarten Seilverspannungen auf die Honsellbrücke und das nördliche Mainufer mit der Großmarkthalle und dem Neubau der Europäischen Zentralbank. | View from the Osthafen Bridge with the elegant oval arches and delicate cable bracing on the Honsell Bridge and the north bank of the Main with the wholesale market and new European Central Bank building.

Grundriss | Plan

FLORIAN NAGLER ARCHITEKTEN

KULTUR + KONGRESS FORUM
ALTÖTTING

TEXT YORCK FÖRSTER

10

ARCHITEKTEN | ARCHITECTS
Prof. Florian Nagler
Theodor-Storm-Straße 16
81245 München | Munich
www.nagler-architekten.de

MITARBEITER | TEAM
Projektleitung
Project management:
Stefan Lambertz
Annette Heilmann, Sebastian Streck, Irina Auerhammer, Britta Weiss

BAUHERR | CLIENT
Stadt Altötting, vertreten durch Ersten Bürgermeister Herbert Hofaue

AUSFÜHRUNGSPLANUNG
EXECUTION PLANNING
Florian Nagler Architekten

BAULEITUNG / PROJEKTSTEUERUNG
SITE MANAGEMENT / PROJECT MANAGEMENT
Städtische Projektleitung:
Hubert Rabenbauer, Abteilungsleiter Hochbau, Altötting

TRAGWERK | STRUCTURE
Merz Kley Partner GmbH, Dornbirn (Österreich | Austria**)**
Prüfstatik | review of structural calculations:
LGA Landesgewerbeanstalt Bayern, München | Munic

BRANDSCHUTZ
FIRE PREVENTION
Konzept | conception**: PHIplan Pavic & Hinterstoißer Ing., Grabenstätt**
Prüfsachverständiger Brandschutz
fire prevention consultant:
Prüfsachverständigenbüro für Brandschutz, M. Eng., Wolfgang Edbauer, Traunstein

ENERGIEKONZEPT
ENERGY CONSULTANT
Transsolar, München | Munich

BÜHNENTECHNIK
STAGE TECHNOLOGY
Bühnenplanung W. Kottke Ing. GmbH, Bayreuth

HAUSTECHNIK | M & E ENGINEERS
Planungsbüro Schwein, Neuötting

BAUPHYSIK + AKUSTIK
BUILDING PHYSICS + ACOUSTICS
Müller BBM GmbH, München | Munich

KÜCHENPLANER
KITCHEN PLANNING
ITM Ingenieurteam Rosenheim, Rosenheim
GTS Großküchen Technik Straubing GmbH, Straubing

BELEUCHTUNG | LIGHTING
Die Lichtideenschmiede, Ottobrunn

ELEKTROTECHNIK
ELECTRICAL ENGINEERING
Gesellschaft für Elektro- und Nachrichtentechnik mbH, Burghausen

LANDSCHAFTSARCHITEKTUR
LANDSCAPE ARCHITECTURE
Christina Kautz Landschaftsarchitektur, Berlin
Link Landschafts-Architekten, Altötting

KUNST AM BAU | ART
Prof. Franz Ackermann, Berlin

FERTIGSTELLUNG | COMPLETION
Januar | January **2013**

STANDORT | LOCATION
Zuccalliplatz 1
84503 Altötting
www.forumaltoetting.de

FOTOS | PHOTOS
Stefan Müller-Naumann, München | Munich

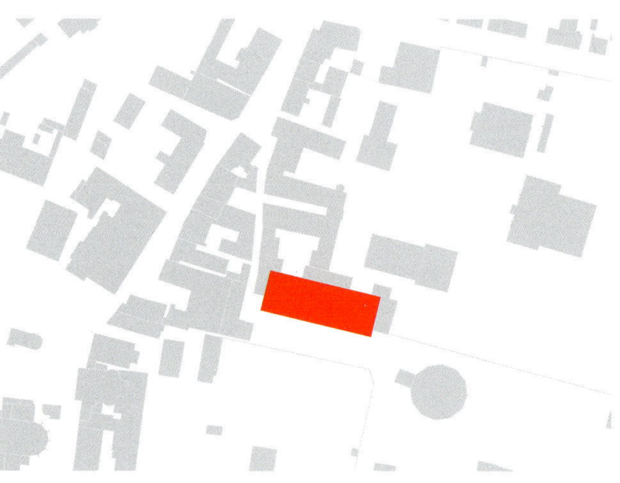

Lageplan | Site plan

Die Süd- und die Ostfassade des Forums. Das steile, schindelgedeckte Satteldach fügt sich ganz selbstverständlich in die Stadtsilhouette ein.
The southern and eastern façades of the Forum. The steep, shingled pitched roof blends in quite naturally with the town's silhouette.

An festlich großen Hallenbauten besteht in Altötting an sich kein Mangel. Doch sind sie allesamt Sakralbauten. Seit über 500 Jahren gibt es die Marienwallfahrt zur „Schwarzen Madonna". Ziel der Pilger ist die bescheidene Gnadenkapelle in der Stadtmitte, um die im 17. Jahrhundert der prachtvolle Kapellplatz angelegt wurde.
Gerade dieser Luxus ist in einem gewissen Sinn aber die Bürde Altöttings. Denn dem fulminanten Auftritt an Orten der religiösen Sammlung gegenüber stand ein Mangel an Orten für das städtische Gemeinschaftsleben. Der größte profane Saal war in einem Hotel zu finden. Das überraschende Scheitern eines Gastwirts bot der Stadt Altötting plötzlich die einmalige Chance, einen kommunalen Saalbau im Stadtzentrum zu entwickeln. Ein Teil des Gasthofs sowie angrenzende Grundstücke im Osten zwischen denkmalgeschützten Klostergärten wurden erworben. Ein städtebaulicher Wettbewerb und ein nachgeschaltetes VOF-Verfahren folgten.
Der Entwurfsansatz von Florian Nagler Architekten besteht stadträumlich aus einer Abfolge von kleinen Plätzen und Gassen, die das Areal mit der Umgebung verzahnen. Eine neue kleine Passage durch ein Bestandsgebäude dient als Erschlie-

Altötting has no shortage of large festive halls per se. All of them, however, are sacred buildings. The Marian pilgrimage to the 'Black Madonna' has been in existence for over 500 years. The pilgrims' destination is the modest Gnadenkapelle (Chapel of Grace) in the town centre, around which the splendid Kapellplatz was built in the seventeenth century. In some sense, this very luxury is Altötting's burden – because in contrast to its impressive appearance at the sites of religious gatherings, the town was lacking in suitable locations for civic community life. The town's largest secular hall was located in a hotel. An hotelier's unexpected bankruptcy suddenly offered the city of Altötting the unique opportunity to develop a communal hall in the centre of town. The city purchased part of the hotel along with adjacent property to the east, between the monastic gardens, a protected heritage site. An urban development competition and a subsequent procedure for the award of contracts for professional services soon followed.

ßung vom Kapellplatz aus. Eine längsrechteckige Platzanlage bildet den Vorplatz des neuen Veranstaltungshauses und befreit nebenbei auch einen Zentralbau mit dem Panoramagemälde Jerusalems aus der vormaligen Hinterhoflage. Östlich davon entstand eine Tiefgarage, über der ein innerstädtischer Park angelegt wurde.

Das Forums-Gebäude ist ein langgezogener Riegel, von dem zunächst das steile Satteldach als das bestimmende Bauelement wahrgenommen wird. Im Kontext von Altötting ist der Bezug zu dieser Bauform ein gelungener Kunstgriff. Denn die steilen Dächer und Türme der Kirchen bestimmen die Silhouette der Stadt. Ganz beiläufig tritt nun ein weiteres hohes Dach in das Ensemble, aber ohne Turm und mit einer Eindeckung nicht aus Ziegeln, sondern aus Holzschindeln. Das ist architektonisch reinstes Understatement, denn sowohl die Dimension als auch der elegant-silbergraue Farbton der inzwischen bewitterten Schindeln weist durchaus selbstbewusst darauf hin, dass hier nun das Bürger- und Kulturzentrum der Stadt entstanden ist. Die unmittelbare Außenwirkung des Baues ist sowohl von elementarer Klarheit als auch feiner Sinnlichkeit. Die Längs- und Giebelwände bilden eine deutliche Kontur. Das Dach ist davon durch eine tiefe Fuge, die die Entwässerung aufnimmt, abgetrennt. Die Großelemente Dach und Wand haben eine

From a town-planning standpoint, the design concept by Florian Nagler Architekten consists of a series of small squares and pathways that link the site with the surrounding area. A new small passageway through an existing building provides access to and from the Kapellplatz. An oblong space serves as the forecourt of the new event hall and at the same time, it frees the area around a centrally planned building containing a panoramic painting of Jerusalem, which had previously been hidden in a rear courtyard. An underground garage was built to the east of this, on top of which a park was created. The Forum building is an elongated block whose steep pitched roof is the first defining feature to catch the eye. In the context of Altötting, the reference to this structural form is a successful device, since the steep church roofs and towers define the silhouette of the town. Quite incidentally, another tall roof has now joined the ensemble – but this time without a tower, and with a covering of wood shingles rather than tiles. From an architectural standpoint, this is sheer understatement, since both the dimensions of the building as well as the elegant,

Der Vorplatz im Süden. Im Hintergrund rechts der Zentralbau mit dem Jerusalem-Panorama.
The forecourt on the south side. In the background on the right is the centrally-planned building with the Jerusalem panorama.

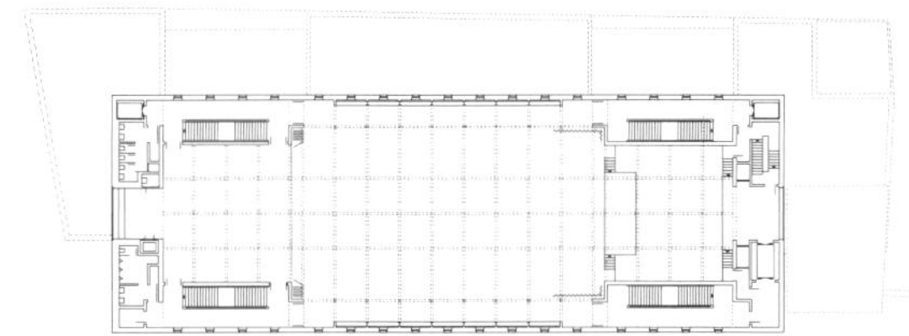

Grundriss 1. Obergeschoss | Plan of 1st floor

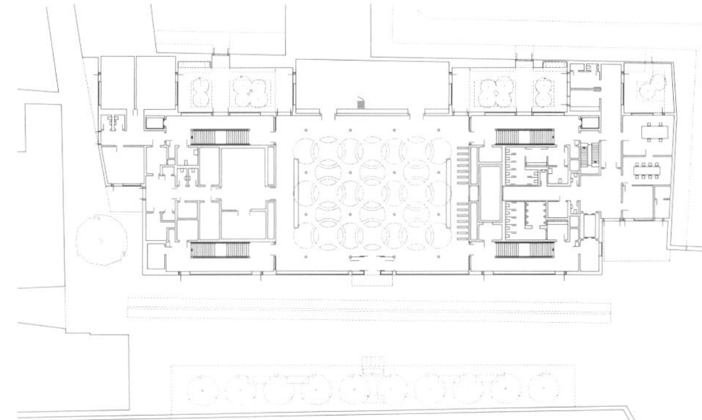

Grundriss Erdgeschoss | Plan of ground floor

Das Satteldach ist mit Holzschindeln gedeckt, der Putz fein strukturiert. The pitched roof is covered with wooden shingles; the plaster is finely structured.

Binnengliederung durch die jeweilige Oberflächentextur: Der Wandputz zeigt eine horizontale Besenstrich-Bearbeitung, das Dach wiederum wird durch den unregelmäßigen Verlauf der Schindelkanten belebt.

Das mittig im Erdgeschoss platzierte Foyer ist als wandelbare Eingangshalle und Veranstaltungsort zugleich ausgelegt. Gastronomieelemente können hineingerollt, Garderobeneinrichtungen aus den Wandzonen ausgefahren werden. Obwohl der Raum fast nur von seiner Zugangsseite her belichtet wird und eine Tiefe von gut 20 Metern aufweist, wirkt er dank der durchgängig hellen Oberflächen niemals düster und gedrückt. Markant ist die Deckengestaltung aus sich überlagernden Kreisbögen. Im Norden an das Foyer anschließend nimmt ein eingeschossiger Baukörper zwei koppelbare Tagungsräume auf, die über seitlich gelegene begrünte Innenhöfe belichtet werden. Dieser fast klösterliche Luxus des umschlossenen Gartens zur Belichtung findet sich auch in der Gestaltung des im Nordosten gelegenen Verwaltungstrakts wieder.

Das Herzstück des Langhauses ist aber der imposante Raiffeisen-Saal im Obergeschoss. Die lichte Höhe des offenen hölzernen Dachstuhls bis zum First beträgt stolze 18 Meter. In der größten Ausgestaltung – wenn das im Westen gelegene

silver-grey colour of the already weathered shingles self-confidently make it clear that the city's new community and cultural centre has been built here. The building makes an immediate external impression of elemental clarity and refined sensuousness. The long sides and gable ends form clearly-defined contours. The roof is separated from the walls by a deep groove that serves as a drainage gutter. The large elements of roof and walls are internally differentiated by their respective surface textures: the wall plaster has a horizontal broom-stroke finish, while the roof is enlivened by the irregular arrangement of the shingle edges.

The foyer, located in the centre of the ground floor, is laid out both as a convertible entrance hall and event venue. Catering elements can be rolled in; cloakroom furnishings can be pulled out from the recessed wall sections. Even though the room is lit almost entirely from the entrance side, and is over 20 metres deep, thanks to its consistently light-coloured surfaces the atmosphere is never gloomy or oppressive. The ceiling design, with its overlapping circular arcs, is a

Das vielseitig nutzbare Foyer mit den charakteristischen Kreissegmenten an der Decke | The flexible, multi-purpose foyer with its characteristic circular segments on the ceiling

Einer der drei Innenhöfe mit klosterartiger Atmosphäre | One of the three courtyards with a monastery-like atmosphere

Besonders abends gut erkennbar sind die Wandgemälde, die Franz Ackermann für die Treppenhäuser geschaffen hat. The wall paintings created for the staircases by Franz Ackermann are most clearly visible in the evenings.

„Kleine Foyer" zugeschaltet wird – ist Platz für 900 Besucher. Der Saal ist auf maximale Wandelbarkeit hin konzipiert. Für Tanzveranstaltungen, Kongresse oder Messen kann er auf einer Bodenebene genutzt werden, bei Konzert oder Theaterveranstaltungen kann durch Hubpodeste das Auditorium gestaffelt werden. Bei geringen Besucherzahlen verkleinern große Vorhänge optisch den Raum. Eine höchst flexible Bühnentechnik mit Hubpodium sowie ein großes Tor in der Ostwand erlauben auch große Showveranstaltungen und die Andienung sperriger Objekte. Streng genommen ist das Gebäude ein variabler Technologieträger vom Küchen- und Cateringbereich über Proberäume bis hin zu verschiedensten Bühnenszenarien. Dass dieses breite Nutzungsspektrum nicht in eine mit Technikdetails überfrachtete pragmatische Eigenschaftslosigkeit der Gestaltung mündete, sondern klar und einfach wirkt, ist die besondere Leistung der Architekten. Das Forum in Altötting ist sowohl artifiziell minimalistisch als auch ein archetypisches Bild einer regionalen Architektur.

striking feature. Adjacent to the foyer on the north side, a single-storey structure houses two combinable conference rooms, which are lit from laterally-placed greened courtyards. This almost monastery-like luxury, in the form of an enclosed garden, can be seen again in the design of the administrative wing on the northeast side.

The heart of the main building, however, is the imposing Raiffeisen Hall on the upper level. The vertical clearance up to the ridge of the open wooden roof truss is an impressive 18 metres. Its most spacious arrangement – when it is connected with the 'small foyer' on the western side – provides room for 900 guests. The hall was designed for maximum flexibility. For dance events, conferences or trade fairs, it can be used at a single floor level; for concerts or theatre productions, the auditorium can be gradated using lifting platforms. Large curtains provide the option of visually reducing the size of the space for smaller numbers of visitors. Highly flexible stage technology – including a lifting podium and a large gate in the eastern wall – also allows for the staging of large show events and the delivery of bulky objects. Strictly speaking, this building displays various technologies, ranging from a kitchen and catering area via rehearsal rooms to a wide range of stage scenarios. The fact that this broad spectrum of uses did not result in a pragmatic and featureless creation, overloaded with technical details, is the architects' great achievement. The Forum in Altötting is both sophisticatedly minimalist as well as an archetypal image of regional architecture.

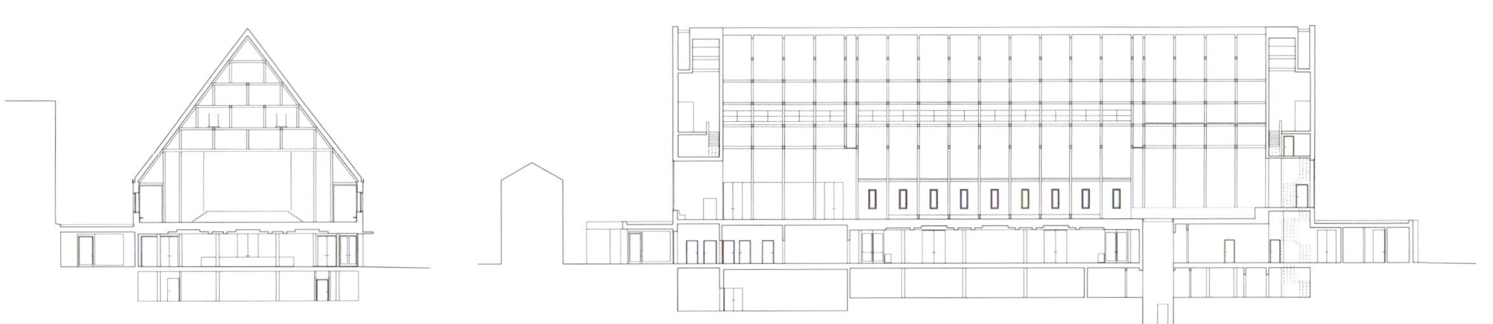

Der Hauptsaal mit seinem beeindruckenden offenen Dachstuhl | The main hall with its impressive open roof truss

Querschnitt | Cross-section

Längsschnitt | Longitudinal section

GLASS KRAMER LÖBBERT / UTA GRAFF

GEBÄUDE | BUILDING

:ENVIHAB
RAUMFAHRTMEDIZINISCHES INSTITUT DES DLR KÖLN-PORZ

TEXT KAREN JUNG

ARCHITEKTEN | ARCHITECTS

Glass Kramer Löbbert Architekten
bda, Berlin
Schlesische Straße 27
10997 Berlin
www.glasskramerlöbbert.de

mit | with **Prof. U. Graff
Architektin bda,
Berlin / München
www.utagraff.de**

MITARBEITER | TEAM

Johannes Löbbert, Uta Graff,
Johan Kramer, Jürgen Ochernal,
Patrick Lau, Hanna Rohrbach,
Christoph Conrad, Johannes Thoma

BAUHERR | CLIENT

Deutsches Zentrum für Luft- und
Raumfahrt e. V., Köln-Porz

AUSFÜHRUNGSPLANUNG
EXECUTION PLANNING

Glass Kramer Löbbert
Architekten bda
mit | with **Prof. U. Graff
Architektin bda**

BAULEITUNG | SITE MANAGEMENT

BIG Architekten und Ingenieure
GmbH, Bonn / Berlin

TRAGWERK | STRUCTURE

IDK Kleinjohann GmbH & Co. KG,
Köln | Cologne

HAUSTECHNIK | M & E ENGINEERS

Carpus + Partner,
Aachen

AKUSTIK | ACOUSTICS

Akustikbüro Szabunia, Berlin

BAUPHYSIK | BUILDING PHYSICS

IB Rahn,
Berlin

BRANDSCHUTZ
FIRE PREVENTION

HHP Nord-Ost,
Braunschweig

LEUCHTEN | LUMINAIRES

Zumtobel, Dornbirn
ERCO, Lüdenscheid

ELEKTROSCHALTER
ELECTRICAL SWITCHES

Berker, Blieskastel

FERTIGSTELLUNG | COMPLETION

September 2013

STANDORT | LOCATION

DLR-Campus Köln-Porz
Linder Höhe
51147 Köln-Porz
www.dlr.de/envihab

FOTOS | PHOTOS

Christian Gahl,
Berlin

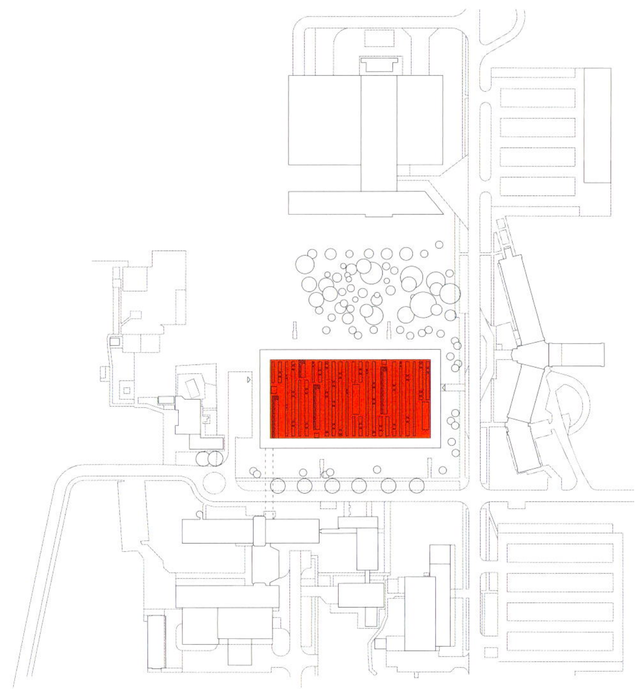

Lageplan | Site plan

Die Südfassade | Southern façade

Der Campus des DLR (Deutsches Zentrum für Luft- und Raumfahrt), seit 1959 auf einem weitläufigen und baumbestandenen Areal vor den Toren Kölns gelegen, erscheint auf den ersten Blick als ein hoch gesichertes Gelände. Umfriedet durch einen meterhohen Zaun gibt das DLR nur wenig von seinem Inneren preis. Doch dieser Eindruck täuscht, sagt das DLR. „Die hermetische Abriegelung ist vielleicht mehr unserem Nachbarn – dem größten Luftwaffenstandort des Landes – als uns geschuldet" und „Wir sind eigentlich gar nicht so", lässt der Pressesprecher wissen. Tatsächlich zeigt sich das DLR seinen Besuchern gegenüber aufgeschlossener als erwartet und macht seit einigen Jahren auch dadurch, dass man versucht, starke zeitgenössische architektonische Akzente auf dem Campus zu setzen, auf sich aufmerksam. Dem Neubau des Kasinos (ASTOC Architects & Planners, 2011) und einer Reihe weiterer Bauten folgte der Neubau der zentralen Forschungsanlage des Raumfahrtmedizinischen Instituts mit dem Namen „:envihab".

:envihab verbindet die Begriffe „environment" (Englisch für Umwelt) und „habitat" (aus dem Lateinischen abgeleitet für Lebensraum) und ist Forschungseinrichtung, Trainingszentrum und Nachsorgestation für die europäischen Astronauten, die bislang nach ihren Missionen auf die Station der NASA in Houston / Texas angewiesen waren.

At first glance, the campus of the DLR (German Aerospace Center), which has been situated on an expansive, wooded site on the outskirts of Cologne since 1959, appears to be a high-security facility. Enclosed by a fence several metres high, the DLR reveals very little about its interior. But, says the DLR, this impression is deceptive. 'The hermetic enclosure has more to do with our neighbours – the largest Air Force base in the country – than it does with us,' and 'We're not really like that,' the press spokesman says. In fact, the DLR seems more open toward visitors than one might expect, and for some years now it has been calling attention to itself – not least by making an effort to incorporate striking contemporary architectural highlights into the campus. The construction of a new cafeteria (ASTOC Architects & Planners, 2011) and a number of additional new buildings was followed by the building of the new central research facility of the Institute of Aerospace Medicine, which was given the name ':envihab'.

:envihab combines the terms 'environment' and 'habitat'; it is a research facility, training centre and follow-up healthcare station for European astro-

Die weiße Scheibe scheint über dem Boden zu schweben. | The white slab seems to float above the ground.

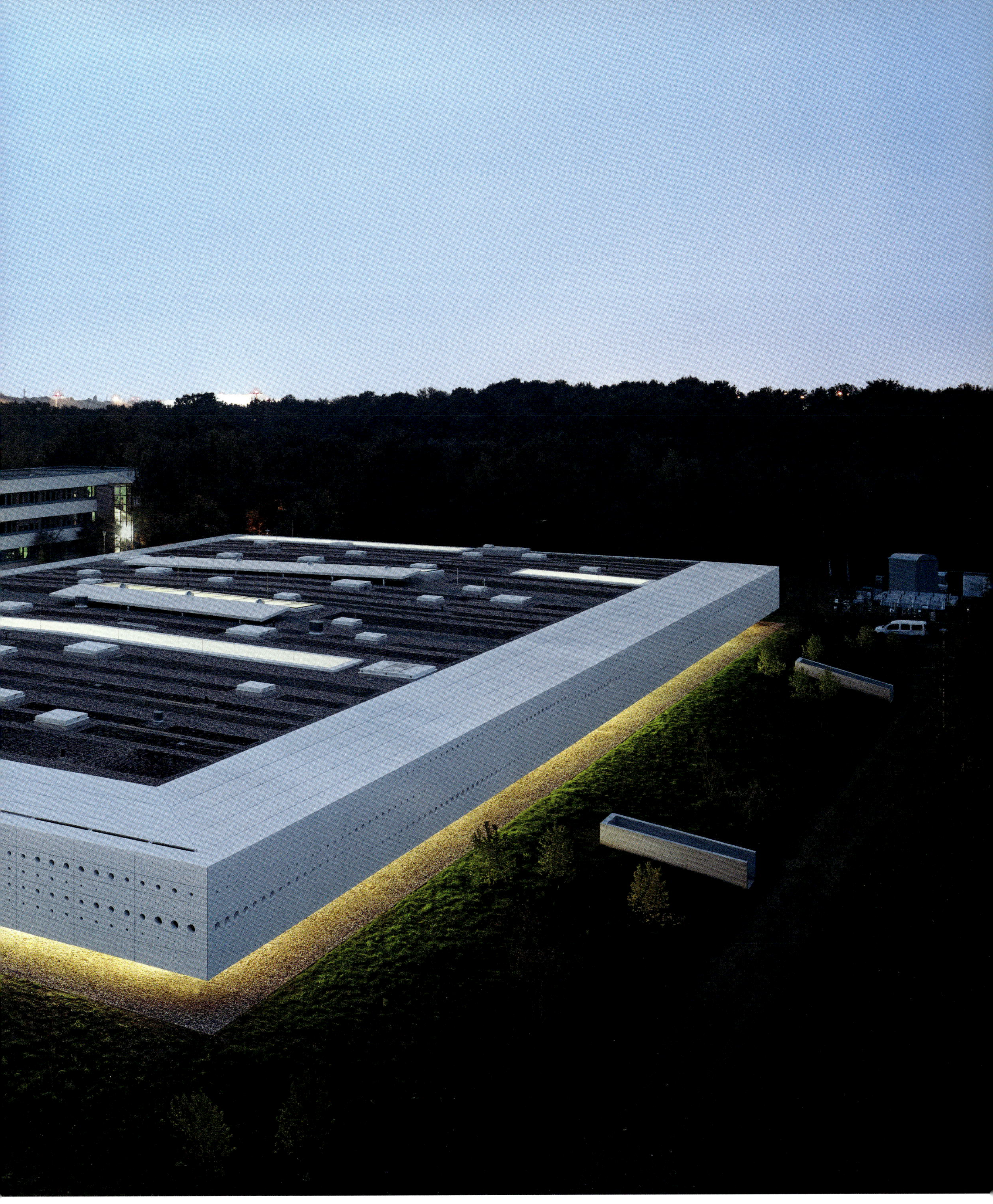

Gebäudeecke; die weiße Scheibe hat einen weiten Überstand und ist mit gelochtem Streckmetall verkleidet.
Corner of the building: the white slab has a broad overhang and is clad in perforated expanded metal.

„Einen Raum für die Forschung zu schaffen, der autark ist – gelöst vom irdischen Kontext – und doch gleichzeitig dem Interessierten die Möglichkeit bietet, Einblicke zu gewinnen und Zusammenhänge mit unserem gewohnten Erlebnisraum herzustellen", war der Wunsch des DLR. Dabei sollte es den Architekten gelingen, Diskretion und Klausur der Wissenschaft mit dem Anspruch an ein öffentliches, eindrucksvolles Raumkonzept zu verbinden.

Auf einem geböschten Gelände schufen die Architekten Glass Kramer Löbbert aus Berlin zusammen mit der Architektin Uta Graff einen flachen, horizontal in zwei Zonen gegliederten, futuristisch anmutenden Kubus mit einer gläsernen Basis. Die oberen zwei Drittel des Bauwerks umhüllt eine weiße, perforierte Aluminiumfassade als Schutz für die komplexe haustechnische Infrastruktur; eine dahinter angeordnete himbeerrote Fassadenebene schimmert dezent hindurch. Das eigentliche Gebäude verbirgt sich jedoch unterhalb dieses gewaltigen Dach-

nauts, who up to now have had to rely on the NASA station in Houston, Texas, after completing their missions.

The DLR wanted to '...create a space for research that is self-sufficient – detached from the terrestrial context – yet at the same time offers interested people the opportunity to gain insight into and establish connections with our familiar area of experience.' Therefore, the architects needed to succeed in combining the discretion and seclusion required by science with the demand for a public, impressive spatial concept.

On a sloping site, the Berlin architects Glass Kramer Löbbert, together with architect Uta Graff, created a low, futuristic-looking cuboid, divided horizontally into two zones, with a glass base. The upper two thirds of the building are enveloped in a white perforated aluminium façade which provides protection for the complex building technology infrastructure; behind it, a raspberry-red surface shimmers subtly through. The actual building, however, is hidden underneath this massive roof structure, shielded from its surroundings, below the earth's surface.

Behind the glass strip of the façade, the descent begins into the building's lower level, which is also the facility's main functional area. Embedded in an enclosure of walls and earth, the many room modules of :envihab seem to be arranged freely inside the approximately 3000 square-metre cuboid. This level receives natural lighting on the one hand through the glass façade, on the other from six atria

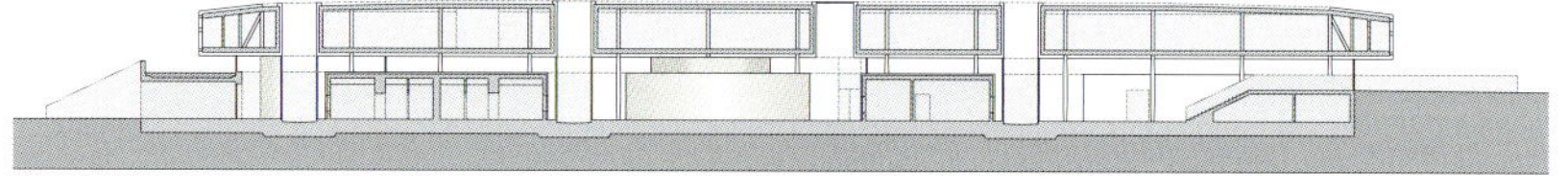

Längsschnitt | Longitudinal section

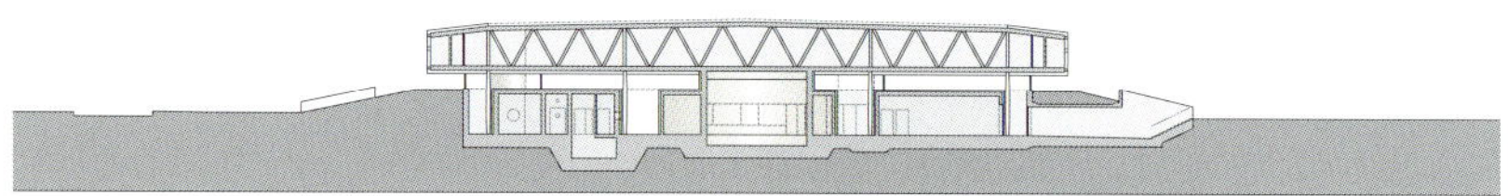

Querschnitt | Cross-section

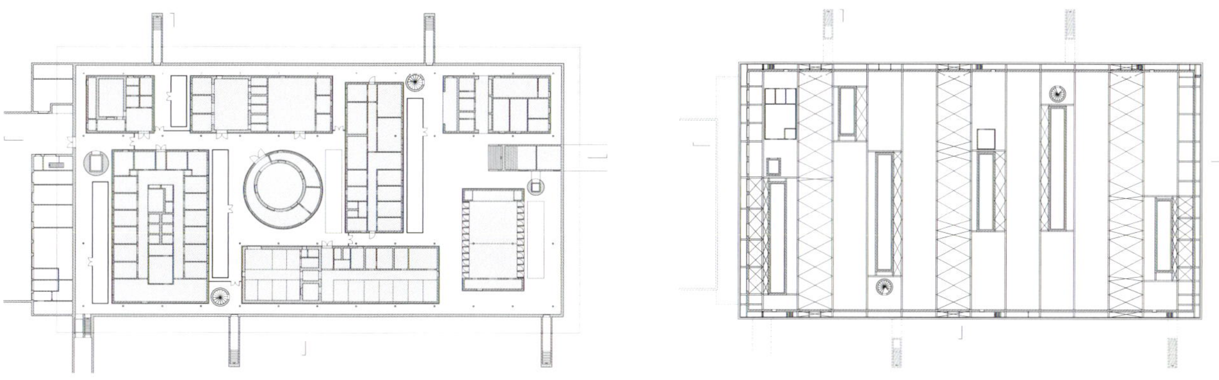

Die eigentliche, glasummantelte und teils eingegrabene Nutzungebene | The semi-basement for actual use, encased in glass

Grundrisse der acht Funktionsmodule im Erdgeschoss
Plans of the eight functional moduls on the ground floor

Grundriss Technikgeschoss
Plan of technical floor

Die Raummodule sind außen weiß…, | The room modules are white on the outside…,

körpers, abgeschirmt von seiner Umgebung, im Erdinneren. Hinter dem gläsernen Fassadenband steigt man hinab in die untere und damit die Hauptnutzungsebene des Gebäudes. Eingebettet in die Umfassung aus Mauer und Erdreich sind sämtliche Raummodule des :envihab scheinbar frei in dem etwa 3000 Quadratmeter großen Kubus arrangiert. Belichtet wird diese Ebene zum einen durch das gläserne Fassadenband, zum anderen durch sechs in den Baukörper eingeschnittene Lichthöfe, die in ihrer Gestaltung mit großen Findlingen zugleich irdisch und mondlandschaftlich anmuten. Alle Wände dieses Kernbereichs sind in einem strahlenden Weiß gehalten und wirken zusammen mit den Sichtbetonelementen und dem naturfarbenen Terrazzoboden klar und ruhig. Der durch die Raummodule differenziert gegliederte Erschließungsbereich verbindet alle acht Funktionseinheiten des :envihab miteinander. Die vollständig autarken Raummodule sind einzeln oder in Kombination gegenüber der Umwelt in Hinblick auf Akustik, Klima, Sauerstoffgehalt und Druck abriegelbar. Hier werden sogenannte Probanden isoliert, immobilisiert und gezielt Stresssituationen ausgesetzt. Einige der Raummodule nehmen medizinische Geräte wie eine Ganzkörper-MRT/PET-Anlage und große Trainings- oder Simulationsgeräte auf. Ein Raum für eine „Kurzarm-Humanzentrifuge" zur Analyse der Effekte erhöhter Schwerkraft auf das Herz-Kreislauf-System sowie auf Muskeln und Knochen ergänzt das Raumprogramm. Hinzu kommen Laboratorien zur Untersuchung der Wirkung von Sauerstoffreduktion und Druck, Technikräume sowie ein teilbarer Vortragssaal.

cut into the structure which, thanks to their decoration with large boulders, are reminiscent of both terrestrial and lunar landscapes. All of the walls in this core area have been painted gleaming white, and – together with the exposed concrete elements and natural-coloured terrazzo flooring – create a clear and calming atmosphere. The access area, which is structured and differentiated by the spatial modules, connects all eight functional units of :envihab to each other. The completely self-sufficient room modules can be sealed off from the environment in terms of acoustics, climate, oxygen content and pressure – either individually or in combination. Here, the experimental subjects can be isolated, immobilized and exposed to specific stress situations. Some of the modules include medical apparatus such as a full-body MRI/PET scanner and large pieces of training and simulation equipment. The room arrangement is supplemented by space for a 'short-arm human centrifuge', used to analyse the effects of increased gravity on the cardiovascular system as well as on the muscles and bones. In addition, there are laboratories for studying the effects of reduced oxygen and pressure, utility rooms, and a lecture hall, which can be partitioned.

The eight room modules also contrast sharply with the access area in terms of colour. An intense,

Auch farblich unterscheiden sich die acht Raummodule stark von der Erschließungshalle. Ein intensives, fast grelles Gelbgrün an Wänden, Decken und Böden taucht diese Räume in ein ungewöhnliches, künstlich wirkendes Licht und lässt die einzelnen architektonischen Elemente regelrecht miteinander verschmelzen. Einen weiteren farblichen Akzent setzen Treppenhauskerne und die Aufzüge in Himbeerrot.

Es ist den Architekten in der Tat gelungen, eine „Raumstation auf der Erde" zu errichten, ohne formale Klischees zu bemühen. Doch zeigt dieses Projekt auch, dass Bauen immer eine zutiefst irdische Angelegenheit ist. Hier war es die handwerkliche Ausführung des Terrazzobodens, der Architekten und Bauherren verzweifeln ließ und der daher auf eine weitere Überarbeitung wartet.

almost garish yellow-green on the walls, ceilings and floors immerses these rooms in an unusual, almost artificial-looking light that causes the individual architectural elements to positively blend into one another. The raspberry-red stairwell cores and elevators add a further accent.

The architects have truly succeeded in building a 'space station on earth' without resorting to any formal clichés. Nevertheless, this project demonstrates once again that construction is a thoroughly earthly endeavour. In this case, it was the technical realization of the terrazzo flooring that drove the architects and their clients to distraction, and which therefore now awaits further reworking.

...innen in kräftigen Farben gehalten. | ... with intense colours in the interiors.

PROJEKTGEMEINSCHAFT IFAU UND JESKO FEZER | HEIDE & VON BECKERATH

GEBÄUDE | BUILDING

BAUGRUPPENPROJEKT R50
BERLIN

TEXT MICHAELA BUSENKELL

12

ARCHITEKTEN | ARCHITECTS

Projektgemeinschaft ifau
und Jesko Fezer |
HEIDE & VON BECKERATH

ifau und Jesko Fezer
Dresdenerstraße 26
10999 Berlin
www.ifau.berlin.heimat.de
www.jeskofezer.de

HEIDE & VON BECKERATH
Kurfürstendamm 173
10707 Berlin
www.heidevonbeckerath.com

BAUHERR | CLIENT

Baugemeinschaft Ritterstraße 50
Planungs- und Bau GbR
Geschäftsführung:
Bärbel Ackermann,
Tim Müller-Heidelberg

MITARBEITER | TEAM

Vladimir Fialka, Adrian Heintz,
Tobias Luppold, Noa Marom,
Wolfgang Rehn, Verena Schmidt

AUSFÜHRUNGSPLANUNG
EXECUTION PLANNING

Projektgemeinschaft ifau
und Jesko Fezer |
HEIDE & VON BECKERATH
Projektsteuerung
project management:
Winfried Härtel, Büro für
Projektentwicklung, Berlin
Bauleitung | site management:
DIMaGB, Berlin

TRAGWERK | STRUCTURE

StudioC Nicole Zahner, Berlin

HAUSTECHNIK | M & E ENGINEERS

Ingenieurbüro N.Lüttgens,
Berlin

BAUPHYSIK | BUILDING PHYSICS

Ingenieurbüro für Bauphysik
und Baukonstruktion GmbH,
Potsdam

AUFZUG | ELEVATOR

OSMA Aufzüge, Stahnsdorf

TÜRKLINKEN UND BESCHLÄGE
HANDLES AND FITTINGS

FSB, Brakel

FERTIGSTELLUNG | COMPLETION

Februar | February 2013

STANDORT | LOCATION

Ritterstraße 50
10969 Berlin

FOTOS | PHOTOS

Andrew Alberts, Berlin

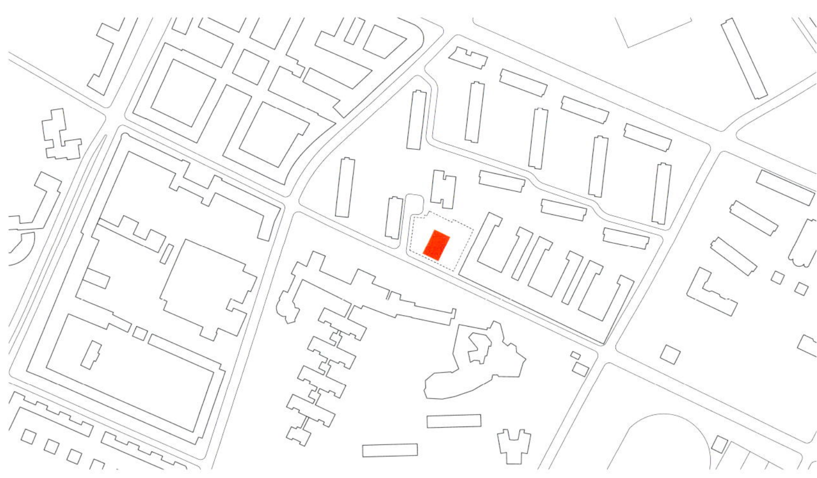

Lageplan | Site plan

Das einzeln stehende Baugruppenhaus R50; offene Grünflächen verbinden es mit einer Siedlung aus den 1960er-Jahren.
The free-standing cooperative building group house R50: open ground areas connect it with a housing estate dating from the 1960s.

Baugruppen gelten als alternatives und soziales Modell für die Stadtentwicklung ebenso wie für die Individualisierung von privatem Wohneigentum. Gleichzeitig gehen sie konform mit den Deregulierungen des Neoliberalismus und der geforderten Übernahme von Verantwortlichkeiten durch die Bürger. Inwiefern aber setzen Baugruppenprojekte auch Potenziale und Wertvorstellungen um, die über herkömmliche wirtschaftspolitische Perspektiven hinausgehen? Ein Gegenmodell, das die Fragen nach dem guten Leben, Wohnen, Bauen und Besitzen in der Stadt mit dem Motiv der Gemeinschaft verknüpft, ist das urbane Wohnhaus für 19 Parteien in Berlin-Kreuzberg.

Das Grundstück, eine seit den 1970er-Jahren vorgehaltene, etwa 2000 Quadratmeter umfassende Verkehrsfläche, wurde im Sommer 2010 vom Berliner Senat zum Festpreis an eine Baugruppe veräußert. Ausschlaggebend für die Vergabe und Umwidmung war das zuvor von den Architekten in Zusammenarbeit mit Interessierten entwickelte Konzept einer gemeinschaftlichen Wohnnutzung und dessen Realisierbarkeit, auch im Zusammenhang mit der Stadtentwicklungspolitik Berlins.

Die Idee der Gemeinschaft war dem Projekt von Anfang an eingeschrieben. Die erste Planungsentscheidung galt der Kooperation zweier Planungsbüros, um unterschiedliche Ansätze und Erfahrungswerte zu verbinden. Das Institut für angewandte Urbanistik (ifau) mit Jesko Fezer und das Architekturbüro HEIDE & VON BECKERATH entwickelten das Gebäude gemeinsam mit den künftigen Bewohner. Ziel war es, ein kostengünstiges Bauprojekt zu realisieren, bei dem einer kollektiven Dimension des alltäglichen Zusammenlebens ein zentraler Wert und eine entsprechende räumliche Ausprägung beigemessen wird. Bereits die frei stehende Platzierung des Hauses

Cooperative building groups are seen as an alternative and social model for urban development, as well as for the personalization of private residential property. At the same time, they are consistent with the deregulation policies of neo-liberalism and the demand for citizens to assume responsibility. To what extent, however, do cooperative building group projects realize possibilities and values that reach beyond conventional economic policy perspectives? An alternative model that connects the desire for the good life and living, building and property-ownership in the city with the theme of community is this 19-unit urban block of flats in Berlin's Kreuzberg district.

Berlin city council sold the property – a public thoroughfare covering approximately 2000 square metres, which had been available since the 1970s – at a fixed price to a cooperative building group in the summer of 2010. The decisive factor in the allocation and conversion of the site was a concept for collective residential use that had been previously developed by the architects in co-operation with interested parties, as well as that concept's feasibility in connexion with Berlin's urban development policies.

The idea of a community was written into the project from the very beginning. The first planning decisions required the co-operation of two planning offices in order to combine the different existing approaches and levels of experience. The Institut für

**Die durchlaufenden Balkonstege
sind ein beliebter Treffpunkt.**
The wrap-around balconies are a
favourite meeting place.

**Die Süd- und
die Ostfassade**
Southern and
eastern façade

Eine Rampe führt zum Souterrain mit Eingang und dem Gemeinschaftsraum.
A ramp leads to the lower level, the entrance area and the community space.

Die Wohnungen sind individuell aufteilbar. | The flats may be divided up individually.

auf dem Grundstück an der Ritterstraße ist auf maximale Öffnung ausgerichtet. Die Gartenflächen verbinden sich mit den Siedlungsstrukturen der benachbarten Otto-Suhr-Siedlung aus den 1960er-Jahren zu einer fließenden Landschaft als verbindendem Miteinander.

Das grundlegende konstruktive System des Gebäudes wurde als Stahlbetonskelettbau mit einer Holzmodulfassade, einem Treppenhaus, zwei festgelegten Installationsschächten und drei Wohnungsgrundtypen entwickelt, das robust genug ist, um im Planungsverlauf größtmögliche Partizipation und die Variabilität der Grundrisse zu ermöglichen. Das Aufgabenspektrum der Architekten umfasste außer den Planungsleistungen auch die Konzeption und Moderation des dialogischen Planungsprozesses der Baugruppe: mit Gesprächen, Fragen, Matrizes, Einzelinitiativen sowie kollektiven Entscheidungsprozessen in Hinblick auf die divergierenden Wünsche und Vorstellungen zum „normalen" Stadtleben. Mit der Erarbeitung von Wohnreporten wurden Dimensionierungen, Raumstrukturen oder gemeinschaftliche Bezugnahmen, vor allem die einheitlichen Ausstattungs- und Bauteilstandards erörtert: Die Oberflächen aller Wände und Decken blieben roh und unbehandelt; imprägnierter Heizestrich wurde durchgängig für die Böden der Wohnungen, Erschließungs- und Treppenräume verwendet. Erschließungsflächen fungieren hier auch als zuschaltbare Räume mit ambivalenten Doppelnutzungen. Die private Wohnfläche kann, bei durchgängiger Materialität, in den gemeinschaftlichen Bereich erweitert werden; oder die Minimal-Bäder der Wohnungen in den davorliegenden Gang.

Die individuellen Grundrisse wurden mit Hilfe von Darstellungsmethoden wie einer Graphen-Matrix zu den gewünschten Raumgrößen und -bezügen entwickelt. Zukünftige Umbauten sind ebenso möglich wie der partielle oder vollständige Selbstausbau und die Zonierung mit Möblierung oder Bauteilen. Fassadenmodule wie Holzpaneele, Fenstertüren oder Glasfaltelemente können auf die jeweiligen Anordnungen der Innenräume abgestimmt werden. Alle inneren Wohnflächen wie auch die allgemeinen Erschließungsräume haben einen Ausgang auf den gemeinschaftlichen Umgang, der das Gebäude in jedem Stockwerk umfasst – als Teil des Gemeinschaftseigentums.

angewandte Urbanistik / Institute for Applied Urbanism (ifau) with Jesko Fezer and the architectural office of HEIDE & VON BECKERATH developed the building design together with the future residents. Their goal was to realize a cost-effective building project in which the collective dimension of day-to-day co-existence would be of central value, and the appropriate spatial manifestation of this value would be given primary importance. The free-standing placement of the building on the Ritterstrasse plot is already geared toward maximum openness. The garden area adjoins the residential structures of the neighbouring Otto Suhr Housing Estate, built in the 1960s, creating a flowing landscape of co-existence and connectivity.

The basic structural system of the building was developed as a reinforced-concrete skeleton construction with a wooden module façade, a stairwell, two fixed installation shafts and three basic types of apartments that is robust enough to allow for the greatest possible participation and variability in floor plans during the planning process. In addition to their planning services, the architects' range of tasks also included the conception of, and mediation in, the planning dialogues within the building group: with meetings, questions, matrices, individual initiatives as well as collective decision-making with regard to the group members' divergent wishes and ideas of 'normal' life in the city. In the context of preparing studies of living conditions, dimensioning, spatial structures and community references were discussed, particularly the uniform standards for fittings and components. All of the wall and ceiling surfaces were left bare and unfinished; waterproof heating screed was used on all the floors in the apartments, access spaces and stairways throughout the building. The access and utility areas also function here as connectible spaces with ambivalent double usages. Thanks to the homogeneity of the

Mit einer gemeinsamen Werkstatt und Waschküche, Dachterrasse (40 Quadratmeter) mit Sommerküche und dem doppel-
geschossigen Gemeinschaftsraum (130 Quadratmeter) neben
dem Eingangsbereich – der auch dem umliegenden Quartier zur
Verfügung gestellt wird – sind die offenen Umgänge ein radi-
kales Statement für das Neudenken sozialer und räumlicher
Beziehungen.
Die einfachen Standards als ökonomisches und soziales Prinzip
sind situative, auf den spezifischen Kontext bezogene Festle-
gungen. Der durchschnittliche Quadratmeterpreis der Wohnfläche einschließlich anteiliger Gemeinschaftsfläche liegt bei
2350 Euro. Der Mehrwert liegt in den Relationen: einfache,
„normale" Flächen oder Bauteile, private und gemeinschaftliche Räume, Innen- und Außenbereiche werden so zueinander
in Beziehung gesetzt, dass sich die Nutzungsmöglichkeiten
vervielfachen und zu Aneignung, Aushandlung und Umdeutung
auffordern. Mit diesem Baugruppenprojekt wurde das Potenzial
von gemeinschaftlichen Wohnformen und programmatischer
Offenheit ausgelotet. Was eine solche außerordentliche Architektur schließlich zu leisten vermag, erweist sich im alltäglichen
Gebrauch durch die Bewohner.

materials, private living spaces can be expanded into
the communal areas; or the apartments' minimal
bathrooms can be extended into the corridors in
front of them.
The individual floor plans were developed to create
the desired room sizes and spatial relationships
with the help of presentation methods such as a
graph matrix. Future conversions are possible, as
are partial or complete self-finishing as well as
zoning using furniture or building components.
Façade modules such as wood panels, French
doors, or plate glass elements can be tailored to the
individual arrangements of the interiors. All of the
interior living spaces, as well as the common access
areas, contain exits onto the shared all-around
balconies which encircle the building on each level
– as part of the communal property. Along with a
common workshop and laundry room, a 40-square-
metre roof terrace including a summer kitchen and
a two-storey, 130-square-metre community space
next to the entrance area – which is also available
for use by the surrounding neighbourhood – the
open wrap-around balconies are a radical statement
in favour of a new way of thinking about social and
spatial relationships.
The simple standards as an economic and social
principle are situational specifications that apply to
this particular context. The average price per square
metre living space, including a pro rata share in the
communal space, is 2350 euros. The added value
lies in the relationships: simple, 'normal' spaces or
building components, private and communal rooms,
interior and exterior spaces are linked to one another in such a way that the possibilities for use are
multiplied and encourage appropriation, negotiation
and re-interpretation. This co-operative building
group project has explored the potential for communal forms of living and programmatic openness.
What can be accomplished by unusual architecture
such as this will prove itself in day-to-day use by
the residents.

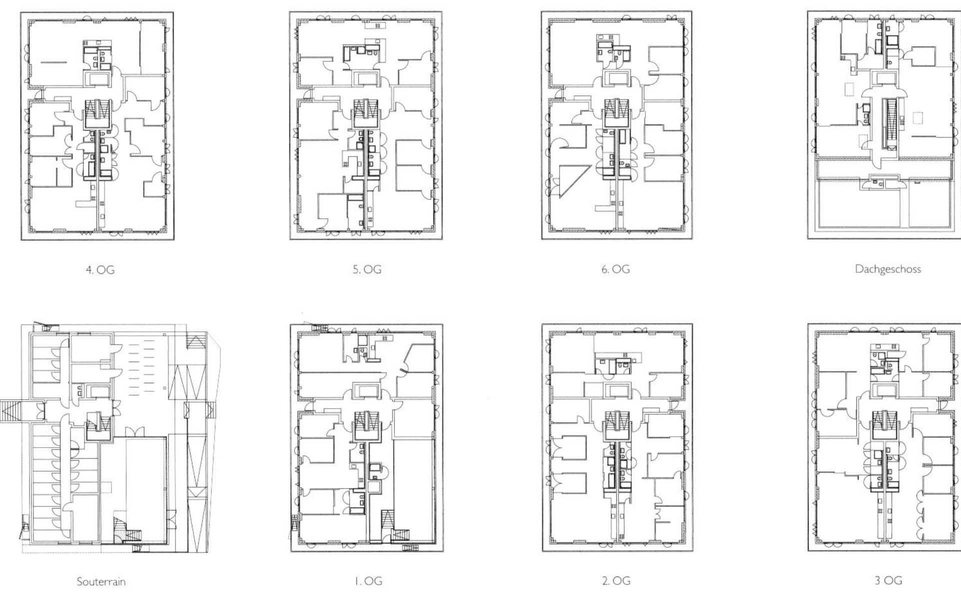

Flexible Grundrisse Souterrain bis Dachgeschoss | Flexible floor plans from souterrain to attic

Das bewusst roh belassene Treppenhaus | The stairwell was deliberately left unfinished.

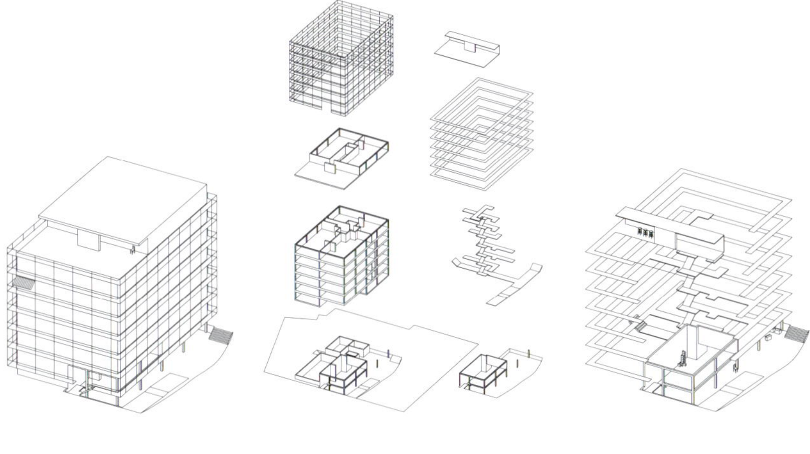

Isometrie der Bauteile | Isometric building components

Der zweigeschossige Gemeinschaftsraum | The two-storey community space

KADAWITTFELDARCHITEKUR

GEBÄUDE | BUILDING

ARCHÄOLOGISCHE VITRINE
AACHEN

TEXT PAUL ANDREAS

13

ARCHITEKTEN | ARCHITECTS

kadawittfeldarchitektur
Aureliusstraße 2
52064 Aachen
www.kwa.ac

MITARBEITER | TEAM

Projektleitung
project management:
Ben Beckers, Jonas Kröber
Projektteam | team:
Sascha Thomas, Maxim König,
Daniel Trappen, Oliver Venghaus
Bauleitung | site management:
Michael Wetstein, Jonas Kröber

BAUHERR | CLIENT

Stadt Aachen
Gebäudemanagement E26

TRAGWERK | STRUCTURE

Imagine structure GmbH,
Frankfurt am Main

WERKSTATTPLANUNG
(STAHLBAU) | WORKSHOP
PLANNING (STEEL CONSTRUCTION)

Tries Ingenieure,
Kastellaun

BAUPHYSIK | BUILDING PHYSICS

TOHR Bauphysik,
Bergisch Gladbach

LICHTPLANUNG
LIGHTING CONSULTANT

Licht Kunst Licht, Bonn

ELEKTROTECHNIK
ELECTRICAL ENGINEERING

Ingenieurbüro Walter Sturm,
Krefeld

AUSSTELLUNGSGESTALTUNG
EXHIBITION DESIGN

Studio Kaiser Matthies, Berlin

METALLBAU
METAL CONSTRUCTION

Schneider Metallbau GmbH,
Kastellaun

FERTIGSTELLUNG | COMPLETION

April 2013

STANDORT | LOCATION

Elisengarten
52062 Aachen
www.archaeologische-vitrine.de

FOTOS | PHOTOS

Jens Kirchner, Düsseldorf
Jörg Hempel, Aachen

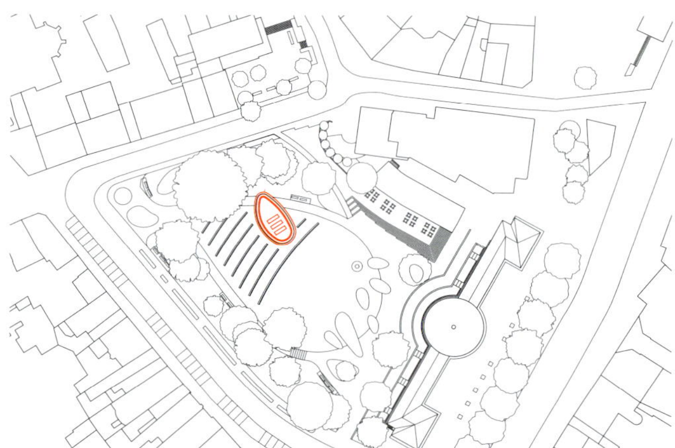

Lageplan | Site plan

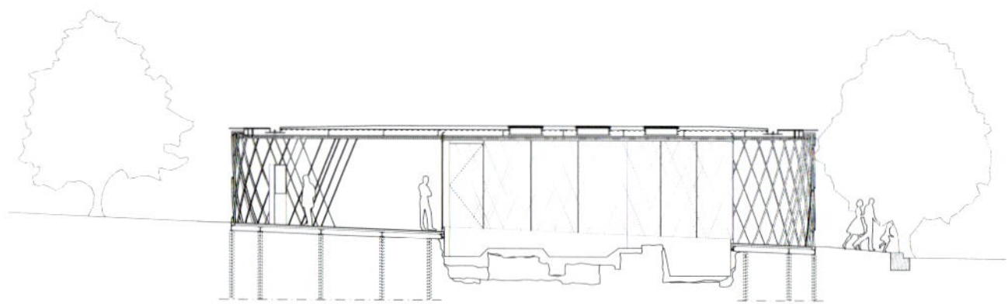

Längsschnitt | Longitudinal section

Die Archäologische Vitrine im Aachener Elisengarten | The archaeological pavilion in Aachen's Elisengarten

Ob Schinkel es wohl ahnte, als er die beiden Wandelhallen des klassizistischen Elisenbrunnens in gebührendem Abstand an die Südkante des Areals setzen ließ? Und Peter Joseph Lenné, der Potsdamer Landschaftsarchitekt, der 1852 den verödeten Klostergarten der Ursulinen in einen belebten Volks-Kurgarten verwandelte? Bei den Modellierungsarbeiten dürften seinen Gärtnern die nur wenige Zentimeter unter Bodenniveau liegenden Trümmer-Gesteinsschichten nicht verborgen geblieben sein. Und doch sollten noch 150 Jahre vergehen, bis die Landschaftsarchitekten des Berliner Büros Lützow7 im Jahr 2007 den Auftrag zur Wiederherstellung des Parks als öffentlichen Ort bekamen – und dabei mit mehr Akribie unter den Rasen schauten. Was da zutage trat, war eine Sensation für die lokale Stadtarchäologie: Fünf Jahrtausende Siedlungsgeschichte verdichteten sich hier in geringer Tiefe auf einem nicht ganz fußballplatzgroßen Grabungsfeld. Einziger verbliebener Hinweis auf die Erdbewegungen bei der Suche nach vergangenen Zivilisationen ist heute ein ovaler Pavillon am höchsten Wegpunkt des Gartens. Mit seinem matt metallischen Flimmern scheint er mehr ephemere Erscheinung als fest gebautes Gefüge zu sein; sein filigranes Maschenwerk leitet den Blick sanft hindurch. Die Außenhaut aus einer doppelten Schicht diagonal aneinander gefügter Duplex-Stahl-Flachlamellen trägt das flache, neigungslose Dach mit geringem, gläsernem Kranzüberstand. Man muss

Could Schinkel have suspected this when he had the two promenade halls of the Neo-classical Elisenbrunnen (Elisa Fountain) placed at a respectful distance on the southern edge of the park? What about Peter Joseph Lenné, the Potsdam landscape architect who converted the abandoned garden of the Ursuline convent into a lively public spa garden in 1852? The stone debris that lay just a few centimetres below the surface of the earth could not have escaped his gardeners' notice during the landscaping work. Nevertheless, another 150 years would pass before the landscape architects of the Berlin firm Lützow7 were awarded the contract to restore the park as a public space in 2007 – and in doing so, conducted a more meticulous exploration underneath the lawns. What came to light was a sensation for the local archaeology: five millennia of settlement history lie concentrated here close beneath the surface, on an excavation site slightly smaller than a football field. Today, the only remaining evidence of the earth-moving operations conducted in search of past civilizations is an oval pavilion situated at the highest point along the garden's paths. With its matte metallic shimmer, it seems to be more of an

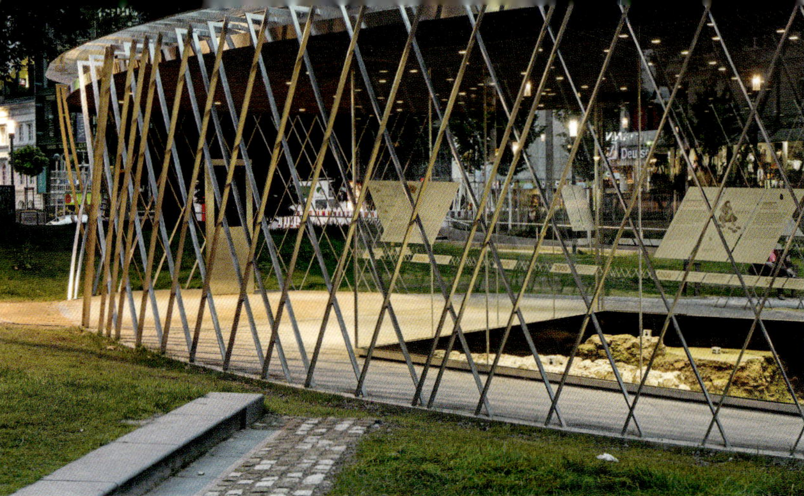

Die drei Schichten des Pavillons: das äußere Gitterwerk, der umlaufende Pfad und die gläserne Vitrine mit den Ausgrabungen | The three layers of the pavilion: the outer meshwork, the circular path and the glass display window showing the excavation

Durch die Gitterstruktur schimmern die Ausgrabungsstelle und Informationstafeln. The excavation site and the information plaques shimmer through the meshwork structure.

sich dem mit aller archäologischer Vorsicht auf Mikrobohrpfählen gegründeten Bau schon auf wenige Meter nähern, um den inneren Glaskörper zu bemerken, der aus einer doppelten, profillosen Schicht von hochtransparentem Weißglas zusammengefügt wurde. Der bis unter die stählernen Deckenroste geführte sechseckige Schaukörper zieht den Zuschauer geradezu in die Geschichte und das Geschehen hinein. In einem etwa 60 Quadratmeter großen offenen Grabungsfenster zeichnen sich bis in zwei Meter Tiefe sandwichartig geschichtet die Epochen ab. Der darum geführte, barrierefreie Parcours lässt die archäologischen Bodenfunde, die tagsüber natürlich, nachts durch LED-Downlights beleuchtet werden, aus verschiedenen Perspektiven erleben und inszeniert sie zu einer zirkulären Zeitreise: Unter Ausnutzung des Bodengefälles und der dem Glas mit angenehmer Zurückhaltung aufgedruckten Erläuterungen steigt man hinab zu den Faustkeilsplittern der Jungsteinzeit, den Fundamenten eines römischen Thermenhotels, entdeckt darin spätantik errichtete Mikro-Tempel, um mit den versprengten Gräbern der Karolingerzeit und den Murmelspielfunden des Spätmittelalters geschwind der Jetztzeit wieder entgegenzugehen. Am Ende dieser Reise weiß man, wie sehr das Schulgeschichtsbuch doch Unrecht hatte, wenn es Karl den Großen ein spätantik völlig verwaistes Aachen heroisch wachküssen ließ. Detailliertere Hintergründe zu den Ausgra

ephemeral phenomenon than a solid structure; its delicate meshwork guides the gaze gently through it. The outer shell, made from a double layer of diagonally crossing duplex steel slats, supports the flat roof with its narrow glass projecting rim. Only when standing just a few metres away from the structure – which was erected with the greatest archaeological care and precision on micro-drilled piles – does one notice the inner glass housing, which was assembled from a smooth double layer of highly transparent flint glass. The hexagonal display structure, extending all the way up to the steel ceiling grille, veritably draws the viewer into the history and events of the past. In an approximately 60-square-metre excavation display window, the eras are revealed in sandwich-like layers to a depth of two metres. The disability-friendly path that encircles it allows visitors to experience the archaeological finds – displayed under natural light in the daytime and illuminated by LED downlights at night – from various perspectives, and stages them in a circular journey through time: exploiting the slope of the ground and the pleasantly unobtrusive explanations printed on the glass, visitors descend to the hand-axe fragments from the Neolithic Age, then to the foundations of a Roman spa hotel. They discover micro-temples constructed in Late Antiquity; then, with the scattered graves of the Carolingian era and the games of marbles dating from the Late Middle Ages, they quickly head back toward the present day. At the end of the journey, it is clear just how wrong the school history books were to claim that Charlemagne heroically brought the city of Aachen, completely deserted in Late Antiquity, back to life. Detailed background information about the excavation can be accessed from a digital display screen stele, which also pays discreet tribute to the pavilion's sponsor. A

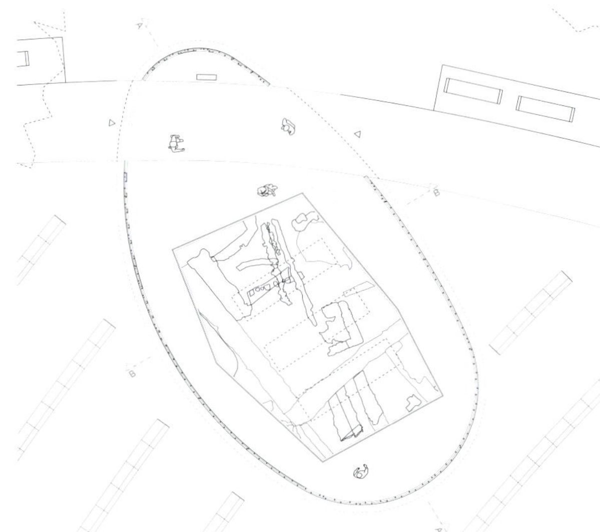

Grundriss | Plan

Die Ausgrabungsstelle hinter Glas im Inneren des Pavillons | The excavation site behind glass in the interior of the pavilion

Ein bereits vorhandener Weg kreuzt jetzt den Pavillon.
A previously existing path now leads through the pavilion.

Das zarte Geflecht des Pavillons fügt sich unauffällig in die Umgebung ein. | The pavilion's delicate meshwork subtly blends into its surroundings.

bungen sind an einer digitalen Screen-Stele abrufbar, die zugleich dezente Reminiszenz an den Stifter ist: Ein weltweit operierendes Aachener Datentechnik-Unternehmen machte das aus einem kleinen Wettbewerb hervorgegangen Projekt erst möglich, weil es für den ungedeckten Kostenanteil der Kommune einstand. Im 1200. Sterbejahr Karls des Großen ist die archäologische Vitrine längst zu einem beliebten öffentlichen Treff- und Verweilpunkt geworden. Mehr als in jedem Museum lässt sich hier en passant das dünne Eis erleben, auf dem die Gegenwart gebaut ist.

globally-operating, Aachen-based information technology firm made this project – the result of a small competition – possible in the first place by assuming responsibility for the municipality's uncovered costs. Now, in the 1200th anniversary year of Charlemagne's death, the archaeological pavilion has long since become a popular place for members of the public to meet and linger. More than in any museum, one is reminded here en passant of the thin ice on which our present-day world is built.

ARCHITEKT | ARCHITECT

LÖSER LOTT ARCHITEKTEN

GEBÄUDE | BUILDING

DOPPEL-HAUS „DUETT“

WARNEMÜNDE

TEXT ULRICH HÖHNS

14

ARCHITEKTEN | ARCHITECTS

Löser Lott Architekten GmbH
Pappelallee 6
10437 Berlin
www.loeserlott.de

MITARBEITER | TEAM

Katharina Löser, Sieghart Löser, Johannes Lott, Andrè Sternitzke

BAUHERR | CLIENT

L&L Gesellschaft für schlüsselfertiges Bauen mbH, Gornsdorf im Erzgebirge

AUSFÜHRUNGSPLANUNG | EXECUTION PLANNING

Löser Lott Architekten GmbH

GENERALUNTERNEHMER | GENERAL CONTRACTOR

L&L Gesellschaft für schlüsselfertiges Bauen mbH, Gornsdorf

BAULEITUNG / PROJEKTSTEUERUNG | SITE MANAGEMENT / PROJECT MANAGEMENT

L&L Gesellschaft für schlüsselfertiges Bauen mbH, Gornsdorf im Erzgebirge
Sieghart Löser

TRAGWERK UND BRANDSCHUTZ | STRUCTURE AND FIRE PREVENTION

Ingenieurbüro für Baustatik
Dr.-Ing. Egon Looks, Rostock

HAUSTECHNIK | M & E ENGINEERS

H.S.W. GmbH, Rostock mit KuK Wärmetechnik GmbH, Rostock

BAUPHYSIK + AKUSTIK | BUILDING PHYSICS + ACOUSTICS

Ingenieurbüro für Baustatik
Dr.-Ing. Egon Looks, Rostock

KÜCHENPLANER | KITCHEN PLANNING

Löser Lott Architekten mit Möbeltischler Röthig+Hampel GbR, Stollberg

AUFZUGPLANER | LIFT PLANNING

Kone GmbH, Hamburg

ARMATUREN | FIXTURES

GROHE

FERTIGSTELLUNG | COMPLETION

2012 / 2013

STANDORT | LOCATION

Ostseebad Warnemünde, Rostock

FOTOS | PHOTOS

Stefan Müller, Berlin
Thomas Spier, Berlin

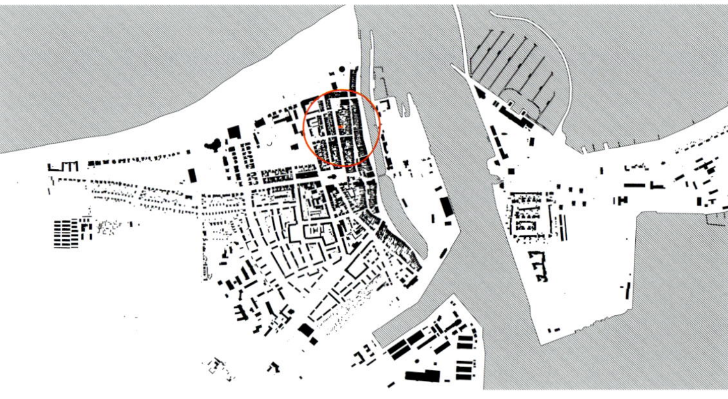

Lageplan | Site plan

Das „Duett", links mit steilem, rechts mit kaum erkennbarem flachen Satteldach | The 'Duett': on the right with a scarcely recognizable shallow pitched roof, on the left with a steep one.

Warnemünde ist Rostocks Seehafen. Der kleine Ort an der Ostsee entwickelte sich am Westufer der Warnow-Mündung aus einer Fischersiedlung zur heutigen Hafenstadt. Die dichteste Bebauung folgt dem „Alten Strom", dem ehemaligen Mündungsarm der Warnow. Heute ist dies ein abgeriegeltes Hafenbecken, und der viel breitere „Neue Strom" weiter östlich übernahm die Aufgaben der Wasserstraße. Westlich der Uferreihe verlaufen Parallelstraßen, bebaut mit zwei- und dreigeschossigen Häusern, die durch extrem schmale Gänge, sogenannte „Tüschen", voneinander getrennt sind, die zu winzigen Höfen und Gärten führen.

Dieses eigenartige Raumbild einer kleinen Stadt am Meer mit dicht zusammengerückten Häusern wird durch abwechslungsreich gestaltete Veranden vor den Erdgeschossen vieler Häuser bereichert. Einst als Läden oder Räume für Feriengäste genutzt, oft improvisiert anmutend, gliedern sie den Straßenraum und lassen ihn lebendig erscheinen – ein erzählerisches Moment im Stadtbild von kaum zu überschätzender Bedeutung für die Identität des Ortes.

Warnemünde is Rostock's seaport. This small village on the Baltic coast grew up on the western shore of the Warnow River estuary, evolving from a fishing settlement to the present-day port. The densest development took place along the 'Alter Strom' ('Old Channel'), the formerly navigable branch of the Warnow. Today, this is a sealed-off harbour basin, and the much wider 'Neuer Strom' ('New Channel') further to the east has taken over the role of active waterway. Parallel streets run to the west of the shoreline, lined with two and three-storey houses divided from one another by extremely narrow passageways called 'Tüschen', which lead into tiny courtyards and gardens.

This unusual spatial image of a small town by the sea, with its houses lined up close together, is enhanced by the variously decorated verandas built on the ground floor in front of many of the houses. At one time used as shops or guest rooms

In den offenen Spalt zwischen den Haushälften ist das Treppenhaus geschoben.
The stairwell is inserted into the open space between the two houses.

Die Gartenseite des Doppelhauses mit Maisonette-Wohnungen und Dachterrassen
The garden side of the semi-detached houses with maisonette apartments and roof terraces

Das „Duett" wurde behutsam in die Straßenabwicklung eingefügt. | The 'Duett' was sensitively integrated into the street landscape.

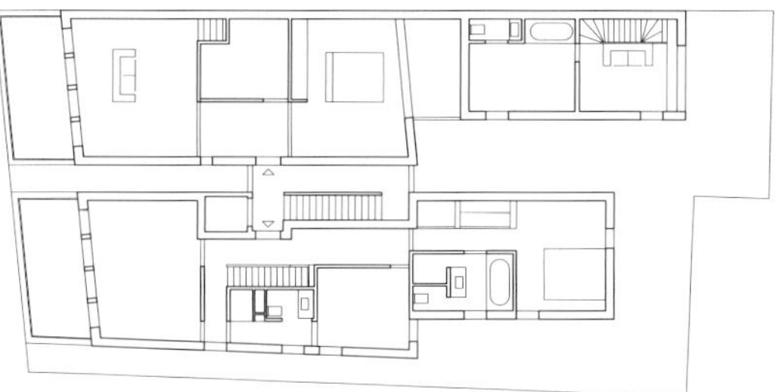

Grundriss 1. Obergeschoss | Plan of 1st floor

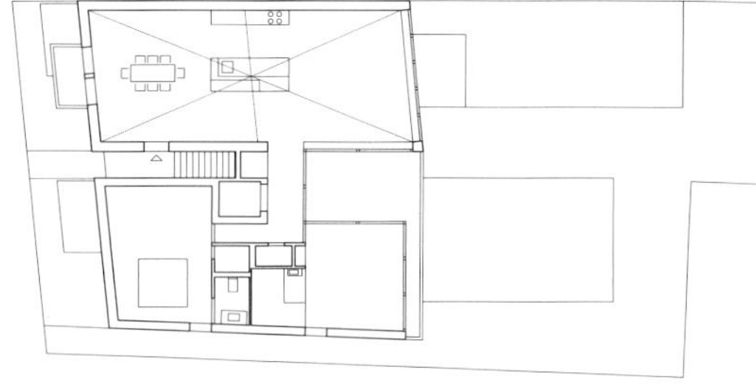

Grundriss Dachgeschoss | Plan of attic floor

Grundriss Erdgeschoss | Plan of ground floor

Grundirss 2. Obergeschoss | Plan of 2nd floor

Löser Lott Architekten haben beim Entwurf ihres Doppel-Hauses auf zwei unbebauten Parzellen diese geschriebenen und ungeschriebenen Regeln befolgt und sich innerhalb dieses Rahmens frei bewegt. Sie entwickelten die „richtige" Gestalt zweier nebeneinander stehender, im Hintergrund aber miteinander verbundener Häuser. Es ist eine strahlend weiße, von naturfarbenen Eichenholzfenstern gegliederte, in verschiedenen Schichtungen und Staffelungen angelegte Architektur, die sich wie selbstverständlich in das Nachbarschaftsgefüge einpasst. Zur Straße hin wahrt sie den Kontext der Lochfassaden und einfachen Giebelformen, die sich dank faltbarer Sonnenläden auch zu ganz anderen, gebrochenen oder hermetischen Bildern verändern lassen. Zur Rückseite hingegen wird der Wildwuchs der umliegenden Nebenbauten und Schuppen als Thema aufgegriffen und in ein modernistisches Vokabular kubischer Formen und Freiräume übersetzt, horizontal wie vertikal. Auf kleinem Raum realisiert, entfaltet sich jenseits der „Tüsche" eine private, helle und großzügig erscheinende Wohnwelt, ein Ausschnitt aus der Stadt, der alles hat, was auch die Nachbarschaft auszeichnet.

Die rationalistisch aufgeräumte Fassade mit stehenden Tür-Fenster-Formaten und zwei „Veranda"-Vorbauten – der linke für die Einfahrt in die gemeinsame Tiefgarage, daneben ein schmaler Laden mit zurückgezogenem Eingang, der rechte als Ausbau einer von zwei Ferienwohnungen im Erdgeschoss – lässt nicht erkennen, dass sich hinter dem steilen Giebelfeld des linken Hauses eine Zeltdachkonstruktion verbirgt, die den schönsten Raum des Ensembles birgt. Über Einschnitte, halb offene Terrassen und ein angedeutetes Atrium verbindet er sich mit dem Nachbarhaus zu einer Wohnung auf einer Ebene.

for holiday-makers, often seemingly improvised, they subdivide the street space and give it a lively appearance – a narrative element in the urban vista whose significance for the town's identity can scarcely be overestimated.

In designing their pair of semi-detached houses on two undeveloped plots of land, Löser Lott Architekten have followed these written and unwritten rules, and have operated freely within this framework. They developed the 'correct' form of two houses which stand side by side, while being connected to one another in the background. The architecture is gleaming white, subdivided by natural-coloured oak windows and structured in various layers and echelons – and it blends almost naturally into the fabric of the neighbourhood. On the side facing the street, it maintains the context of perforated façades and simple gable shapes, whose folding vertical sun blinds allow the houses to assume a very different appearance – either broken or hermetically closed off. In the rear, on the other hand, the architects have picked up on the proliferation of surrounding annexes and sheds as their theme, translating it into a modern vocabulary of cubic forms and open spaces, both horizontal and vertical. Realized in a small space, on the other side of the 'Tüsche' a living area unfolds which is private, light and spacious – a slice of the town which has everything that makes this neighbourhood distinctive.

Das Whiskygeschäft im Erdgeschoss | The whisky shop on the ground floor

Sie wird entweder über eine frei durch den Gebäudeschlitz geführte Treppe – als Himmelsleiter mit Ausblick über die Stadt – erreicht, oder über den Aufzug, der alle Wohnungen direkt anfährt. Das rechte Haus hat, anders als vermutet, kein Flachdach, sondern ein sehr flaches Satteldach. Dahinter staffeln sich kleinere Kuben mit abfallenden Höhen in die Tiefe des Grundstücks – bis hin zum „Gartenhaus" ganz hinten auf der linken Seite. Auf minimaler Grundfläche zweigeschossig und unter fast vollständiger Einbeziehung der Verkehrsräume in die Wohnzonen erscheint es, was den geringen Raumbedarf betrifft, wie ein legitimer Nachfolger der „Wohnung für das Existenzminimum". Die außergewöhnliche Tiefe der beiden Maisonette-Wohnungen im ersten und zweiten Obergeschoss bei geringer Breite wird nie zum Problem, sondern im Gegenteil zum Vorteil für die Wohnvielfalt. Es bilden sich differenzierte, auch voneinander trennbare, Wohnzonen mit einem Maximum an erzielbarer Belichtung der Ost-West-orientierten Häuser heraus. Den begrenzten Flächen in den schmalen Bewegungszonen wird im Detail mit Schiebetüren, in Wandnischen schlagende Türen oder Möglichkeiten des Rundgangs begegnet, so dass auch ein kleines Badezimmer von zwei Seiten erreichbar ist. Alle, auch die kleineren Räume in diesen Wohnungen, vermitteln stets den Eindruck von Weite, gewähren Ausblicke auf die Nachbarschaft, das Geflecht der Rückseiten und Höfe und in die Straße. Bei allem Wohnluxus und der durchweg gehobenen Ausstattung sind sie legitime Nachfahren der schmalen, langen Häuser, die dieses Viertel prägen.

The 'rational' clean façade with 'perpendicular' door and window formats and two 'veranda' extensions – the one on the left is for the entrance to the shared underground garage, and next to it a small shop with a recessed entrance, while the structure on the right is an extension of one of the two holiday flats located on the ground floor – does not provide any clue that behind the steep gable of the left-hand house is hidden a tented roof construction which contains the most beautiful room in the whole ensemble. Connected to the neighbouring house by means of incisions, half-open terraces and a hinted-at atrium, it forms a single apartment on one level. It can be reached either by means of the freestanding outdoor staircase in the gap between the buildings – like a stairway to heaven with a view over the town – or using the elevator that provides direct access to all the flats. Contrary to one's first assumption, the roof of the right-hand house is not flat, but very slightly pitched. Behind it, smaller cubes are arranged in descending order of size into the deepest part of the plot – all the way to the 'garden house' at the very back on the left side. Built in two storeys on a minimal floor area, and almost completely incorporating the communication areas in the living-zones, this seems – in terms of its small space requirements – to be a legitimate successor to the 'Dwelling for Minimum Subsistence'. The unusual depth of the two maisonette apartments on the first and second floors compared with their narrow width never becomes a problem; on the contrary, it provides an advantage in terms of flexibility. Differentiated, even partitionable, living zones with a maximum of attainable light can be created within these east-west oriented houses. The limited area of the narrow communication zones is counterbalanced by details such as sliding doors, doors that open into wall niches, or circular routes through the space, so that even a small bathroom is accessible from two sides. All of the rooms in these apartments – even the small ones – constantly communicate a feeling of spaciousness; they provide views of the neighbourhood, the network of house backs and backyards, and the street. Despite all their luxury and consistently upscale design elements, they are legitimate descendants of the long, narrow houses that characterize this district.

Der große Raum im Dachgeschoss mit seiner zeltartigen Deckengeometrie | The large room on the top floor, with its tent-like ceiling geometry

Ausschnitt der strahlend weißen und sorgfältig komponierten Straßenfassade | Detail of the gleaming white, carefully composed street façade

O&O BAUKUNST

GEBÄUDE | BUILDING

LANDESARCHIV NRW
DUISBURG

TEXT URSULA KLEEFISCH-JOBST

15

ARCHITEKTEN | ARCHITECTS

**O&O Baukunst
Justinianstraße 16
50679 Köln** | Cologne
www.ortner-ortner.com

Fachplanung Leistungsphasen 1–4, künstlerische Oberleitung | expert planning: work phases 1–4, senior artistic management

MITARBEITER | TEAM

Christian Heuchel, Sebastian Wiswedel, Shidokht Shalapour, Defne Saylan

BAUHERR | CLIENT

Bau- und Liegenschaftsbetrieb NRW, Düsseldorf

AUSFÜHRUNGSPLANUNG
EXECUTION PLANNING

Hochtief Solution AG

BAULEITUNG / PROJEKTSTEUERUNG
SITE MANAGEMENT / PROJECT MANAGEMENT

zarinfar bauprojektmanagament, Köln | Cologne

TRAGWERK | STRUCTURE

Turm | tower**: office for sturctural design (osd), Frankfurt am Main
Welle** | wave**: LWS-Ingenieursgesellschaft, Duisburg**

HAUSTECHNIK | M & E ENGINEERS

Arup GmbH

BAUPHYSIK | BUILDING PHYSICS

THOR Bauphysik GmbH, Bergisch Gladbach

BRANDSCHUTZ
FIRE PREVENTION

Ökotec, Schwalmtal

AUFZUGPLANER | LIFT PLANNING

Lift Consulting Planungsgesellschaft GmbH, Wiesbaden

LICHTPLANUNG
LIGHTING CONSULTANT

ag Licht Gesellschaft beratender Ingenieure für Lichtplanung b. R., Bonn

REGALANLAGENPLANUNG
SHELVING SYSTEM PLANNING

Obermeyer-ALBIS Bauplan GmbH, Chemnitz

LANDSCHAFTSARCHITEKTUR
LANDSCAPE ARCHITECTURE

FSWLA Landschaftsarchitekten, Düsseldorf

BERATUNG FASSADE
FAÇADE CONSULTANTS

Gödde Architekt, Neuss

ARMATUREN | FITTINGS

Grohe, Porta Westfalica

TÜRKLINKEN UND BESCHLÄGE
HANDLES AND FITTINGS

FSB, Brakel

ELEKTROSCHALTER
ELECTRICAL SWITCHES

Albrecht Jung GmbH & Co. KG, Schalksmühle

FERTIGSTELLUNG | COMPLETION

2013 / 2014

STANDORT | LOCATION

**Schifferstraße 30
47059 Duisburg
www.archive.nrw.de**

FOTOS | PHOTOS

**O&O Baukunst
Thomas Mayer, Neuss**

Vor dem Umbau | Before the conversion

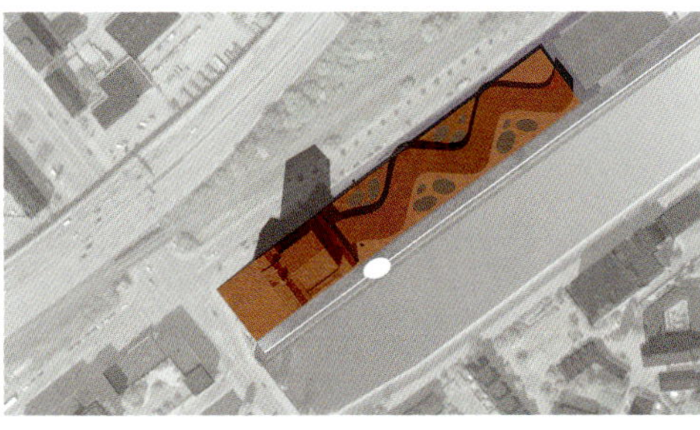

Lageplan | Site plan

Der neue Archivturm wächst aus dem alten Speicher; rechts schließt sich die „Welle" an. | The new archive tower emerges from the old silo. The 'wave' is connected on the right side.

Duisburg hat ein neues Wahrzeichen: einen schon von der Autobahn A 40 weithin sichtbaren roten Turm mit einem steilen Satteldach. Kein Dachfirst, keine Regenrinne, keine Auskragung beeinträchtigen die monolithische, skulptural anmutende Form des Turms. Es ist der Speicherturm des neuen Landesarchivs NRW. Nach langen Querelen um das Baugrundstück und vergeudeten Millionen hat das Landesarchiv nun eine neue Heimat im Duisburger Innenhafen gefunden.

Der Duisburger Hafen am nördlichen Rand der Innenstadt war einst aufgrund der dort angesiedelten Getreidemühlen und großen Speicher der „Brotkorb des Ruhrgebietes". Mit dem Niedergang der Mühlen in den 1960er-Jahren verlor der Hafen an Bedeutung. Während der IBA Emscher Park begann man ab 1991, das 89 Hektar große Hafenareal auf der Grundlage eines von Foster + Partners entwickelten Masterplans mit Erfolg zu einem neuen städtischen Areal zu entwickeln.

Aus einem geladenen Wettbewerb ging 2007 der Entwurf von O&O Baukunst aus Wien / Köln als Sieger hervor. Der Komplex des Landesarchivs besteht aus zwei Teilen: dem denkmalgeschützten RWSG-Speicher von 1936 und einem daran anschließenden wellenförmigen Neubau. Die Idee der Architekten war, den historischen Getreidespeicher aufgrund seiner kompakten und massiven Bauweise auch weiterhin als Speicher, nun für das Archivgut, zu nutzen und durch einen weiteren Speicher als einen

Duisburg has a new landmark: a red tower with a steep, pitched roof, which can already be seen from afar when approaching on the A 40 autobahn. No roof ridge, rain gutter or overhang interferes with the monolithic, almost sculptural shape of the tower. This is the storage tower of the new State Archive of North Rhine-Westphalia. After long bickering over the building site and millions of wasted euros, the state archive has found a new home in Duisburg's Innenhafen (Inner Harbour).

Duisburg harbour on the northern edge of the city centre was once known as the 'breadbasket of the Ruhr' by dint of the grain mills and large silos located there. With the decline of the mills in the 1960s, the harbour became less important. Starting in 1991, during the IBA Emscher Park (International Building Exhibition at Emscher Park), the council began successfully developing the 89-hectare harbour area into a new city district, based on a master plan developed by Foster + Partners.

In a closed competition held in 2007, the design by the Vienna / Cologne firm of O&O Baukunst emerged as the winner. The State Archive complex consists of two sections: the historic and protected

Der Blick auf die Flussseite mit der optisch deutlich abgesetzten „Welle" | View of the riverside façade; visually, the 'wave' stands out clearly from the older structure.

Die Darstellung zeigt, dass die Fassade der „Welle" ursprünglich wie das alte Speichergebäude und der neue Archivturm verklinkert und gegliedert werden sollte.
This illustration shows that the façade of the 'wave' was originally intended to be clinkered and structured like the old silo building and the new archive tower.

Die Straßenseite der „Welle" | The street façade of the 'wave'

Der alte Speicher mit dem Archivturm | The old silo with the archive tower

„Speicher im Speicher" in Gestalt eines mächtigen Archivturms in der Mitte des historischen Bauwerks zu ergänzen. Der Bau der 1930er-Jahre ist eine Stahlbetonkonstruktion, die mit rotbraunen Vollziegeln im alten Reichsformat (25 x 12 x 6,5 Zentimeter) verkleidet ist. Um das äußere Fassadenbild zu bewahren, wurde die erforderliche Wärmedämmung auf der Innenseite angebracht. Die Ziegelhaut des historischen Bauwerks griffen O&O für den neuen Archivturm auf und verwendeten für die Verkleidung ebenfalls Vollziegel im gleichen Format. Jetzt aber wurden die Ziegel in einem rautenförmigen Muster verlegt. Je nach Sonneneinstrahlung ist das subtile Muster mehr oder weniger deutlich sichtbar. Auch das steile Satteldach besteht aus Ziegeln. Von der Ferne wirkt es monolithisch, aber der Eindruck täuscht. Eine raffinierte Konstruktion aus speziellen Hohlziegeln, die auf Stahlrohren aufgefädelt sind, ermöglicht schmale, offene Fugen, durch die die technischen Anlagen auf dem Dach belüftet werden.

Der 20-stöckige Archivturm ruht auf einer eigenen Gründung aus 505 Bohrpfählen. Seine Konstruktion wurde aufgeteilt in einen äußeren Stahlbetonturm, der die Horizontallasten abträgt sowie die Funktion der Gebäudehülle übernimmt, und eine innere Stahlkonstruktion zur Abtragung der Archivlasten. Die strengen Anforderungen zur Aufbewahrung der Archivalien – Raumtemperatur 16° Celsius und Luftfeuchtigkeit 50 Prozent – wurden durch eine effektive Wärmedämmung zum Schutz vor Klimaschwankungen und eine schwere Konstruktion zur Stabilisierung der Temperatur erreicht.

Östlich an den RWSG-Speicher schließt sich der Neubau an, der zum Hafenbecken hin wellenförmig geschwungen ist. Am Schnittpunkt von Speicher und „Welle" befinden sich Eingang und Foyer des Archivs. Im Erdgeschoss der Welle wurden Lese- und Vortragssaal untergebracht. Die Obergeschosse sind zurzeit als Büroetagen ausgebaut und werden zunächst vermietet. Langfristig aber sollen auch hier mit steigendem Bedarf weitere Archivalien eingelagert werden. Später ist beabsichtigt, wie auch im historischen Speicher, die Fensteröffnungen nach und nach zu schließen.

silo of the RWSG (Rheinisch-Westfälische Speditions-Gesellschaft), dating from 1936, and an adjoining, wave-shaped new building. The architects' idea was to continue using the historic granary, with its compact and solid construction, as a storage space – but this time for archival material. It would be augmented by an additional storage building to create a 'silo within a silo' in the form of a massive archive tower in the centre of the historic structure. The 1930s building is made of reinforced concrete clad in solid red-brown bricks in the old imperial format of 25 x 12 x 6.5 centimetres. In order to preserve the appearance of the outer façade, the necessary thermal insulation was installed on the inside. O&O adopted the brick shell of the historic building for the new archive tower and used solid bricks in the same format for the cladding here as well. This time, however, the bricks were laid in a diamond-shaped pattern. Depending on the angle of the sun, the subtle pattern is more or less clearly visible. The steep pitched roof is likewise constructed out of bricks. From a distance, it seems monolithic, but this appearance is deceptive. An ingenious construction of special hollow bricks strung onto steel rods allows for the creation of narrow, open joints through which the technical facilities on the roof are ventilated. The 20-storey archive tower rests on its own foundation of 505 bored piles. Its structure was divided into an outer reinforced-concrete tower which supports the horizontal loads as well as functioning as the building envelope, and an inner steel structure which supports the archive loads. The strict requirements for the preservation of archival material – an indoor temperature of 16º Celsius and a relative humidity of 50 percent – were achieved through effective thermal insulation to protect against climate fluctuations and a heavy structure to stabilize the temperature.

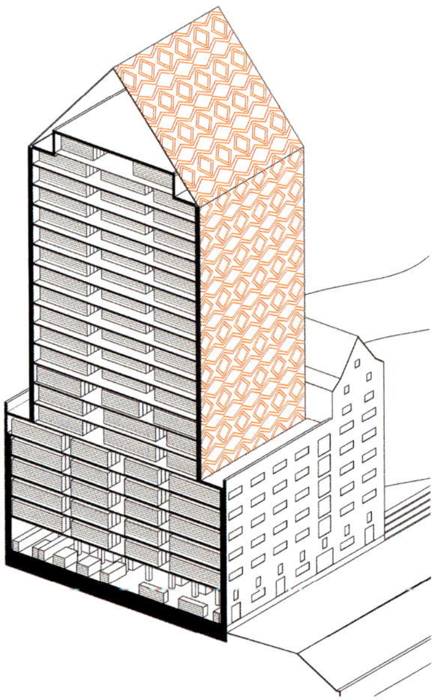

Schnitt Archivturm | Section of archive tower

Die Fassaden der Welle bestehen aus einem rot eingefärbten Dämmputz. Der rote Farbton wirkt wie der vergebliche Versuch, die beiden so unterschiedlichen Gebäudeteile zu einem Ensemble zusammenzufügen. Nach den ursprünglichen Planungen von O&O sollte auch der Neubau eine Ziegelhaut erhalten. Da das dem Bauherrn zu teuer war, entschied man sich im Einvernehmen mit den Architekten für die Putzlösung. Allerdings war vorgesehen, die Fassaden der Welle nach den Planungen von O&O mit einem lisenenartigen Rastersystem zu gliedern. So wäre der Neubau nicht nur strukturiert worden, sondern es hätte sich mit den leicht vor- und zurückspringenden Flächen, verstärkt durch das allmähliche Verschließen der Fensteröffnungen, eine sichtbare Analogie zu dem Umgang mit den Fassaden an dem historischen Speichergebäude ergeben. Die Stimmigkeit aus Kontur, Textur und Farbigkeit, die den Umbau des historischen Speichergebäudes auszeichnet, ist in dem Neubau gänzlich verloren gegangen. So mögen die Worte von Christian Heuchel von O&O dem Bauherrn in den Ohren klingen: „Kulturelle Bauten wie das Landesarchiv NRW sind letztlich eine stabilisierende Investition in die nächsten 300 Jahre. Jeglicher kurzfristige und spekulative Umgang mit Architektur wirkt dagegen lächerlich. In den Archiven wird in Zukunft unsere Vergangenheit geschrieben."

Adjoining the RWSG silo to the east is the new construction, which curves toward the harbour basin in an oscillating wave shape. The entrance and foyer of the archive are located at the point of intersection between the silo and the 'wave'. The ground floor of the wave houses the reading room and lecture hall. Currently, the upper storeys have been constructed as offices, and initially, these will be rented out. In the long term, however, additional archival material will be stored here as the need increases. Future plans call for the window openings to be successively blocked, as they are in the historic silo. The façades of the wave are covered in red insulating plaster. The red colour gives the appearance of a vain attempt to unite the two very different sections of the building into a single ensemble. According to O&O's original plans, the new building was also supposed to be covered in bricks. Since the client found this too expensive, a decision was reached together with the architects in favour of the plaster solution. O&O's intention, however, was to structure the wave's façade with a pilaster-like grid system. Not only would this have lent the new building a more structured appearance, but with its subtly protruding and receding surfaces – underscored by the gradual closing of the window openings – this solution would have resulted in a visible analogy to the treatment of the façades on the historic silo building. The coherency of contour, texture and colour that distinguishes the renovation of the historic silo has been completely lost in the case of the new structure. Therefore, may the words of O&O's Christian Heuchel ring in the ears of the client: 'Cultural buildings like the NRW State Archive are ultimately a stabilizing investment in the next 300 years – whereas any kind of short-term or speculative handling of the architecture appears ridiculous. In the future, our past will be recorded in these archives.'

Blick in das Foyer | View of the foyer

Die „aufgefädelten" Ziegel des steilen Satteldachs auf dem Archivturm
The 'strung' bricks on the steep pitched roof of the archive tower

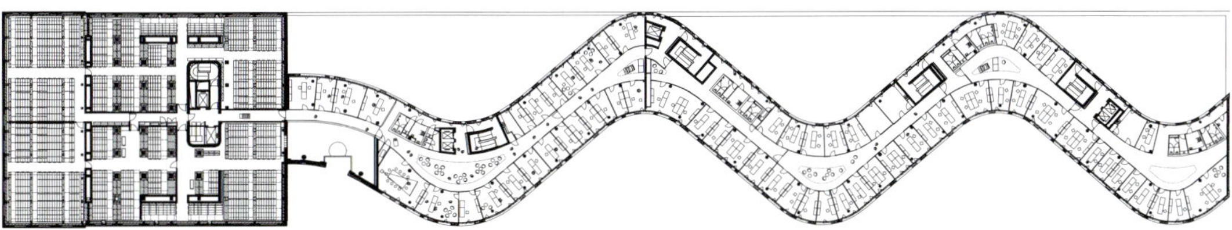

Grundriss 1. Obergeschoss | Plan of 1st floor

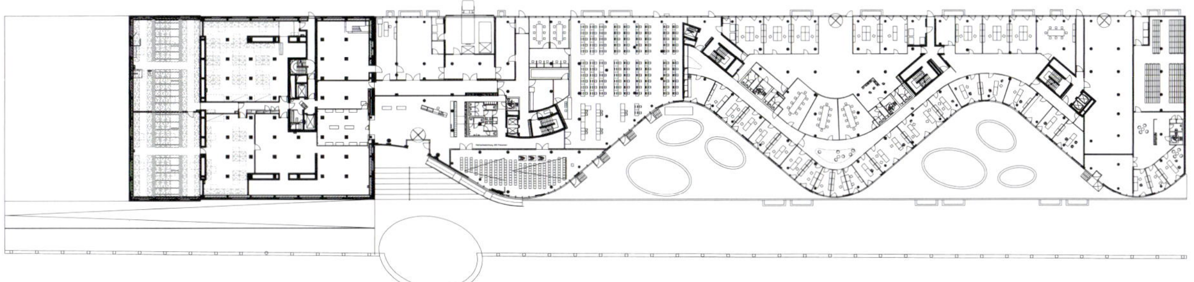

Grundriss Erdgeschoss | Plan of ground floor

RITTER JOCKISCH ARCHITEKTUR INNENARCHITEKTUR

GEBÄUDE | BUILDING

ARCHÄOPARK VOGELHERD
NIEDERSTOTZINGEN-STETTEN

TEXT KARIN LEYDECKER

16

ARCHITEKTEN | ARCHITECTS

Ritter Jockisch Architektur
Innenarchitektur
Fürstenstraße 10
80333 München | Munich
www.ritterjokisch.de

BAUHERR | CLIENT

Stadt Niederstotzingen,
vertreten durch
Hr. Bürgermeister Kieninger

AUSFÜHRUNGSPLANUNG
EXECUTION PLANNING

Ritter Jockisch Architektur
Innenarchitektur

ÖRTLICHE BAULEITUNG
SITE MANAGEMENT

Ingenieurbüro Gall,
Niederstotzingen

TRAGWERK UND BRANDSCHUTZ
STRUCTURE AND FIRE PREVENTION

Prof. Feix Ingenieure GmbH,
München | Munich

HAUSTECHNIK | M & E ENGINEERS

Schreiber Ingenieure GmbH,
Ulm

BAUPHYSIK + AKUSTIK
BUILDING PHYSICS + ACOUSTICS

Müller-BBM,
Planegg

SZENOGRAFIE INNENRAUM
INTERIOR SCENOGRAPHY

Arbeitsgemeinschaft
Ritter Jockisch Architektur
Innenarchitektur mit
Lutzenberger & Lutzenberger,
Bad Wörishofen

SZENOGRAFIE PARK
PARK SCENOGRAPHY

Lutzenberger & Lutzenberger,
Bad Wörishofen

**WISSENSCHAFTLICHE
BETREUUNG**
SCIENTIFIC CONSULTING

Institut für Ur- und Frühgeschichte
der Universität Tübingen,
Prof. Nicholas J. Conard,
M. A. Ewa Dutkiewicz

LEUCHTEN | LUMINAIRES

ERCO, Lüdenscheid

AUSSENANLAGEN
OUTDOOR FACILITIES

Keller Damm Roser
Landschaftsarchitekten,
München | Munich

FERTIGSTELLUNG | COMPLETION

Mai | May **2013**

STANDORT | LOCATION

Am Vogelherd 1
89168 Niederstotzingen
www.archaeopark-vogelherd.de

FOTOS | PHOTOS

Brigida González, Stuttgart

Lageplan | Site plan

Das Museum Archäopark ist in das Gelände hineingeschoben. | The Archäopark Museum is nestled into the park landscape.

Damals war Eiszeit. Von einem gnadenlos blauen Himmel schickte die Sonne ihre Strahlen auf den im Permafrost erstarrten Boden einer steppenähnlichen Landschaft. Der steinzeitliche Mensch lebte unter extremen äußeren Bedingungen in Gruppen mit klar definierten Aufgabenbereichen. Es gab Jäger und Sammler, man fertigte Kleidung und man liebte Musikinstrumente und Schmuck aus Knochen. Tiere wurden gejagt und erlegt, über dem Feuer zubereitet und verspeist, Pflanzen und Samen ergänzten den Speiseplan. Die Wohnungen waren Zelte oder natürliche Höhlen. So oder ähnlich vollzog sich das steinzeitliches Leben vor 40 000 Jahren in Europa. Die Quellen des Wissens über diese Zeit basieren auf Zufallsfunden und gezielten Grabungen an bekannten Siedlungsorten wie zum Beispiel dem Lonetal auf der Schwäbischen Alb. Dort entdeckten Archäologen in der Vogelherdhöhle nahe dem schwäbischen Niederstotzingen winzige Tierskulpturen aus dem Jungpaläolithikum: Ein kleines Mammut und ein Löwe aus Mammutelfenbein – die wohl ältesten Kunstwerke der Menschheit.

In those days it was the Ice Age. Out of a mercilessly blue sky, the sun's rays shone down on the permafrost-hardened earth of a steppe-like landscape. Stone Age humans lived in extreme conditions, in groups with clearly defined areas of responsibility. There were hunters and gatherers; people made clothing, and they loved musical instruments and jewellery made of bone. Animals were hunted and killed, cooked over fires and eaten; the menu was supplemented with plants and seeds. Dwellings were tents or natural caves. Stone Age life in the Europe of 40,000 years ago was lived in this or a similar manner. Our sources of knowledge about this time are based on chance discoveries and targeted excavations at known settlements – such as, for example, in the Lone Valley in the Swabian Alb. Here, in the Vogelherd Cave near the Swabian city of Niederstotzingen, archaeologists have discovered tiny animal sculptures dating from the Upper

Die Sitzstufen sind mit Fellen belegt. | Animal skins are laid out on the seating steps.

Um einige dieser Funde unmittelbar am Grabungsort präsentieren zu können und in Form eines Archäoparks die steinzeitliche Lebenswelt unserer Vorfahren aufleben zu lassen, lobte die Stadt Niederstotzingen einen Architekturwettbewerb für ein Ausstellungsgebäude aus, den das Architekturbüro Ritter Jokisch mit einem ersten Preis für sich entschied.

Das neue Gebäude des „Archäopark Vogelherd" liegt 200 Meter südöstlich von der Fundstelle in einer Talsenke in der Nähe des Ortes Niederstotzingen-Stetten. Organisch eingebettet in die Hügel des Lonetals mit Ackerland, Wiesen und Wäldern, schmiegt sich das Besucherzentrum fast unmerklich in die fließende Geschichtslandschaft. Wer auf dem Zickzackweg vom Parkplatz kommt, sieht zunächst nur einen sanften grünen Grashügel, der integraler Bestandteil des Archäoparks zu sein scheint. Beim Näherkommen erkennt man in diesem lang gestreckten Hügel zwei Einschnitte: Einen großen für den Freisitz der verglasten Cafeteria und einen engen schmalen für den Eingang. Dieses Entree, das als ein dunkler, von Betonwänden gesäumter Gang ausgebildet ist, wirkt zwar unprätentiös, spielt aber mit der expressiven Kraft des ritualisierten Zugangs in einen Höhlenraum: Der Mensch tritt ein in C. G. Jungs „schützende Höhle".

Palaeolithic period – a small mammoth and a lion carved out of mammoth ivory – possibly the oldest works of art in human history.

In order to display these finds directly at the excavation site, and to bring the Stone Age world of our ancestors back to life in the form of an archaeological park, the town of Niederstotzingen sponsored an architectural competition for the design of an exhibition building; the first prize was awarded to the Ritter Jokisch architectural firm.

The new building at the 'Archäopark Vogelherd' ('Vogelherd Archaeological Park') is located 200 metres southeast of the discovery site, in a valley basin near the village of Niederstotzingen-Stetten. Nestled organically among the hills of the Lone Valley, among farmlands, meadows and forests, the visitor centre blends almost unnoticed into the flowing historical landscape. Visitors who follow the zigzag path from the car park will first see only a green grassy hillock, which seems to be an integral part of the park. Coming closer, one can make out two incisions in this elongated

Ansicht von Westen | View from the west

Ansicht von Osten | View from the east

Im Prinzip hat diese weich gewölbte Höhle zwei Seiten: Ihr Rückgrat aus hellem Sichtbeton fügt sich sichelförmig in den begrünten Wall und in die biomorphe Struktur der Landschaft. Ihre Vorderfront zum Hof ist ganz aus Glas und gibt den Blick frei auf das Panorama des Vogelherdhügels. Integriert in das Halbrund des Höhlenraums sind der Empfangsbereich mit der puristisch möblierten Cafeteria und den teilweise mystisch abgedunkelten Ausstellungsflächen. Das von den Architekten konzipierte Design der Innenraumgestaltung gibt sich im Kontrast zu den im Außenbereich vielfältig präsenten Naturmaterialien sehr zurückhaltend und verzichtet angenehm auf jegliche Bricolage. Informationen zu Ort und Zeit erhält der Besucher über Texte, die auf von der Decke baumelnde satinierte Plexiglasschalen gedruckt sind oder über filmische Animationen. Das Allerheiligste des Hauses ist die stimmungsvoll dämmrige Schatzkammer mit zwei Originalfundstücken – dem Mammut und der Löwenfigur – aus dem Vogelherd. Zentral in jeweils eigenen Vitrinen präsentiert beherrschen diese winzigen Figuren den Raum, in dem eine umlaufende, mit Fellen belegte

mound: a large one for the open-air seating at the glazed cafeteria and a smaller, narrower one for the entrance. This entranceway, which is designed as a dark corridor lined with concrete walls, may seem unpretentious; in fact, however, it draws on the expressive power of a ritual approach to a cave chamber: the human being is entering C. G. Jung's 'protective cave'.

In principle, this gently domed cave has two sides: its sickle-shaped spine, made out of pale exposed concrete, is integrated into the green wall and the biomorphic structure of the landscape. Its front side, facing the courtyard, is constructed completely of glass and offers a panoramic view of the Vogelherd hill. Integrated into the semicircle of the cave chamber are the entrance area with its puristically-furnished cafeteria, and the exhibition spaces, some of which are bathed in mystical darkness. In contrast to the outdoor area, with its highly visible variety

Der Zugang an der konvex gebogenen Seite des Museums
The entrance on the outer side of the museum

Der nach Westen ausgerichtete Museumsraum
The west-facing museum space

Eines der „Highlights": das Miniatur-Mammut | One of the 'highlights': the miniature mammoth

Betonbank zur kontemplativen und filmisch begleiteten Betrachtung einlädt. Im benachbarten Auditorium sitzt man auf mit Fell bedeckten ansteigenden Betonstufen wie in einem intimen Hörsaal und lauscht kurzen Hörgeschichten zu steinzeitlichen Themen, die ganz pragmatisch auch Kochrezepte einschließen.
Ausgerüstet mit einiger Theorie und der Archäopark-App folgt nun die tätige Praxis im Freigelände, das die Besucher im ansteigenden Hang automatisch zum Höhepunkt des Ortes – zur Vogelherdhöhle – geleitet. „Sich auf den Weg machen" – „Forschen – Entdecken – Erleben" sind die Mottos des Rundgangs in die Eiszeit und zurück. Einzelne anschaulich inszenierte und nachdrücklich didaktisierte Themenplätze wie Waffenherstellung, Speerwerfen oder Feuermachen lassen den Besucher mit allen Sinnen in die Lebenswelten des paläolithischen Menschen eintauchen. Und wenn man dann ermüdet vom Abenteuer zu den Ursprüngen am großen Rund des Feuerplatzes ausruht, wieder ganz bei sich im Jetzt sein darf und von fern in die gerundete Guckkastenbühne des Ausstellungsgebäudes hineinsieht, dann fühlt man sich frei nach Meister Goethe gewiss „nur halb so gelehrt, aber doppelt beglückt".

of natural materials, the interior design conceived by the architects is extremely restrained, pleasantly dispensing with any type of bricolage. Visitors can obtain information about the place and the time period from texts printed on curved frosted acrylic-glass plates suspended from the ceiling, or from animated films. The holy of holies of the building is the atmospherically darkened treasure chamber containing two original artefacts – the mammoth and the lion figure – from the Vogelherd cave. Each placed in the centre of its own display case, these minuscule figures dominate the room, in which a fur-covered concrete bench lining the walls invites visitors to contemplative observation, accompanied by a film. In the adjacent auditorium, visitors sit on ascending, fur-covered concrete steps, as if in an intimate lecture hall, and listen to short audio reports on Stone Age topics – including, very pragmatically, some recipes.

Armed with some theoretical information and the Archäopark App, visitors are now ready for actual practice in the outdoor area, whose rising slope automatically leads them to the park's highlight – the Vogelherd Cave. 'Sich auf den Weg machen' ('Set out on your journey') and 'Forschen – Entdecken – Erleben' (Search – Discover – Experience) are the mottos of this tour into the Ice Age and back. Individual vividly staged and emphatically didactic 'thematic sites' such as weapon production, spear-throwing or fire-making let visitors immerse themselves in the world of Palaeolithic human life with all of their senses. Then, while resting on the large circular steps around the fire site, exhausted from the journey to their origins, the visitors can once again be completely with themselves in the present day, gazing at the rounded proscenium stage of the exhibition hall from a distance. Then one surely feels – to paraphrase Goethe – 'only half a scholar but twice as contented'.

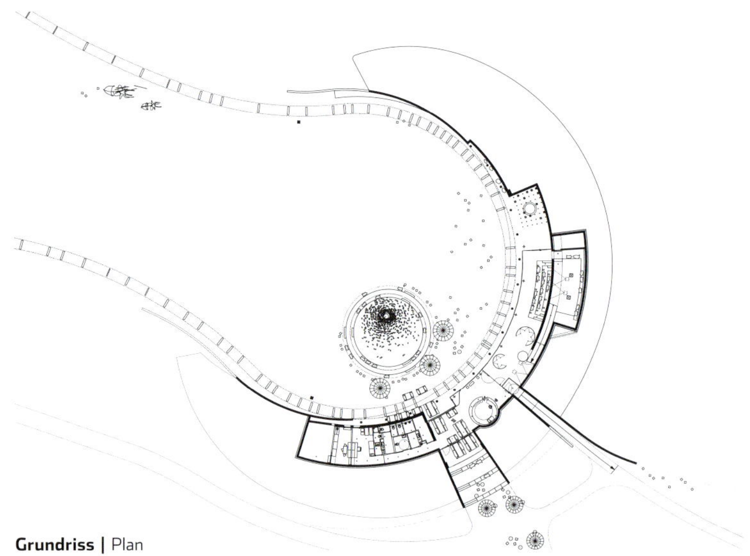

Grundriss | Plan

Die sichelmondförmige Fassade des Museums tagsüber ... | The crescent façade of the museum by day ...

... und in der Abendstimmung | ... and by evening light

SCHNEIDER+SCHUMACHER

GEBÄUDE | BUILDING

ÖLHAFENBRÜCKE RAUNHEIM

TEXT CHRISTOF BODENBACH

17

ARCHITEKTEN | ARCHITECTS

schneider+schumacher
Planungsgesellschaft mbH
Poststraße 20A
60329 Frankfurt am Main
www.schneider-schumacher.de
mit | with
SPI Schüßler-Plan
Ingenieurgesellschaft mbH,
Frankfurt am Main

MITARBEITER | TEAM

Projektarchitekt | project architect:
Michael Schumacher
Projektleitung Planung | planning
project director: Karlo Filipovic
Team: Christian Simons, Kyriakos
Chatziparaskevas

BAUHERR | CLIENT

Stadt Raunheim,
Stadt Rüsselsheim,
Stadt Kelsterbach

AUSFÜHRUNGSPLANUNG
EXECUTION PLANNING

schneider+schumacher
Planungsgesellschaft mbH
SPI Schüßler-Plan
Ingenieurgesellschaft mbH

BAULEITUNG | SITE MANAGEMENT

SPI Schüßler-Plan
Ingenieurgesellschaft mbH

PROJEKTSTEUERUNG
PROJECT MANAGEMENT

NH ProjektStadt
SPI Schüßler-Plan
Ingenieurgesellschaft mbH

TRAGWERK UND BRANDSCHUTZ
STRUCTURE AND FIRE PREVENTION

SPI Schüßler-Plan
Ingenieurgesellschaft mbH

FERTIGSTELLUNG | COMPLETION

Mai | May 2013

STANDORT | LOCATION

Raunheim

FOTOS | PHOTOS

Jörg Hempel, Aachen

Luftbild von Nordwesten aus gesehen | Aerial view seen from northwest

Der elegante Schwung der Brücke am Eingang zum Raunheimer Ölhafen | The elegant curve of the bridge at the entrance to the Raunheim oil terminal

Das Büro schneider+schumacher besteht nun schon über 25 Jahre. Seine Gründer Till Schneider und Michael Schumacher gehören nicht erst seit gestern der „Generation 50plus" an. Im BauNetz-Ranking lagen die Architekten im Februar 2014 national auf Rang vier und international auf Rang acht. An den drei Standorten – neben der Zentrale in Frankfurt am Main gibt es Niederlassungen in Wien und im chinesischen Tianjin – werden gut einhundert Mitarbeiter beschäftigt. Das nennt man etabliert. Und dennoch haftet den beiden Inhabern erstaunlicherweise noch immer das Etikett der Jugendlichen, Experimentierfreudigen an!

Woran mag das liegen? Wer sich das Œuvre von schneider+schumacher anschaut, der stellt fest, dass es schon immer unkonventionelle, abseits des Mainstream liegende Projekte gab. Das war bereits ganz am Anfang so, und die experimentellen „Sonnenflecke" von 1988 belegen das überzeugend. Auch die knallrote, lange als eine Art Markenzeichen fungierende 1994

The architectural office of schneider+schumacher has been in existence for over 25 years. Its founders, Till Schneider and Michael Schumacher, have been members of the '50-plus generation' for some time now. In February 2014, they ranked fourth on the BauNetz-Ranking at the German national level; on the international level they were rated eighth. The firm employs more than one hundred workers in three locations: in addition to the headquarters in Frankfurt, there are branch offices in Vienna, Austria and Tianjin, China. That's what you call an established company. But astonishing as it may seem, the two associates still can't shake off the label of 'young and willing to experiment'!

Why is that? Anyone who takes a look at the œuvre of schneider+schumacher can see that it has always included projects which were unconventional and

Die unterschiedlichen Brüstungen: als Schutzwand zum Ölhafen, durchlässig und mit Aussicht zum Fluss hin | The contrasting balustrades: a security wall facing the harbour; open with a view facing the river

entstandene „Info-Box" am Potsdamer Platz in Berlin – ein Glücksfall für das Büro – kann so gelesen werden. Das ist bis heute so geblieben, nimmt man die „Autobahnkirche Siegerland", 2013 fertiggestellt, oder die Talstation für die Rüdesheimer Seilbahn, die 2016 den Betrieb aufnehmen soll, als Beispiele. Auch das Möbeldesign spielte schon früh eine Rolle im Schaffen der Rheinländer – und seit ein paar Jahren finden sich, ungewöhnlich genug für Architekten, auch Brücken im Werkverzeichnis.

Ein schönes Beispiel dafür ist die zeitgleich mit der Autobahnkirche in Betrieb genommene Ölhafenbrücke bei Raunheim, von Frankfurt gut 20 Kilometer flussabwärts am Main gelegen. Die Betonung liegt hier auf am Main, denn die Fußgänger- und Radfahrerbrücke überspannt nicht etwa den Fluss, sondern die Schiffszufahrt zum namensgebenden Ölhafen. Vom hiesigen Tanklager wird hauptsächlich der in Sicht- und vor allem Hörweite gelegene, kaum drei Kilometer entfernte Frankfurter Flughafen mit (Flug-)Benzin versorgt, und fast 50 Jahre lang unterbrach die Hafenzufahrt den traditionellen Weg am südlichen Mainufer. Die von schneider+schumacher gemeinsam mit den Ingenieuren von Schüßler-Plan entwickelte Brücke schließt nun eine der letzten Lücken im Mainuferweg zwischen Frankfurt und Mainz.

Als lange, flach auf- und wieder absteigende Rampe kann sie von Radlern, Skatern und auch Rollstuhlfahrern benutzt werden. Die Überwindung der knapp 70 Meter breiten Hafen-

outside the mainstream. This has been true from the very beginning; the experimental 'Sonnenflecke' ('Sun Spots') project from 1988 is convincing proof. Likewise, the bright red 'Info-Box' on Berlin's Potsdamer Platz, built in 1994, which has long functioned as a kind of city landmark – and a stroke of luck for the office – can be seen in this way. It is still true to this day: the 'Autobahnkirche Siegerland' (Siegerland Autobahn Church), completed in 2013, or the lower cable car terminal in Rudesheim, which is due to begin operations in 2016, are some recent examples. Interior design also played a role in the Rhinelanders' repertoire from early on; and for a few years now – strangely enough for an architectural firm – bridges can also be found in their catalogue of works.

A beautiful example of these is the Oil Terminal Bridge outside Raunheim, a little over 20 kilometres downstream from Frankfurt on the River Main; it was put into operation at the same time as the Autobahn church. The emphasis here is on the word on, because this bridge for pedestrians and cyclists does not actually span the river, but rather the ships' entrance to the eponymous oil terminal harbour. The local oil depot primarily supplies Frankfurt Airport – located within sight, and especially within earshot, scarcely three kilometres away – with aviation fuel. For almost 50 years, the harbour entrance interrupted the traditional path along the southern bank of the Main. The bridge, developed by schneider+schumacher in co-operation with engineers from Schüssler-Plan, now closes one of the last remaining gaps in the riverside path along the Main between Frankfurt and Mainz.

As a long, gently ascending and then descending ramp, the bridge can be used by cyclists, skaters as well as wheelchair users. In this way, a journey across the nearly 70-metre-wide harbour entrance adds up to 170 metres of bridge length. Since highly flammable fuels are transferred and stored in the giant oil tank, and their transport route runs under the bridge, strict safety requirements needed to be met. And of course, the view of the river from the bridge needed to be impaired as little as possible – better still, it should be facilitated.

The solution was an almost sculptural superstructure in the form of a five-part continuous girder that

Die ringförmige Auffahrt am nördlichen Ende der Brücke | The spiral ramp on the north end of the bridge

Blick von Westen | View from the west

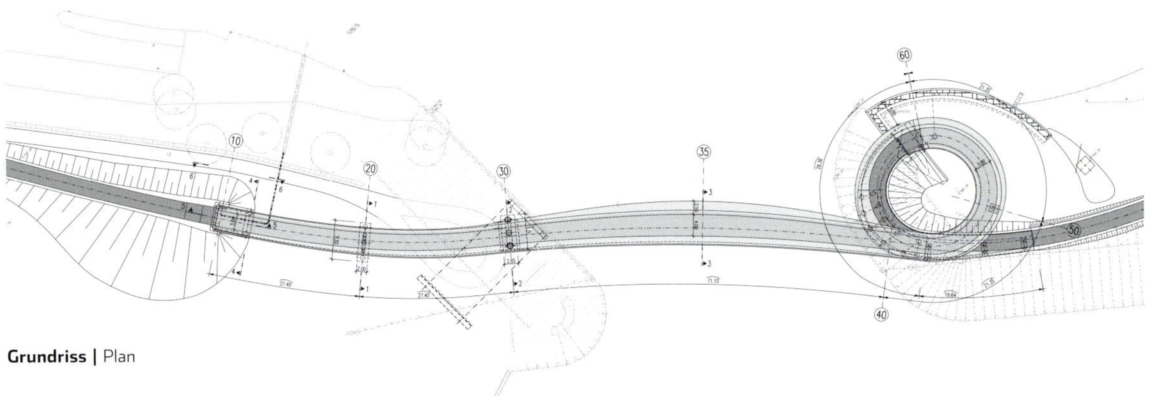

Blick in Richtung Norden | View facing north

Grundriss | Plan

Eine der X-förmigen Stützen am Südufer | One of the X-shaped supports on the southern bank

zufahrt summiert sich so auf 170 Meter Brückenlänge. Da Im Großtanklager hochentzündliche Treibstoffe umgeschlagen und gelagert werden und ihr Transport unter der Brücke hindurch geht, waren hohe sicherheitstechnische Vorgaben zu erfüllen. Und natürlich sollte der Blick von der Brücke auf den Fluss so wenig wie möglich behindert – am besten sogar unterstützt – werden.

Gelöst wurde dies mit einem beinahe skulpturalen Überbau als fünfteiligem Durchlaufträger, der die Hafenzufahrt frei überspannt. Beim Begehen oder Befahren bietet die im Süden leicht S-förmig geschwungene und am Nordufer kreisrunde Linienführung vielfältige Blicke auf den Main und die Umgebung. Auf der dem Hafen zugewandten Seite baut sich der Brückenkörper aus weißem Beton zu einer weich geschwungenen, schwer überwindlichen Sicherheitswand auf. Zum Main hin lässt das filigrane Geländer die Blicke nahezu ungehindert schweifen. Wie funktioniert das? Der untere Halbkreis der Spirale besteht aus einer Winkelstützwand, die sich fließend aus der Geometrie des stählernen Überbaus entwickelt und in der anschließenden Betonwand fortgesetzt wird. Die Stahlrohrstützen, die monolithisch mit Überbau und Fundament verbunden sind, wurden als aussteifende Kreuze ausgeführt, um eine Gabellagerung des Überbaus zu gewährleisten. Interessant ist auch die Konstruktion des Brückenquerschnitts: Bestehend aus einem L-förmigen Stahlhohlkasten weist die senkrechte Seitenwand des Kastens eine Höhe bis zu 2,80 Meter ab Oberkante Lauffläche auf und bildet so die geforderte Abschirmung zum Hafen. Auf der Mainseite hingegen wird der Brückenkörper um bis zu 2,50 Meter über die Geländerlinie hinaus verbreitert. Das Geländer selbst neigt sich zudem den Nutzern entgegen und hält sie so von der Brückenkante fern.

Der unkonventionelle, aber gestalterisch einfache Leitgedanke, „ein Band, das wie ein geschwungener Pinselstrich beide Seiten des Raunheimer Ölhafens verbindet" (Michael Schumacher), ist aus der Vogelperspektive besonders gut ablesbar und übersetzt die komplexen Anforderungen in eine bildhafte Form.

freely spans the harbour entrance. When crossing on foot or by bicycle, the bridge's layout – a slightly undulating S-shape to the south and a spiral on the northern bank – provides multifaceted views of the Main and the surrounding area. On the side that faces the harbour, the white concrete bridge structure rises into a gently curving, nearly unscalable security wall. On the Main side, the openwork railing allows the viewer's gaze to wander almost unobstructed. How does this work? The lower half circle of the spiral consists of an angle supporting wall that emerges fluently from the geometry of the steel superstructure and is continued in the adjacent concrete wall. The tubular steel supports, which are monolithically connected to the superstructure and the foundation, were designed as reinforcing crosses in order to create a fork bearing for the superstructure. The construction of the bridge cross section is also interesting: consisting of an L-shaped hollow steel box, the vertical side wall of the box extends a height of up to 2.80 metres from the top edge of the bearing surface, thus forming the necessary shield from the harbour. On the Main side, on the other hand, the bridge structure stretches up to 2.50 metres past the railing line. At the same time, the railing itself inclines toward the users, thus keeping them away from the edge of the bridge.

The unconventional, but creatively simple design approach – 'A swiftly-rendered stroke of a paintbrush, connecting the two sides of the Raunheimer Ölhafen' (Michael Schumacher), is particularly recognizable from a bird's eye view, and it translates the complex demands of the project into a vivid form.

SPEECH, SERGEI TCHOBAN, SERGEY KUZNETSOV

TCHOBAN FOUNDATION
MUSEUM FÜR ARCHITEKTURZEICHNUNG BERLIN

TEXT JÜRGEN TIETZ

18

ARCHITEKTEN | ARCHITECTS

Entwurf | design development:
Sergei Tchoban, Sergey Kuznetsov
SPEECH Tchoban & Kuznetsov
16, Krasnoproletarskaya
127473 Moskau | Moscow,
Russland | Russia
www.speech.su
www.npstv.de

MITARBEITER | TEAM

Projektleitung | project architect:
Philipp Bauer, Ulrike Graefenhain;
Planung, Bauleitung | construction
management planning: **Nadja
Fedorova, Katja Fuks, Dirk Kollendt**

BAUHERR | CLIENT

**Tchoban Foundation. Museum für
Architekturzeichnung, Berlin**

AUSFÜHRUNGSPLANUNG
EXECUTION PLANNING

nps tchoban voss, Berlin

**BAULEITUNG /
PROJEKTSTEUERUNG**
SITE MANAGEMENT /
PROJECT MANAGEMENT

nps tchoban voss, Berlin

TRAGWERK UND BRANDSCHUTZ
STRUCTURE AND FIRE PREVENTION

Tragwerk | Structure: **PPW
Dipl.-Ing. D. Paulisch, Berlin;
Brandschutz** | Fire Prevention
Consultant: **Rössel Brandschutz,
Berlin**

HAUSTECHNIK | M & E ENGINEERS

Planungsbüro Thye, Berlin

BAUPHYSIK | BUILDING PHYSICS

Planungsbüro Thye, Berlin

AUFZUGPLANER | LIFT PLANNING

**Tepper Aufzuganlagen GmbH,
Münster**

ARMATUREN | FIXTURES

Hansgrohe Axor, Schiltach

LEUCHTEN | LUMINAIRES

**RZB Rudolf Zimmermann,
Bamberg**

FERTIGSTELLUNG | COMPLETION

Mai | May **2013**

STANDORT | LOCATION

**Christinenstraße 18a
10119 Berlin
www.tchoban-foundation.de**

FOTOS | PHOTOS

**Roland Halbe, Stuttgart
Patricia Parinejad, Berlin
Thomas Spier, Berlin**

Lageplan | Site plan

Blick von Nordwesten: das Museum auf dem Areal der ehemaligen Brauerei „Pfefferberg" | View from the northwest: the museum on the site of the former 'Pfefferberg' brewery

Im Zeitalter glamouröser Renderings aus dem Computer erscheinen von Hand gefertigte Architekturzeichnungen wie die Dinosaurier des Entwurfs. Nichts an ihnen ist genormt, jeder Strich individuell. Fast wirkt es, als würden sie mit ihren mal feinen, mal fetten Strichen, ihrer wackeligen Linienführung und der gezielten Unschärfe eine architektonische Gedankenwelt öffnen, die einen Kontrast zur konstruktiven Endgültigkeit eines fertigen Gebäudes heraufbeschwört. In den Architekturzeichnungen fallen Abbild und Aneignung der gebauten Umwelt in eins, zugleich überlagern sich in ihnen Vision und Wirklichkeit. Dennoch ist ihre große Zeit vorbei. Daran ändert auch das Bekenntnis renommierter Architekten wie Álvaro Siza Vieira, Frank O. Gehry oder Ben van Berkel wenig, dass sie nicht am Bildschirm entwerfen würden, sondern mit dem Stift in der Hand. Und wie alles, was nicht mehr ganz zur Gegenwart zählt, aber auch noch nicht vollends dem Vergessen anheimfallen soll, wandern die Architekturzeichnungen in die Museen. Ein Haus wie die Berliner Tchoban

In the age of glamorous computer-generated renderings, hand-executed architectural drawings seem like the dinosaurs of drafting. Nothing about them is standardized; every stroke is unique. It almost seems, with their sometimes fine, sometimes broad strokes, their wobbly lines and intentional blurring, that they open up a world of architectural thought that evokes a contrast to the constructive finality of a completed building. In architectural drawings, the image and the appropriation of the constructed environment are merged into one, and vision and reality overlap within them. Nevertheless, their golden age is past. Even the avowals of acclaimed architects such as Álvaro Siza Viera, Frank O. Gehry or Ben van Berkel – that they do not create their designs on a screen, but with pen or pencil in their hand – can do little to change this. And like everything else that no longer quite belongs to the

Die Eingangsnische an der Nordwestseite; die hölzerne Tür fügt sich nahtlos in die profilierte Betonwand ein. | The entrance niche on the northwest side: the wooden door blends in seamlessly with the contoured concrete wall.

Foundation, das sich ausschließlich der Architekturzeichnung widmet, ist jedoch eine Besonderheit, ja geradezu eine Sensation. Entworfen und gebaut hat es der zwischen Moskwa und Spree pendelnde Architekt Sergei Tchoban, selbst ein hervorragender Zeichner, in Zusammenarbeit mit Sergey Kuznetsov und seinem Moskauer Büro SPEECH.

Dabei ist ihnen ein Haus gelungen, das einer Architekturzeichnung gleicht. Jenseits des normierten Blicks schwört es jeglichem Minimalismus ab, tanzt selbstbewusst und individuell aus der Reihe. Wie Erker schieben sich die gegeneinander versetzten Betonkuben der einzelnen Geschosse in lichtem Sandgelb vor und zurück. So entstand auf einem gerade einmal acht Meter breiten Restgrundstück am Zugang zum Kunstcampus des Pfefferbergs in Berlin auf vier Geschossen eine bewegte Architekturplastik mit 270 Quadratmetern Nutzfläche.

Kleinteilig bewegt zeigt sich auch das Fassadenrelief. In die Matrize der Betonschalung ließ Tchoban eine abstrahierte Zeichnung einritzen. Sie ist eine Referenz an die allererste Architekturzeichnung, die der leidenschaftliche Sammler 2001 erwarb – ein Bühnenbildentwurf Pietro di Gottardo Gonzagas

present day, but which we still do not wish to forget completely, architectural drawings are making their way into museums. An institution such as Berlin's Tchoban Foundation, however, which is devoted exclusively to architectural drawings, is certainly an anomaly – it can practically be called a sensation. It was designed and built by Sergei Tchoban – an architect who shuttles back and forth between the Moskva and the Spree and who is an outstanding draftsman in his own right – in cooperation with Sergey Kuznetsov and his Moscow office, SPEECH. They have succeeded in building a house that itself resembles an architectural drawing. Reaching beyond any standardized vision, it renounces all forms of minimalism and marches, unique and self-assured, to its own drummer. The light sandy-yellow concrete cubes of the individual storeys protrude back and forth, offset from one another like bay windows. In this way, it was possible to build an animated architectural sculpture with 270 square metres of floor space divided over four storeys on a vacant plot just eight metres wide at the entrance to the Pfefferberg arts campus in Berlin.

The building's façade relief is equally animated, if on a smaller scale. Tchoban had an abstract drawing carved into the matrices of the concrete formwork. It is a reference to the very first architectural drawing that the passionate collector acquired in 2001 – a stage design by Pietro di Gottardo Gonzaga (1751–1831). Here, however, the drawing is not simply portrayed as a copy; it has, so to speak, been transcribed. Like a musical composition by Philip Glass, certain parts are constantly repeated and strung together in new combinations. On the ground floor, strange, cubically-shaped window sections have been carved out of the concrete sketch. The building is crowned by a glazed pent-

Die Nordost- und Nordwestfassade; die vorstehende Glasbox ist an der Unterseite mit spiegelndem Edelstahl verkleidet. | The northeastern and northwestern façades: the underside of the protruding glass box is clad in reflecting stainless steel.

(1751–1831). Doch die Zeichnung wird nicht lediglich als Kopie abgebildet, sondern gleichsam transkribiert. Wie in einem Musikstück von Philip Glass werden Teile stets aufs Neue wiederholt und aneinandergereiht. Im Erdgeschoss sind zudem seltsam kubisch geformte Fensterausschnitte aus der Betonskizze herausgeschält. Ein gläsernes Staffelgeschoss mit Büro- und Besprechungsraum samt Dachterrasse bekrönt das Haus, das ganz unbefangen mit Motiven des russischen Konstruktivismus spielt.

Eine eigenwillige Handschrift zeigt auch das Museumsentree. Hinter der schweren Eingangstür aus Holz schließt sich ein Foyer an, das zugleich als kleine Bibliothek dient. Hier herrscht ein ungewohntes Neo-Art-déco-Ambiente, das durch die dunklen Paneele der Nussbaumverkleidung mit eingeritzter Zeichnungsstruktur eine bemerkenswerte Schwere erhält. Sie wird auch von der auf Hochglanz polierten Stahldecke nicht

house – including office and conference rooms and a roof terrace – which quite un-self-consciously plays with motifs from Russian Constructivism. The museum entrance also displays an individual signature. Behind the heavy door, it is connected to a foyer which simultaneously serves as a small library. An unusual Neo-Art Deco atmosphere prevails here, which is lent a strange severity by the dark panels of the walnut cladding with its etched drawing structure. The high-gloss polished steel ceiling does nothing to alleviate this effect. It is a house cast from a single mould – all the way to the washbasin and the door handles –whose design was also the work of the St. Petersburg-born Tchoban. Via a narrow staircase with glass balustrades and an elegant brass handrail, visitors make

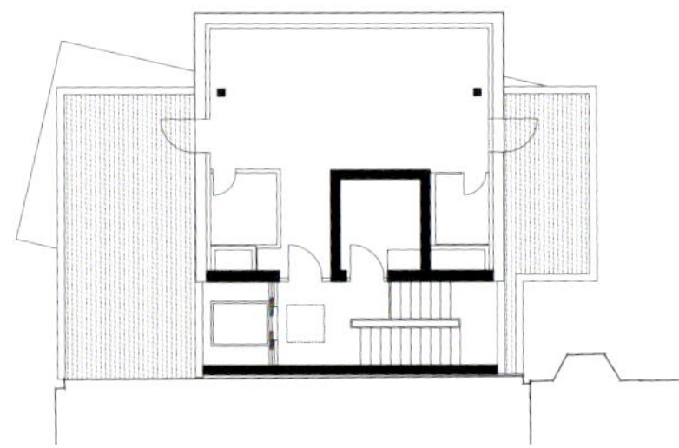

Grundriss Dachgeschoss
Plan of attic floor

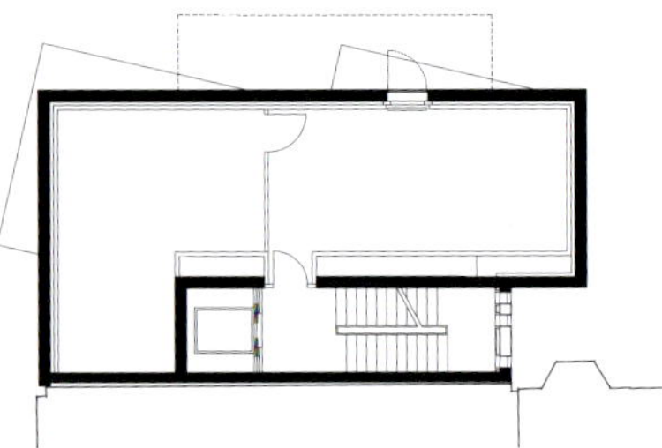

Grundriss 3. Obergeschoss
Plan of 3rd floor

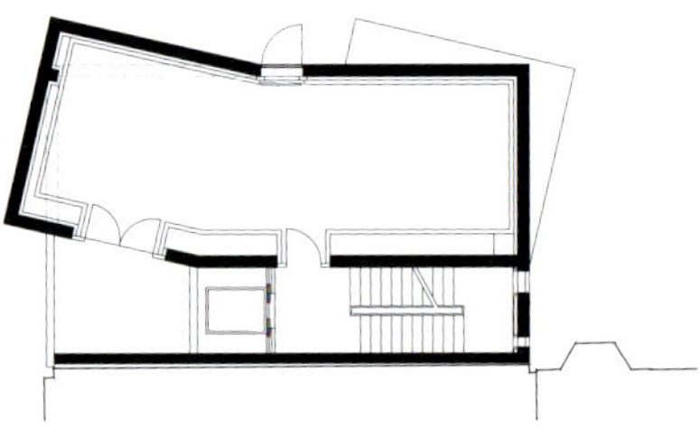

Grundriss 2. Obergeschoss
Plan of 2nd floor

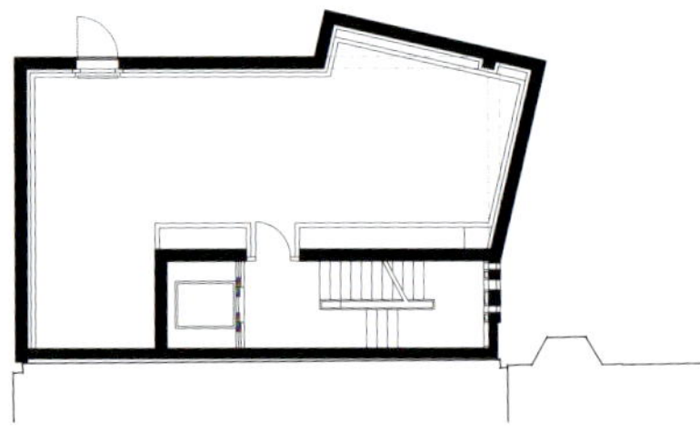

Grundriss 1. Obergeschoss
Plan of 1st floor

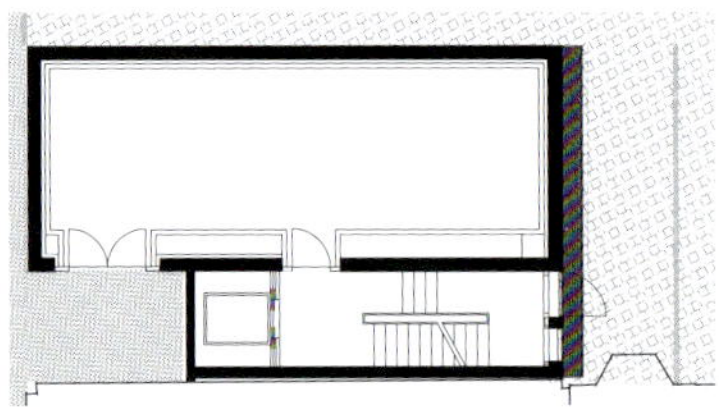

Grundriss Erdgeschoss
Plan of ground floor

Das nussbaumgetäfelte Foyer mit spiegelnder Decke aus poliertem Edelstahl | The walnut-paneled foyer with its mirrored ceiling made of polished stainless steel

Der Ruheraum im 2. Obergeschoss mit Ausblick auf den Teutoburger Platz
The relaxation room on the 2nd floor, with a view of Teutoburger Platz

Ausstellungsraum im 2. Obergeschoss | Exhibition space on the 2nd floor

aufgehoben. Es ist ein Haus aus einem Guss – bis hin zum Waschtisch und den Türdrückern, deren Entwürfe ebenfalls aus der Hand des gebürtigen St. Petersburgers Tchoban stammen. Über ein schmales Treppenhaus mit Glasbrüstung und edlem Messinghandlauf gelangen die Besucher empor zu den beiden Ausstellungsgeschossen. Darüber schließt sich noch ein Sammlungsarchiv an, das Forschern für Studienzwecke offensteht. So gesprächig sich das kleine Haus nach außen hin aufplustert, so introvertiert gibt es sich in seinen beiden Ausstellungsräumen. Blackboxes, die klimatisch und technisch für jede Präsentationsform des empfindlichen Ausstellungsgutes geeignet erscheinen.

Nicht weniger bemerkenswert als das Haus ist dessen Sammlung. Sie basiert auf jenen Architekturzeichnungen, die Sergei Tchoban in seine 2009 gegründete Stiftung eingebracht hat. Es handelt sich um Hunderte eigener Zeichnungen, Blätter von bemerkenswerter Ausdruckstärke, die mehrfach ausgestellt wurden. Hinzu kommen Werke internationaler Architekten des 20. und 21. Jahrhunderts. Zugleich kann das kleine Museum auf Tchobans private Sammlung zurückgreifen, die sich auf Blätter des 18. und 19. Jahrhunderts konzentriert. Der bestens etablierte Kreativcampus am Pfefferberg, Heimat der Architekturgalerie Aedes, gewinnt mit der Tchoban Foundation einen weiteren Baustein von überregionaler Bedeutung. Das verändert zwar den Prenzlauer Berg – ist aber gut für Berlin.

their way up to the two exhibition floors. Above these is a collection archive which is open to researchers for study purposes. As invitingly as the small building fluffs up its feathers on the outside, its two exhibition rooms are correspondingly introverted in their presentation. They are black boxes that seem climatically and technically suitable for every form of presentation of the sensitive exhibition material. No less remarkable than the house itself is what it contains. Its basis is the collection of architectural drawings that Sergei Tchoban acquired through his foundation, which was established in 2009. There are more than one hundred of his own drawings – strikingly expressive works that have been exhibited numerous times. These are joined by compositions by international architects of the twentieth and twenty-first centuries. At the same time, the small museum houses Tchoban's private collection, which is centred on works from the eighteenth and nineteenth centuries. With the Tchoban Foundation, the already firmly-established creative campus at Pfefferberg, home of the Aedes Architecture Forum, has gained another component of supra-regional importance. This may change the Prenzlauer Berg district – but it is good for Berlin.

STAAB ARCHITEKTEN

GEBÄUDE | BUILDING

KUNSTMUSEUM AHRENSHOOP

TEXT CHRISTINA BUDDE

ARCHITEKTEN | ARCHITECTS

Staab Architekten, Berlin
Schlesische Straße 27
10997 Berlin
www.staab-architekten.com

MITARBEITER | TEAM

Wettbewerb | competition:
Antje Bittorf, Katherina Ortner,
Johannes Thoma, Anna Hüper,
Bettina Schriewer,
Matthias Tscheuschler
Planung und Bauleitung | planning
and construction management:
Per Pedersen, Anke Hafner
(Projektleitung | project architects),
Sonja Hehemann, Michael Zeeh,
Daniel Angly, Marcus Ebener,
Hagen Groß, Johan Jensen,
Manuela Jochheim,
Zuzanna Kaluzna, Dalia Karg,
Dominik Schendel, Tobias Steib,
Fabian Weber, Sabine Zoske,
Nicole Braune (örtliche Bauleitung
construction mangement on site)

BAUHERR | CLIENT

Kunstmuseum Ahrenshoop e. V.

AUSFÜHRUNGSPLANUNG
EXECUTION PLANNING

Staab Architekten, Berlin

BAULEITUNG | SITE MANAGEMENT

Staab Architekten, Berlin

TRAGWERK | STRUCTURE

ifb Frohloff Staffa Kühl Ecker,
Berlin

HAUSTECHNIK | M & E ENGINEERS

PHA Planungsbüro für
Haustechnische Anlagen GmbH,
Breuna

LICHTPLANER
LIGHTING CONSULTANT

LichtKunstLicht AG, Berlin

FREIRAUMPLANUNG
OUTDOOR GROUNDS PLANNING

Levin Monsigny
Landschaftsarchitekten,
Berlin

BAUPHYSIK + AKUSTIK
BUILDING PHYSICS + ACOUSTICS

Müller BBM GmbH, Berlin

BRANDSCHUTZ
FIRE PREVENTION

Ingenieur- und
Sachverständigenbüro für
Brandschutz / Arbeitssicherheit,
Wolgast

ARMATUREN | FITTINGS

VOLA GmbH

TÜRKLINKEN UND BESCHLÄGE
HANDELS AND FITTINGS

FSB, Brakel

FERTIGSTELLUNG | COMPLETION

August 2013

STANDORT | LOCATION

Weg zum Hohen Ufer 36
18347 Ostseebad Ahrenshoop
www.kunstmuseum-ahrenshoop.de

FOTOS | PHOTOS

Stefan Müller, Berlin
Thomas Spier, Berlin

Lageplan | Site plan

Die Eingangsseite des Museums-Ensembles | The entrance side of the museum ensemble

Ein Museum zu entwerfen ist unbestritten eine der begehrtesten Bauaufgaben, bietet sie doch beachtliches Entfaltungspotenzial für architektonische Höhenflüge. Wenn aber nicht der spektakuläre Wurf das Gebot der Stunde ist, sondern die große Kunst der kleinen Geste, die sich dem Kontext des Ortes verpflichtet und das Neue dem Vertrauten unterordnet, kann eigentlich nur von Staab Architekten die Rede sein.

Ahrenshoop, ein kleines Seebad auf der Halbinselkette Fischland-Darß-Zingst zwischen Ostsee und Boddenküste hat eine ruhmreiche Vergangenheit als Künstlerkolonie. Auf der Suche nach dem einfachen Leben, unberührt von industrieller Entwicklung und aufkommender Großstadthektik, siedelten sich ab 1890 zahlreiche Künstler in der Abgeschiedenheit des Fischerdorfs an, in deren Gefolge so berühmte Namen wie Alexej von Jawlensky, Marianne von Werefkin oder auch Lyonel Feininger auftauchten.

Um dieses Vermächtnis materiell und ideell für die Gegenwart zu sichern und ihm, buchstäblich, den gebührenden Raum zu geben, gründete sich 2005 der Förderverein des Kunstmuseums Ahrenshoop. Mit bemerkenswertem bürgerschaftlichem Engagement gelang es den Mitgliedern, finanzielle Mittel in einer Höhe zusammenzutragen, die es ihnen erlaubte, das Wagnis einer

Without a doubt, designing a museum is one of the most sought-after building assignments possible, since it offers substantial potential for architectural flights of fancy. However, when the demand is not for a spectacular stroke, but rather the fine art of the subtle gesture, which is committed to the context of the location and in which the new is subordinated to the familiar, then the only logical choice can be Staab Architekten.

Ahrenshoop, a small seaside resort on the Fischland-Darss-Zingst peninsula between the Baltic Sea and the Bodden coast, has a glorious past as an artists' colony. In search of the simple life, untouched by industrial developments and the increasingly hectic pace of the cities, numerous artists relocated to the seclusion of this fishing village from around 1890; they were followed by such famous names as Alexej von Jawlensky, Marianne von Werefkin and Lyonel Feininger.

In order to safeguard this legacy materially and otherwise for the present day – and to literally

Der Haupteingang des Museums | Main entrance of the museum

Die golden glänzende Baubronze dunkelt im Lauf der Zeit nach. | The gleaming gold-coloured brass sheeting will darken over time.

Bauherrenschaft einzugehen. 2008 folgte der Einladungswettbewerb für die Realisierung eines Kunstmuseums, aus dem das Büro Staab einstimmig als Sieger hervorging.

Ortsbezug war das handlungsleitende Entwurfskriterium der Architekten. Inspiration und ständige Vergewisserung in Zeiten planerischer Zweifel war die alte Fotografie eines norddeutschen Gehöfts, das aus unregelmäßig angeordneten reetgedeckten Häusern gebildet wurde.

Analog entstanden fünf Einraumhäuser in Massivbauweise aus Stahlbeton, in Form und Maßstab dem ortsüblichen Bautypus angepasst. Fassade und Dachflächen wurden mit einer Gebäudehaut aus unregelmäßig gefälteltem Messingblech geradezu hermetisch überzogen – eine Abstraktion des norddeutschen Rohrdachs, übersetzt in zeitgemäße Architektursprache. Das war mutig, denn anfangs haben sich die Ahrenshooper schwer getan mit der „Blechbüchse", dieser ungewöhnlichen Auffassung ihres traditionellen Daches. Nicht nur die metallene Hülle rief Irritationen hervor, auch der anfängliche goldene Glanz war gewöhnungsbedürftig. Also entwickelten Staab Architekten neben dem Bauprozess, gemeinsam mit dem Bauherrn, einen strategisch ausgeklügelten Vermittlungsprozess, um den Skeptikern Interpretationshilfen zu liefern. Ein vorpatiniertes Dachmodell beispielsweise zeigte, dass die Baubronze der Fassade ähnlich altert wie ein Rohrdach und sich farblich dem natürlichen Vorbild allmählich angleicht – die Akzeptanz wuchs zusehends. Die Häuser sind durch einen flachen Trakt miteinander verbunden. Ein Terrazzoboden bildet einen fließenden Übergang zwischen innen und außen, der den Besucher geradezu auffordert, das Museum zu betreten. Das ist symbolisch nicht unwichtig für ein Haus, das eben nicht nur den museumserfahrenen Besucher anspricht, sondern Kunst auch dem Strandtouristen in Flipflops näher bringen möchte. Im Foyer sind Kasse und Museumsshop untergebracht. Bei Bedarf kann es kurzerhand in einen Veranstaltungssaal umfunktioniert werden. Eines der Häuser beherbergt einen Raum für die Abteilung Museumspädagogik und kleinere Veranstaltungen. Im Obergeschoss ist die Verwaltung untergebracht, im Kellergeschoss das Depot, die Technik und die Besuchertoiletten.

provide it with the necessary space – the Association of Friends of the Ahrenshoop Art Museum Foundation was established in 2005. Thanks to outstanding community participation, the members were able to raise sufficient financial means to embark on a construction project. A competition for the realization of an art museum was held in 2008, and the Staab architectural firm was unanimously chosen as the winner.

A connexion to the location was the guiding principle of the architects' design. For inspiration and continuous reassurance at times of uncertainty in the planning process, they drew on old photographs of a northern German farmstead, which was made up of irregularly arranged, thatched-roof houses. Following this example, they created five one-room buildings constructed of solid reinforced concrete that matched the local building style in terms of shape and scale. The façades and roof surfaces were clad almost hermetically in an envelope of folded brass sheeting – an abstraction of the typical north-German thatched roof, translated into contemporary architectural language. This was a daring step, since to start with, the residents of Ahrenshoop had their difficulties with the 'tin cans' – this unusual version of their traditional roofs. Not only the metallic shells were cause for irritation; the buildings' initial golden shine also took some getting used to. Therefore, parallel to the building process, Staab Architekten joined together with the client to develop an ingenious communication strategy that could aid sceptics in their interpretation of the project. For example, a pre-patinated model roof demonstrated that the architectural bronze used for the façades would age in a similar manner to a thatched roof, with the colour gradually approximating that of the natural original. Public acceptance of the project increased appreciably.

Schnitt | Section

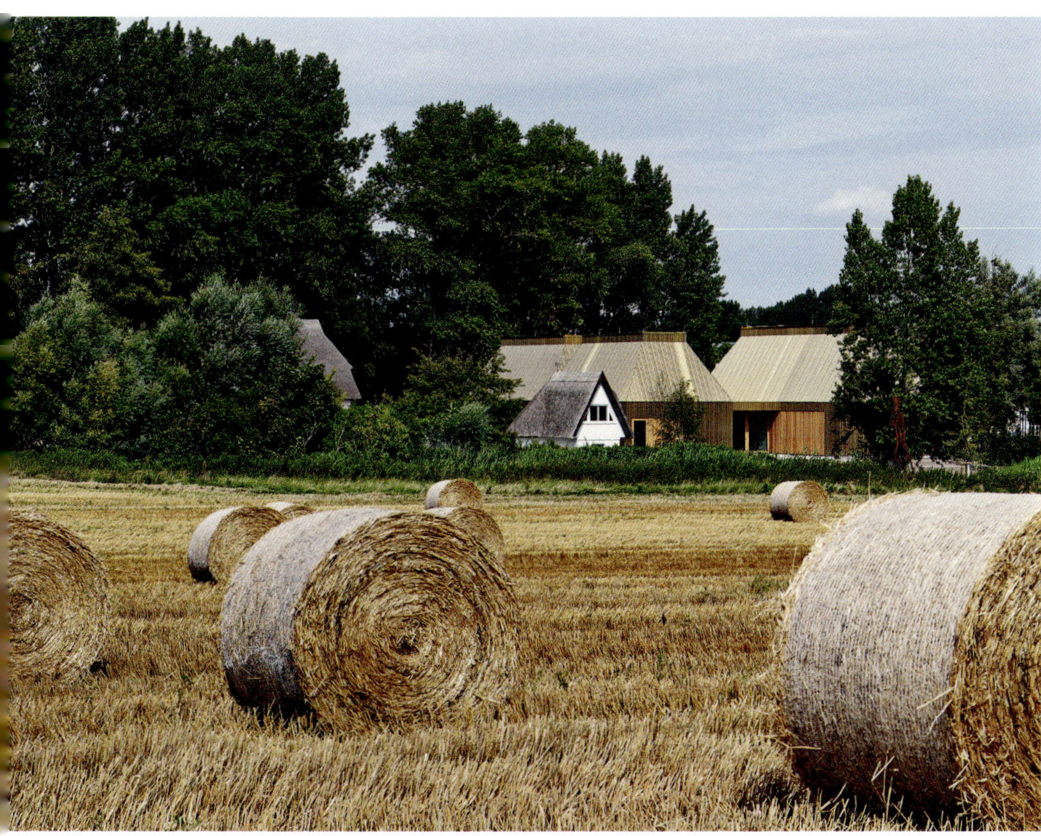

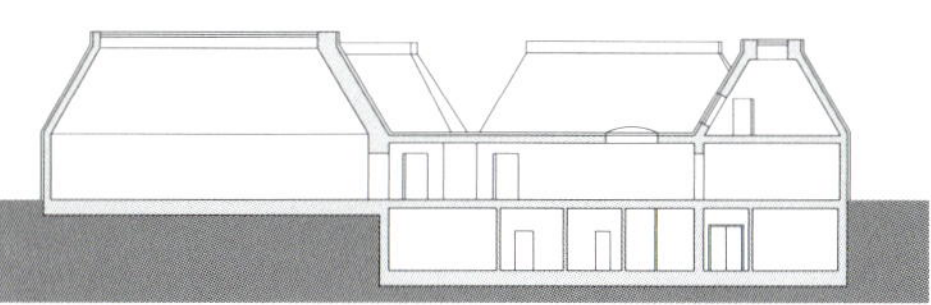

Das Museums-Ensemble eingebettet in die Umgebung | The museum ensemble, integrated into the surroundings

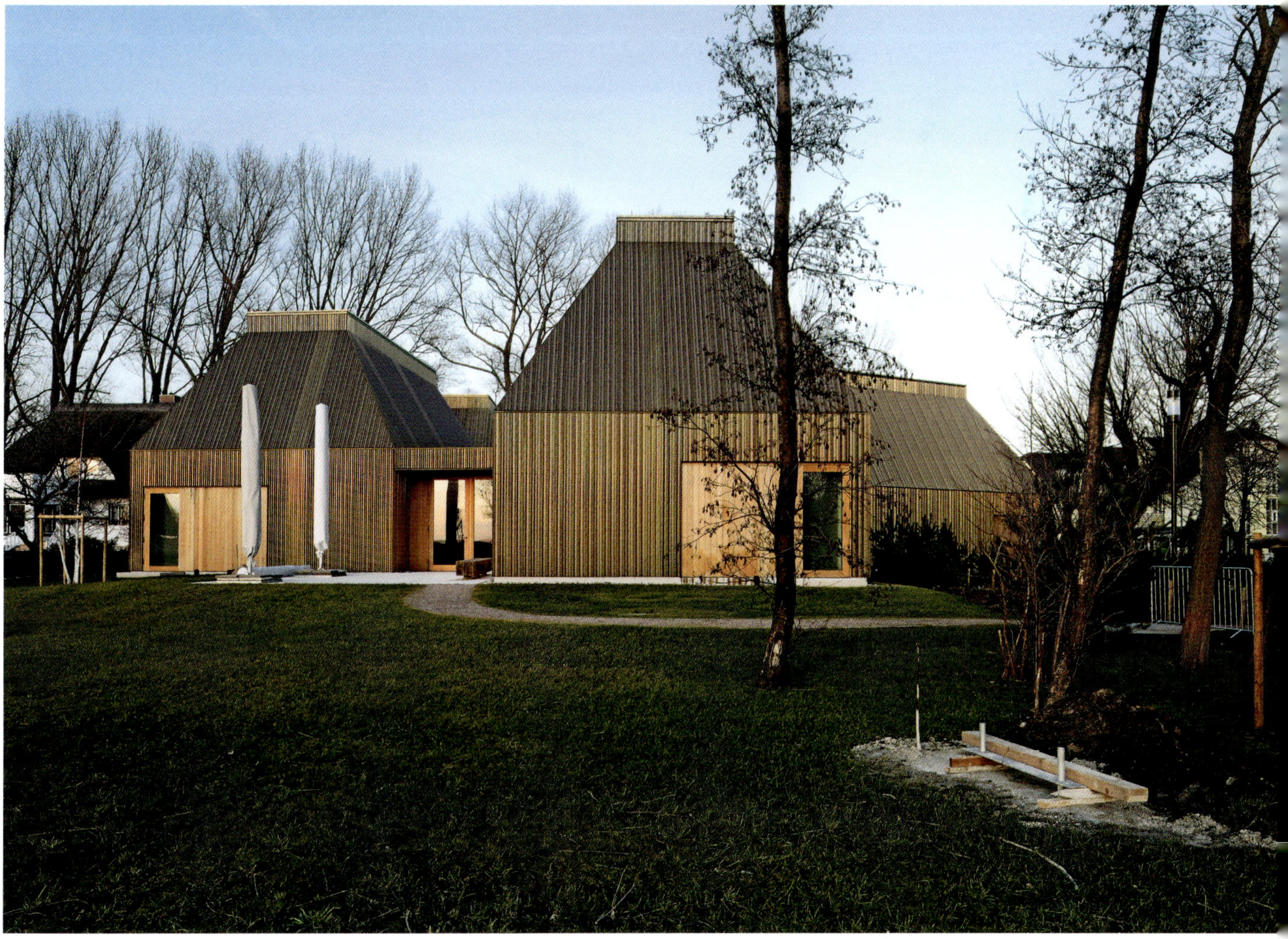

Die Gartenseite und Westansicht des Museums | The garden side and western view of the museum

Im Foyer treffen die Gebäudeteile sternförmig zusammen. | In the foyer, the building sections come together in a star formation.

Die vier Ausstellungshäuser sind klassische „white cubes", fensterlos bis auf jeweils einen verglasten Einschnitt in einer Raumecke, der Blickbeziehungen nach draußen herstellt und gleichzeitig als Notausgang dient.

In die abgeschnittenen, aufgekanteten Dachfirste sind Tageslichtbänder eingelassen. Integrierte Prismen sorgen für die blendfreie Verteilung des Lichts. Zusammen mit der Raumhöhe, die immer wieder für Überraschungsmomente sorgt, sind das perfekte Bedingungen, um Kunst ins rechte Licht zu setzen.

Im ursprünglichen Entwurf war das Volumen des Ensembles mit drei weiteren Häusern, allesamt zweigeschossig, wesentlich umfangreicher angelegt. Ökonomische Zwänge erforderten jedoch eine Überarbeitung des Raumprogramms. Letztendlich war das „ein Segen für das Projekt", so Volker Staab. Konzentriert nun auf das Wesentliche, fügen sich die Häuser einmal mehr in die norddeutsche Landschaft ein. Der nicht nur versprochene, sondern inzwischen eingetretene Alterungsprozess der Metallhaut macht die Referenz an das Rohrdach auch für die letzten Zweifler sichtbar und hat die Ahrenshooper mit dem neuen Nachbarn längst versöhnt.

The buildings are connected by a low covered walkway. A terrazzo floor creates a flowing transition between the interior and exterior spaces, which virtually invites the visitor to enter the museum. Symbolically, this is not unimportant for a structure that aims not only to appeal to experienced museumgoers, but also hopes to bring art closer to the seaside holidaymakers in their flip-flops. The foyer houses the ticket office and the museum shop. If required, it can be transformed at short notice into an event venue. One of the buildings contains a room for the museum education department and for small-scale events. The administrative offices are located on the upper level; the basement houses the museum's depository, technical equipment, and the visitors' toilets.

Inside, the four exhibition buildings are classic 'white cubes' (though they are not, strictly speaking, cubes) – windowless except for a glass incision in one corner of each, which creates a visual connection to the outside world and at the same time serves as an emergency exit.

Natural light strips have been inserted into the cropped, upstanding roof ridges; integrated prisms ensure the glare-free distribution of light. Combined with the height of the space, which time and again provides an element of surprise, they create the perfect conditions for viewing art in the best possible light.

Grundriss Erdgeschoss
Plan of ground floor

Einer der Ausstellungsräume mit offener Decke und Oberlicht | One of the exhibition rooms with its open ceiling and skylight

STEFAN FORSTER ARCHITEKTEN

GEBÄUDE | BUILDING

GEMEINDEZENTRUM UND WOHNHAUS
FRANKFURT AM MAIN

TEXT AXEL SIMON

20

ARCHITEKTEN | ARCHITECTS

Stefan Forster Architekten
Hedderichstraße 108–110
60596 Frankfurt am Main
www.stefan-forster-architekten.de

MITARBEITER | TEAM

Sandra Söhnel, Julia Goldschmidt,
Ute Streit

BAUHERR | CLIENT

Evangelischer Regionalverband
Frankfurt am Main

AUSFÜHRUNGSPLANUNG
EXECUTION PLANNING

Stefan Forster Architekten

**BAULEITUNG & AUSSCHREIBUNG
/ PROJEKTSTEUERUNG**
SITE MANAGEMENT & TENDERING /
PROJECT MANAGEMENT

Ingenieurbüro Schmid
Ges. für Projektsteuerung
und Bauüberwachung mbH,
Frankfurt am Main

**TRAGWERK UND BRANDSCHUTZ,
WÄRMESCHUTZNACHWEIS**
STRUCTURE & FIRE PREVENTION,
THERMAL PROTECTION
CERTIFICATION

Kannemacher + Dr. Sturm
Beratende Ingenieure für
Bauwesen VBI,
Frankfurt am Main

HAUSTECHNIK | M & E ENGINEERS

pb Planungsbüro für
Haustechnische Anlagen
G. Bieger Ing., Ingelheim

AKUSTIK | ACOUSTICS

AC Bauphysik Consult
Ingenieurgesellschaft mbH,
Frankfurt am Main

KÜCHENPLANER
KITCHEN PLANNING

Sakristei | sacristy: **Rotpunkt
Küchen, Cubica HG**

AUFZUGPLANER | LIFT PLANNING

Fa. Zehner

ZIEGEL | BRICKS

Ziegelei Hebrok, Natrup-Hagen

LEUCHTEN | LUMINAIRES

Zumtobel, Dornbirn

FERTIGSTELLUNG | COMPLETION

Oktober | October 2012

STANDORT | LOCATION

Hafenstraße 5–7
60327 Frankfurt am Main

FOTOS | PHOTOS

Lisa Farkas,
Frankfurt am Main

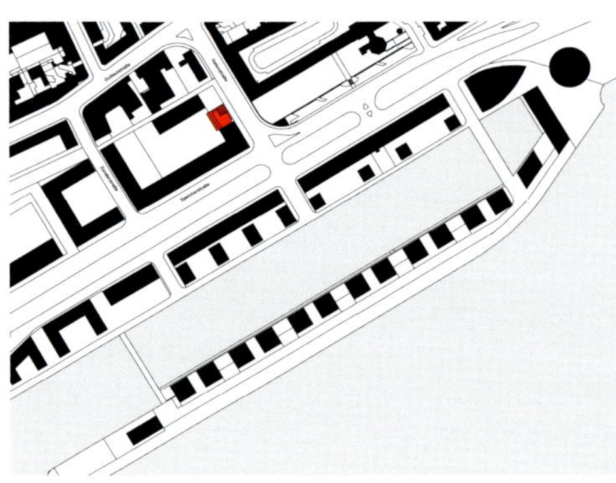

Lageplan | Site plan

Das kombinierte Wohn- und Gemeindehaus mit der turmartigen Nordecke | The combination apartment building and community centre with its tower-like north corner

Kaum steigt der Architekt von seinem Rennrad, folgt eine vernichtende Analyse der Gesellschaft. Nun sei auch der Wohnungsbau in Investorenhand und die Investorenarchitekten verstünden nichts davon. „Sehen Sie!" Beim Nachbarhaus ist der Sockel zu niedrig, die Erdgeschosswohnungen zu offen, die Eingänge „designt". Aber es geht auch anders! Die Loggien seines Hauses sind tief genug, um das private Leben zu bergen, die Eingänge sind sorgfältig gestaltet, die Fenster wohlproportioniert. Ein Haus, das sein schönes anonymes Gesicht dem Straßenraum zuwendet, der Stadt. Der Architekt heißt Stefan Forster. Er sagt: „Wir haben eine Verantwortung gegenüber der Gesellschaft! Wir müssen zurück zur Mitte!"

Zur Mitte? Forster wirkt nicht wie jemand, der Maß hält. Seine Lobeshymnen auf Vorbilder aus der Schweiz oder Berlin sind genauso überschwänglich wie seine Kritik ätzend. Doch das Radikale seiner Person findet sich nicht in seinen Bauten. Oder,

The architect has scarcely dismounted from his racing bike when he begins a scathing analysis of society. Even residential construction is now in the hands of investors – and the investors' architects don't know anything about it. 'Look at that!' he says: the base of the neighbouring house is too low; the ground-floor flats are too open; the entranceways are 'designed'. But there are other ways! The loggias on his house are deep enough to keep private lives private; the entranceways are carefully constructed; the windows are well-proportioned. It is a house that turns its attractive, anonymous face toward the public street – toward the city. The architect's name is Stefan Forster. He says: 'We have a responsibility to society! We need to go back to the middle!'

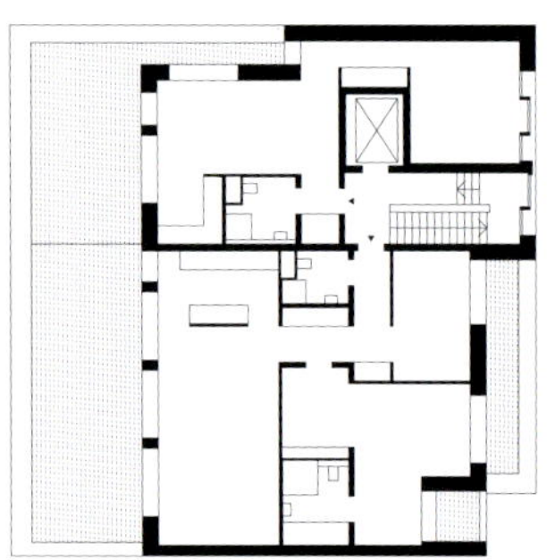

Grundriss 6. Obergeschoss
Plan of 6th floor

Grundriss Regelgeschoss
Standard storey plan

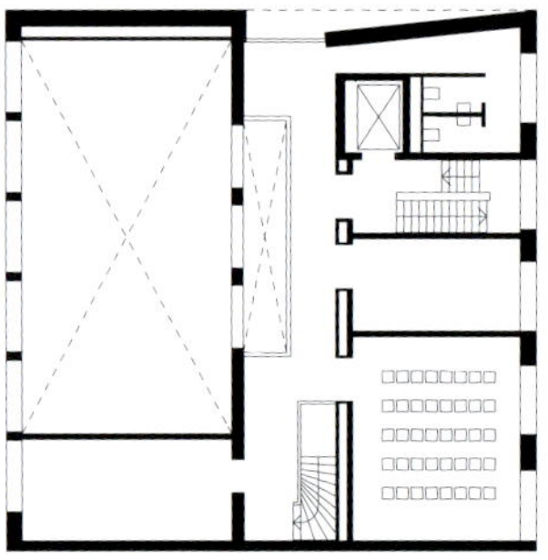

Grundriss 1. Obergeschoss
Plan of 1st floor

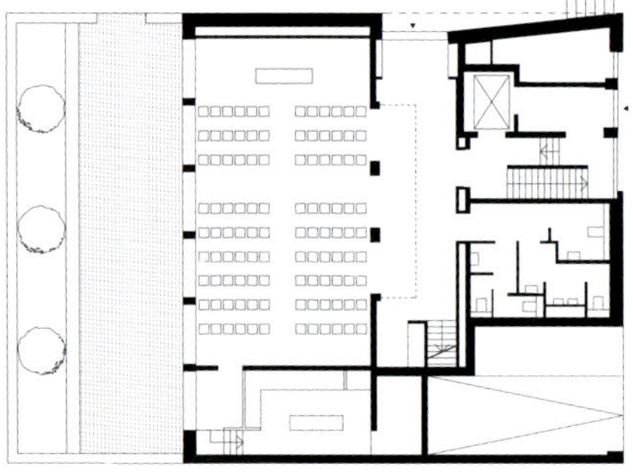

Grundriss Erdgeschoss
Plan of ground floor

Das farblich fein abgestimmte Treppenhaus | The colour of the stairwell is finely harmonized.

anders: Forsters Bauten verbinden die radikalen Gegensätze und lassen sie in der Mitte zusammentreffen. Es sind schöne Häuser, Alltagshäuser, Sowohl-als-auch-Häuser.

Das Haus, vor dem wir stehen, ist Gemeindezentrum und Wohnhaus zugleich. In Frankfurts konvertiertem Westhafen schließt es einen Stadtblock, den Stefan Forster vor zehn Jahren mit seinem ersten größeren Wohnhaus begründete. Das erste ist mit Ziegeln verkleidet, das letzte auch. In der Straßenfassade vor uns hat das Treppenhaus die gleichen Fenster wie die Wohnungen. Das in die Wand eingeprägte zwei Geschosse hohe Sockelrelief verläuft von der Straßenfassade um die Ecke zum seitlichen Vorplatz. Ein großes Ziegelkreuz leitet dort die Gemeinde ins Innere, die Steine türmen sich darüber zum Eckturm. An der Rückseite wird die Fassadenfläche zur viergeschossigen Pfeilerreihe aufgelöst. Die Betonböden und Stahlgeländer der Loggien drücken zwischen den Pfeilern nach außen, kokettieren mit deren Monumentalität. Vicenza oder Dessau? „Beides!", sagt der Architekt.

Die Pfarrerin Jutta Jekel sagt, ihr Gemeindezentrum und der Supermarkt im ersten Forster-Haus seien die einzigen Orte, wo sich alle träfen, sowohl die Bewohner der Häuser mit Yachtgarage vorn am Westhafen, als auch die aus dem alten Gutleutviertel, die Armen und die Künstler. Der Evangelische Regionalverband finanzierte den Neubau mit dem Verkauf alter Liegenschaften, auch der Gutleutkirche aus den 1950er-Jahren im alten Blockrand.

Die Pfarrerin erzählt begeistert vom Musiker aus der Nachbarschaft, der in ihrem neuen Saal Konzerte gibt. Sie erzählt von

To the middle? Forster doesn't seem like someone who does things in moderation. When he sings the praises of examples from Switzerland or Berlin, he seems as effusive as his criticisms are biting. Yet his radical personality is not reflected in his buildings. Or to put it another way: Forster's buildings bring radical opposites together and allow them to meet in the middle. These are attractive buildings, everyday buildings, buildings that are a bit of both. The house that stands before us functions both as a parish centre and an apartment building. Located in Frankfurt's converted Westhafen (western harbour) district, it completes a city block that Stefan Forster established ten years ago with his first large apartment building. The first house is clad in brick, and the last one is as well. On the street façade that faces us, the stairwell contains the same type of windows as the flats. The two-storey base relief embossed in the wall extends from the street façade around the corner to the courtyard. Here, a large

Durchlaufende Loggia auf der Gartenseite
Continuous loggia on the garden side

Der eingeschnittene Eingang zum Gemeindezentrum mit dem reliefartigen Kreuz
The recessed entrance to the parish community centre with its relief-style cross

Die Nordwestfassade | The northwestern façade

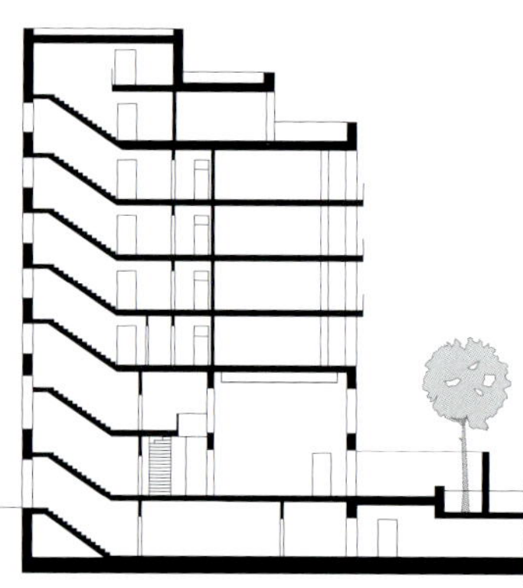

Schnitt | Section

der Predigtreihe mit Schlagzeug und von Gottesdiensten mit Essen. Sie schwärmt von der Akustik und berichtet von Paaren, die sich spontan entschließen, in diesem Raum getraut zu werden, ihr Kind zu taufen. „Das Auseinanderdividieren von Gottesdienst und allem anderen, das stimmt nicht mehr. Heute muss ein Raum beides können." Die heutige Kirche ist eine Sowohl-als-auch-Kirche.

Ist das denn noch eine Kirche? Dieser gediegene, recht weltliche Saal, der sich über hohe Fenstertüren zum introvertierten Hof hin öffnet? Die Fenster sind, wie im ganzen Haus, aus Holz, lasiert in einem Orange-Ton, der gerade noch die Assoziation „Holz" zulässt. Einfache Glaszylinder dienen als Lüster, ein Eichentisch als Altar, eine Teeküche als Sakristei. „Das ist ein würdiger Raum", sagt die Pfarrerin. Die gute Predigt und die gute Musik brauchten eine gewisse Nüchternheit. Der Architekt strahlt.

brick cross leads the parishioners inside; above it, the stones are stacked up to form a corner tower. In the rear, the façade surface is broken up into a four-storey row of piers. The concrete floors and steel railings of the loggias press outward between the piers, flirting with their monumental character. Vicenza or Dessau? 'Both!' says the architect.

Pastor Jutta Jekel says that her parish centre and the supermarket in the first Forster house are the only places where everyone comes together – both the residents of the houses with the yacht garages up ahead at the harbour and the people from the old Gutleutviertel district, the poor people and the artists. The Protestant Regional Association financed the new construction through the sale of older properties, including the 1950s' Gutleut Church at the edge of the old city block.

The pastor speaks enthusiastically about the neighbourhood musician who performs concerts in her new hall. She tells of sermon series with percussion accompaniment and church services that include meals. She praises the acoustics and recounts stories of couples who have spontaneously decided to be married or have their children baptized in this space. 'The separation of church services from everything else – that doesn't exist anymore. Nowadays, a space has to be able to accommodate both.' Today's church is a 'a bit of both' church.

But is it then still a church? This dignified, quite secular hall whose tall French doors open on to an introverted courtyard? As in the rest of the house, the window frames are made of wood, varnished in an orange tone that just barely retains an association with 'wood'. Simple glass cylinders serve as chandeliers, an oak table as an altar and a kitchenette as a sacristy. 'This is a dignified space,' says the pastor. Good sermons and good music require a certain degree of austerity. The architect beams.

This hasn't always been the case. The old pastor, Jekel's predecessor, thought an 'open church' should be architecturally open as well. 'Made of glass! A church!' Forster gestures toward the high, white walls; the slender openings – both to the entrance area and to the courtyard – lend them a rhythmic structure. Here, he says, it is possible to meditate, to be alone with oneself. He wanted a wall that would separate the forecourt from the street. That could

Das war nicht immer so. Der alte Pfarrer, Jekels Vorgänger, sah die „offene Kirche" auch architektonisch offen. „Gläsern! Eine Kirche!" Forster weist auf die hohen weißen Wände: rhythmisiert von schlanken Öffnungen, zum Eingangsraum wie auch zum Hof. Hier sei Meditation möglich, Bei-sich-sein. Eine Mauer, die den Vorplatz zur Straße hin abgrenzt, wollte er. Sie kam nicht, aber diejenige zum Blockinnenhof. Das Haus ist Monument und anonyme Stadtstruktur, Solitär und Blockrand. Es ist Kirche und Wohnhaus.

In der ersten Etage befinden sich die Räume der Gemeinde. Ein weiter Gang blickt als Galerie in den Saal hinunter und durch ihn hindurch ins grüne Innere des Blocks. Die 14 Wohnungen darüber zeigen den geübten Wohnungsplaner: knappe, gut möblierbare Zimmer. Raumfolgen verbinden Straße und Hof. Loggien geben den Räumen etwas Höhlenartiges. Die zu Bändern gereihten Straßenfenster springen in ihrer Laibung mal nach innen, mal nach außen. Das Entree des Treppenhauses ist hoch und geräumig, die Farben frisch, die Materialien robust und hochwertig. Eine Adresse! „Sehen Sie?" Stefan Forster steigt auf sein Fahrrad und fährt davon. Manchmal übrigens auch in einem Porsche. Der Sowohl-als-auch-Architekt.

not be realized, but a wall to the block's shared inner courtyard was possible. The house is both a monument and an anonymous city structure; a solitary edifice and a border to the city block. It is both a church and an apartment house.

The first floor contains the rooms belonging to the parish. An additional corridor functions as a gallery, looking down into the hall below and through it into the green inner court of the city block. The 14 flats located above it are a testament to an experienced interior-design planner: economical, easily furnished rooms. The arrangement of the space connects the street and the courtyard. The loggias lend the rooms a somewhat cavernous atmosphere. In a ribbon-like arrangement, the street-side windows alternately protrude and recess. The entrance to the stairwell is high and spacious; the materials are robust and high-quality. Some address! 'You see?' Stefan Forster climbs on his bike and rides away. By the way, he sometimes drives a Porsche. He is the 'bit of both' architect.

Die turmartige Nordecke | The tower-like north corner

Die Gartenseite zeigt nach Südwesten. | The garden side faces southwest.

TKA THOMAS KRÖGER ARCHITEKT

GEBÄUDE | BUILDING

WERKHAUS SCHÜTZE
GERSWALDE

TEXT ULRICH MÜLLER

21

ARCHITEKTEN | ARCHITECTS

Thomas Kröger Architekt
Schöneberger Ufer 59
10785 Berlin
www.thomaskroeger.net

MITARBEITER | TEAM

Georg Bosch, Urs Walter

BAUHERR | CLIENT

Gerhard Schütze, Gerswalde

AUSFÜHRUNGSPLANUNG
EXECUTION PLANNING

Thomas Kröger Architekt

**BAULEITUNG /
PROJEKTSTEUERUNG**
SITE MANAGEMENT /
PROJECT MANAGEMENT

Thomas Kröger Architekt

TRAGWERK UND BRANDSCHUTZ
STRUCTURE AND FIRE PREVENTION

Studio C, Nicole S. Zahner,
Berlin

BRANDSCHUTZ
FIRE PREVENTION

Rössel Brandschutz, Beate Rössel,
Berlin

FERTIGSTELLUNG | COMPLETION

Dezember | December 2012

STANDORT | LOCATION

Friedenfelder Weg 13
17268 Gerswalde
www.gehard-schuetze.de

FOTOS | PHOTOS

Thomas Heimann,
Berlin

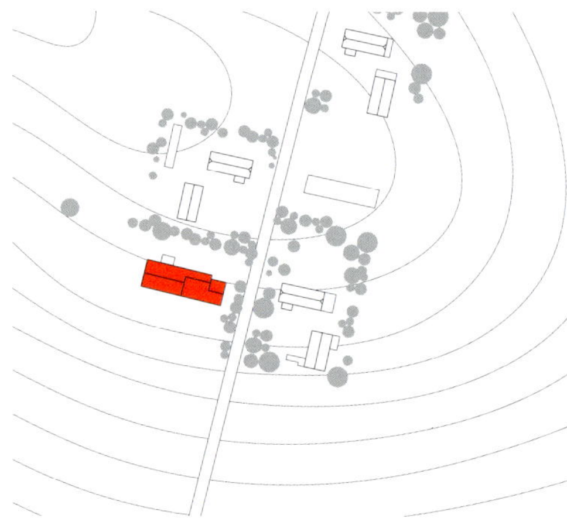

Lageplan | Site plan

Die Nordostecke; die Giebelwände sind holzverkleidet, die übrige Außenhaut besteht aus grünem Wellblech. | The northeast corner: the gable ends are wood-panelled; the rest of the building is clad in green corrugated sheet metal.

Auf der einen Seite: Grashügel und Feldwege, Nebeldunst trotz Sonne. Auf der anderen: Lebenstraum und Realität, Askese und Fantasie. Auch wenn Architektur ohne Geschichten verständlich sein sollte: Das Ausblenden dieser Umstände würde einen Beschreibungsversuch des Werkhauses höchst unvollständig lassen. Bereits der Weg zum Bauplatz ist nicht nur schlicht ein räumlicher, sondern ein atmosphärischer. Und er offenbart Wesentliches über den Bauherrn, einen auch an den eigenen Ansprüchen feilenden Tischler und Möbelentwerfer. Denn naturnahe Abgeschiedenheit bedeutet zugleich Verzicht auf die schnellen Annehmlichkeiten städtischer Infrastruktur. Aber auch für den Architekten ist ein derartiges Projekt nur mit sehr hohem Aufwand realisierbar. Für Thomas Kröger ist es jedoch nicht das erste Projekt in der nördlich von Berlin gelegenen Uckermark – dem neuen Sehnsuchtsort zumeist gut betuchter Berliner. Bereits sein 2010 fertiggestelltes, archetypisch anmutendes Einfamilienhaus im nahe gelegenen Pinnow sorgte für große Aufmerksamkeit.

Beim Werkhaus Schütze – je nach Sichtweise Wohnhaus mit angeschlossener Werkstatt beziehungsweise umgekehrt – auf dem Gelände einer alten DDR-Schlosserei ist ihm nun jedoch ein

On one side: grassy hills and dirt roads; a hazy mist even in the sunlight. On the other side: a lifelong dream and reality; asceticism and fantasy. Even if architecture is supposed to be comprehensible without a backstory, omitting these circumstances would leave any attempt at describing this workshop very incomplete. Even the path to the building site itself is not simply a spatial journey but an atmospheric one. And it reveals a great deal about the client – a carpenter and furniture designer who is also polishing his own standards. After all, seclusion in harmony with nature also means forgoing the quick convenience of urban infrastructure. But for the architect as well, a project of this kind can only be realized with great effort. However, for Thomas Kröger, this is not his first project in the Uckermark region – the new idyllic retreat for mostly well-heeled Berliners. His seemingly archetypal single-family house in nearby Pinnow, completed in 2010, has already attracted a great deal of attention.

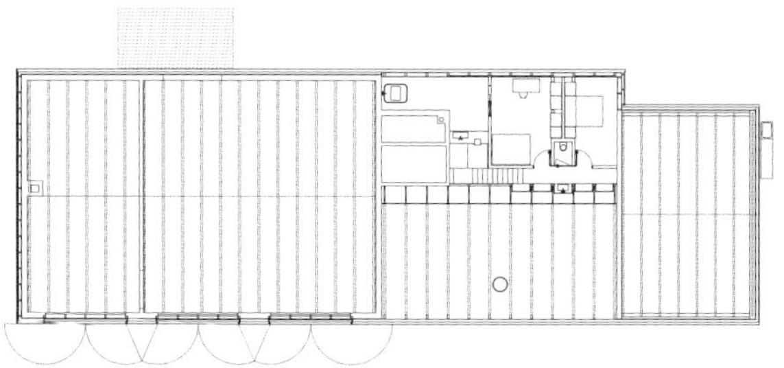

Grundriss Obergeschoss | Plan of upper floor

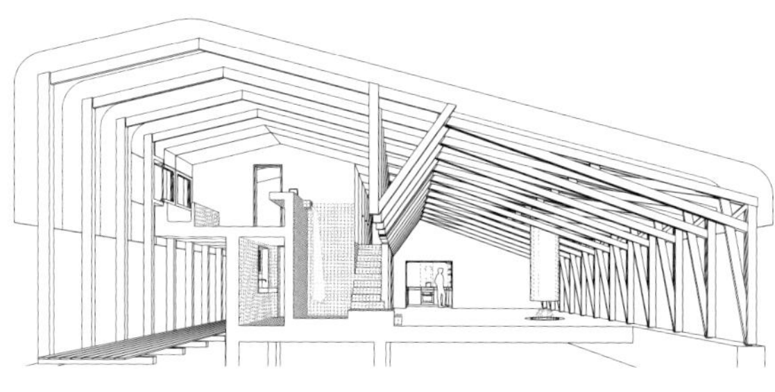

Perspektivischer Schnitt | Perspective section

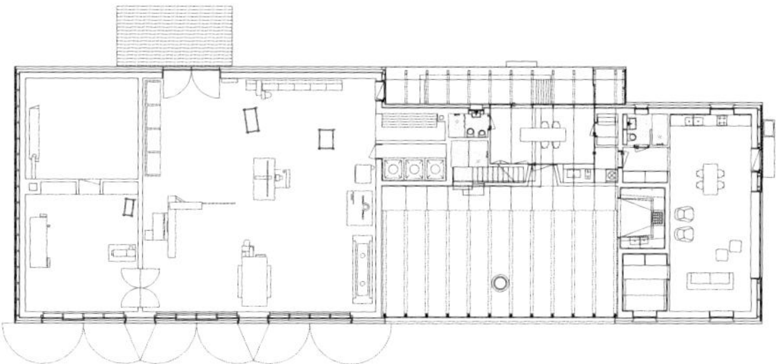

Grundriss Erdgeschoss | Plan of ground floor

Projekt gelungen, das in seiner Eigenart nur schwer zu übertreffen ist. Seine Besonderheit beruht darin, dass Kröger den Entwurf scheinbar aus dem Landschaftsbild generiert, das sanften Wellen gleich an den Bauplatz heranrollt. Der entwerferische Transformationsprozess gelingt vor allem durch die Wand und Dach gleichermaßen bedeckende Metallhaut, ihre Staffelung, Farbe und Ausprägung im Detail. Sie bedeckt die drei aneinandergereihten, unterschiedlich hohen und langen Baukörper – eine bestehende Werkhalle, einen zum Wohnbereich umgebauten Mittelteil sowie eine hinzugefügte Gästewohnung – wie ein sorgfältig ausgebreitetes Tuch. Die Struktur des grünen Wellblechs wirkt dabei wie ein feines Faltenwerk und lässt eine sanfte Großfigur entstehen. Ihr industrieller Charakter wird an den Stirnseiten durch die raue Stulpschalung aus baumstarken Schalbrettern ergänzt, die zugleich eine Reminiszenz an alte ortstypische Bautechniken ist. Das perfekt einheitliche Bild dieses zeitgenössischen Nurdachhauses entsteht jedoch durch die abgerundeten Formteile am Übergang zwischen Dach und Wand. Erst dieses Fehlen einer klassischen Traufe verleiht dem Bau die konsequente Körperhaftigkeit und Abstraktion. Auch die notwendigen Fenster der Nebenräume und die Tore in der Produktionshalle folgen diesem Diktat.

With the Werkhaus Schütze – a residential house with an attached workshop, or vice versa, depending on your point of view – located on the site of an old communist-era locksmith's shop, he has now successfully realized a project which is difficult to surpass in its uniqueness. Its distinctive quality comes from the fact that Kröger appears to have generated his design from the scenery of the landscape, whose gently rolling hills ripple all the way up to the site. The design's transformative process has been achieved primarily through the metal cladding that covers the walls and the roof alike, its staggered arrangement, colour and expressive detail. It covers the row of three main structures of different heights and lengths – the existing workshop, a middle section which has been converted into a living space, and an additional guest apartment – like a carefully spread blanket. Here, the structure of the corrugated sheet metal has the effect of a fine drapery, allowing a soft overall figure to emerge. On the front end, its industrial character is enhanced by the rough weatherboard siding made of solid shuttering boards, which is at the same time reminiscent of the traditional building techniques typical of the region. However, the perfectly unified appearance of this contemporary A-frame house is achieved through the rounded mouldings at the junction between roof and wall. It is this lack of traditional eaves that ultimately lends the structure its consistent corporality and abstract nature. The necessary windows in the adjoining space and the gates in the production hall also follow this dictate. Instead of openings, here the corrugated metal is finely perforated; the resulting shading allows one at most to guess what is behind them. Of course, this method also means that the view from the windows behind into the surrounding environment is 'filtered' – however,

Die Südfassade mit dem großzügig verglasten „Showroom"
The southern façade with its generous glass 'showroom' window

Blick von Westen, vorne die Werkstatt. Die großen Öffnungen sind mit fein perforiertem Wellblech geschützt. | View from the west; the workshop is in front. The large openings are protected by finely perforated corrugated metal.

Die Schlafkoje; der hölzerne Innenausbau stammt vom Bauherrn selbst.
Sleeping loft: the wooden interior furnishings were built by the client himself.

Innenraum des mittleren Gebäudeteils mit Betondecke und Gussasphaltboden
Interior of the middle section with concrete ceiling and poured asphalt floor

Anstelle von Öffnungen ist das Wellblech hier fein perforiert und die dadurch entstehende Schattierung lässt das Dahinter allenfalls erahnen. Diese Maßnahme hat zwar zur Folge, dass der Blick aus den dahinterliegenden Fenstern in die Umgebung „gefiltert" ist, aber auch in der Uckermark gibt es Nachbarn, die man nicht immer im Blick haben möchte. Lediglich das über die gesamte Raumbreite spannende Fensterband des Wohnraums im Süden und der gedeckte Eingangsbereich auf der Nordseite sind offen und rhythmisieren die Fassade. Sie zeigen ebenso wie das Panoramafenster der Gästewohnung im Westgiebel an, welche Ausblicke wirklich wichtig sind. Im Bereich der Werkstatt lässt sich die Fassade vor den drei großen Werktoren zudem öffnen, so dass der Bauherr bei gutem Wetter im „gefühlten Freien" arbeiten kann. In der Dunkelheit wiederum strahlen die perforierten Flächen ein geheimnisvolles Licht aus und geben dem geschlossenen Baukörper einen neuen Rhythmus.

Im Inneren setzt sich der industrielle Habitus durch den schwarzen Gussasphaltboden fort. Nur in den privaten Räumen im Obergeschoss erzeugt der Holzdielenboden eine warme Atmosphäre. Der zentrale, hallenartige Raum mit den vom Bauherrn selbst angefertigten Dachbindern ist eine Synthese aus Denkraum und Werkstatt. Seine Decke steigt von der Fassade zum zweigeschossigen Privatbereich an und führt das Motiv der gewellten Landschaft innen fort. Eine überraschende Ergänzung ist der höhlenartige Duschraum an der inneren Längswand, den Thomas Kröger nach Anregungen des Bauherrn entworfen hat.

even in Uckermark, there are some neighbours that one doesn't want to see all the time. Only the band of windows that span the entire width of the living space on the south side and the covered entrance area on the north side are open, lending rhythm to the façade. Like the picture window in the western gable in the guest apartment, they show us which views are truly important. In the workshop area, the façade that covers the three large workshop gates can also be opened, allowing the client to work in an 'open-air atmosphere' when the weather is good. After dark, on the other hand, the perforated surfaces emit a mysterious light and give the closed-off structure a new rhythm.

In the interior, the industrial habitus is maintained in the poured asphalt flooring. Only in the private rooms on the upper floor does a wooden board floor provide a warm atmosphere. The central, hall-like space, whose roof trusses were constructed by the client himself, is a synthesis of study and workshop. Its ceiling extends from the façade to the two-storey private area, and continues the motif of the rolling landscape on the inside. A surprising addition is the cave-like shower room on the interior longitudinal wall, which Thomas Kröger designed at the client's suggestions. From here, one has an unobstructed diagonal view across the room

„Showroom"; die im Boden eingelassene Feuerstelle betont den Charakter des Rohen und Ländlichen. | 'Showroom': the recessed fire pit in the floor accentuates the building's raw, rural character.

Von hier aus hat man quer durch den Raum einen freien Blick auf die Landschaft. Dass sämtliche Einbauten vom Bauherrn präzise und ohne Furnier gebaut wurden, versteht sich von selbst.

Mit seiner grünen Wellblechhaut könnte das Werkhaus Schütze, aus der Ferne betrachtet, ebenso ein modernes landwirtschaftliches Nutzgebäude sein wie ein Überbleibsel ehemaliger militärischer Einrichtungen. Unabhängig davon, ob solche Bilder beabsichtigt waren oder nicht: Ein derartig exakt im Kontext verhaftetes und gleichzeitig fantasievoll darüber hinausreichendes Projekt sieht man in unserer bildgesättigten, auf Effekte getrimmten Welt leider viel zu selten.

of the landscape outside. It goes without saying that all of the fixtures were precision-built without veneer by the client himself.

From a distance, the Werkhaus Schütze, with its green corrugated metal skin, could just as easily be taken for a modern agricultural utility building or a remnant left over from former military installations. Regardless of whether or not such associations were intentional, a project like this – which is anchored precisely in its context, while at the same time extending imaginatively beyond it – is seen far too seldom in our image-saturated, effect-oriented world.

DER AMERIKANISCHE FREUND
THE AMERICAN FRIEND
WARUM BEHNISCH ARCHITEKTEN SO GERNE IN DEN USA BAUEN
WHY BEHNISCH ARCHITEKTEN LOVE TO WORK IN THE USA

WOLFGANG BACHMANN

E2

Skyscrapers bloom in America
Cadillacs zoom in America
Industry boom in America
Twelve in a room in America

Lots of new housing with more space
Lots of doors slamming in our face
I'll get a terrace apartment
Better get rid of your accent.

Life can be bright in America
If you can fight in America
Life is all right in America
If you're all white in America

West Side Story, Filmversion | film version

Behnisch Architekten, Genzyme Center, Cambridge

Behnisch Architekten, Genzyme Center

Seit 25 Jahren leitet Stefan Behnisch sein Architekturbüro, das er aus, mit und neben der legendären Unternehmung seines Vaters gegründet hat. Nach wechselnder Firmierung und mittlerweile an drei Standorten liegt ein Großteil des internationalen Engagements von Behnisch Architekten in den USA. Man kann sagen: antizyklisch zum allgemeinen Trend.

Man kann als Architekt im Nahen und im Fernen Osten bauen. Was die dort erfolgreich tätigen Kollegen reizt, wäre neben schnellen Antworten zur wirtschaftlichen Sicherung ihrer großen Büros eine tiefenpsychologische Untersuchung wert. Welche Rolle spielen der Ehrgeiz, die Suche nach Anerkennung, die Gelegenheit, unter neuen Konditionen Architektur zu liefern? Verstehen sich ihre Schöpfer als Weltenbauer, die mit ihrer Export-Moderne rückständige Länder kolonisieren? Auf jeden Fall setzen sie sich seit geraumer Zeit der Kritik aus, dass ihre Leistung der Stabilisierung und Verbrämung von Regimen dient, die von unserer humanistischen und demokratischen Räson Lichtjahre entfernt sind.

Stefan Behnisch hat sich anders entschieden. Er möchte sicher sein, dass sein Leistungstransfer, den er als gebaute Architektur in einem anderen Land hinterlässt, dort allen Menschen zugute kommt. Da liegen Sotschi, Katar und Beijing plötzlich dicht beieinander. Also besser, man liefert den Schurken erst gar keine Stadien.

GO WEST!

Wie viel sympathischer ist es dagegen, bei den Amerikanern zu bauen. Behnischs Engagement in den USA beruht allerdings auf keiner politisch motivierten Fluchtbewegung. Er hatte sein Büro vom väterlichen Architekturbetrieb rasch unabhängig gemacht. Sein Start war zwar leicht, denn man hatte ihm zugetraut, dass er was bauen kann. Aber es wurde auch sofort Leistung erwartet, keine juvenilen Grillen. Es musste ohne Aufwärmphase gehen, ohne lässiges Ausprobieren und Herumsuchen. Ein Behnisch repräsentierte die Marke Behnisch.

In der Schule und während des Studiums hatte er Sprachen gelernt. Sein Verhältnis zur weiten Welt war ein anderes, als man es im Partnerbüro seines Vaters pflegte. Dort war man für den Wiederaufbau zuständig gewesen, und es gab genug zu tun. Etwas Schulenglisch reichte da fürs Geschäft, man hatte sich ja erfolgreich mit dem deutschen Wettbewerbswesen arrangiert. „Mein Vater hat sich mit seinem kulturellen Verständnis hier zu Hause gefühlt", erinnert sich der Sohn.

For 25 years, Stefan Behnisch has headed the architectural firm that he founded out of, together with, and alongside his father's legendary company. Following company name changes, and now with a total of three locations, a large portion of Behnisch Architekten's international activity takes place in the United States. One might say this is anti-cyclical to the general trend.

As an architect, one can work in the Middle or Far East. It would be interesting to conduct a depth-psychological study on the attractiveness of these regions for the members of our profession who are active there – in addition to the obvious answers concerning the economic security of their large offices. How significant are factors such as ambition, the desire for recognition, and the opportunity to produce architecture under novel conditions? Do these creators see themselves as builders of civilizations, colonizing underdeveloped countries with their exported modernity? In any case, for some time now, they have been exposing themselves to the criticism that their work is contributing to the stability and glamorization of regimes which are light years removed from our humanitarian and democratic ideals.

Stefan Behnisch decided on a different path. He wants to be sure that the services he leaves behind in another country in the form of completed buildings will benefit all the people in that location. From this point of view, Sochi, Qatar and Beijing suddenly seem to be positioned neck-and-neck. The best choice is not to build a stadium for any of these scoundrels.

GO WEST!

By comparison, it is so much more pleasant to build for the Americans. However, Behnisch's activity in the US is not based on any kind of politically-motivated emigration movement. He quickly made his office independent of his father's architectural firm. He had quite an easy start, since people had faith that he knew how to build. On the other hand, they also expected immediate performance, and no youthful messing around. It had to work without a warm-up period, without any casual trial-and-error or fumbling about. A Behnisch represented the Behnisch brand.

In school and at university, Stefan Behnisch studied languages. His relationship to the world was different from the one cultivated in his father's partner office. That firm had been responsible for Germany's rebuilding, and there was plenty to be done in that area. A little classroom English was enough to get by in the business, and the firm dealt successfully with the German competition system. 'With his cultural understanding, my father felt very at home here,' the son remembers.

Behnisch Architekten, Allston Science Complex, Harvard University

Behnisch Architekten, Allston Science Complex, Harvard University

Sein eigener Weg schien von glücklichen Zufällen gesäumt. Er hatte in Los Angeles gearbeitet. Für seine Generation galt eine Amerikareise als Bildungsreise schlechthin. „Nicht mehr die Grand Tour zur Medici-Venus und zum Apoll von Belvedere und zu Raffael, überhaupt keine Kunst- und Kulturreise mehr, sondern eine Reise ausschließlich zu einer Lebensart"[1], heißt es bei Martin Walser, dem die Entfernung vom bundesrepublikanischen Kulturbetrieb nach Amerika immer wie ein Kuraufenthalt vorgekommen war. Zurück in Deutschland blieb Behnisch über Praktikanten in Kontakt mit den USA. Später, in seinem eigenen Büro, beschäftigte er ausländische Mitarbeiter, die irgendwann darauf drängten, sich in ihren Herkunftsländern zu engagieren. Das animierte, 1992 bei einem internationalen Verfahren in Wageningen/Niederlande als Nachrücker teilzunehmen – übrigens auch der Auftakt zu dem, was sein Büro künftig auszeichnen sollte: Das Gebäude galt als Pilotprojekt für nachhaltiges Bauen. Das amerikanische Magazin „Architectural Record" hat es gebührend veröffentlicht.

Damit waren die Weichen gestellt. Einige Zeit später (2000) wurden die Stuttgarter, die inzwischen eher hobbymäßig einen Arbeitstisch in Los Angeles stehen hatten, zu einer Architekturkonkurrenz in Cambridge, Massachusetts, eingeladen. Die übrigen Teilnehmer rekrutierten sich aus den international erfolgreichen Büros. Die Behnischs machten mit, erwarteten nichts und dachten sich: Zwei Freiflüge nach Boston, das ist doch auch nicht schlecht. Die Präsentation für den Neubau des Genzyme Centers muss indes beeindruckend gewesen sein. Die etablierten Kollegen lieferten für die Bewerbung Zeichnungen und Modelle, wie man sie bei uns nicht einmal für die Ausführungsplanung anfertigen würde. Also keine Chance? Es kam anders. Stefan Behnisch präsentierte comicartige Skizzen und eröffnete der Jury ein Szenario möglicher Lösungen, die sich vom routinierten Erfolgsversprechen drastisch unterschieden. Tatsächlich erhielt er den Auftrag.

Damit war das Eis war gebrochen. Man hatte kapiert, wie man mit den Amerikanern umgehen musste. Ihre Mentalität gehorchte „dem Appell an den Geschäftssinn genauso wie der Aufforderung Gefühle zu zeigen"[2]. Humor war unerlässlich. Wenn zum Beispiel Fernsehmoderatoren das nicht schafften, wurden sie „durch niedrige Einschaltquoten bestraft"[3]. Daran musste man sich orientieren, um von Stuttgart in die neue Welt zu kommen. Zum emotionalen Auftritt gehörte das originale Erläutern der eigenen Arbeit. Die Leute müssen einen „amüsant

His own path seemed to be accompanied by lucky coincidences. He worked in Los Angeles. For his generation, a trip to America was the ultimate educational journey. 'No longer the grand tour to the Medici Venus, the Apollo Belvedere and Raphael; or art and culture of any kind; rather, a journey exclusively to a lifestyle,'[1] wrote Martin Walser, who always likened leaving West German cultural institutions for America to a stay at a health resort. After he returned to Germany, Behnisch stayed in contact with the USA through interns. Later, in his own office, he hired employees from other countries, who sooner or later insisted on working in their lands of origin. This prompted him to take part, as a substitute, in an international project in Wageningen in the Netherlands. This, by the way, was the start of something for which his firm would become known in the future: the building was seen as a pilot project for sustainable construction. The American magazine 'Architectural Record' gave it the publicity it deserved.

With this, the groundwork was laid. A short time later (in 2000), the Stuttgart firm – which by now had a small workplace in Los Angeles, more as a hobby than anything else – was invited to take part in an architectural competition in Cambridge, Massachusetts. The other participants were recruited from internationally successful companies. The Behnisches took part, expecting nothing. They thought: two free airfares to Boston, that's already pretty good. Nevertheless, the presentation for the construction of the new Genzyme Center must have been impressive. Their established colleagues provided drawings and models with their entries which surpassed anything one might produce even for the actual execution planning in this country. Not a chance? It turned out very differently. Stefan Behnisch displayed comic-style sketches and presented the jury with a scenario of possible solutions which differed drastically from well-rehearsed promises of success. Sure enough, he was awarded the contract.

Now the ice had been broken. The architects understood how to deal with the Americans. Their mentality responded to 'both an appeal to business sense and an invitation to show emotion'.[2] Humour was essential. If television hosts, for example, did not have it, they would be 'punished with low viewer ratings'.[3] One had to adapt to this in order to move from Stuttgart to the New World. Emotional presentation included explaining one's own work in an original manner. People have to 'find you amusing,' says Stefan Behnisch. What a contrast to the torture track of German competitions, where you had to hide your accomplishments behind an anonymous six-digit number sequence! In the USA it was a big show. From that time on, company members referred to these presentations as a 'beauty contest'. They

Behnisch Architekten, Donelly Center, Toronto, Canada

Behnisch Architekten, Donelly Center

finden", sagt Stefan Behnisch. Was für ein Unterschied gegenüber der Marterstrecke deutscher Wettbewerbe, bei denen man
anonym hinter einer sechsstelligen Ziffernfolge seine Leistung versteckte! In den USA gab es großes Kino. Fortan hießen
diese Präsentationen im Büro „Beauty-Contest". Hinzu kam
der Bonus des Exotischen: Behnisch Architekten waren Deutsche. Damit erhielten sie von vornherein bessere Arbeitsbedin-
gungen.

Zunächst versicherten sie sich noch der Kooperation europä-
ischer Partner wie Happold Consulting: die Projektbearbei-
tung übernahm das Stuttgarter Büro, die Bauleitung ein Büro
in Los Angeles. Alles, was an fortschrittlicher Gebäudetechnik
gebraucht wurde, also Heliostaten, außen laufende Jalousien,
Tageslichtlenkung, musste damals noch importiert werden. Mit
Erfolg: Das Genzyme Center erhielt als erstes Gebäude in den
USA eine LEED-Platinum-Zertizierung. Es bedeutete für den
Bauherrn, für Happold und für Behnisch den Durchbruch in den
USA. Was der Mieter in seinen Laboren entwickelt, ist in der
Öffentlichkeit weniger populär als die Architektur seiner Firma.
Sie gilt bis heute als Anziehungspunkt für alle, die an der
Gestaltung nachhaltiger Gebäude interessiert sind. 6000 Besu-
cher werden jedes Jahr durch die Räume geführt.

Daraufhin folgte eine weitere Wettbewerbseinladung nach
Massachusetts. Nach Harvard. Und wieder konnte sich
Behnisch platzieren. Aber das riesige Wissenschaftszentrum
wurde ein Opfer der Finanzkrise und nimmt nach einer Umpla-
nung erst allmählich wieder Konturen an. Dafür waren andere
Aufträge ins Portfolio gewandert. In Toronto das Donelly Center
for Cellular and Biomolecular Research (2005). Zwar gab es mit
dem Harvarderfolg inzwischen ein weiteres Büro in Boston, das
kleinere Aufträge und ein Laborgebäude in New Haven (2010)
baute, aber die Planung blieb weiterhin in Stuttgart.

COME ON, LET'S WORK TOGETHER!

Das Kleingedruckte hatte dem Deutschen offenbar zu keiner Zeit
Schwierigkeiten bereitet. Für Stefan Behnisch war die Lizenzie-
rung beim National Council of Architectural Registration Boards
(NCARB) unproblematisch, das American Institute of Architects
(AIA) hatte ihn als honorary member aufgenommen. Was ängst-
liche Naturen üblicherweise beunruhigt – Akquise, Vertrags-
gestaltung, Honorierung, Zulassung in anderen Bundesstaaten
und natürlich die Gewährleistung –, scheint Behnisch in den
Schoß gefallen zu sein. Manches ist unserem Standard offenbar

also enjoyed the extra bonus of being something exotic: Behnisch
Architekten were German, and this helped them obtain better working
conditions from the very beginning.

First of all, they secured the co-operation of European partners such
as Happold Consulting: the Stuttgart office took over responsibility
for the project management; the office in Los Angeles supervised the
construction. At that time, all of the advanced building technology
needed – heliostats, exterior blinds, daylight control – had to be im-
ported. It was a success: the Genzyme Center was the first building
in the United States to be awarded LEED Platinum status. For the
clients, for Happold and for Behnisch, this represented a breakthrough
into the US market. The architecture is more popular with the public
than the products developed within it. To this day, it serves as a point
of reference for all those who are interested in designing sustainable
buildings. Six thousand visitors tour the space every year.

This accomplishment was followed by an invitation to a competition in
Massachusetts – at Harvard. Once again, Behnisch was a frontrunner.
However, the gigantic research centre fell victim to the financial crisis,
and following a re-planning phase, it is only gradually taking shape
again. But in the meantime, other contracts have entered the firm's
portfolio. In Toronto, for example, is the Donelly Center for Cellular
and Biomolecular Research (2005). Thanks to the firm's success at
Harvard, they opened an additional office in Boston to handle smaller
assignments, and built a laboratory building in New Haven (2010);
however, the planning office remained in Stuttgart.

COME ON, LET'S WORK TOGETHER!

Apparently, bureaucratic details never posed any difficulties for the
Germans. Stefan Behnisch's licensing by the National Council of
Architectural Registration Boards (NCARB) was problem-free, and the
American Institute of Architects (AIA) accepted him as an honorary
member. The issues that are often troubling to people of a more
anxious disposition – finding clients, drafting contracts, remuneration,
certification in other states, and of course, guarantees – seem to have
simply fallen into Behnisch's lap. Many standards seem to be quite
similar to ours, or they can be co-ordinated by mutual agreement.
While litigation seems to be the order of the day in Germany, Behnisch
recalls, he only experienced one dispute among ten projects in the
USA. Even the liability risks are lower, he says. In the USA, the
architect's intent is what matters; the construction firms are responsible for the technical aspect. Nevertheless, one has to attend to every
detail. You make your plans with thoroughness; otherwise, the result
will be American mediocrity. Behnisch wants to transfer Europe's

Behnisch Architekten, Donelly Center

Behnisch Architekten, Park Street Clinical Laboratory Building, New Haven

Behnisch Architekten, Park Street Clinical Laboratory Building

sehr nahe, oder es lässt sich einvernehmlich regeln. Gerichtliche Auseinandersetzungen seien in Deutschland an der Tagesordnung, in den USA habe es bei zehn Projekten ein einziges Mal einen Streitfall gegeben, erinnert er sich. Sogar die Haftungsrisiken seien geringer. In den USA zählt der intent, also die Absicht des Architekten, für die Technik sind die Baufirmen verantwortlich. Allerdings muss man sich um jedes Detail kümmern. Da plant man doch mit deutscher Gründlichkeit, andernfalls entsteht amerikanischer Durchschnitt. Behnisch will eben den kulturellen Hintergrund Europas nach amerikanischen Regeln übertragen. Vielleicht entspricht das dem, was Baudrillard als „eine bestimmte Art der Verinnerlichung der eigenen Kultur" [4] bezeichnet hatte. Offenbar sind sich dabei demokratische Gesellschaften näher und vertrauter als nach Bedeutung suchende Regime in anderen Weltgegenden.

Wann immer es geht, treten Behnisch Architekten als Generalplaner an, sie regeln vertraglich alle „specifications" mit einem „general contractor" oder vereinbaren ein „construction management"-Verfahren. So lässt sich die Verantwortung für Qualität und Quantität einvernehmlich trennen. Selbst die Honorierung nach den AIA-Sätzen ist ihnen lieber als die HOAI: „Ich mag Amerika, mir ist es da gut gegangen, die haben mich anständig behandelt", fasst Behnisch seine Erfahrung zusammen. Gerade wenn alles nicht bis zum letzten Reißnagel festgelegt ist, lasse sich angenehmer arbeiten. Was überhaupt für Länder gelte, in denen sich die Berufsstände gerade erst organisatorisch etablierten.

Ein anderer Wesenszug unter amerikanischen Planern sei die Kollegialität. Ob es daran liegt, dass die Architektendichte in den USA nur ein Fünftel der Baden-Württembergischen beträgt, ist eine Mutmaßung. Zu erkennen sei eine ungenierte Kooperation. Man empfiehlt sich, man gibt sich Tipps, bittet unbeteiligte Kollegen vor der Wettbewerbsabgabe um einen kritischen Kommentar zu seiner Arbeit. Behnisch war sogar zu Werkvorträgen in amerikanische Büros eingeladen, und das wurde passabel honoriert. So etwas gehört zu den Leistungen, die er für sein eigenes Geschäft mitgenommen hat: die Fähigkeit zur Kommunikation und zur unangestrengten Auseinandersetzung mit der Architektur.

Der Sektor, auf dem Stefan Behnisch in den USA arbeitet, ist überschaubar. Es handelt sich um Hochschulbauten (private und staatliche), um Institute und Forschungseinrichtungen. Daraus lässt sich kein Erfolgsmodell zur Nachahmung ableiten.

cultural background into American standards. Perhaps this is something like what Baudrillard described as 'a kind of internalization of one's own culture'. [4] In this regard, democratic societies seem to be closer and more familiar than regimes that are searching for significance in other parts of the world.

As often as possible, Behnisch Architekten steps in as the general planner: the firm regulates all the specifications contractually with a general contractor or agrees on a construction management process. In this way, the responsibilities for quality and quantity can be separated amicably. They even prefer remuneration according to AIA guidelines to that of the HOAI (Honorarordnung für Architekten und Ingenieure / German Fee Regulations for Architects and Engineers). Behnisch sums up his experience: 'I like America. Things have gone well for me there, and they have treated me fairly.' Especially when everything is not determined down to the last thumbtack, it is a more pleasant way to work. This is true in general, he says, of countries in which professions have just recently been established at an organizational level.

Another trait characteristic of American planners is their collegial nature. One might speculate that this has something to do with the fact that the concentration of architects in the United States is only one-fifth of what it is in Baden-Württemberg. A spirit of open cooperation is noticeable here. People recommend one another, give each other advice; they ask non-participating colleagues for their critical opinions before submitting work to a competition. Behnisch has even been invited to give expert lectures at American firms, and was paid reasonably for it. These are some of the benefits he has taken with him for his own business: the ability to communicate and engage in relaxed interchanges with architecture.

The sector in which Stefan Behnisch works in the United States is a manageable one. He designs university buildings (both private and public), institutions and research facilities. This is not necessarily a successful business model to imitate. Behnisch is recommended further, quite incidentally, he says. A client will say, 'I know the facilities person at this or that university – they're called "head of capital projects" – send him some of your stuff. That's how it works.' His company's most recent projects were a residence hall in Berkeley (2012), a multi-storey car-park in Santa Monica (2013), and most recently, the Law Center at the University of Baltimore (2013, see p. 162 ff.) – a broad geographical spread. One would actually expect to find Behnisch Architekten located on the West Coast, but the opposite is the case. Even though they don't work with bricks, brownstones and punched windows, their meticulously detailed glass

Behnisch Architekten, Student Housing Complex, University of California, Berkeley

Behnisch Architekten, Student Housing Complex

Behnisch wird weiterempfohlen, ganz beiläufig, erzählt er. Da sagt ein Bauherr: „Ich kenn' den Facilities-Typ bei der und der Uni – „head of capital projects" heißen die –, schick doch dem mal ein bissl Zeug von euch. So läuft das." Die letzten Bauten seines Büros waren ein Studentenwohnheim in Berkeley (2012), ein Parkhaus in Santa Monica (2013) und schließlich das Justizzentrum der Universität Baltimore (2013, siehe S. 162 ff.). Ein geografischer Spagat. Eigentlich würde man Behnisch Architekten eher an der Westküste vermuten, aber das Gegenteil ist der Fall. Obwohl sie nicht mit bricks, brownstones und punched windows bauen, stehen ihre gewissenhaft detaillierten Glashäuser gut im Raster der konservativen Hochhausstädte. „Schon von der Mentalität und der Arbeitsweise passen wir besser an die Ostküste. Das ist ein ernsthafteres Geschäft", erläutert Behnisch. Und fügt hinzu: „Gehry, dem sein Zeug funktioniert nur in Kalifornien. Berlin, die DG-Bank (heute DZ Bank; Anm. d. Hrsg.) war die Ausnahme." Man kann eben nicht ungestraft jede Architektur an jedem Ort der Welt aufschlagen.

CAUTION: OBJECTS IN MIRROR MAY BE CLOSER THAN THEY APPEAR

Behnisch Architekten liefern keine Absichtserklärungen, die der Bauherr als „signature-building" kauft und dann von irgendeiner Bauabteilung ungefähr ähnlich ausführen lässt. Wer Behnisch bestellt, kriegt Behnisch. Was er heute baut, wäre mit der Arbeitsweise der Vätergeneration gar nicht zu leisten gewesen. Das ist auch eine Folge veränderter Anforderungen. Während Behnisch und Partner ein Gebäude aus Bauteilen, aus Schichten zusammengesetzt haben und jedem schwachen Ding seine Bedeutung geben wollten, konstruieren Behnisch Architekten bereits im Rohbau ein fertiges Gehäuse, weil in den speicherfähigen Flachdecken und wärmegedämmten transparenten Fassaden bereits unzählige technische Besonderheiten enthalten sein müssen. Dies hat die Architektur nicht langweiliger gemacht. Sie ist intelligenter, verlässlicher geworden, „sie hat eine viel höhere Planungsdichte". Vater Behnisch hat noch den Luftraum erobert, Sohn Behnisch bietet bereits reguläre Flugpläne. Denn heute müsse man viel früher komplexe Zusammenhänge erkennen, nicht baubegleitend entscheiden, was gerade nötig sei, „wie das mein Vater gemacht hat". Camping-Architektur darf man sich nicht mehr leisten, man muss die Materialien reduzieren, ihre Herkunft und ihre Entsorgung

buildings fit in well with the pattern of conservative high-rise cities. 'Even our mentality and way of working fit in better on the East Coast,' Behnisch explains, 'this is a more serious business.' He adds, 'Gehry's stuff only works in California. The DG Bank [now the DZ Bank] in Berlin was the exception.' One cannot simply put up any kind of architecture in any part of the world with impunity.

CAUTION: OBJECTS IN MIRROR MAY BE CLOSER THAN THEY APPEAR

Behnisch Architekten do not deliver letters of intent which the client then purchases as a signature building, assigning some construction department or another to execute something like it. Anyone who hires Behnisch gets Behnisch. The projects that he builds today would not have been affordable using the working methods of his father's generation. This is also the result of changing demands. Whereas Behnisch und Partner would put a building together out of components or layers, and tried to give significance to every little thing, Behnisch Architekten construct a finished housing even at the shell stage, because a countless number of technical specifications already need to be included in the energy-storing trabeated ceilings and thermally insulated transparent facades. This has not made architecture more boring. It has become more intelligent, more reliable – 'it is much more densely planned'. Behnisch Senior conquered the air space; Behnisch Junior is already offering regular flight schedules. After all, today one needs to recognize complex interactions much earlier, and not simply decide what is necessary at any given moment during the building process 'like my father used to'. 'Camping architecture' is no longer affordable: one has to reduce the use of materials and take their origins and disposal into account. In this regard, the Americans – whom we like to accuse of unchecked consumption as part of their constitutionally guaranteed pursuit of happiness – are quite advanced as far as the construction industry is concerned. Moreover, says Stefan Behnisch, 'I studied with Fritz Haller. From him, I acquired a certain fondness for order. And from Ottokar Uhl, a certain fondness for discussion.' He still likes architectural gestures, but he advises his staff, 'Don't make too many moves per square metre'. Not everything needs to flutter. Baudrillard wrote: 'America is the original version of the modern; we are the second version, or the one with subtitles.'[5] It is fitting therefore, that Behnisch should deliver his purified forms to the New World.

America is no longer the 'image tank, a storehouse of images for the avant-garde'.[6] In the 1920s, architects sailed across the pond, hungry for experience. With his photo essay, Erich Mendelsohn concluded

Behnisch Architekten, Public Parking Structure #6, Santa Monica

Behnisch Architekten, Public Parking Structure #6

berücksichtigen. Da seien die Amerikaner, denen man gerne den ungebremsten Konsum als Beitrag ihres verfassungsgarantierten „pursuit of happiness" nachsagt, beim Bauen ganz fortschrittlich aufgestellt. Im Übrigen, sagt Stefan Behnisch, „ich habe bei Fritz Haller studiert. Von ihm hab' ich eine gewisse Vorliebe für eine Ordnung mitgebracht. Und von Ottokar Uhl eine gewisse Vorliebe für die Diskussion." Architekturgesten mag er schon noch, aber er rät seinen Leuten „macht nicht zu viele moves pro Quadratmeter". Es muss nicht alles flattern. Bei Baudrillard heißt es: „Amerika ist die Originalausgabe der Moderne, wir sind die Zweitfassung oder die mit Untertiteln."[5] Da passt es doch, geläutert die Neue Welt zu beliefern. Denn Amerika ist nicht mehr der „Bildertank, ein Bilderspeicher für die Avantgarde"[6]. Architekten waren in den 1920er-Jahren erlebnishungrig über den großen Teich gefahren. Erich Mendelsohn brachte mit seinem Fotoessay die Erkenntnis mit, dass es nach der Erfahrung „Amerika" leichter sei „nun von der Spitze der Zeit zurückzurechnen, auf sich selbst zu schließen, anstatt ohne seine Kenntnis vom alten Nullpunkt aufzusteigen zum höchsten Stand".[7] Diese Faszination hielt offensichtlich noch eine geraume Weile an. Mitte der 1980er-Jahre brachen ein Dutzend gestandener deutscher Architekten mit ihrem Verleger auf, um amerikanische Ateliers und ihre Arbeiten zu bestaunen und die Eindrücke in einem Buch mitzuteilen.[8] Heute wäre das eine Semesterexkursion für Studenten.

that after his 'America' experience, it was easier 'now to calculate backwards from the pinnacle of time and draw conclusions about oneself, instead of climbing from the old zero point to the highest level without any knowledge of it.'[7] This fascination apparently continued for quite some time. In the mid-1980s, a dozen well-established German architects set off with their publisher to marvel at American studios and their work, and to share their impressions in a book.[8] Nowadays, that would be a student excursion during semester break.

[1] André Ficus, Martin Walser, Die Amerikareise. Versuch, ein Gefühl zu verstehen. Frankfurt am Main 1990 (Weingarten1986), p. 102.

[2] Dieter Kronzucker, Klaus Emmerich: Das amerikanische Jahrhundert. Düsseldorf, Vienna, New York 1989, p. 70.

[3] Ibid.

[4] Jean Baudrillard, Amerika. Munich 1987 [1986], p. 108.

[5] Baudrillard, ibid., p. 109.

[6] Jean-Louis Cohen, Zur Amerikanisierung der Architektur – Leitbild oder Feindbild? In: Positionen 1968–1998, Institut Grundlagen moderner Architektur und Entwerfen, University of Stuttgart, Stuttgart 2000, p. 93.

[7] Erich Mendelsohn, Amerika. Bilderbuch eines Architekten. Berlin 1926 [1925], p. IX.

[8] Architektur USA. Selected, compiled and edited by Harald Deilmann and Gerhard Schwab, published by Karl H. Krämer. Stuttgart 1985.

[1] André Ficus, Martin Walser, Die Amerikareise. Versuch, ein Gefühl zu verstehen. Frankfurt am Main 1990 (Weingarten 1986), S. 102.

[2] Dieter Kronzucker, Klaus Emmerich: Das amerikanische Jahrhundert. Düsseldorf, Wien, New York 1989, S. 70.

[3] a. a. O.

[4] Jean Baudrillard, Amerika. München 1987 [1986], S. 108.

[5] Baudrillard, a. a. O., S. 109.

[6] Jean-Louis Cohen, Zur Amerikanisierung der Architektur – Leitbild oder Feindbild? In: Positionen 1968–1998, Institut Grundlagen moderner Architektur und Entwerfen, Universität Stuttgart, Stuttgart 2000, S. 93.

[7] Erich Mendelsohn, Amerika. Bilderbuch eines Architekten. Berlin 1926 [1925], S. IX.

[8] Architektur USA. Ausgewählt, zusammengestellt und bearbeitet von Harald Deilmann und Gerhard Schwab, hrsg. von Karl H. Krämer. Stuttgart 1985.

Gerber Architekten, Olaya Metro Station, Riyadh

BAUKUNST ALS SPRACHROHR
ECKHARD GERBER

Was bewegt einen Schriftsteller zu schreiben, einen Musiker zu komponieren, einen Maler zu malen oder einen Architekten zu planen und zu bauen? Was ist der Antrieb zum künstlerischen Schaffen? Für wen schreibt ein Schriftsteller oder komponiert ein Musiker? Für eine westliche oder östliche Welt, für gewisse Staatssysteme? Sie tun es wohl eher für alle Menschen, die sich daran erfreuen. Auch als Architekten schließen wir uns da ein. Wir bauen für die Menschen, die sich in unseren Gebäuden aufhalten, in ihnen leben, für die Menschen in den Städten, in denen unsere Gebäude stehen. Wir sind auch der festen Überzeugung, dass unsere Gebäude Botschafter einer neuen Welt sind, dass sie Menschen befindlich machen, glücklich, fröhlich oder nachdenklich, sie anregen und aktivieren. Die meisten Künste haben es dabei einfach: Sie sind im Gegensatz zur Baukunst frei. Ein Bauwerk ist jeweils fest mit einem Ort verbunden, hat funktionale und andere Bindungen und braucht immer einen Auftraggeber. Auf Grund der medialen Internationalisierung haben viele Architekten heute das Glück, nicht nur im eigenen, sondern auch in anderen Ländern zu bauen. Und es ist egal, für welches Land sie bauen, auf die Botschaft unserer Baukunst kommt es an. Sie kann mithelfen, zu verändern: „Wandlung durch Annäherung". Im Planungsprozess beginnen wir, das Land, seine Kultur, seine Menschen zu verstehen und zu begreifen, warum vieles anders ist als bei uns. Auch diese vielen Gespräche dienen zur kulturellen und politischen Verständigung. Unsere fertigen Gebäude sind letztlich die Sprachrohre für unsere Botschaft, sie kommunizieren mit den Menschen und sie können sie überzeugen. Im Ausland zu bauen ist deshalb eine große Chance, nämlich mitzuhelfen, mit Gebäuden Prozesse des Wandels anzustoßen und einzuleiten, vor allem in Staaten, die politisch anders als wir aufgestellt sind. Die Ostpolitik von Willy Brandt hat gezeigt, dass nur das Gespräch mit den Regimen Erfolg zum Wandel verspricht. Aufgeklärte Baukunst kann zu solchen Botschaftern werden und Brücken bauen zwischen Ländern und Menschen.

ARCHITECTURE AS A MOUTHPIECE
ECKHARD GERBER

What motivates an author to write, a musician to compose, an artist to paint or an architect to design and build? What drives artistic creation? For whom does an author write or a musician compose? For a Western or an Eastern world – for particular systems of government? More likely, they do it for all the people who will take enjoyment from it. As architects, we also include ourselves among these artists. We build for the people who will spend time in our buildings – those who will live in them, and the people in the cities where our buildings are located. We also strongly believe that our buildings are messengers of a new world: that they can affect people's moods, make them happy, joyful or thoughtful; they can inspire or stimulate. Most art forms have an easier time with this: in contrast to architecture, they are free. A building is always permanently connected with a place; it has functional obligations and other relationships; it always needs a customer. Thanks to the internationalizing effects of the media, many architects today have the good fortune to build not only in their own countries, but in other countries as well. It does not matter in which country they build: the message of our architecture is what is essential. It can help to create change: 'change through rapprochement'. During the planning process, we begin to understand the country, its culture and its people, and to comprehend the reasons why many things are different then they are where we live. The many discussions that take place can also contribute to cultural and political understanding. Finally, our finished buildings provide a mouthpiece for our message: they communicate with the people, and they can win them over. Building in other countries is therefore a great opportunity to make a contribution: through our buildings, we can initiate and set in motion processes of change – particularly in countries whose political positions are different from our own. Willy Brandt's 'Ostpolitik' demonstrated that only communication with these regimes can bring the promise of successful change. Enlightened architecture can serve as this type of ambassador, building bridges between countries and people.

DEUTSCHER ARCHITEKTUR EXPORT
GERMAN ARCHITECTURE EXPORT

22–24

INTERNATIONAL
INTERNATIONAL

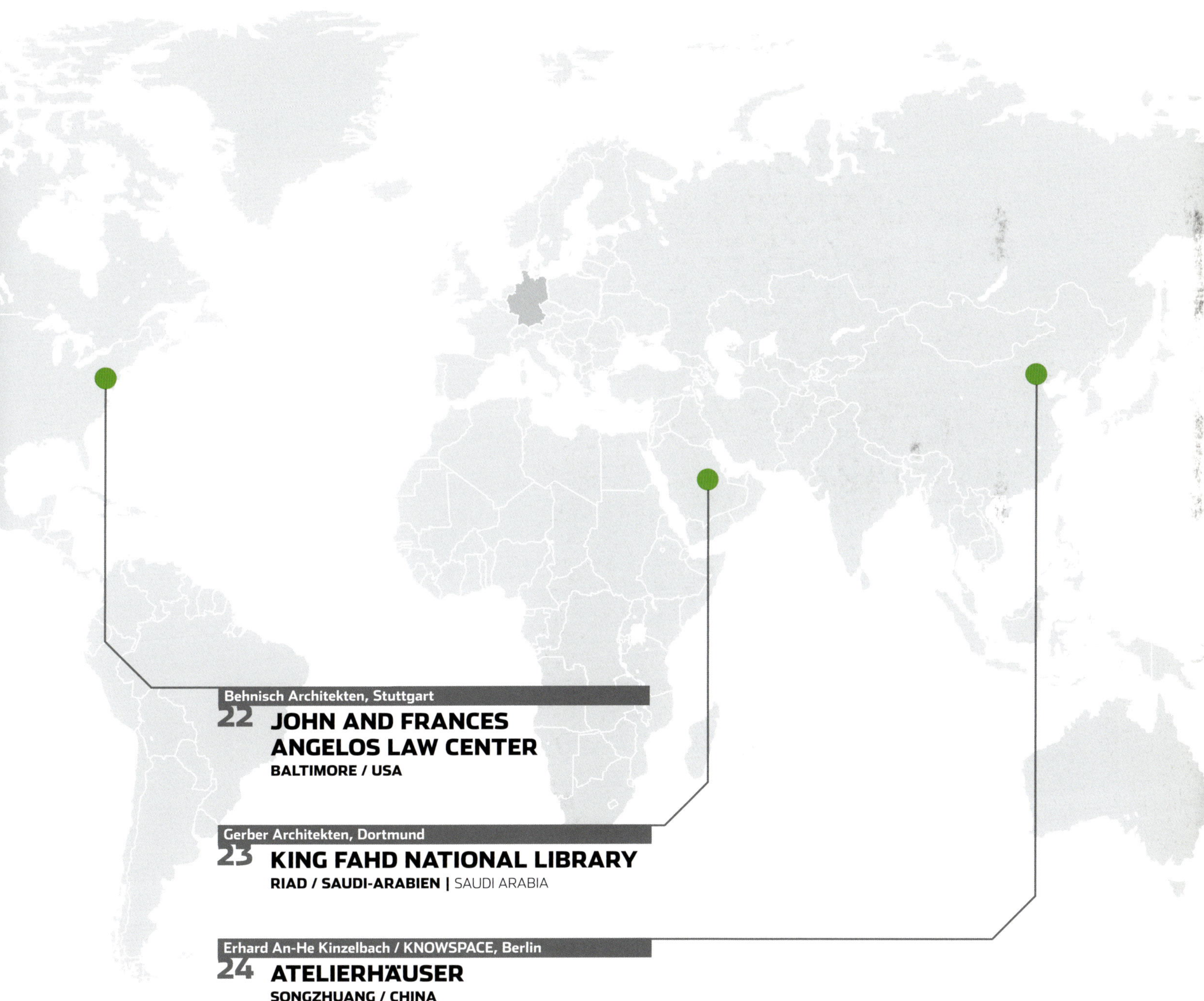

BEHNISCH ARCHITEKTEN

GEBÄUDE | BUILDING

JOHN AND FRANCES ANGELOS LAW CENTER
BALTIMORE, USA

TEXT KLAUS PHILIPSEN

22

ARCHITEKTEN | ARCHITECTS
Behnisch Architekten
Rotebühlstraße 163 A
70197 Stuttgart
www.behnisch.com

mit | with
Ayers Saint Gross,
Baltimore, MD, USA

MITARBEITER | TEAM
Projektleitung | project management
Behnisch Architekten:
Andrea Crumbach, Taylor Rogers
Mitarbeiter | staff
Behnisch Architekten:
Shir Gale, Alex Hirsig,
Maryjane King, Michael Kocher,
Christine Napolitano,
Stefanie Platsch, Gavin Ruedisueli,
Meghan Webster, Thomas Weitzel,
Aaron Vaden-Youmans

Projektleitung | Project management
Ayers Saint Gross:
Michael Barber, Steve Eastwood
Mitarbeiter | staff
Ayers Saint Gross:
Brett Gullborg, Dan McKelvey

BAUHERR | CLIENT
University of Maryland Baltimore,
University of Baltimore

AUSFÜHRUNGSPLANUNG
EXECUTION PLANNING
Behnisch Architekten mit | with
Ayers Saint Gross

**BAULEITUNG /
PROJEKTSTEUERUNG**
SITE MANAGEMENT /
PROJECT MANAGEMENT

Generalunternehmer
general contractor:
The Whiting-Turner
Contracting Group, USA

TRAGWERK UND BRANDSCHUTZ
STRUCTURE AND FIRE PREVENTION
Cagley & Associates, Rockwell,
MD, USA

HAUSTECHNIK | M & E ENGINEERS
Mueller Associates, Baltimore,
MD, USA

AKUSTIK | ACOUSTICS
Shen Milson & Wilke, USA

FERTIGSTELLUNG | COMPLETION
April 2013

STANDORT | LOCATION
1401 N. Charles Street
Baltimore
MD 21201, USA
www.law.ubalt.edu

FOTOS | PHOTOS
David Matthiessen, Stuttgart
Brad Feinknopf, Columbus, USA

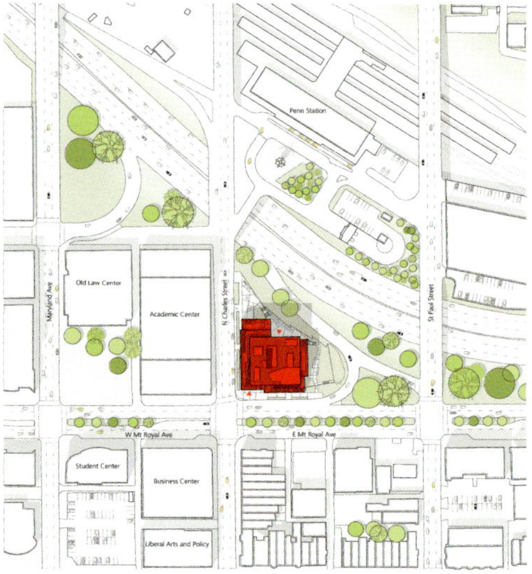

Lageplan | Site plan

Das Law Center steht als neue Landmarke in seiner Umgebung. | The Law Center represents a new landmark in its surroundings.

In jeder Stadt gibt es Plätze, an denen ein Wahrzeichen angemessen ist. Hier, wo sich Baltimores Charles Street zum Bahnhof hin öffnet und ein Fluss eine Bruchstelle schafft, an der sich eine Stadtautobahn in Tieflage entlangschlängelt, hier auf einem ehemaligen Parkplatz der University of Baltimore, braucht man keine Anpassungsarchitektur. Von allen Seiten voll im Blick, ist an dieser Stelle schon etwas „Bravado" angebracht, selbst wenn die nahe gelegene historische Substanz auch Respekt verlangt. Das neue Gebäude der juristischen Fakultät ist so ein Leuchtturm, denn der zwölfgeschossige weiße Würfel, zusammengesetzt aus drei versetzten Raumelementen, ist nicht zu übersehen.

Der Entwurf von Behnisch Architekten, realisiert in Partnerschaft mit dem örtlichen Büro Ayers Saint Gross, konnte sich in einem internationalen Wettbewerb der Universität Baltimore gegen die Konkurrenz von Stars wie Norman Foster, Dominique Perrault und Moshe Safdie durchsetzen. Das gelang ihm, weil er präzise und durchdacht zeigte, wie sein Zauberwürfel flexibel sowohl auf die komplizierten Sichtbeziehungen als auch auf die sich ändernde Welt der Juristenausbildung reagieren kann. Als

Each city has a few places that are appropriate for architectural landmarks. The plot belonging to the University of Baltimore at Charles Street and Mount Royal Avenue, a former parking lot, is such a spot. In full view from all sides, this strategic location demanded a bold move that can shine all around. That is what the new law school became. The 12-storey white cube, assembled from three basic elements, is in your face, whether you exit the glorious Beaux Arts train station, come up Charles Street or speed by on the expressway located along the fault line that used to be the Jones Falls river. The design of Behnisch Architekten goes back to an international design competition organized by the University of Baltimore, in which Behnisch and his local partner, Ayer Saint Gross, beat some of the most renowned stars in architecture, including Norman Foster, Dominique Perrault and Moshe Safdie. Behnisch won by thoughtfully demonstrating how his Rubik's Cube could flexibly

Der abgesenkte Vorplatz an der Nordseite
The sunken forecourt on the north side

das Gebäude im April 2013 im Beisein des US-Vizepräsidenten Biden eingeweiht wurde, sahen die Gäste genau das, was sich der Bauherr gewünscht hatte: ein Wahrzeichen für Stadt und Campus, das die gesamte Universität in neuem Licht erscheinen lässt.

Der mit 18 000 Quadratmetern beachtliche Koloss ist der bauliche Schlussakkord für den denkmalgeschützten Bezirk Mount Vernon und Anker des Universitätsbereichs. Behnisch setzt den Würfel aus den drei Funktionsbereichen Lehre, Verwaltung und Bücherei zusammen und bildet die jeweils eigene „DNA" dieser Bausteine subtil in der Fassade ab. Damit bricht er nicht nur das Volumen, sondern nimmt auch geschickt den Dialog mit der Umgebung auf. Aus der Ferne fällt zunächst die schachbrettartige Fassade des Büchereibereichs auf. Aus der Nähe erschließt sich die komplexere Glas-Doppelfassade vor den unregelmäßigen großen Fensterflächen der Seminarräume, der zurückgesetzte Eingangsbereich mit Sonnenschutzlamellen und die feine Differenzierung des hellgrau gehaltenen Unterrichtsbereichs. Die moderne Helligkeit und Leichtigkeit kontrastiert nicht nur mit den weit weniger ehrgeizigen Universitätsgebäuden der Umgebung, sondern auch mit dem bei US-Universitäten beliebten neugotischen Stil, den auch die nahe University of Maryland in ihrem Neubau für die Rechtswissenschaften jüngst verwendete.

Wie bei seinem ersten großen US-Projekt, dem Genzyme Haus in Cambridge, hat Stefan Behnisch das Atrium als das Herz des Gebäudes entwickelt: ein Marktplatz, der die Interaktion erlaubt. Seine Vorliebe für Leichtigkeit, Farbe, Helligkeit und Transparenz sind dieselben architektonischen Tugenden, die seinen Vater Günter Behnisch weltberühmt machten, als er 1972 die Münchner Olympiazelte als spielerische Gegenthese zum damals vorherrschenden Image des spröden Deutschen entwarf. Stefan Behnisch hat diese Philosophie weiterentwickelt und seiner Auffassung von Nachhaltigkeit untergeordnet.

respond to the changing world of legal education. When the building opened in April 2013 with US Vice President Biden as guest, the University of Baltimore and its president had accomplished precisely what he had aimed for: an architectural gem and iconic attention-grabber that moves UB's Law Center to the next level and establishes the university as an urban anchor.

The building, bursting with nearly 18,000 square metres of programme space, respects historic Mount Vernon district, neatly completes the campus and buttons up the historic neighbourhood. It responds to the challenges as a large cube of interlocking components. Classrooms, administration and the library make up the three main puzzle pieces, each signalling its own distinctive DNA on the building's façade and taking up the dialogue with the various surroundings. The distant view offers a simple chequerboard. The more intimate, close-up experience reveals the layers of the glazed double façade, the sunshades and the slight grey of the classroom tract. The new flagship departs from the blandness of UB's campus and from the typical law-school classicism as exemplified by the new pseudo-Gothic law school building of the nearby University of Maryland.

Though Behnisch had clearly taken cues from his first American project, a biotech building in Cambridge, Mass., the Baltimore Law Center was custom-designed around the programme 'from the inside out', as he said.

As in the Cambridge design, the atrium is the building's heart and forum, allowing openness, interaction, transparency and light — all hallmarks of Behnisch architecture since Stefan Behnisch's father, Günter Behnisch, entered the world stage in 1972 with his Munich Olympic 'tents', designed as a clear antithesis to the prevailing image of the German as broody and heavy.

Stefan Behnisch has taken this philosophy to new heights and enriched it with his broad definition of sustainability, consisting not only of high-tech but happily communicating use and efficient organization.

Die Südfassade des schachbrettgemusterten Gebäudes | The southern façade of the checkerboard-patterned building

Die Nordostecke; hier sind die ineinandergesteckten Kuben besonders gut ablesbar. | The northeast corner: the interlocked cuboids are particularly visible here.

Grundriss Erdgeschoss | Plan of ground floor

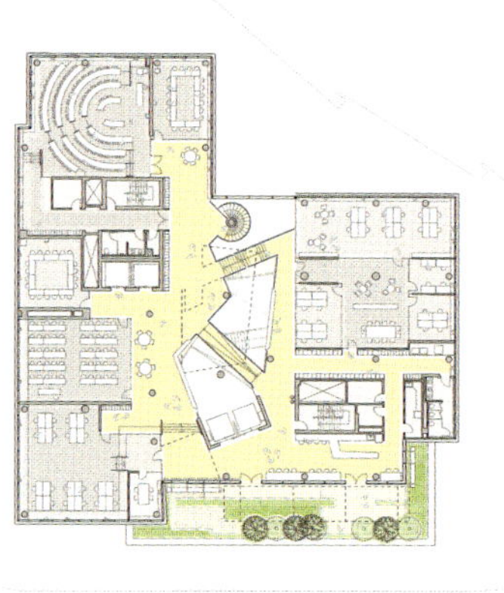

Grundriss 6. Obergeschoss | Plan of 6th floor

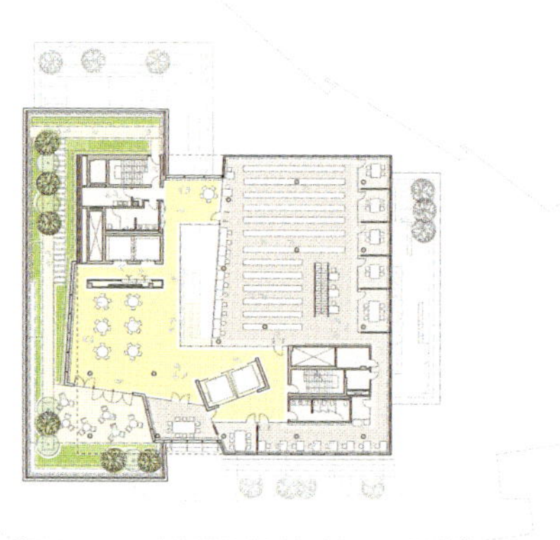

Grundriss 12. Obergeschoss | Plan of 12th floor

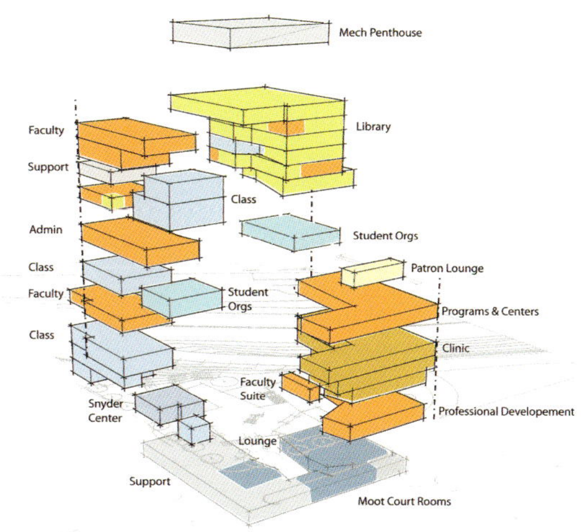

Raumprogramm | Room arrangement

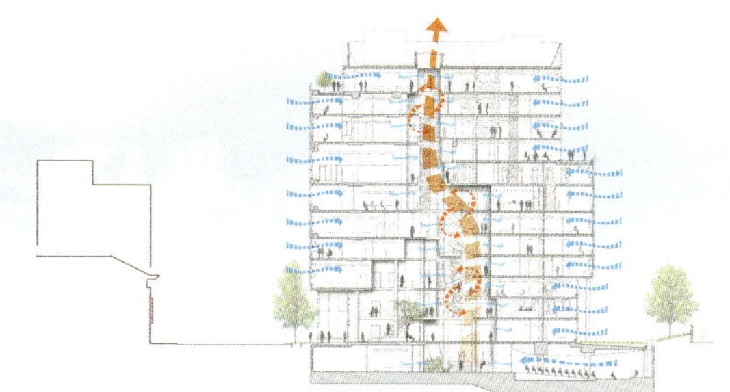

Das helle und freundliche Foyer vermittelt nicht den Eindruck einer spröden Jurafakultät. | The bright and welcoming foyer does not suggest an aloof law department.

Der Schnitt zeigt die natürliche Belüftung.
The section shows the natural ventilation.

Das beindruckende Schauspiel eines zwölfgeschossigen lichtdurchfluteten Atriums mit Staffelungen, Aufweitungen und Verengungen, verknüpft mit einem komplexen Geflecht von Brücken, Treppen und Aussichtspunkten, die es fröhlich miteinander kommunizierenden Nutzern erlauben, das Atrium von oben bis unten zu durchwandern, wie die langen Lichterketten aus LEDs in lumineszierenden weißen Plexiglasplatten sind genauso Zeichen von Nachhaltigkeit wie beheizte Betonböden, fast vollständig vermiedene abgehängte Decken, vorgehängte Vollglasfassaden und bedienbare Fenster. Alles ein für US-Verhältnisse ungewöhnlicher Aufwand, der dem Gebäude die LEED-Platinum-Bewertung einbrachte und demonstriert, dass Nachhaltigkeit nicht nach Birkenstock aussehen muss. Dieses Bauwerk ist keineswegs nur eine große Geste. Überall finden sich ungewöhnliche, wohldurchdachte Details. Da sind zum Beispiel die zur Ablage erweiterten Geländer, auf denen man Getränkebecher abstellen kann, während man dem Getriebe im Innenhof zuschaut. Hier wurde nicht einmal an den Nottreppen gespart, geschweige denn am Gerichtssaal, in dem sich die künftigen Juristen üben und der mit seinem kunstvoll ausgelegten Stabparkett aus Bambus alle Gerichtssäle der Region ästhetisch aussticht.

Man staunt, wie sehr das Endprodukt dem Wettbewerbsentwurf gleicht. Das ist sicherlich einer nicht ganz undeutschen Sturheit geschuldet, mit der Behnisch amerikanischen Sehgewohnheiten trotzt. Und hier steht es nun: ein luftig helles und durchaus fröhliches Wahrzeichen, das sich und seine Nutzer so schamlos feiert, dass in diesem Haus selbst Jura Spaß machen muss.

Baltimore's first dual façade with an exterior rainscreen of pure glass, the 12-storey atrium in which one can walk from top to bottom on crisscrossing, open stairs and slender bridges for seeing and being seen, the 50 miles of hydronic tubing for heated floors, the operable windows, the LED light chains of luminescent acrylic-glass plates, and the notably absent hung ceilings, all this demonstrated that sustainability does not have to be as bland as a Birkenstock sandal, and achieved the Platinum level on the LEED sustainability scale .

This landmark is not just about big gestures, though. Behnisch and his local architect partner drove surprise and love for detail into every nook and cranny, even the emergency exit stairways. Custom classroom furniture, the moot court with elaborate bamboo woodwork, which easily outdoes any actual courtroom in the region, and creative little gestures such as atrium guardrails which become shelves for the caffe latte, show a creative hand throughout. One can marvel at how close the final product resembles the competition design. There certainly is a somewhat Germanic bluntness and rigour in how Behnisch defied Baltimore's traditional architectural expectations. Yet, here it is: a landmark, light and airy, indeed, joyful. It celebrates itself and its occupants so brazenly that even law, as studied here, promises to be fun.

GERBER ARCHITEKTEN

KING FAHD NATIONAL LIBRARY
RIAD, SAUDI-ARABIEN

TEXT FRANK R. WERNER

23

ARCHITEKTEN | ARCHITECTS

Gerber Architekten
Tönnishof 9–13
44149 Dortmund
www.gerberarchitekten.de

MITARBEITER | TEAM

Gesamtleitung | general management**: Eckhard Gerber**
Projektleitung | project architect**:**
Thomas Lücking
Britta Alker, Olaf Ballerstedt,
Carolin Balkenhol, Hans Christoph
Bittner, Markus Görtz,
Juana Grunwald, Thomas Helms,
Nicole Juchems, Alexandra Kranert,
René Koblank, Nils Kummer,
Stefan Lemke, Jörg Schönweis,
Van Hai Nguyen

BAUHERR | CLIENT

Königreich Saudi Arabien

AUSFÜHRUNGSPLANUNG / KÜNSTLERISCHE OBERLEITUNG
EXECUTION PLANNING / SENIOR ARTISTIC MANAGEMENT

Gerber Architekten

GENERALUNTERNEHMER
GENERAL CONTRACTOR

Saudi Bin Laden Group

TRAGWERK UND BRANDSCHUTZ
STRUCTURE AND FIRE PREVENTION

Wettbewerb | competition**:**
Schlaich Bergermann und Partner,
Stuttgart
Ausführung | execution**:**
Bollinger & Grohmann Ingenieure,
Frankfurt am Main |
Saudi Consulting Services, Riad

LANDSCHAFTSARCHITEKTUR
LANDSCAPE ARCHITECTURE

Gerber Architekten mit | with
Kienle Planungsgesellschaft,
Stuttgart

HAUSTECHNIK | M & E ENGINEERS

Wettbewerb | competition**:**
HL-Technik AG, München | Munich
Ausführung | execution**:**
DS-Plan (Drees & Sommer Group)

ARMATUREN | FITTINGS

Grohe, Porta Westfalica

FERTIGSTELLUNG | COMPLETION

November 2013

STANDORT | LOCATION

King Fahd Road, Riad
Königreich von Saudi Arabien

FOTOS | PHOTOS

Christian Richters, Berlin

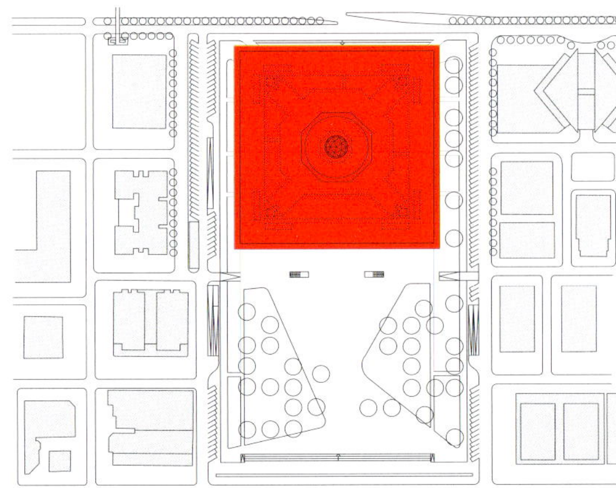

Lageplan | Site plan

Die Nordostfassade mit dem davor gelegenen Platz | The northeast façade with the large square in front

Als Eckhard Gerber 1999 zum Wettbewerb für einen Neubau der King Fahd Nationalbibliothek im Zentrum von Riad eingeladen wurde, da lag der avisierte Bauplatz noch an einer ganz anderen Stelle der Stadt. Mit dem Beschluss, die neue Bibliothek dann aber doch auf dem Grundstück des älteren Vorgängerbaus zu errichten, wurde der siegreiche Entwurf Mario Bottas ad acta gelegt. Aufgrund eines ebenso signifikanten wie zurückhaltenden Konzepts ging Eckart Gerber unangefochten als Gewinner aus dem zweiten Wettbewerbsverfahren hervor. Dieses hatte es den Teilnehmern freigestellt, den denkmalverdächtigen Bestandsbau abzubrechen oder in den Neubau zu integrieren. Gerber entschied sich für das Letztere, wobei er dem Bauplatz auf einem schmalen, überwiegend mit Hochhäusern bebauten Band zwischen den vielspurigen Stadtautobahnen King Fahd Road und Olaya Street unaufgefordert hohe städtebauliche Qualitäten abzutrotzen wusste.
Bei der Ende 2013 vollendeten Nationalbibliothek handelt es sich also weniger um einen Bau ex novo als vielmehr um ein spannungsreiches Gefüge nach dem Haus-im-Haus-Prinzip.

In 1999, when Eckhard Gerber was invited to participate in the architectural competition for a new King Fahd National Library in the centre of Riyadh, the proposed site was in a completely different location in the city. However, when the decision was made to construct the new library on the site of the previous structure after all, the winning design by Mario Botta was set aside. Based on his concept, which was as significant as it was restrained, Eckart Gerber emerged as the undisputed winner in the second competition process. This competition gave the participants the option of demolishing the existing building – a candidate for heritage protection – or integrating it into the new structure. Gerber decided on the latter, and in doing so, he was able to coax unexpectedly high city-planning qualities out of the building site – which is located on a narrow strip dominated by high-rise buildings, between the multilane highway King Fahd Road and Olaya Street.

Die Nordecke der Bibliothek | The north corner of the library

Blick entlang der Nordostfassade auf den Faisaliah Tower | View along the northeast façade to the Faisaliah Tower

So ging es Eckhard Gerber vorrangig darum, den schönen, mit weißen Marmor- und Keramikplatten verkleideten sowie von einer Kuppel bekrönten Altbau aus den frühen 1980er-Jahren in den Bibliotheksneubau zu integrieren und dabei funktional für das 21. Jahrhundert zu ertüchtigen. Der Kerngedanke des Entwurfs bestand darin, den bestehenden Altbau in einen großzügig bemessenen Erweiterungsbau einzuhausen. So schmiegt sich der Neubau als quadratischer, vielfach geschichteter und vergleichsweise flacher Kubus um den kreuzförmigen Altbau, mit dem er räumlich komplett verschmolzen ist. Das ehemalige Flachdach des Altbaus fungiert gleichsam als Boden für den neuen, hoch gelegenen, lichtdurchfluteten Lesesaal, während sich im dunklen Inneren der alten Bibliothek die Magazine befinden. Den Freihandbereich im dritten Obergeschoss des Neubaus erreichen die Besucher über Brücken vom Lesesaal aus. Eine neue Stahl-Glas-Konstruktion ersetzte die alte geschlossene Kuppel im Zentrum des Altbaus. Das Flachdach des Neubaus umschließt sie weiträumig, so dass sie stadträumlich nur noch aus der Vogelperspektive in Erscheinung tritt. Das neue Dach überdeckt zudem den Altbau, die neu entstandenen Innenhöfe, das neue Foyer sowie alle angrenzenden Räumlichkeiten und besteht aus einer komplexen Stahlfachwerkkonstruktion. An deren Unterseite wurden weiße Membranen gespannt. Diese filtern das über unsichtbare Oberlichtbänder

Thus, the National Library, completed at the end of 2013, is less an ex novo building than a dynamic structure built on the principle of a house-within-a-house. Eckhard Gerber's priority, therefore, was to integrate the old building dating from the early 1980s – which was clad in white marble and ceramic slabs and crowned with a cupola – into the new library structure and thereby upgrade its functionality for the twenty-first century. The core idea of his design was to enclose the existing building inside a generously-proportioned extension. Thus, the new building – in the shape of a square, many-layered and comparatively squat cuboid – wraps itself around the cross-shaped older structure, with which it has been spatially completely merged. What was once the flat roof of the old building more or less functions as a floor for the new, brightly lit upper-level reading room, while the stacks are located in the dark interior of the old library. From the reading room, visitors can reach the open stacks area on the third floor of the new building via walkways. A new steel-and-glass construction replaced the old closed cupola in the centre of the old building. The flat roof of the new building generously encloses it, so that

einfallende Tageslicht. Auf angenehme Weise werden somit
alle Räume gleichmäßig mit blendfreiem Licht versorgt.
Nachts dienen oberhalb der Membran versteckte Leuchten als
Lichtquelle. Im Erdgeschoss gruppieren sich um den Altbaukern
hohe Ausstellungsräume, das Restaurant sowie eine Buchhand-
lung, vor allem aber die neue repräsentative Eingangshalle.
Letztere reicht vom Eingangsniveau bis zur Dachmembran und
beherbergt V-förmig angeordnete Rolltreppen und Aufzüge.
Der im ersten Obergeschoss des neuen Südwesttrakts nur für
Frauen reservierte und durch abstrakt gemusterte Glaspaneele
abgeschirmte Bibliotheksbereich wird separat erschlossen.
Die peripheren Geschosse des Neubaus sind ansonsten von
Leseplätzen und Regalen, administrativen Großraumbüros, der
repräsentativen Suite des königlichen Bauherrn sowie Bespre-
chungsräumen belegt.
Besondere Aufmerksamkeit verdient die Bibliotheksfassade, die
den Bau auf einem gänzlich neu geschaffenen, parkähnlichen
Vorplatz, der von Gerber Architekten gleichsam als Zugabe und
städtebaulicher Mehrwert konzipiert wurde, ebenso selbstbewusst wie zurückhaltend auftreten lässt. Seriell aneinander-
gereihte weiße Membranen, die wie Segel in ein tief geschich-

in city-planning terms, it is visible only from above.
The new roof, which is made from a complex steel
lattice construction, also covers the old building,
the newly-created inner courtyards, the new foyer
as well as all the adjacent spaces. White membranes have been stretched across the underside of
this framework; they filter the daylight which enters
through invisible skylight strips. This creates a
pleasant way of evenly supplying all the rooms with
glare-free daylight. At night, lamps hidden above
the membrane serve as a light source. Grouped
around the old building core on the ground floor are
high-ceilinged exhibition spaces, a restaurant and a
book shop; however, the space is dominated by the
elegant new entrance hall. The latter, which extends
upward all the way from the entrance level to the
roof membrane, contains a V-shaped arrangement
of escalators as well as elevators. Built as a separate
addition, a library area reserved for women only is
located on the first floor of the new southwest wing
and shielded by glass panels with abstract patterns.

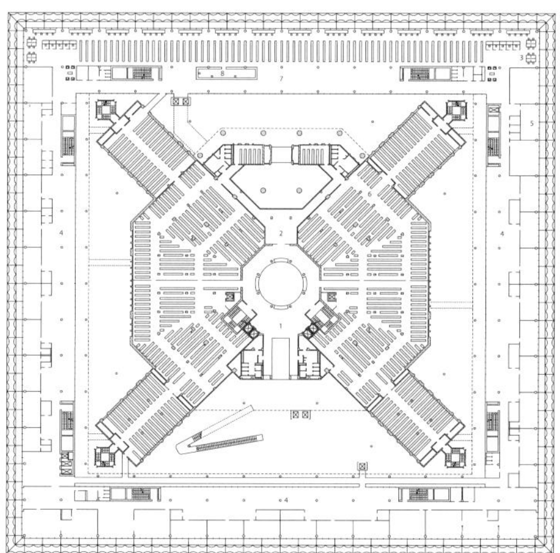

Grundriss 1. Obergeschoss | Plan of 1st floor

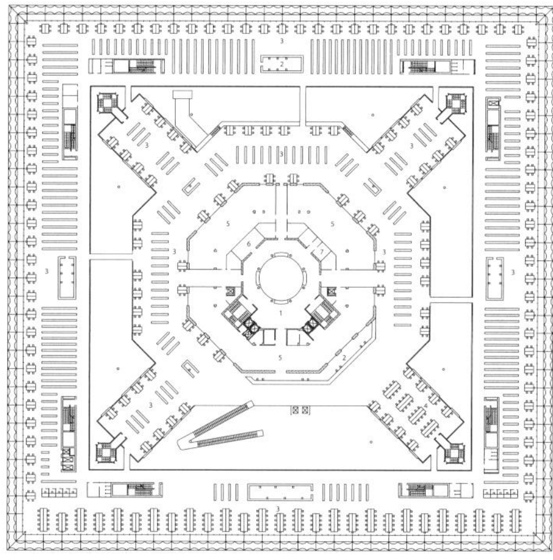

Grunddriss 3. Obergeschoss | Plan of 3rd floor

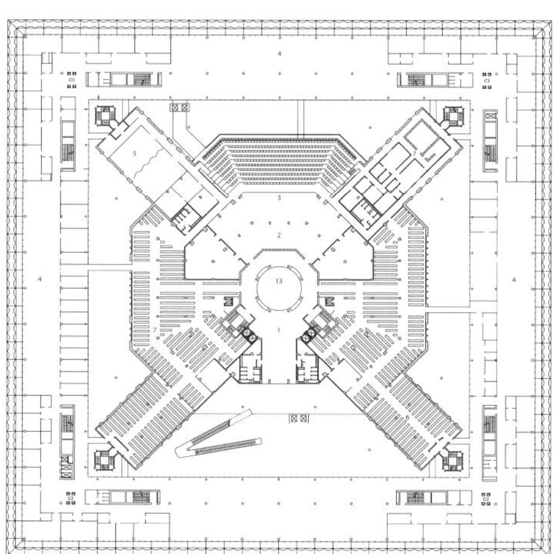

Grundriss Erdgeschoss | Plan of ground floor

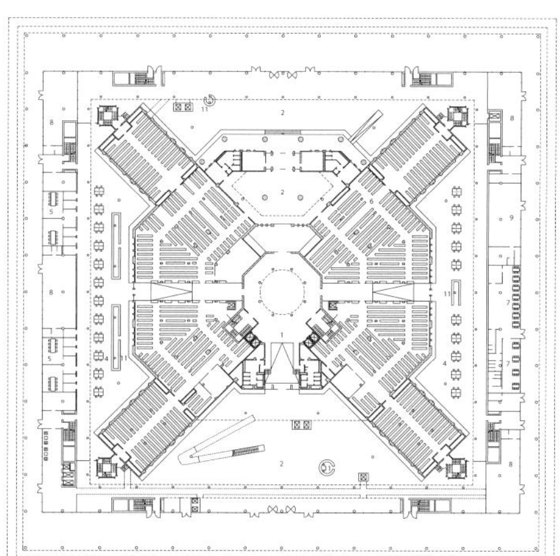

Grundriss 2. Obergeschoss | Plan of 2nd floor

Blick in die raffinierte Konstruktion der Membransegel | The sophisticated construction of the sail membranes

Das Foyer mit einer eleganten, leuchtenden Rolltreppe
The foyer with its elegant illuminated escalator

tetes Netz aus sichtbaren Stahlseilen eingespannt sind, dienen umlaufend als Sonnenschutz für die Obergeschosse. Gleichzeitig verleihen sie der Fassade Plastizität und Tiefe. Unterschwellig verweisen sie auch auf die nomadische Tradition temporärer Zeltbauten und lassen beflügelnde Reminiszenzen an Frei Ottos Wirken in Riad anklingen. Weitaus wesentlicher erscheint jedoch der geglückte Umgang mit der in der arabischen Welt tief verwurzelten Tradition des Gegensatzes von Verhüllung und Offenlegung. Mit der Implementierung dieses dialektischen Gegensatzes ist Eckhard Gerber ausgerechnet hier in Riad, wo Verhüllungsstrategien tonangebend sind, eine programmatische Ausweitung des Transparenzbegriffs gelungen. Altes und Neues verdichten sich bei diesem Bau bis in Details hinein zu einer zurückhaltenden, repräsentativen Zeichenhaftigkeit, welche in Riad qualitativ ihresgleichen sucht. Bei Nacht setzen im Widerschein changierender Lichtreflexe die Segel diesen wie traumhaft bauliche Gestalt gewordenen „nordsüdlichen" beziehungsweise „westöstlichen Divans" stadtwirksam in Szene.

The other peripheral floors of the new building are occupied by reading areas and shelves, open-plan offices, conference rooms and the luxurious suite of the royal client.

The library façade deserves special attention here: it lends a self-assured yet restrained appearance to the building, facing the completely new, park-like forecourt which was conceived by Gerber Architekten as something of an encore and for added urban value. Serially aligned white membranes, stretched like sails on a deeply layered network of visible steel cables, serve as sunshades around the entire circumference of the upper storeys. At the same time, they lend plasticity and depth to the façade, while making subliminal reference to the nomadic tradition of temporary tent construction and evoke inspiring reminiscences of Frei Otto's work in Riyadh. The successful treatment of the traditional opposition between what is concealed and what is revealed, which is deeply rooted in the Arab world, seems far more fundamentally important. With the implementation of this dialectical opposition, Eckhard Gerber has succeeded in creating – here in Riyadh, of all places, where strategies of concealment set the tone – a programmatic expansion of the concept of transparency. In this building, the old and the new are condensed – down to the smallest details – into a restrained, prestigious semiotic character which is unequalled in quality in Riyadh.

At night, in the glow of oscillating reflections of light, the sails provide a vibrant urban setting for this 'nordsüdliche' or 'westöstliche Diwan' ('North-southern or 'West-eastern Divan') which, as if in a dream, has become an architectural reality.

Fassadenausschnitt mit den rautenförmigen Sonnenschutzsegeln | Detail of the façade with its diamond-shaped solar protection sails

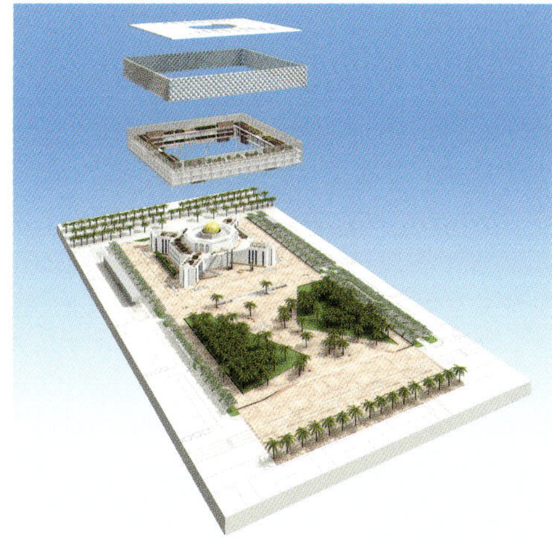

Die Isometrie verdeutlicht das Haus-im-Haus-Prinzip. The isometric diagram illustrates the house-within-a-house principle.

Blick wie in ein Regal über verschiedene Etagen | Bookcase-like view of the different storeys

ERHARD AN-HE KINZELBACH / KNOWSPACE

ATELIERHÄUSER
SONGZHUANG, CHINA

TEXT ZHI WENJUN, ZHOU ZEWO

24

ARCHITEKTEN | ARCHITECTS

**KNOWSPACE / Erhard An-He
Kinzelbach Architekt BDA
Prinzenstraße 85D
10969 Berlin
www.knowspace.eu**

MITARBEITER | TEAM

Manuela Wind

BAUHERR | CLIENT

Wang Xingwei, Qin Qi

AUSFÜHRUNGSPLANUNG
EXECUTION PLANNING

**KNOWSPACE / Erhard An-He
Kinzelbach Architekt BDA**

**BAULEITUNG /
PROJEKTSTEUERUNG**
SITE MANAGEMENT /
PROJECT MANAGEMENT

Qin Lichao

TRAGWERK UND BRANDSCHUTZ
STRUCTURE AND FIRE PREVENTION

Cao Shanghui

HAUSTECHNIK | M & E ENGINEERS

Cao Shanghui

FERTIGSTELLUNG | COMPLETION

Anfang | beginning of **2013**

STANDORT | LOCATION

**Songzhuang,
China**

FOTOS | PHOTOS

**Erhard An-He Kinzelbach
Zhou Zewo**

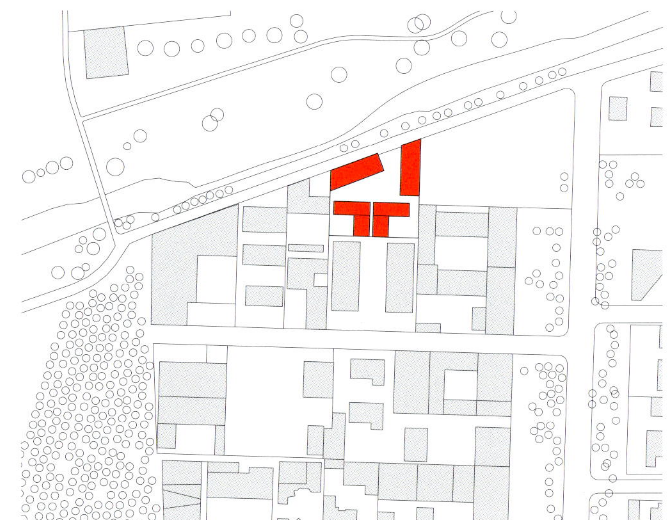

Lageplan | Site plan

Die Atelierhäuser in einem Künstlerdorf östlich von Beijing | The studio houses in an artists' colony east of Beijing

Ungefähr 30 Kilometer vom Platz des Himmlischen Friedens Richtung Osten, in Verlängerung der Changan-Straße und zwischen den beiden Quellflüssen des Kaiser-Kanals im Tong-Zhou-Bezirk liegt das Künstlerdorf Songzhuang. Im Jahr 1994 beschlossen mehrere bekannte chinesische Maler aus der Künstlerkolonie Yuanmingyuan in der Innenstadt Pekings nach Songzhuang zu ziehen, auf der Suche nach Ruhe und Raum für Kreativität. Heute ist es das größte Künstlerdorf Chinas. Es besitzt als typisches nordchinesisches Dorf noch immer seine traditionelle Struktur, die aus einer dichten, niedrigen Bebauung aus meist mit rotem Backstein ummauerten Höfen besteht. Die Bebauung folgt dem Typus des chinesischen Hofhauses. Jeder Haushalt hat einen eigenen Innenhof und alle Gebäudeöffnungen sind auf diesen Hof hin orientiert. Während dies zu einem sehr geschlossenen Eindruck von außen führt, bieten die Gebäude nach innen sehr viel Raum und Offenheit. Die Atelierhäuser des zurzeit in Berlin ansässigen Architekten Erhard An-He Kinzelbach gehören den Malern Wang Xingwei und Qin Qi. Durch gemeinsame Freunde lernten die beiden Maler Kinzelbachs Büro KNOWSPACE kennen und beauftragten es mit dem Entwurf und Bau dieses Projekts. Die Bauherren hatten eine klare Vorstellung über ihre räumlichen Bedürfnisse, ohne jedoch detaillierte Vorgaben zu machen: Es sollte ein Lebensraum für zwei Maler geschaffen werden, der zugleich

Approximately 30 kilometres to the east of Tiananmen Square, in a continuation of Chang'an Avenue and between the two source rivers of the Grand Canal in the Tongzhou District, lies the artists' community of Songzhuang. In 1994, a number of well-known Chinese painters from the Yuanmingyuan artists' colony in the centre of Beijing made the decision to relocate to Songzhuang in search of space and tranquillity for the pursuit of their creative goals. Today, it is the largest artists' community in China. It still maintains the structure of a typical northern Chinese village, consisting of a low, dense development of courtyards, mostly enclosed by red brick walls, in keeping with the traditional structure of the Chinese courtyard house. Each household has its own inner courtyard, and all of the openings in the building are oriented toward this court. While this creates an extremely closed-off appearance from the outside, the buildings provide a great deal of space and openness on the inside. The studio houses designed by architect Erhard An-He Kinzelbach, who is based in Berlin, belong to the painters Wang Xingwei and Qin Qi. The two artists became acquainted with

trennend als auch verbindend sein kann, und zwar sowohl in Hinblick auf die beiden Individuen als auch hinsichtlich der Funktionen des Wohnens und Arbeitens. Ein egalitäres Neben- und Miteinander von Außen- und Innenräumen war gewünscht. Der Gebäudekomplex liegt im Herzen des Künstlerdorfs. Da er im Norden nur durch einen Bach und Felder begrenzt wird, ergibt sich eine direkte Verbindung zur Landschaft. Wenn man sich von der Straße aus nähert, lassen die Gebäudeformen im Nebeneinander mit den Nachbarbauten ein außerordentliches Maß an Form- und Proportionsgefühl erkennen. Der Architekt bediente sich für seinen Entwurf der ortstypischen Materialität sowie Bauweise und wählte die Typologie des traditionellen chinesischen Hofhauses Siheyuan mit einer umschließenden Mauer als Ausgangspunkt der architektonischen Überlegungen. Zwei Baukörper mit den Arbeitsräumen gruppieren sich um die Nordseite des Grundstücks. Die gezackten Sheddach-Oberlichter gewährleisten eine gleichmäßige Belichtung. Zwei Wohnhöfe sind südorientiert und damit quasi wie von selbst von der Straße maximal abgeschieden. Die insgesamt vier separaten Baukörper sind zweigeschossig und orientieren sich in ihrer Ausrichtung an den Grundstücksgrenzen, die sich wiederum an den topografischen Bedingungen von Straße und Bach ausrichten. Daraus resultiert die versetzte Lage der beiden Atelierbaukörper und ein natürlicher Eingang zum Gebäude-

Kinzelbach's office, KNOWSPACE, through mutual friends, and offered the firm a commission to design and build this project. While not making any detailed specifications, the clients nevertheless had a clear idea of their spatial demands: the architects should create a living space for two painters which can both separate and connect them – as far as the two of them as individuals are concerned as well as in terms of its functions as a residential and work space. Their wish was for the egalitarian existence of exterior and interior spaces – side-by-side as well as shared.

The building complex is located in the heart of the artists' village. Bordered to the north only by fields and a stream, it is directly connected to the landscape. When one approaches from the street, the shapes of the buildings reveal an extraordinary sensitivity to form and proportion in relationship to the surrounding structures. In creating his design, the architect drew on the characteristic local materials and construction style, choosing the typology of the traditional Chinese siheyuan quadrangle house, with the surrounding wall as a starting point for his architectural concept. Two structures containing the workspaces are grouped together on the north side of the property. The zigzag sawtooth skylights provide uniform light exposure. The two residential courtyards face toward the south, shielding them more or less automatically from the street. There are a total of four separate two-storey buildings whose alignment is oriented toward the borders of the site, which in turn are aligned to the topographical constraints of the street and the brook. This creates a staggered positioning of the two studio structures and a natural entrance into the building complex. From the street, it appears closed and protected. Nevertheless, the expressive shapes of the roofs and the simplicity of the façades lend the complex an iconic character which provides clues to some of its functions and to the ensemble's identity.

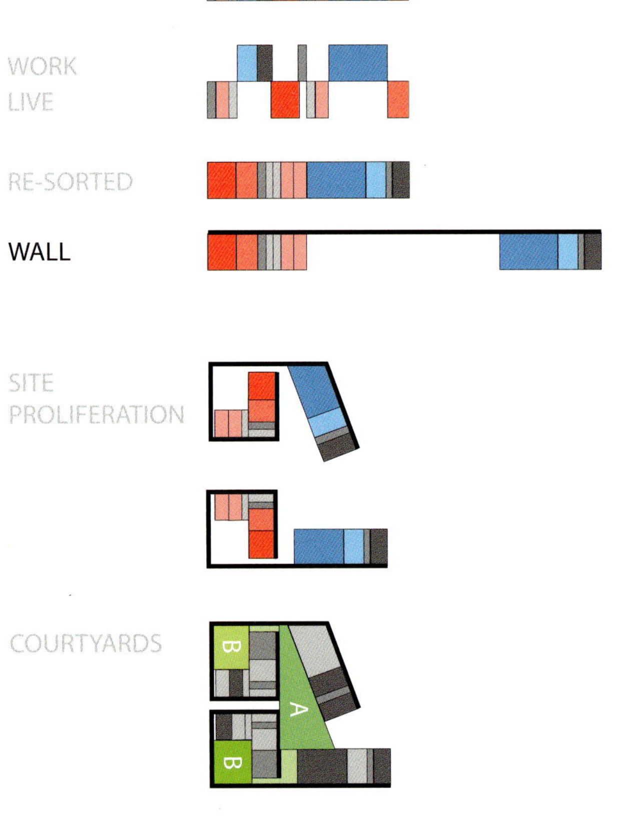

Das Raumprogramm: Wohnen, Arbeiten, Grünflächen
The spatial programme: living, working, green space

Grundriss Erdgeschoss | Plan of ground floor

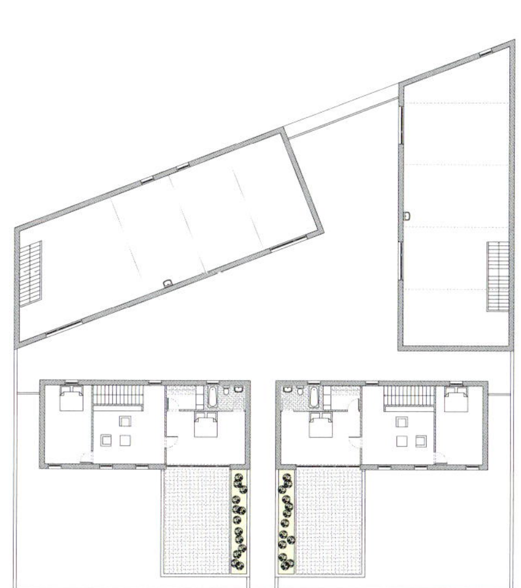

Grundriss Obergeschoss | Plan of upper floor

Die Häuser gruppieren sich um einen gemeinsamen und zwei individuelle Höfe. | The houses are grouped around one shared and two individual courtyards.

Atelierraum; durch die Sheddächer fällt gefiltertes Licht ins Innere.
Studio space: sawtooth skylights allow filtered light to enter.

Das Ensemble von außen und im Inneren
The ensemble from the outside and the inside

komplex. Dieser erscheint von der Straße aus geschlossen und geschützt. Die expressiven Dachformen und die Einfachheit der Fassade erzeugen jedoch einen ikonischen Charakter, der bereits Hinweise auf Teile seiner Funktion und die Identität des Ensembles gibt.

Der Architekt verfolgte in diesem Projekt eine Strategie der typologischen Transformation. Das Siheyuan mit seinen typischen offenen und geschlossenen Räumen wird dahingehend neu interpretiert, dass öffentlicher und privater Raum der Atelierhäuser in einem modernen Gebäudekomplex vereint werden und sich optimal in das dörfliche Gefüge eingliedern. Wie in dem Künstlerdorf üblich, wurden auch diese Ateliers von lokalen Bauern errichtet, so dass der Entwurf mit einfachen Techniken zu realisieren sein musste. Die Hauptproblematik der Entwurfsaufgabe war es, architektonisch zwischen Innen und Außen, Arbeiten und Wohnen und zwischen dem Individuum und der Gemeinschaft zu vermitteln.

Das schwierigste der drei Gegensatzpaare ist vermutlich das des Individuums und der Gemeinschaft. Wenn man zwischen den beiden Atelierhäusern den gemeinschaftlichen Hof betritt, erreicht man zunächst einen halb-öffentlichen Raum, die Schnittstelle zur Straße. Hier findet der gemeinschaftliche Teil des Lebens statt. Entlang der östlichen und westlichen Umschließungsmauern gelangt man jeweils in die spiralförmig vom Wohnhaus umschlossenen kleineren Innenhöfe. Ihr Charakter ist sehr privat. Nach Eintritt durch das Haupttor ergibt sich daher über die Folge der Hofräume ein kontinuierlicher und gradueller Übergang von der Öffentlichkeit der Straße bis hin zum Privaten des eigenen Wohnhauses.

Die Raumsequenz der Außenräume, die Nutzung der Hofräume, die Gassenbildung, das Falten der Umschließungsmauer, die Formensprache – all das sind schlussendlich die architektonischen Elemente, mit denen die typologische Transformation des Hofhaus-Typus und seine Überführung in einen zeitgenössischen Atelierhauskomplex vollzogen wird.

With this project, the architect followed a strategy of typological transformation. The siheyuan, with its typical open and closed spaces, is reinterpreted in such a way that the public and private spaces of the studio houses are united in a modern building complex and optimally integrated into the fabric of the village. As is customary in this artists' community, the studios were constructed by local farmers; therefore, the design needed to be realizable using simple techniques. The primary challenge of the design task was to mediate on an architectural level between interior and exterior, work and living, and between the individual and the community.

Probably the most difficult of these juxtapositions is that between the individual and the community. When you enter the shared courtyard between the two studio houses, you are first entering a semi-public space, the interface with the public street. This is where the communal part of life takes place. Following the eastern or western perimeter walls, you reach one of the small inner courtyards, enclosed in a spiral shape by the respective residential buildings. These are very private in character. Thus, after entering through the main gate, you experience – through the progression of the courtyard spaces – a gradual and continuous transition from the public sphere of the street to the private space of a person's own home.

The spatial sequence of the exterior spaces, the use of the courtyards, the creation of pathways, the folds of the perimeter wall, the formal structure – ultimately, all of these things are the architectural elements that complete the typological transformation of the traditional courtyard house into a contemporary studio-house complex.

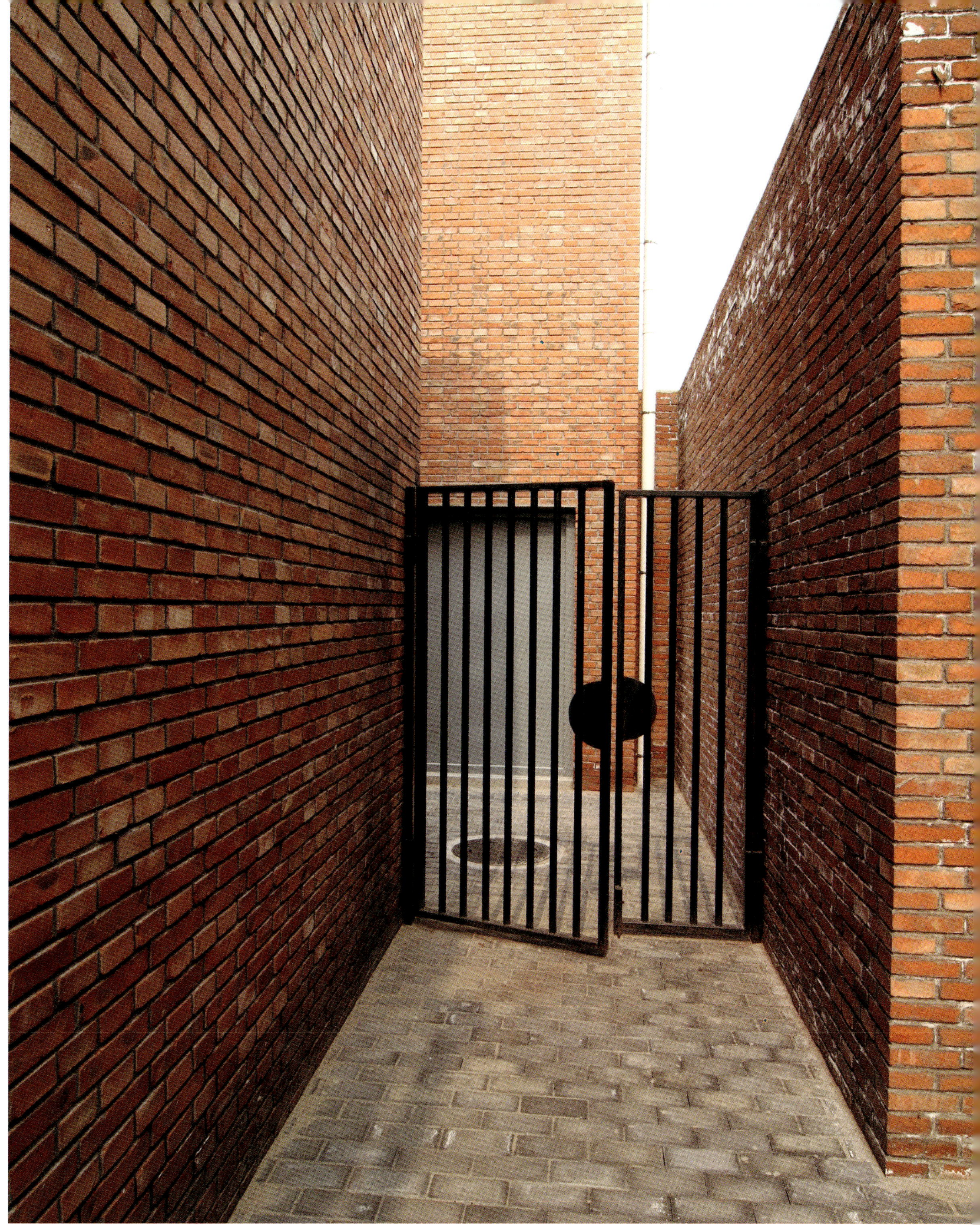

Eines der Hoftore | One of the courtyard gates

DAM JAHRESBERICHT 2014
DAM ANNUAL REPORT 2014

**Das Deutsche Architektur-
museum zeigte 2014
folgende Ausstellungen**
In 2014 the Deutsches
Architekturmuseum hosted
the following exhibitions

INTERFERENZEN
INTERFÈRENCES
Deutschland Frankreich
Architektur 1800–2000
02. 10. 2013 – 12. 01. 2014

DAM PREIS FÜR ARCHITEKTUR
IN DEUTSCHLAND 2013
Die 22 besten Bauten in/aus
Deutschland
DAM AWARD FOR ARCHITECTURE
IN GERMANY
The 22 best buildings in/from
Germany
01. 02. – 11. 05. 2014

MIES VAN DER ROHE PREIS |
AWARD **1988–2013**
Preis der Europäischen Union für
zeitgenössische Architektur
European Union Prize for
Contemporary Architecture
08. 02. – 20. 04. 2014

PLAYBOY ARCHITEKTUR
1953–1979
PLAYBOY ARCHITECTURE
1953–1979
15. 02. – 20. 04. 2014

EINE INTERKULTURELLE REISE
IN DIE GEBAUTE UMWELT
Ergebnisse zweier Schulprojekte
AN INTERCULTURAL JOURNEY
INTO THE BUILT ENVIRONMENT
Results of two school projects
27. 02. – 27. 04. 2014

MISSION: POSTMODERN
Heinrich Klotz und die
Wunderkammer DAM
Heinrich Klotz and the
Wunderkammer DAM
10. 05. – 19. 10. 2014

BRÜCKENSCHLAG OSTEND
Momentaufnahmen aus
nächster Nähe
BRIDGING OSTEND
Points of Time at closest Range
24. 05. – 24. 08. 2014

SUOMI SEVEN
Junge Architektur aus Finnland
Emerging Architects from Finland
06. 09. – 09. 11. 2014

HÄUSER DES JAHRES 2014
Die besten Einfamilienhäuser
BUILDINGS OF THE YEAR 2014
The best single-family dwellings
17. 09. 2014 – 19. 01. 2015

HOCHHAUSSTADT FRANKFURT
Bauten und Visionen seit 1945
HIGH-RISE CITY FRANKFURT
Buildings and visions since 1945
08. 11. 2014 – 19. 04. 2015

BEST HIGH-RISES 2014/15
Internationaler Hochhaus Preis
2014
International High-Rise Award 2014
20. 11. 2014 – 18. 01. 2015

SPRINGER
Digitales Arbeiten der Zukunft
Digital Working Spaces of the Future
01. 11. 2014 – 02. 02. 2015

Dauerausstellung im DAM
Permanent exhibition at the DAM

Von der Urhütte zum
Wolkenkratzer
From Primitive Hut to Skyscraper

**DAM Ausstellungen auf Tour
2014**
DAM touring exhibitions in 2014

BAUHAUS ZWANZIG-21
BAUHAUS Twenty-21
Memphis, Art Museum of the
University of Memphis
21. 09. 2013 – 04. 01. 2014
Bartlesville, Oklahoma USA,
Prize Tower Art Center
23. 01. – 04. 05. 2014

UNESCO WELTKULTURERBE
Eine Deutschlandreise
UNESCO WORLD HERITAGE
A Tour of Germany
Trier, Thermen am Viehmarkt
05. 10. 2013 – 05. 01. 2014

Dresden, Deutsche Werkstätten
Hellerau
23. 01. – 04. 04. 2014
Koblenz, Festung Ehrenbreitstein
13. 04. – 29. 06. 2014

IM BRENNPUNKT
FOCUS OF ATTENTION
Stuttgart, vhs-photogalerie
28. 11. 2013 – 31. 01. 2014
Kassel, KAZimKUBA
12. 02. – 23. 02. 2014
Gelsenkirchen, Wirtschaftspark
11. 04. – 21. 06. 2014

NOVE NOVOS – NEUN NEUE
Emerging Architects from Brazil
CIVA, Bruxelles
Oktober – Dezember 2014

GROSSE ARCHITEKTEN
Fotografiert von Ingrid von Kruse
EMINENT ARCHITECTS
Photographed by Ingrid von Kruse
Venezia, Palazzo Flangini
06. 06. – 28. 09. 2014

**Vortragsreihen und
Veranstaltungen**
Lecture Series and Events

STADTplus
DIE STADT + IHRE ANDERE SEITE
Christian Setzepfandt
05. 03. 2014

DIE STADT + DAS FEUER
Reinhard Ries
02. 04. 2014

DIE STADT + DER FUSSBALL
Michael Horeni
07. 05. 2014

DIE STADT + DIE 80ER
Claus-Jürgen Göpfert
04. 06. 2014

Freunde vor Ort
In Planung:
06 / 2014: Kindergarten Pesta-
lozzistraße, Hoidn Wang Partner
Führung DAM Archiv,
Europäische Zentralbank,
Taunus Tor

Baukultur ohne Wettbewerb?
Barbara Ettinger-Brinckman,
Brigitte Holz, Peter Cachola
Schmal, Felix Waechter, Kirsten
Worms, Alexander Wetzig
27. 01. 2014

**Medienpreis Architektur der
Vfa Hessen**
12. 02. 2014

**Baukultur – fächerübergreifend,
fächerverbindend**
Eva-Maria Kabisch, Stefan
Neuhaus, Christine Sauerbaum-
Thieme, Karlheinz Schaedler,
Kristina Hasenpflug
14. 03. 2014

Pecha Kucha Night
KN 030@ HfG
Hochschule für bildende Kunst,
Offenbach
04. 02. 2014

PKN 031@Luminale
Museum für Angewandte Kunst,
Frankfurt am Main
29. 03. 2014

ARCH+ FEATURE
Anh-Linh Ngo, Oliver Elser,
Myriam Pflugmann,
Franziska Stein
10. 05. 2014

Architektursommer Rhein-Main
ASRM 2015
Visionen für die Metropolregion
Rhein-Main
Visions for the Rhine Main Region
AWP Paris, feld72 Wien,
KCAP Rotterdam, Lola landscape
architects Rotterdam,
Magma Architecture Berlin,
SKT Umbauplan Bonn,
Superpool Istanbul, Urbed
Manchester & London
20. 05. 2014

**Exkursionen im Rahmen der
Ausstellung Mission: Postmodern**
TOUREN ZUR POSTMODERNE
Tour 1 City:
**17. 05. / 14. 06. / 28. 06. /
12. 07. / 20. 09. /
04. 10. 2014**

Tour 2 Museumsufer:
**24. 05. / 21. 06. / 05. 07. /
19. 06. / 27. 09. / 11. 10. 2014**

Sondertour Deutsche Bundesbank
Jourdan & Müller, Berghof
Landes Rang
27. 06. / 19. 09. 2014

BDB im DAM
Sonderführungen zu den
Ausstellungen des DAM
Yorck Förster
**23. 10. 2013 / 20. 11. 2013
12. 02. 2014 / 12. 03. 2014
09. 04. 2014**

**Verleihung Internationaler
Hochhauspreis 2014**
19. 11. 2014

Vorträge | Lectures

**Interferenzen. Abschied
von nationaler Architektur-
geschichte. Ein Erfahrungs-
bericht**
Jean-Louis Cohen, Hartmut Frank
08. 01. 2014

**Franco-German Romanticism
in Architecture 1830–1880**
Barry Bergdoll
12. 01. 2014

Mies van der Rohe Award 2013
Osbjørn Jacobsen, María Langarita
07. 02. 2014

**Hugh Hefner: Playboy,
Activist and Rebel**
Brigitte Berman
06. 03. 2014

**Territories of Poverty:
Urban Informality in a
Rearranged South-North
World**
Ananya Roy
17. 06. 2014

Dean´s Honory Lecture
Elisabeth Diller
03. 07. 2014

**Postmoderne der 1980er
Jahre in Frankfurt**
Oliver Elser
10. 07. 2014

**Panoptikum der Postmoderne.
Terry Gilliams Film „Brazil"
und sein Drehort,
Ricardo Bofills
„Les Espaces d'Abraxas"**
Anne Kockelkorn, ETH Zürich
16. 07. 2014

Symposien | Symposia

Media Facade Summit 2014
Hank Haeusler, Gernot Tscherteu,
Tapio Rosenius, Veronika Pauser,
Susanne Seitinger, Susa Pop,
Johan Bettum, Mirco Becker,
Alexander Wiethoff
02. 04. 2014

Ausstellung „Mies van der Rohe Preis 1988–2013" | 'Mies van der Rohe Award 1988–2013' exhibition

30. Geburtstag des DAM
Eduard Beaucamp, Roland
Burgard, Diethelm Fichtner,
Andrea Gleininger, Hans-Erhard
Haverkamp, Hans-Peter Schwarz
31. 05. 2014

**Architekturvermittlung
für Kinder / Jugendliche /
Erwachsene**
Education in architecture for
children / young people / adults

LegoBaustelle im DAM
26. 07. – 31. 08. 2014

Bauakademie im DAM
27. 10. – 30. 10. 2014

Bauwerkstatt im DAM
14. 06. 2014
12. 07. 2014
14. 09. 2014
12. 10. 2014
02. 11. 2014
14. 12. 2014

Satourday
Wunderkammer!
28. 06. 2014

Architektur-Marken
29. 11. 2014

Raumwaben
25. 10. 2014

Projekte: „Architekturmuseum
macht Schule", Museum in a Box
Paul-Hindemith-Schule,
Frankfurt am Main
15. 01. – 17. 12. 2014

Stadtteildetektive – Kinder
entdecken ihr Frankfurt
Henri-Dunant-Schule,
Frankfurt am Main
16. 05. – 28. 05. 2014

Gruneliusschule,
Frankfurt am Main
Herbst 2014

Joblinge machen Architektur,
im DAM
02. 06. – 06. 06. 2014

Raum für Kunst
Otto-Hahn-Schule
Frankfurt am Main
30. 06. – 12. 07. 2014

10 ArchitekturTage + 1 BauWoche
+ 1 AusStellung
Herbst 2014

Modellbau! Kann ich das auch?
Musterschule Frankfurt am Main
21. 07. – 25. 07. 2014

**Fortbildungen für Lehrkräfte
und andere Interessierte**
Seminars for teachers and other
interested persons

Architektur kommunizieren –
Formen in Raum und Stadt
23. 06. 2014

Expressionismus
27. 09. 2014

Was ist postmoderne
Architektur?
04. 10. 2014

Architektur vor Ort
Postmodern. Saalgasse revisited
Arne Winkelmann
09. 07. 2014

**Folgende Kataloge und
Veröffentlichungen sind
erschienen**
The following catalogues and
books have been published

NOVE NOVOS – NEUN NEUE
Emerging Architects from Brazil
Hrsg. | ed. **Peter Cachola
Schmal, Ricardo Ohtake,
Anna Scheuermann,
Fernando Serapião**
Jovis Verlag, Berlin
Mit Beiträgen von | with text
contributions by: **Peter Cachola
Schmal, Ricardo Ohtake,
Fernando Serapião**

Playboy architecture 1953–1979
Texte | texts: **Beatriz Colomina**
NAIM / Bureau Europa, Maastricht

**Die Klotz-Tapes. Das Making-of
der Postmoderne**
The Klotz tapes. The making of
postmodernism
Arch + Verlag, Aachen
Mit Beiträgen von | with
articles by: **Nikolaus Kuhnert /
Anh-Linh Ngo, Franziska
Stein, Jasper Cepl, Julia Voss,
Oliver Elser / Simon Schulz,
Heinrich Klotz**

Suomi Seven
Emerging Architects from Finland
Hrsg. | ed. **Peter Cachola
Schmal, Anna Scheuermann,
Juulia Kauste**
MFA, Helsinki
Mit Beiträgen von | with
contributions by: **Ulf Meyer,
Christophe Pourtois**

Hochausstadt Frankfurt
Hrsg. | ed. **Peter Cachola
Schmal, Philipp Sturm,**
Mit Beiträgen von | with
contributions by:
**Peter Cachola Schmal, Philipp
Sturm, Michael Kummer,
Dieter von Lüpke, Loïse Lenne,
Marianne Rodenstein, Matthias
Alexander, Evelyn Steiner**

20 Best Highrises 2014/15
**Internationaler Hochhaus
Preis** | International Highrise
Award 2014
Hrsg. | ed. **Peter Cachola
Schmal, Peter Körner**

Ausstellung „Playboy Architektur 1953–1979" | 'Playboy Architecture 1953–1979' exhibition

Ausstellung „Mission: Postmodern. Heinrich Klotz und die Wunderkammer DAM"
'Mission: Postmodern. Heinrich Klotz and the DAM's Chamber of Wonders' exhibition

Erschienen im | published by:
Prestel Verlag, München
Mit Beiträgen von | with
contributions by: **Peter Cachola
Schmal, Stefano Boeri, Corinne
Elsesser, Peter Körner etc.**

**DEUTSCHES ARCHITEKTUR
JAHRBUCH 2014/15**
German Architecture Annual 2014/15
Hrsg. | ed. **Peter Cachola
Schmal, Yorck Förster,
Christina Gräwe**
Erschienen im | published by:
Prestel Verlag München
Deutsch / Englisch
German / English

**Zu den wichtigsten Neuer-
werbungen des DAM zählen**
The DAM's most important new
acquisitions include

**architekturbild. Europäischer
Architekturfotografie-Preis**
**prämierte Wettbewerbsbei-
träge der Jahrgänge 2009
und 2011**
Schenkung | donation by
architekturbild e. V., Stuttgart

FAR frohn & rojas, Berlin
Modell | model
**Temporärer Sitz des
Goethe-Instituts,
Santiago de Chile, 2011**
Schenkung Architekten |
donation by architects

Rolf Janke, München
Fotoabzüge und Dias
Schenkung | donation by
Rolf Janke

**Firmenarchiv RoLu Normbau,
Rottenburg / Neckar**
Schenkung | donation by
Rosemarie Lupfer-Meyer

Nachlass Walter A. Noebel
Schenkung | donation by
Irina Noebel, Berlin

**Charles Percier, Pierre Francois
Léonard Fontaine**
Druck | print
Anlage der Rue de Rivoli
Ankauf | purchase

**Endo Shuhei Architect Institute,
Osaka**
Modell | model
Rooftecture S, 2006
Schenkung Architekt |
donation by architect

Simon Ungers
Druck | print
Pan Am Projekt, Manhattan
Schenkung | donation by
Helge Bofinger, Wiesbaden

Haus-Rucker-Co., Wien
Zeichnung | drawing
**Kunstprojekt „Matterhorn",
Kunstverein
Braunschweig, 1974**
Ankauf der Gesellschaft

**der Freunde des DAM
Dauerleihgabe** | permanent
loan

Giorgio Grassi, Mailand
**Lichtprint, signiert
Abbiategrasso Castello, 1980
Ankauf der Gesellschaft der
Freunde des DAM
Dauerleihgabe** | permanent loan

James Wolfson
300 Zeichnungen | drawings
Schenkung | donation by
Stephen Farthing, London

Hans Peter Petri, Wien
3 Zeichnungen | drawings
Schenkung Architekt |
donation by architect

**9 Modellschenkungen zur
Ausstellung**
Nove Novos – Neun Neue
Arquitetos Associados.
Belo Horizonte – Minas Gerais
Burle Marx Bildungszentrum,
Brumadinho, 2006–09

BMCF Arquitetos,
Belo Horizonte – Minas Gerais
**Nationales Schießsport-
zentrum PAN,** Rio de Janeiro,
2005–07

Carla Juçaba, Rio de Janeiro
Humanidade 2012 Pavillon,
Rio de Janeiro, 2011–12

Corsi Hirano Arquitetos,
São Paulo
TRT Landesarbeitsgericht,
Goiânia, 2007–12

**Jacobsen Arquitetura,
Gávea ML Residenz,**
Porto Feliz, 2008–10

Metro Arquitetos Associados,
São Paulo
Nestlé Schokoladenmuseum,
Caçapava, 2009–11

**Nitsche Arquitetos
Associados,** São Paulo
**João Moura 1144
Bürogebäude,** São Paulo,
2008–12

Rizoma, Belo Horizonte
Lygia Pape Galerie,
Brumadinho, 2010–12

Studio Paralelo, Porto Alegre
Hauptsitz CREA-PB, Campina
Grande, 2010–12

ARCHITEKTURPREISE
ARCHITECTURAL AWARDS

Das DAM ist an der Auslobung wichtiger Architekturpreise beteiligt: Seit 2007 zeichnet das DAM eines der im Deutschen Architektur Jahrbuch präsentierten Bauten mit dem DAM Preis für Architektur in Deutschland aus. Die Auszeichnung für das beste Gebäude 2007 wurde an Wandel Hoefer Lorch & Hirsch aus Saarbrücken für die Gedenkstätte Hinzert, 2008 an Peter Zumthor aus Chur für das Kölner Kolumba Museum, 2009 an Barkow Leibinger aus Berlin für das Betriebsrestaurant Trumpf in Ditzingen, 2010 an David Chipperfield Architects aus Berlin für das Neue Museum Berlin, 2011 an Diener & Diener-Architekten aus Berlin für das Naturkundemuseum Berlin, 2012 an Max Dudler Architekten aus Berlin für den Um- und Weiterbau des Hambacher Schlosses, 2013 an Lederer Ragnarsdóttir Oei für das Kunstmuseum Ravensburg und 2014 an Hess Talhof Kusmierz für die Grundschule am Arnulfpark in München verliehen.

Der Internationale Hochhaus Preis (IHP) wird seit 2004 alle zwei Jahre von der Stadt Frankfurt am Main vergeben. Initiiert und organisiert wird er in partnerschaftlicher Kooperation vom DAM und der DekaBank, die außerdem den IHP finanziert. 2004 gewannen KPF Europe für De Hoftoren in Den Haag, 2006 Jean Nouvel aus Paris für Torre Agbar in Barcelona, 2008 Foster and Partners, London, für Hearst Headquarters in New York, 2010 WOHA aus Singapur für The Met in Bangkok und 2012 ingenhoven architects aus Düsseldorf & Architectus aus Sydney für „1 Bligh Street" in Sydney. Der Preis besteht aus einer Statue des Künstlers Thomas Demand und einem Geldpreis von 50 000 Euro.

Der Europäische Architekturfotografie-Preis, alle zwei Jahre ausgelobt, wurde 2013 zum zehnten Mal vergeben. Zum dritten Mal fanden die Preisverleihung und die Ausstellung der besten Wettbewerbsbeiträge im DAM statt, denn seit 2008 kooperieren der Auslober architekturbild e. v. und das DAM. Aus Anlass der zehnten Preisverleihung fand im DAM eine große Ausstellung statt, die neben dem aktuellen auch einen Querschnitt aller Preisträger der letzten 20 Jahre zeigte.

Der DAM Architekturbuchpreis wurde 2012 zum vierten Mal vergeben. Er wird jährlich gemeinsam mit der Frankfurter Buchmesse ausgelobt und zu diesem Zeitpunkt verliehen. Die zehn Preisträger 2013 waren:
A Blessing in Disguise – War and Town Planning in Europe 1940 – 45. Jan Düwel, Niels Gutschow, Dom publishers, Berlin / Borrowed City. Hyunji Lee, Junki Jeong, Dambdi Publishing Publishing, Seoul / Bürgermeisterzimmer in Deutschland. Jörg Winde, Kerber Verlag, Bielefeld / City of God, Marc Angélil, Rainer Hehl mit Something Fantastic, Ruby Press, Berlin / Conrete – Fotografie und Architektur. Daniela Janser, Thomas Seelig, Urs Stahel, Scheidegger & Spiess, Zürich / Simón Vélez Architecte / La Maitrise Du Bamboo. Jean-Paul Capitani, Actes Sud, Arles / Mensa im Park – Vom Gebrauchen und Verbrauchen Jüngster Architektur. Florian Kirfel, Moritz Fritz, M Books, Weimar / Stadt entwerfen. Grundlagen – Prinzipien – Projekte. Leonard Schenk, Birkhäuser de Gruyter, Berlin / Unbuildable Tatlin!? Klaus Bollinger, Florian Medicus, Springer, Wien, New York / The Western Town. Alex Lehnerer, ETH Zürich, Hatje Cantz, Ostfildern.

Bereits zum vierten Mal findet die Zusammenarbeit des DAM mit dem Callwey Verlag beim Preis „Häuser des Jahres" statt, der an die schönsten Einfamilienhäuser in Deutschland, Österreich, Schweiz und Südtirol vergeben wird. 2011 wurde der Preis an Ruinelli Associati, Soglio, für ein Haus in Soglio, 2012 an Daniele Marques, Luzern, für „Drei Einfamilienhäuser in Luzern" und 2013 an HHF, Basel, mit einem Haus in Nuglar verliehen. Preisträger 2014 ist Thomas Kröger, Berlin, für das Werkhaus Schütze in Gerswalde. Die Verleihung fand am 16. 09. 2014 im DAM statt. Auszeichnungen gingen an A1I et al, München (Haus Gemini, Weissenbach), Thomas Kröger, Berlin (Haus Pinnow), Gian Salis, Zürich (Haus, Wyhlen), Think (Vier Hofhäuser, Zumikon). Anerkennungen gingen an Bearth + Deplazes, Zürich (Haus, Schaan), bergmeisterwolf, Brixen (Hanghaus, Brixen), Bernardo Bader, Dornbirn (Haus, Krumbach), clavienrossier, Genf (Haus, Genf).

Das DAM ist seit 2010 Mitglied des wissenschaftlichen Beirats und der Jury für den alle zwei Jahre verliehenen European Prize for Public Urban Space vom Centre of Contemporary Culture of Barcelona (CCCB). Gemeinsame Preisträger 2014 waren Michael Desvigne Paysagiste MDP mit Foster and Partners, Tangram, INGEROP und AIK AIK für die Sanierung des Alten Hafens von Marseille und Grupo Aranea, Alicante, für „The Braided Valley" in Elche, Spanien.

Das DAM ist außerdem Mitglied des Steering Committees für den EU Mies van der Rohe Preis für zeitgenössische Architektur in Europa. Der Preis 2013 ging an Henning Larsen Architects, Kopenhagen und Batteríid architects, Reykjavik; sowie Studio Olafur Eliasson, Berlin, für das Harpa – Concert Hall & Conference Centre in Reykjavik. Der Nachwuchspreis wurde Langarita-Navarro Arquitectos, Madrid, für die Red Bull Music Academy / Nave De Música Matadero in Madrid verliehen.

The DAM (German Architecture Museum) participates in the awarding of some important architecture prizes: Since 2007, the DAM has selected one of the projects presented in the German Architecture Annual to receive the DAM Award for Architecture in Germany. The award for the best building in 2007 went to Wandel Hoefer Lorch & Hirsch from Saarbrücken for their Hinzert Memorial, in 2008 to Peter Zumthor from Chur for the Kolumba Museum in Cologne, in 2009 to Barkow Leibinger from Berlin for the Trumpf company restaurant in Ditzingen, in 2010 to David Chipperfield Architects from Berlin for the Neues Museum Berlin, in 2011 to Diener & Diener Architekten from Berlin for the Natural History Museum in Berlin, in 2012 to Max Dudler Architekten from Berlin for the conversion and enlargement of Hambach Castle, in 2013 to Lederer Ragnarsdóttir Oei for the Kunstmuseum Ravensburg, and in 2014 to Hess Talhof Kusmierz for the Grundschule am Arnulfpark in Munich. The city of Frankfurt am Main has awarded its International Highrise Award every second year since 2004. The award is initiated and organized in partnership with the DAM and DekaBank, which also funds the IHP. In 2004, the winner was KPF Europe for the Hoftoren in The Hague, in 2006 Jean Nouvel from Paris for the Torre Agbar in Barcelona, in 2008 Foster and Partners of London for the Hearst Headquarters in New York, in 2010 WOHA of Singapore for The Met in Bangkok, and in 2012 ingenhoven architects from Düsseldorf & Architectus from Sydney for '1 Bligh Street' in Sydney. The prize consists of a statue by the artist Thomas Demand and a cash award of 50,000 euros.

The European Architectural Photography Prize, awarded every two years, was presented for the tenth time in 2013. For the third time,

the awards ceremony and exhibition of the best competition entries took place at the DAM, which joined architekturbild e.v. as co-sponsor of the award in 2008. In celebration of the tenth presentation of the award, a large exhibition was held at the DAM which, in addition to the current entries, displayed a cross-section of all the winners from the past 20 years.

The DAM Architectural Book Award was presented for the fifth time in 2013. Prizes are awarded annually in partnership with the Frankfurt Book Fair and coinciding with that event. The ten winners for 2013 were:

'A Blessing in Disguise – War and Town Planning in Europe 1940-45', Jan Düwel, Niels Gutschow, Dom publishers, Berlin; 'Borrowed City', Hyunji Lee, Junki Jeong, Dambdi Publishing, Seoul; 'Bürgermeister-zimmer in Deutschland', Jörg Winde, Kerber Verlag, Bielefeld; 'City of God', Marc Angélil, Rainer Hehl with Something Fantastic, Ruby Press, Berlin; 'Concrete – Fotografie und Architektur', Daniela Janser, Thomas Seelig, Urs Stahel, Scheidegger & Spiess, Zürich; 'Simón Vélez Architecte / La Maitrise Du Bambou', Jean-Paul Capitani, Actes Sud, Arles; 'Mensa im Park – Vom Gebrauchen und Verbrauchen Jüngster Architektur', Florian Kirfel, Moritz Fritz, M Books, Weimar; 'Stadt entwerfen. Grundlagen – Prinzipien – Projekte', Leonard Schenk, Birkhäuser de Gruyter, Berlin; 'Unbuildable Tatlin?!' Klaus Bollinger, Florian Medicus, Springer, Vienna, New York; 'The Western Town', Alex Lehnerer, ETH Zürich, Hatje Cantz, Ostfildern.

For the fourth time this year, the DAM co-operated with Callwey Verlag in presenting the Houses of the Year award, which is bestowed on the most beautiful single-occupancy homes in Germany, Austria, Switzerland and South Tyrol. In 2011, the prize was awarded to Ruinelli Associati from Soglio for a house in Soglio, in 2012 to Daniele Marques of Lucerne for 'Three Single-Family Homes in Lucerne', and in 2013 to HHF, Basel for a house in Nuglar. The winner for 2014 is Thomas Kröger of Berlin for the Werkhaus Schütze in Gerswalde. The awards ceremony took place on 16 September 2014 at the DAM. Prizes were awarded to AI1 et al from Munich for Haus Gemini in Weissen-bach, Thomas Kröger of Berlin for a house in Pinnow, Gian Salis of Zürich for a house in Wyhlen, and Think for four courtyard houses in Zumikon. Special mentions were given to Bearth + Deplazes of Zürich for a house in Schaan, bergmeisterwolf of Brixen for a hillside house in Brixen, Bernardo Bader of Dornbirn for a house in Krumbach, and clavienrossier of Geneva for a house in Geneva.

Since 2010, the DAM has been a member of the board of experts and jury of the European Prize for Public Urban Space, which was founded by the Centre of Contemporary Culture of Barcelona (CCCB) and is awarded every two years. The joint winners in 2014 were Michael Desvigne Paysagiste MDP with Foster and Partners, Tangram, INGEROP and AIK AIK for the renovation of the old port in Marseille and Grupo Aranea, Alicante for 'The Braided Valley' in Elche, Spain. In addition, the DAM is a member of the steering committee for the EU Mies van der Rohe Award for Contemporary Architecture in Europe. In 2013, the prize was awarded to Henning Larsen Architects of Copenhagen and Batterííd Architects of Reykjavik, along with Studio Olafur Eliasson of Berlin, for the Harpa – Concert Hall & Conference Centre in Reykjavik. The award for young talent went to Langarita-Navarro Arquitectos of Madrid for the Red Bull Music Academy / Nave De Música Matadero in Madrid.

DAM SPONSOREN 2014
DAM SPONSORS 2014

Hessische Kulturstiftung, Wiesbaden
Gemeinnützige kulturfonds frankfurt rhein-main GmbH, Bad Homburg v. d. Höhe
DekaBank Deutsche Girozentrale, Frankfurt am Main
FUNARTE & Ministério da Cultura (MinC), Rio de Janeiro
Gesellschaft der Freunde des Deutschen Architekturmuseums e. V., Frankfurt am Main
Finnish Literature Exchange und FINNLAND. COOL.
aurelis Real Estate GmbH & Co. KG, Eschborn
Grundstücksgesellschaft Gateway Gardens GmbH, Frankfurt am Main
Helaba – Landesbank Hessen-Thüringen Girozentrale, Frankfurt am Main
Tishman Speyer, Frankfurt am Main
ACTRIS Grundstückverwaltungsgesellschaft mbH & Co., Frankfurt am Main
Architekten- und Stadtplanerkammer, Wiesbaden
Stiftung Polytechnische Gesellschaft, Frankfurt am Main
HOCHTIEF Projektentwicklung GmbH, Niederlassung Rhein-Main, Frankfurt am Main
s.boehme & co. KGaA, Frankfurt am Main
Bundesministerium für Verkehr, Bau und Stadtentwicklung (BMVBS), Berlin
Bundesministerium für Forschung und Wissenschaft, Berlin
Wüstenrot Stiftung, Ludwigsburg
Commerz Real AG, Wiesbaden
DIC Deutsche Immobilien Chancen AG & Co. KGaA, Frankfurt am Main
KP Investments, Hoevelaken
Messe Frankfurt GmbH, Frankfurt am Main
Hessischer Museumsverband, Wiesbaden
Förderverein der Walter-Kolb-Schule, Frankfurt am Main
Kooperationspool der Stadt Frankfurt am Main
Europäische Zentralbank, Frankfurt am Main
Nassauische Heimstätte, Frankfurt am Main
GLL Real Estate Partners GmbH, Frankfurt am Main

UND FOLGENDE UNTERSTÜTZER
AND THE FOLLOWING SUPPORTERS

Frankfurter Buchmesse, Frankfurt am Main
DESERVE GbR Raum und Medien Design, Wiesbaden
inditec Display & Messegestaltung GmbH, Bad Camberg

GESELLSCHAFT DER FREUNDE DES DAM
THE SOCIETY OF FRIENDS OF THE DAM

Die Gesellschaft der Freunde des Deutschen Architekturmuseums e.V. wurde im Jahr 1985 als eingetragener Verein ins Leben gerufen. Das Hauptanliegen dieser Gesellschaft ist es, das Deutsche Architekturmuseum, Frankfurt am Main, (DAM) in der Verwirklichung seiner öffentlichen Aufgaben ideell und materiell zu unterstützen und zu fördern.

Zu den Aufgaben und Zielen des Vereins gehören:
— Vermittlung, Ankauf und Überlassung von Plänen, Zeichnungen und Modellen deutscher und internationaler Architektur-Projekte und Architekten-Nachlässe bzw. –Vorlässe mit dem Ziel der wissenschaftlichen Bearbeitung und öffentlichkeitswirksamen Vermittlung der Arbeitsergebnisse durch das DAM. Vorhaltung eines großen Kontingents von Dauerleihgaben an das Archiv des DAM.
— Unterstützung bei der Planung, Vorbereitung und Durchführung von Ausstellungen, Auktionen, Veranstaltungen und anderen anstehenden Aufgaben. Einer der Schwerpunkte ist u. a. die Jugendarbeit / Museumspädagogik und die Architekturvermittlung.
— Herstellung von Kontakten zu Personen, Institutionen und Wirtschaftsunternehmen, die für die partnerschaftliche Unterstützung von Aktivitäten des DAM in Frage kommen.
— Unterstützung des DAM bei verschiedenen Maßnahmen im Rahmen der Öffentlichkeitsarbeit.
— Vorhaltung und Überlassung einer Wohnung für Praktikanten.

Mitglieder in diesem Verein sind Personen, Institutionen und Firmen, deren Anliegen es ist, einen Beitrag zur Förderung der Qualität der gebauten Umwelt zu leisten. Der Vorstand wird jeweils über einen Zeitraum von fünf Jahren von der Mitgliederversammlung gewählt. Er setzt sich aus Persönlichkeiten aus den Bereichen Wirtschaft, Politik, Bildung, Bankwesen und Kultur zusammen. Dadurch ist gewährleistet, dass Informationen und Kontakte aus den unterschiedlichsten Bereichen zugunsten der Ziele der Gesellschaft der Freunde des DAM genutzt werden können. Um einen intensiven Kontakt zu den Mitgliedern sicherzustellen, wird jährlich mindestens eine Versammlung durchgeführt, anschließend findet eine Sonderführung durch die laufende Ausstellung statt.

Wie Sie sich vorstellen können, erfordern die Aktivitäten der Gesellschaft in hohem Maße Geld, Ideen, ehrenamtliches Engagement und Idealismus. Unterstützen Sie uns bei unserem Vorhaben! Als Mitglied erhalten Sie das Jahrbuch des DAM bei Abholung unentgeltlich; auf alle anderen Publikationen des DAM erhalten Sie mit Ihrem Ausweis 20 % Rabatt. Nur als Mitglied können Sie an speziellen Previews und Sonderführungen teilnehmen. Die Jahresgaben der Gesellschaft 1998 bis 2005 erhalten Sie zu einem Vorzugspreis. Es werden Architekturreisen für die Mitglieder angeboten.

Der Jahresmitgliedsbeitrag beträgt 95,00 EUR für Einzelmitglieder, für Studenten 50,00 EUR und für juristische Personen und Personenvereinigungen 920,00 EUR.

Vorstand: Marietta Andreas (Vorsitz), Prof. Johann Eisele (Stellvertretender Vorsitz), Martin Seelinger (Schatzmeister), Stefan Boehme, Michael Bahrenberg, Barbara Ettinger-Brinckmann, Kaspar Kraemer, Florian Schlüter, Fritz Straub, Francois Valentiny, Prof. Dr. Martin Wentz

The Society of Friends of the Deutsches Architekturmuseum was founded in 1985 as a registered non-profit organisation. The society's main objective is to support and promote the Deutsches Architekturmuseum, Frankfurt/Main (DAM) both intellectually and materially in the execution of its public duties.

The organization's duties and aims include:
— The mediation, purchase, and sale of plans, drawings and models of German and international architecture projects and architects' estates and bequeathals for the purpose of scientific handling as well as the effective public dissemination of the results of DAM's work. A large contingent of permanent loans is housed in the DAM archive.
— Support in the planning, preparation and realization of exhibitions, auctions, events and other ongoing tasks. Focuses here include youth outreach and museum education.
— Establishing contact with persons, institutions and companies that come into question as potential partners for the support of DAM's activities.
— Supporting DAM with various PR-related measures.
— Maintaining an apartment for use by interns.

The organisation's members include persons, institutions and firms that are committed to making a contribution to improving the quality of our constructed environment. The Board of Directors is elected for a period of five years by the General Meeting of the members. It is made up of representatives from the worlds of business, politics, education, banking and culture. This ensures that information from and contacts with a wide range of fields can be put to maximum use in furthering the objectives of the Society of Friends of DAM. In order to keep in close contact with members, at least one General Meeting is held every year. It is followed by a special guided tour of the exhibition on show at the time.

As you can imagine, the Society's activities require a large amount of money, ideas, voluntary work and idealism. Why not support us in our objectives! As a member you will receive the DAM Annual free of charge when you pick it up yourself, as well as a 20% discount on all other DAM publications on presentation of your membership card. Only society members are entitled to attend special previews and take part in special tours. You can also obtain the society's annual gifts from 1998 until 2005 at a reduced rate. Architecture-related trips are organized for members.

Annual membership costs 95 EUR for private members, 50 EUR for students and 920 EUR for corporate bodies and associations.

The Board: Marietta Andreas (Chairperson), Prof. Johann Eisele
(Deputy Chairperson), Martin Seelinger (Treasurer), Stefan Boehme,
Michael Bahrenberg, Barbara Ettinger-Brinckmann, Kaspar Kraemer,
Florian Schlüter, Fritz Straub, Francois Valentiny, Prof. Martin Wentz

Kontakt | Contact

Gesellschaft der Freunde des Deutschen Architekturmuseums e. V.
Geschäftsstelle | Office**: Deutsches Architekturmuseum**
Schaumainkai 43
60596 Frankfurt am Main
Deutschland | Germany
Telefon | Tel.**:   +49 (0) 69 - 97 20 33 66**
Mobil | Mobile**: +49 (0) 178 - 447 53 63**
E-Mail: freundeskreis.dam@stadt-frankfurt.de
http://www.dam-online.de/ Freunde

Bankverbindung | Bank account

Commerzbank, Frankfurt am Main
Konto-Nr. | Account number**: 198 041 500**
BLZ | Sorting code**: 500 800 00**
IBAN DE83 5008 0000 0198 0415 00
BIC DRESDEFFXXX

Die Gesellschaft dankt folgenden Personen und Institutionen,
die sich in besonderem Maße engagiert haben:
We would like to thank our special sponsors:

ALLMANN SATTLER WAPPNER.ARCHITEKTEN, München
A N P Architektur- und Planungsgesellschaft mbH, Kassel
ARCTEC GmbH Design-Planung-Consulting, Frankfurt am Main
Architekten- und Stadtplanerkammer Hessen, Wiesbaden
Artemide GmbH, Fröndenberg
aurelis Real Estate GmbH, Eschborn/Taunus
Bauverlag BV GmbH, Gütersloh
Beton Marketing Süd GmbH, Ostfildern
s.boehme & Co. KgaA, Frankfurt am Main
Bund Deutscher Architekten im Lande Hessen e. V.,
Frankfurt am Main
Bund Deutscher Baumeister, Architekten und Ingenieure e. V.,
Berlin-Steglitz
cornelsen + seelinger architekten, Darmstadt, Berlin, Amsterdam
Deutsche Werkstätten Hellerau GmbH, Dresden
Dornbracht Deutschland GmbH & Co. KG, Iserlohn
ernst-may-gesellschaft e. V., Frankfurt am Main
Frankfurter Allgemeine Zeitung, Frankfurt am Main
Gainestranslations, Frankfurt am Main
Hentrich-Petschnigg & Partner GmbH & Co. KG, Düsseldorf
HERMANN & VALENTINY et Associés, Remerschen, Luxembourg
und Wien, Österreich
HOCHTIEF Projektentwicklung GmbH, Niederlassung Rhein-Main,
Frankfurt am Main
House of Logistics & Mobility (HOLM) GmbH, Frankfurt am Main
Prof. Dr.-Ing. Katzenbach GmbH, Ingenieursozietät,
Frankfurt am Main

Kunst- und Auktionshaus Wilhelm M. Döbritz, Frankfurt am Main
Landes & Partner, Michael Landes Architekt, Frankfurt am Main
MEIXNER SCHLÜTER WENDT Architekten, Frankfurt am Main
Nassauische Heimstätte Wohnungs- und Entwicklungsges.mbH,
Frankfurt am Main
netzwerkarchitekten, Darmstadt
schneider+schumacher, Architekten Frankfurt am Main und
Wien, Österreich
STEFAN FORSTER ARCHITEKTEN, Frankfurt am Main
Treuhandverwaltung IGEMET GmbH, Frankfurt am Main
unit Gesellschaft für Projektentwicklung mbH, Darmstadt
WENTZ & CO. GmbH, Frankfurt am Main
Xella International GmbH, Duisburg-Ruhrort

AUTOREN KURZBIOGRAFIEN
SHORT BIOGRAPHIES OF THE AUTHORS

PAUL ANDREAS

***1973 in Wolfsburg.
Kunsthistoriker und Kultur-
wissenschaftler M. A. Seit
2000 Journalist, Autor und
Publizist zu Themen der
Architektur und des Designs,
vor allem für die „Neue
Zürcher Zeitung", Fach-
und Publikumszeitschriften,
den Hörfunk sowie diverse
Ausstellungspublikationen.
2007–10 Leitung der Presse-
und Öffentlichkeitsarbeit des
DAM, dabei auch Kurator
der Ausstellungen über
Oscar Niemeyer und Tezuka
Architects. Lebt und arbeitet
in Düsseldorf.**

Born 1973 in Wolfsburg.
Art historian and cultural scholar,
M.A. Since 2000 journalist,
author and publicist specializing
in architecture and design,
especially for the 'Neue Zürcher Zeitung', professional and
popular magazines, radio and
various exhibition publications.
From 2007–10 head of Press
and Public Relations at the DAM,
during which time he also served
as curator of the Oscar Niemeyer
and Tezuka Architects exhibitions.
Lives and works in Düsseldorf.

WOLFGANG BACHMANN

***1951 in Ludwigshafen/Rhein.
Studium der Agrarwissen-
schaften und Architektur.
Diplom 1976 an der RWTH
Aachen. Dissertation über die
Architektur der Anthroposo-
phen. Drei Jahre Berufspraxis
in verschiedenen Architektur-
und Ingenieurbüros, beglei-
tend journalistische Tätigkeit.
1982 Redakteur der Zeit-
schrift „Bauwelt" in Berlin,
seit 1991 Chefredakteur der
Zeitschrift „Baumeister" in
München, von 2011–13 deren
Herausgeber. Außerdem
schreibt er Kritiken, Glossen
und Kurzgeschichten für
Zeitungen, Magazine und
Jahrbücher. 2008 „Fachjour-
nalist des Jahres" (2. Preis).**

Born 1951 in Ludwigshafen am
Rhein.
Studied agriculture and architecture; degree from RWTH Aachen
University in 1976. Dissertation
on anthroposophically inspired
architecture. Three years of
professional practice in various architecture and engineering offices while also working
as a journalist. From 1982 editor of the journal 'Bauwelt' in
Berlin. Since 1991 editor-in-chief
of the magazine 'Baumeister' in
Munich; served as its publisher
from 2011–13. Also writes reviews, glosses and short histories
of architecture and other themes
for newspapers, magazines and
annuals. In 2008, awarded 2nd
prize as 'Specialist Journalist of
the Year'.

CHRISTOF BODENBACH

***1960 in Kestert am Rhein.
Schreinerlehre. Studium in
Darmstadt, Frankfurt am
Main, Kassel und Wiesbaden.
1996 Journalistenpreis. Seit
1997 diverse Lehraufträge an
verschiedenen Hochschulen.
Seit 2004 Pressesprecher der
Architekten- und Stadtplaner-
kammer Hessen. Regelmäßige
Veröffentlichungen über
Architektur und Städtebau.
Lebt in Wiesbaden.**

Born 1960 in Kestert am Rhein.
Apprenticed as a carpenter.
Studied in Darmstadt, Frankfurt/
Main, Kassel and Wiesbaden.
Journalism award in 1996. Since
1997 various teaching posts at
several different universities.
Since 2004 press officer for the
Hessian Chamber of Architects
and Urban Planners. Regular
publications on architecture
and urban planning. Lives in
Wiesbaden.

CHRISTIAN BRENSING

***1960 in Bad Ems.
1982–89 Studium der
englischen Literatur und
Kunstgeschichte in England;
Abschluss M. A. Royal
College of Art (RCA), London.
1989–90 wissenschaftlicher
Assistent am RCA. 1990–92
Zaha Hadid Architects,
London. 1993–2004 Ove
Arup & Partners Consulting
Engineers, London und Berlin.
2004–05 CBP Consulting
Engineers, München. Seit
2006 freischaffender Berater,
Autor und Kurator, gründete
2012 die Christian Brensing
Enterprises Ltd. mit Sitz in
London und Berlin.**

Born 1960 in Bad Ems.
1982–89 studied English literature and history of art in England,
final degree M.A. Royal College
of Art (RCA), London. 1989–90
assistant lecturer, Royal College
of Art, London; 1990–92 Zaha
Hadid Architects, London;
1993–2004 Ove Arup & Partners
Consulting Engineers, London and Berlin; 2004–05 CBP
Consulting Engineers, Munich.
Since 2006 freelance consultant,
author and curator; 2012 founded Christian Brensing Enterprises
Ltd., based in London and Berlin.

CHRISTINA BUDDE

***1954 in Wilhelmshaven.
Studium Lehramt Sekundar-
stufe II (Anglistik/Politik)
in Frankfurt am Main und
Warwick, UK. Referendariat
an einem Frankfurter**

Gymnasium; langjährige pädagogische Mitarbeiterin an der Volkshochschule Frankfurt am Main. Seit 2005 Kuratorin am DAM mit Schwerpunkt Architekturvermittlung.

Born 1954 in Wilhelmshaven. Studied Secondary Level Teaching II (English Language & Literature/Politics) in Frankfurt/Main and Warwick, UK. Traineeship at a Frankfurt high school; many years as a teacher at the Volkshochschule in Frankfurt/Main. Since 2005 curator at the DAM with a focus on architecture appreciation.

MICHAELA BUSENKELL

***1962 in Schleswig. Diplom Architektur TU München, Döllgastpreis. Mitarbeit in Architekturbüros. Volontariat / Redakteurin bei „AIT", Stuttgart. 1999–2005 Mitbegründerin und Chefredakteurin von „a-matter, architecture and related". Seit 2005 freie Autorin und Publizistin. 2007–13 freie Kuratorin am DAM. Seit 2013 Studien zur Stadtforschung. Im Wintersemester 2013 Gastdozentin an der OTH Regensburg. Redakteurin der Literaturzeitschrift „außer.dem". Mitglied der Darmstädter Textwerkstatt / Zentrum für junge Literatur.**

Born 1962 in Schleswig. Degree in architecture from the Technical University of Munich, Döllgast Award. Worked in architecture offices; volunteer/editor of the trade journal 'AIT', Stuttgart. 1999–2005 co-founder and editor-in-chief of 'a-matter, architecture and related'. Since 2005 freelance author and publicist. 2007–2013 freelance curator at the DAM. Has studied urban research since 2013; guest lecturer at the Regensburg University of applied sciences in the 2013 winter semester. Editor of the literary magazine 'außer.dem'. Member of the Darmstädter Textwerkstatt /Zentrum für junge Literatur (Darmstadt Text Workshop / Centre for Young Literature).

OLIVER ELSER

***1972 in Rüsselsheim. Architekturstudium in Berlin. Zahlreiche Architekturkritiken für Zeitungen und Zeitschriften (u. a. „Frankfurter Allgemeine Zeitung", „Süddeutsche Zeitung", „Bauwelt") sowie in Katalogen und Büchern. 2006–07 Lehrtätigkeit in Graz und Wien. Seit 2007 Kurator am DAM. Ausstellungen u. a. „Mission: Postmodern. Heinrich Klotz und die Wunderkammer DAM", 2014; „Bollinger + Grohmann: Hinter den Kulissen", 2013; „Das Architekturmodell – Werkzeug, Fetisch, kleine Utopie", 2012.**

Born 1972 in Rüsselsheim. Studied architecture in Berlin. Has written numerous architectural reviews for newspapers and magazines ('Frankfurter Allgemeine Zeitung', 'Süddeutsche Zeitung', 'Bauwelt' etc.) as well as catalogues and books. Taught in Graz and Vienna 2006–07. Since 2007 curator at the DAM. Exhibitions include: 'Mission: Postmodern. Heinrich Klotz und die Wunderkammer DAM', 2014; 'Bollinger + Grohmann: Hinter den Kulissen', 2013; 'Das Architekturmodell – Werkzeug, Fetisch, kleine Utopie', 2012.

YORCK FÖRSTER

***1964 in Hannover. Studium der Philosophie, Soziologie und Kunstpädagogik an der Universität Frankfurt am Main. Kurator und Publizist. Zahlreiche Vorträge, Publikationen und Ausstellungen. Für das DAM u. a. „Peter Kulka – Minimalismus und Sinnlichkeit" (2005), „Gewahrsam. Räume der Überwachung" (2007), „Heterotopia. Arbeiten von Willem van Genk und anderen" (2008), „Johannes Peter Hölzinger. Psychodynamische Raumstrukturen" (2012). Partner der kuratorenwerkstatt Förster Gräwe Winkelmann.**

Born 1964 in Hanover. Studied philosophy, sociology und art education at the University of Frankfurt am Main. Curator and journalist. Numerous lectures, publications and exhibitions. Publications for the DAM include 'Peter Kulka – Minimalismus und Sinnlichkeit' (2005), 'Gewahrsam. Räume der Überwachung' (2007), 'Heterotopia. Arbeiten von Willem van Genk und anderen' (2008), 'Johannes Peter Hölzinger. Psychodynamische Raumstrukturen' (2012). Partner in kuratorenwerkstatt Förster Gräwe Winkelmann.

DOMINIQUE GAUZIN-MÜLLER

***1960 in Vincennes. Französische Architektin, lebt seit 1986 in Stuttgart. Lehrt an den Architekturschulen in Straßburg und Stuttgart. Internationale Vorträge zum Thema Nachhaltigkeit. Neben der Zusammenarbeit mit europäischen Fachverlagen und -zeitschriften seit 2007 Chefredakteurin des französischen Magazins „EcologiK" (EK). Ihre Bücher wurden in zahlreiche Sprachen übersetzt, darunter ins Deutsche: „Nachhaltigkeit in Architektur und Städtebau", Basel 2002, „Neue Wohnhäuser aus Holz", Basel 2004, „Nachhaltiges Wohnen", Basel 2006, „Ökologische Architektur in Vorarlberg", Wien 2011.**

Born 1960 in Vincennes. French architect living in Stuttgart since 1986. Instructor at the Schools of Architecture in Strasbourg and Stuttgart. International lecturer on the subject of sustainability. In addition to her work with European trade publishers and magazines, she has been editor-in-chief of the French magazine 'EcologiK' (EK) since 2007. Her books have been translated into many languages; German editions include: 'Nachhaltigkeit in Architektur und Städtebau', Basel 2002; 'Neue Wohnhäuser aus Holz', Basel 2004; 'Nachhaltiges Wohnen', Basel 2006; 'Okologische Architektur in Vorarlberg', Vienna 2011. English editions include: 'Sustainable Architecture and Urbanism: Design, Construction, Examples', Basel 2002; 'Wood Houses', Basel 2004; 'Sustainable Living', Basel 2002.

ECKHARD GERBER

***1938 in Oberhain/Thüringen. Architekturstudium an der TH Braunschweig. 1966 Bürogründung „Werkgemeinschaft 66". 1973–75 Assistent an der Universität Dortmund. Seit 1979 Inhaber von Gerber Architekten und Gerber Architekten international. Weitere Bürogründungen 2008 in Hamburg und 2012 in Berlin. 1981–92 Professur an der Gesamthochschule Essen, 1992–2004 Professur an der Bergischen Universität Wuppertal, 1995–99 dort Dekan des Fachbereichs Architektur, seit 2004 Professor im Masterstudiengang Grundlagen des Entwerfens und Entwerfen für Architekten.**

Born 1938 in Oberhain/Thuringia. Studied architecture at the Braunschweig University of Technology. 1966 founded the office 'Werkgemeinschaft 66'. 1973–75 assistant at the University of Dortmund. Since 1979 founder and owner of Gerber Architekten and Gerber Architekten International. Opened additional offices in Hamburg in 2008 and Berlin in 2012. 1981–92 professor at the Comprehensive University of Essen; 1992–2004 professor at the University of Wuppertal, served as its Dean of Architecture from 1995–99; since 2004 professor in the master's degree programme in Fundamentals of Design and Design for Architects.

CHRISTINA GRÄWE

***1965 in Idar-Oberstein. Krankenschwester, Architekturstudium in Berlin. Seit 2003 Volontärin und Kuratorin am DAM. Dort zahlreiche Ausstellungen, u. a. „Martin Elsaesser und das Neue Frankfurt" (2009). Seit 2007 freie Kuratorin und Publizistin. Lehrauftrag am Institut für Baugeschichte, TU Berlin. Weitere Ausstellungen:**

„Modernisierung der Platte" (2009/10), „Stadtvisionen 1910/2010" (Architekturmuseum TU Berlin, 2010). 2012–14 Redakteurin bei „BauNetz". Partnerin der kuratorenwerkstatt Förster Gräwe Winkelmann.
Born 1965 in Idar-Oberstein. Nurse, studied architecture in Berlin. Since 2003 volunteer, then curator at DAM. Exhibitions curated there inclucle 'Martin Elsaesser and the New Frankfurt' (2009). Since 2007 freelance curator and journalist. Teaching post at the Institut für Baugeschichte, Technical University (TU) of Berlin. Additional exhibitions: 'Modernising Pre-Fabricated Panel Buildings' (2009/10), 'City Visions 1910/2010' (Architecture Museum at TU Berlin, 2010). 2012–14 editor at 'BauNetz'. Partner in kuratorenwerkstatt Förster Gräwe Winkelmann.

OLIVER G. HAMM
***1963 in Limburg an der Lahn.**
Dipl-Ing. (FH Darmstadt) Architektur. Freier Autor, Herausgeber, Redakteur und Kurator (u. a. „NEU BAU LAND. Architektur und Stadtumbau in den neuen Bundesländern", DAM, 2007). 1989–92 Redakteur der „db deutsche bauzeitung", Stuttgart, 1992–98 Redakteur der „Bauwelt", Berlin, 2000–07 Chefredakteur „Deutsches Architektenblatt", Berlin, 2008–09 Chefredakteur „greenbuilding", Berlin. Deutscher Preis für Denkmalschutz 2003 (Journalistenpreis). 2003–10 Mitglied im Fachbeirat der IBA Fürst-Pückler-Land. Lebt in Berlin.
Born 1963 in Limburg/Lahn. Qualified architectural engineer (FH Darmstadt). Freelance author, publisher, editor, and curator (e. g. 'NEU BAU LAND. Architektur und Stadtumbau in den neuen Bundesländern' DAM, 2007). 1989–92 editor of 'db deutsche bauzeitung', Stuttgart; 1992–98 editor of 'Bauwelt', Berlin; 2000–07 editor-in-chief

of the 'Deutsches Architektenblatt', Berlin; 2008–09 editor-in-chief of 'greenbuilding', Berlin. German award for monument preservation 2003 (journalist award). Member of the IBA Fürst-Pückler-Land advisory council since 2003–10. Lives in Berlin.

ULRICH HÖHNS
***1954.**
Architekturhistoriker und -kritiker, wissenschaftlicher Leiter des Schleswig-Holsteinischen Archivs für Architektur und Ingenieurbaukunst.
Born 1954.
Architectural historian and critic, research director of the Schleswig-Holstein Archive for Architecture and Engineering.

CHRISTIAN HOLL
Zunächst Kunststudium in Stuttgart und Münster/Westfalen, dann Architekturstudium an der RWTH Aachen, in Florenz und an der Universität Stuttgart. 1997–2004 Redakteur der „db deutsche bauzeitung". 2004 Mitbegründer von „frei04 publizistik". Buchveröffentlichungen, freie Redakteurs-, Journalisten- und Kritikertätigkeit sowie Lehraufträge. 2005–10 akademischer Mitarbeiter am Städtebau-Institut der Uni Stuttgart. Mitglied im Ausstellungsausschuss und Kurator der „architekturgalerie am weißenhof", Stuttgart. Seit 2010 Landessekretär des BDA Hessen.
Studied art in Stuttgart and Münster/Westphalia, then architecture at RWTH Aachen University, in Florence and at the University of Stuttgart. 1997–2004 editor at 'db deutsche bauzeitung'. 2004 co-founder of 'frei04 publizistik'. Has published books, worked as freelance editor, journalist and reviewer and held posts as lecturer. 2005–10 academic assistant at the Institute of Urban Planning at the University of Stuttgart. Member of the exhibition committee and curator of 'architekturgalerie am weißenhof', Stuttgart. Since 2010

state secretary of the Hessian chapter of the German Association of Architects.

KAREN JUNG
***1974 in Münster.**
Studium der Architektur an der Universität Karlsruhe und der ETH Zürich. Mitarbeit in verschiedenen Architekturbüros. 1999–2002 Mitarbeiterin am Institut für Grundlagen der Architektur an der Universität Karlsruhe. 2005 Promotion an der ETH Zürich bei V. M. Lampugnani und À. Moravànsky zum „Porösen Baublock". 2006–08 Volontärin und seit 2008 freie Kuratorin und Autorin am DAM. Seit 2009 freie Kuratorin am M:AI Museum für Architektur und Ingenieurkunst NRW in Gelsenkirchen. Publikationen zu Architektur und Städtebau.
Born 1974 in Münster. Studied Architecture at Karlsruhe University and the Swiss Federal Institute of Technology (ETH) in Zurich. Worked at several architectural firms. 1999–2002: Associate at the Institute for Architectural Principles at University of Karlsruhe. 2005: PhD on the 'Porous Block' at ETH Zurich supervised by V. M. Lampugnani and À. Moravànsky. 2006–08: Trainee at the DAM. From 2008: Curator and author for DAM. 2009–present: freelance curator for M:AI Museum für Architektur und Ingenieurkunst NRW in Gelsenkirchen and the DAM. Publications on architecture and urban construction.

WOLFGANG KIL
*** 1948 in Berlin.**
Architekturstudium in Weimar, danach Arbeit als Architekt in Ostberlin. 1978–82 Chefredakteur der Zeitschrift „Farbe und Raum", anschließend freiberuflicher Kritiker und Publizist. 1992–94 Redakteur bei der „Bauwelt", Berlin. Seither wieder freiberuflich tätig. Schreibt vor allem in Fachzeitschriften. Eigene Bücher u. a.: „Gründerparadiese", Berlin 2000,

„Werksiedlungen – Wohnform des Industriezeitalters", Dresden 2003, „Luxus der Leere", Wuppertal 2004, „Das Wunder von Leinefelde", Dresden 2007, „Wolfgang Hänsch – Architekt der Dresdner Moderne", Berlin 2009. Lebt in Berlin.
Born 1948 in Berlin. Studied architecture in Weimar, then worked as an architect in East Berlin. From 1978 to 1982 editor-in-chief of the journal 'Farbe und Raum', later freelance critic and journalist. 1992–94, editor at 'Bauwelt' in Berlin, since then working on a freelance basis. Writes mainly for specialist journals. Author of books including 'Gründerparadiese', Berlin 2000; 'Werksiedlungen – Wohnform des Industriezeitalters', Dresden 2003; 'Luxus der Leere', Wuppertal 2004; 'Das Wunder von Leinefelde', Dresden 2007; 'Wolfgang Hänsch – Architekt der Dresdner Moderne', Berlin 2009. Lives in Berlin.

URSULA KLEEFISCH-JOBST
***1956 in Stuttgart.**
Studium der Kunstgeschichte, Archäologie und Germanistik in Bonn, München und Rom: Promotion. 1985–88 Forschungsprojekt an der Biblioteca Hertziana in Rom. 1989–90 Mitarbeiterin am Landesdenkmalamt in Berlin. 2001–08 freie Kuratorin am DAM. Seit 2008 leitende Kuratorin am Museum für Architektur und Ingenieurkunst NRW.
Born 1956 in Stuttgart. Studied art history, archaeology and German language & literature in Bonn, Munich and Rome, culminating in doctorate. 1985–88 research project at the Biblioteca Hertziana in Rome. 1989–90 employee at the Berlin Monument Authority. 2001–08 freelance curator at the DAM. Since 2008 head curator at the Museum of Architecture and the Art of Engineering NRW.

KARIN LEYDECKER

***1956 in Speyer.
Studium der Germanistik,
Kunstgeschichte und der
evangelischen Theologie in
Mainz, Heidelberg und Karlsruhe. 1988 Promotion. Lehrtätigkeit zur Architekturwahr-
nehmung an der Universität
und Pädagogischen Hoch-
schule Karlsruhe. Schreibt
regelmäßig für die „Neue
Zürcher Zeitung" sowie für
Fach- und Publikumszeit-
schriften. Zahlreiche Buchveröffentlichungen zur Architektur und Denkmalpflege.**
Born 1956 in Speyer.
Studied German language &
literature, psychology, art history
and Protestant theology in
Mainz, Heidelberg and Karlsruhe.
Doctorate in 1988. Teacher
of architectural perception at
Karlsruhe University and School
of Education. Regularly writes
for the 'Neue Zürcher Zeitung'
newspaper and for trade and
popular journals. Has published
numerous books on architecture
and historic building conservation.

GERHARD MATZIG

***1963.
Studium der Architektur.
Seit 1997 tätig bei der
„Süddeutschen Zeitung".**
Born 1963.
Studied Architecture. Editor
and architecture critic at the
'Süddeutsche Zeitung' since
1997.

ULRICH MÜLLER

***1965 in Merseburg.
Studierte Architektur in
Weimar und Darmstadt. 1993–
2002 bei Ungers & Partner
sowie Büroleiter von Peter
W. Schmidt und als selbst-
ständiger Architekt in Berlin
tätig. 1999 Gründung der
„Architektur Galerie Berlin".
Herausgeber von Architektur-
publikationen, Vorträge zum
Thema Architekturkommu-
nikation. Seit 2009 Herausgeber des Kalenders „AAB
– Architektur-Ausstellungen
Berlin", seit 2012 der Webseite „AAD – Architektur-
Ausstellungen Deutschland"**
und seit 2014 der Webseite
„AEX – Architecture Exhibitions International".
Born 1965 in Merseburg.
Studied architecture in Weimar
and Darmstadt. 1993–2002
worked at Ungers & Partner,
as office manager for Peter
W. Schmidt and as a freelance
architect in Berlin. Founded the
'Architektur Galerie Berlin' in
1999. Edits architectural publications and lectures on the subject of mediation of architecture.
Since 2009 publisher of the
calendar 'AAB – Architektur-
Ausstellungen Berlin' ('Architecture Exhibitions Berlin'); since
2012 publishes the website
'AAD – Architektur-Ausstellungen
Deutschland' ('Architecture Exhibitions Germany) and since 2014
the website 'AEX – Architecture
Exhibitions International'.

KLAUS PHILIPSEN

***1950 in Stuttgart.
FAIA; ist Gründer und Eigner
von „ArchPlan", eines Archi-
tektur- und Stadtplanungs-
büros in Baltimore, Mary-
land (USA) mit Schwerpunkt
in Stadterneuerung, Umnut-
zung, Bestandserhaltung und
öffentlichem Nahverkehr. Für
seinen professionellen Einsatz
im Dienste der Öffentlichkeit
wurde er vom American Institute of Architects zum Fellow
ernannt. Philipsen schreibt
über Architektur und ist regel-
mäßiger Radiokommentator.**
Born 1950 in Stuttgart.
FAIA, LEED AP is president of
'ArchPlan Inc.', an architecture
and urban design firm in Baltimore, MD (USA), specializing in
community revitalization, adap-
tive re-use, historic preservation
and transportation planning
since 1992. He has been named
a Fellow of the American Institute of Architects for using his
profession to affect communities
through advocacy, lately increasingly through writing and as a
radio talk show contributor.

SEBASTIAN REDECKE

***1957 in Osnabrück.
Studium der Architektur
an der Technischen Univer-**
sität Braunschweig und an
der Universität La Sapienza,
Rom. **Seit 1990 Redakteur bei
der „Bauwelt" und Heraus-
geber sowie Autor zahlreicher
Bücher zur aktuellen Architektur in Berlin und Paris.**
Born 1957 in Osnabrück.
Studied architecture at the Technical University of Braunschweig
and the Sapienza University in
Rome. Since 1990 editor at 'Bauwelt' and publisher and author of
numerous books on contemporary
architecture in Berlin and Paris.

PETER CACHOLA SCHMAL

***1960 in Altötting.
Aufenthalte in Multan/Paki-
stan, Mülheim/Ruhr, Jakarta/
Indonesien, Holzminden und
Baden-Baden. Architektur-
studium an der TU Darm-
stadt; 1989 Diplom. Mitar-
beit bei Behnisch+Partner in
Stuttgart 1989. 1990–93 bei
Eisenbach+Partner in Zeppe-
linheim. 1992–97 wissen-
schaftlicher Mitarbeiter an der
TU Darmstadt. 1997–2000
Lehrauftrag für Entwerfen an
der FH Frankfurt am Main.
Ab 2000 Kurator, seit 2006
Direktor des DAM. 2007
Deutscher Generalkommissar
VII. Internationale Architek-
turbiennale São Paulo.**
Born 1960 in Altötting.
Has lived in Multan/Pakistan,
Mülheim/Ruhr, Jakarta/Indo-
nesia, Holzminden and Baden-
Baden. Studied architecture
at the Technical University of
TU Darmstadt; diploma in 1989.
Worked at Behnisch+Partner
in Stuttgart in 1989. 1990–
93 at Eisenbach+Partner in
Zeppelinheim. 1992–97 Assistant
Professor at the TU Darmstadt.
1997–2000 taught architectu-
ral design at the University of
Applied Sciences in Frankfurt/
Main. From 2000 curator, since
2006 director of the DAM . 2007
German Commissioner for the
7th International Architecture
Biennial in São Paulo.

AXEL SIMON

***1966 in Düsseldorf.
Studierte Architektur in
Düsseldorf und Berlin sowie**
Geschichte und Theorie der
Architektur in Zürich. **1999–
2005 Entwurfsassistent
an der ETH Zürich, u. a. bei
Peter Märkli. Ab 2000 freier
Architekturkritiker u. a. beim
„Tages-Anzeiger", der „Welt-
woche" und internationalen
Fachzeitschriften. Seit 2010
Redakteur Architektur bei der
Zeitschrift „Hochparterre".**
Born 1966 in Düsseldorf.
Studied architecture in Düssel-
dorf and Berlin as well as history
and theory of architecture in
Zurich. 1999–2005 design assis-
tant at the Swiss Federal Institute
of Technology Zurich, including
for Peter Märkli. From 2000 free-
lance architecture critic for the
'Tages-Anzeiger', 'Weltwoche'
and other newspapers and for
international trade journals.
Since 2010 architecture editor at
'Hochparterre' magazine.

JÜRGEN TIETZ

***1964 in Berlin.
Studium der Kunstgeschichte
in Berlin. Arbeitet als freier
Architekturkritiker und
-historiker u. a. für die „Neue
Zürcher Zeitung". Lehrtätigkeit in Berlin und Dresden.
Zahlreiche Buchveröffentlichungen zur Architektur und
Denkmalpflege.**
Born 1964 in Berlin.
Studied art history in Berlin.
Work as freelance architecture
critic and architectural historian
for publications including
the 'Neue Zürcher Zeitung'
newspaper. Lecturer in Berlin and
Dresden. Numerous books on
architecture and historic building
conservation.

CHRISTIAN THOMAS

***1955 in Lüdenscheid.
Studierte Germanistik, Philosophie und Kunstgeschichte.
Seit 1993 Redakteur der
„Frankfurter Rundschau",
verantwortlich für Architektur
und Städtebau. Seit 2003
stellvertretender Ressort-
leiter, seit 2010 Leiter des
Feuilletons.**
Born 1955 in Lüdenscheid.
Studied German, philosophy and
art history. Since 1993 editor

of the 'Frankfurter Rundschau' responsible for architecture and urban development. Since 2003 deputy department head; since 2010 head of the arts section.

ALEXANDER WETZIG
***1947.**
Studierte Kunstgeschichte sowie Architektur und Städtebau in München. Mitarbeiter im Büro für Architektur und Stadtplanung Prof. Breitling in München und Graz. 1978–85 Referent für Städtebau und Städtebauförderung im Bayerischen Innenministerium. 1985–91 Leiter des Amtes für Stadtplanung Ulm, seit 1991 dort Bürgermeister, Leiter des Fachbereichs Stadtentwicklung, Bau und Umwelt.
Born 1947.
Studied art history as well as architecture and urban development in Munich. Worked at the Office of Architecture and City Planning Prof. Breitling in Munich and Graz. 1978-85 lecturer on Urban Development and Urban Development Funding at the Ministry of the Interior in Bavaria. 1985–91 head of the Office of City Planning in Ulm; since 1991 Mayor of Ulm as well as that city's head of the Department of Urban Development, Construction and Environment.

FRANK R. WERNER
***1944 Worms am Rhein.**
Studierte Philosophie, Malerei und Architektur in Mainz, Hannover und Stuttgart. Assistent und Dozent für Baugeschichte in Stuttgart. 1983 Direktor der Ausstellung „IBA 1994/97 – Idee, Prozess, Ergebnis". 1990 Professor für Baugeschichte, Architekturtheorie und Designgeschichte in Stuttgart, ab 1994 Professor und Leiter des Instituts für Baugeschichte und Architekturtheorie an der Bergischen Universität Wuppertal, 1999–2003 dort Dekan des Fachbereichs Architektur. Ab 1999 Leitung der „Galerie für Architektur und Arbeit". Diverse Gastprofessuren. Mitglied der Westfälischen Akademie der Wissenschaften und Künste.
Born 1944 in Worms am Rhein. Studied philosophy, painting and architecture in Mainz, Hanover and Stuttgart. Assistant and instructor of architectural history in Stuttgart. In 1983 director of the exhibition 'IBA 1994/97 – Idee, Prozess, Ergebnis' (International Building Exhibition 1994/97 – Idea, Process, Result'). As of 1990 professor of architectural history, architectural theory and design history in Stuttgart; as of 1994 professor and head of the Institute for Architectural History and Architectural Theory at the University of Wuppertal; 1999–2003 Dean of the Department of Architecture there. Since 1999 head of the 'Galerie für Architektur und Arbiet' ('Gallery of Architecture and Work'). Various guest professorships. Member of the North Rhine-Westphalian Academy of Sciences, Humanities and Arts.

ARNE WINKELMANN
***1969 in Ludwigshafen am Rhein.**
Studium der Architektur an der Bauhaus-Universität Weimar, dort 2004 Promotion (Dr.-Ing.) zur „Sozialistischen Moderne". 2006 Promotion (Dr. phil.) an der Humboldt-Universität zu Berlin zu „Kulturfabriken". 2000–06 Redakteur bei „BauNetz". 2006–07 wissenschaftlicher Mitarbeiter am DAM. Seit 2008 freier Publizist und Autor. Partner der kuratorenwerkstatt Förster Gräwe Winkelmann.
Born 1969 in Ludwigshafen am Rhein. Studied architecture at the Bauhaus-Universität in Weimar, doctorate (Dr.-Ing.) there in 2004 on the theme of 'Socialist Modernism'. In 2006 doctorate (Dr. phil.) at the Humboldt University in Berlin on 'Kulturfabriken'. 2000–06, editor at 'BauNetz'. 2006–07 researcher at DAM. Since 2008 freelance journalist and author. Partner in kuratorenwerkstatt Förster Gräwe Winkelmann.

ZHI WENJUN
***1962.**
Studium der Architektur mit dem Abschluss als Bachelor im Jahr 1983 sowie einem Master-Abschluss in Geschichte und Theorie der Architektur an der Tongji University, Shanghai im Jahr 1986. Danach Lehrtätigkeit an der Universität und Arbeit als Redakteur für die einflussreiche chinesische Architekturzeitschrift „Time + Architecture". Derzeit Professor am College of Architecture and Urban Planning der Tongji University und Chefredakteur von „Time + Architecture".
Born 1962.
Got his bachelor's degree in Architecture in 1983 and his master's degree in History and Theory of Architecture in 1986 at Tongji University, Shanghai, China. After his graduation, he began to teach in the university and work for 'Time + Architecture' as an editor, which is the most influential academic architectural journal in China. He is now a professor of the College of Architecture and Urban Planning of Tongji University; the editor-in-chief of 'Time + Architecture'.

GERWIN ZOHLEN
***1950 in Berlin.**
Studium der Literaturwissenschaft, Geschichte und Philosophie in Berlin und Heidelberg; 1978–82 wissenschaftlicher Mitarbeiter am Institut für Allgemeine und Vergleichende Literaturwissenschaft der FU Berlin; 1984–85 Redakteur der IBA Berlin und 1984–87 sowie 1995–96 Chefredakteur von „Foyer", dem Magazin der Senatsbauverwaltung von Berlin. Seit 1982 Autor und Kritiker in Radio, Zeitung, Fernsehen sowie Publikationen in Buchverlagen: „Baumeister des Neuen Berlin", Berlin 2001, „Architektur des Neuen Berlin", Berlin 2002, „Auf der Suche nach der verlorenen Stadt – Berliner Architektur am Ende des 20. Jahrhunderts", Berlin 2002. Beiträge in der „Süddeutschen Zeitung", der „Frankfurter Allgemeinen Zeitung", in „Die Zeit", „Baumeister" und „Bauwelt".
Born in 1950 in Berlin. Studied literature, history and philosophy in Berlin and Heidelberg. 1978–1982 research assistant at the Institute for General and Comparative Literature at the Free University of Berlin; 1984–85 editor at the International Building Exhibition Berlin; 1984–87 and 1995–96 editor-in-chief of 'Foyer', the magazine of Berlin's City Department for Urban Development. Since 1982 author and critic in radio, newspaper and television as well as book publications: 'Baumeister des Neuen Berlin', Berlin 2001; 'Architektur des Neuen Berlin', Berlin 2002; 'Auf der Suche nach der verlorenen Stadt – Berliner Architektur am Ende des 20. Jahrhunderts', Berlin 2002. Contributor to the 'Süddeutsche Zeitung', 'Frankfurter Allgemeine Zeitung', 'Die Zeit', 'Baumeister' and 'Bauwelt'.

IN MEMORIAM

KURT ACKERMANN

(2. 3. 1928 – 6. 5. 2014)

„Schweige Künstler, rede nicht" – dieses Goethe-Zitat hat er Studenten gerne mit auf den Weg gegeben – und hinzugesetzt: „Arbeite!" Wer Kurt Ackermann kannte, wusste, dass er mit gutem Beispiel voranging und selbst diesem Imperativ folgte. Er war kein Mann der großen Worte. Sich durch Reden oder Schriften in den Vordergrund zu spielen war seine Sache nicht. Mag sein, dass das umfangreiche Werk, das er hinterlassen hat, deshalb ein zu wenig beachtetes ist.

Geboren wurde Ackermann 1928 im mittelfränkischen Insingen, erst nach einer Ausbildung zum Maurer und Zimmermann hat er in München Architektur studiert. 1953 gründete er das Büro Ackermann und Partner in München, das heute von seinem Sohn geführt wird. Ackermann war Mitglied der Akademie der Künste und der Bayrischen Akademie der Schönen Künste. Der BDA Bayern hat ihn zu seinem Ehrenmitglied ernannt und die TU Wien ihm die Ehrendoktorwürde verliehen.

1974 wurde er an die Universität Stuttgart berufen, wo er bis zu seiner Emeritierung 1993 Direktor des Instituts für Entwerfen und Konstruieren war. Dort rief Ackermann die integrierte Ausbildung von Architektur- und Bauingenieurstudenten ins Leben. Das enge Zusammenwirken beider Disziplinen war ihm nie akademischer Selbstzweck. Die Zusammenarbeit von Architekt und Ingenieur lebte er, Gestalt und Konstruktion verstand er als Einheit. Er hat viel mit dem Büro Schlaich Bergermann und Partner zusammengearbeitet. Aus dieser Kooperation entstand beispielsweise das Eislaufzelt im Münchner Olympiapark, eine elegant geschwungene, doppelt gekrümmte Holzkonstruktion, die von einem mittigen Stahlfachwerkträger abhängt. Gut sollten Bauten sein, von Schönheit wollte er nicht reden. Gut – das hieß für ihn, dass Funktion, Material und konstruktive Logik in Übereinstimmung gebracht sind. Kurt Ackermann hat viele gute Bauten errichtet. Die Christuskirche in Bad Füssing von 1972, ein Sichtbetonbau von hoher Konzentration und atmosphärischer Dichte, aber auch ein Anker im Einerlei der ihn umgebenden Bauten. Das Klärwerk Gut Marienhof (1987) demonstrierte, wie wichtig es sein kann, auch scheinbar weniger attraktive Bauaufgaben mit größter Sorgfalt zu erfüllen. Für die Faultürme der Kläranlage in Freiham (2009), unweit der Allianz-Arena, konnte auf die Arbeit der 1980er-Jahre zurückgegriffen werden. Für die Fassadenfirma Gartner entstand 1991 in Gundelfingen das Konstruktionsbüro mit idealen Voraussetzungen für unhierarchische Teamarbeit in einer offenen Gebäudestruktur. Die Halle 13 für die Expo 2000 in Hannover wirkte so selbstverständlich, als wäre es keine besondere Herausforderung, eine stützenfreie Halle der Größe von 120 mal 225 Metern zu errichten; auch sie entstand in Zusammenarbeit mit Schlaich Bergermann und Partner.

Kurt Ackermann hat Industriebauten, Brücken sowie Wohnhäuser entworfen. Er hat für Verwaltungen, Universitäten und ebenso für die Kirche gebaut. Der Präzision seiner Bauten entsprach eine Haltung, für die er unmissverständliche Worte fand. Wenn er geredet hat. Am 6. Mai 2014 ist er für immer verstummt.

'Be silent, artist, do not speak.' He liked to this give this quote from Goethe as a piece of advice to his students, adding the behest: 'Work!' Those who knew Kurt Ackermann knew that he led with a good example and followed this imperative himself. He was not a man of many words. It was not his way to draw attention to himself through speeches or writing. Perhaps it is for this reason that the extensive body of work which he left behind has been too little appreciated.

Ackermann was born in 1928 in the Middle Franconian village of Insingen. He trained as a bricklayer and carpenter before studying architecture in Munich. In 1953, he founded the Munich office of Ackermann and Partner which his son heads today. Ackermann was a member of the Akademie der Künste (Academy of Arts) and the Bayrischen Akademie der Schönen Künste (Bavarian Academy of Fine Arts). The BDA (Association of German Architects) in Bavaria appointed him an honorary member, and he was awarded an honorary doctorate by Vienna's University of Technology.

In 1974 he was appointed to the University of Stuttgart, where he served as director of the Institute for Building Design and Construction until his retirement in 1993. Here, Ackermann initiated the integrated training of students in architecture and architectural engineering. For him, the close interaction of the two disciplines was never an academic end in itself. He demonstrated the cooperative work of architect and engineer in his own life; he understood design and construction as a unified entity. He worked extensively with the of-

fice of Schlaich Bergermann und Partner. Among other projects, this co-operation produced the ice skating rink in Munich's Olympic Park, an elegant, doubly curving wooden structure that hangs from a central steel truss girder. Buildings had to be good: he was not interested in talking about beauty. For him, 'good' meant that function, material and structural logic should be brought into mutual harmony. Kurt Ackermann constructed many good buildings: for example, the Christuskirche in Bad Füssing, built in 1972, an exposed concrete church which is highly concentrated and atmospherically dense but also represents a landmark within the monotony of the surrounding buildings. The Gut Marienhof sewage treatment plant (1987) demonstrated how important it can be to execute even seemingly less attractive construction projects with the greatest of care. He was able to refer back to the work from the 1980s for the digestion towers at the treatment plant in Freiham (2009), not far from the Allianz Arena. In 1991, he built a design office for the Gartner façade company which provided the ideal conditions for non-hierarchical teamwork in an open building structure. Hall 13 for the Expo 2000 in Hanover had such an organic appearance that it seemed to have been no great challenge to construct a 120-by-225 metre hall without supports; this project, too, was carried out in co-operation with Schlaich Bergermann und Partner. Kurt Ackermann designed industrial buildings and bridges as well as residential buildings. He constructed buildings for governments and universities as well as for the church. The precision of his construction corresponded to an attitude for which he found unambiguous words – when he did actually speak. On 6 May 2014, he fell silent forever.

Christian Holl

ULRICH CONRADS
(27. 10. 1923 – 28. 9. 2013)

Als Aufmacher für ihren Nachruf hatten die „Bauwelt"-Redakteure ein großartiges Foto gewählt: Es zeigt eine Wohn- und Arbeitslandschaft von berauschender Großzügigkeit, während vorn, nahe zum Bildrand, auf drei Treppenstufen der Hausherr sitzt. Das Haus, vom Scharoun-Schüler Heinz Schudnagies bestellt, war gelebtes Programm. Und der Mann, uneitel privat in Socken und Sandalen, war gerade dabei, die ihm wichtigen Texte zum Vermächtnis zu bündeln: „Zeit des Labyrinths", sein letztes Buch. Ulrich Conrads, 1923 in Bielefeld geboren und als Abiturient noch zur Wehrmacht eingezogen, gehörte zur Generation derer, die ihre Kriegserfahrung mit unkündbarer Skepsis und Moral quittierten. Nach Studien der Kunstgeschichte, Archäologie, Philosophie, Soziologie, Literatur- und Theaterwissenschaft meldete sich da bald ein markanter Streiter, der das Denken über Architektur in der Bundesrepublik herausgefordert, bewegt, mitgestaltet hat wie wenige andere. Die Liste seiner publizistischen Gründungen ist länger als die Œuvres so mancher berühmter Baukollegen: 1952–57 trieb er die heftigen Debatten zum Wiederaufbau in der Zeitschrift „baukunst und werkform" an. Ab 1957 dann wurde die in Berlin erscheinende „Bauwelt" unter seiner Leitung zur unverzichtbaren Instanz in allen Baufragen. Ab 1964 erhielten Stadtplaner viermal im Jahr ihr Themen-Special mit der „Stadtbauwelt", den Freunden baukultureller Höhenflüge wollte er „Daidalos" widmen (1981–92). Doch er sah sein Publikum überall, an die 800 Mal strahlte der RIAS seine Sendung „Neues Bauen in unserer Zeit" aus. 1963 erschien „Programme und Manifeste", der legendäre erste Band der „Bauwelt Fundamente", jener prominenten Buchreihe, die inzwischen auf 150 Bände angewachsen ist. Und sogar in Lobbygefilde konnte er sich begeben, mithilfe der Bank für Gemeinwirtschaft initiierte er 1980 den „Deutschen Städtebaupreis". Zur Diskurskultur der 1960er- und 1970er-Jahre gehörte, über Architektur immer auch politisch zu reden. Doch selbst wenn der „Bauwelt"-Chefredakteur sich manchmal unmodische Begrifflichkeiten leistete, Utopien verteidigte oder auf Tugenden wie Mut, Gewissen, Stehvermögen pochte – nein, ein naiver Träumer sprach da nie. Denn auch um die Bodenfrage und um soziale Gerechtigkeit kreisten seine Texte regelmäßig, und dass man „die Bezeichnung sozial in Sachen Wohnungsbau stets GROSS schreiben" müsse, damit sie nicht zur bürokratischen Floskel verkommt. Seine Ziele verfocht er unerschrocken: 1961 forderte er vom Westberliner Senat, endlich Mies van der Rohe die Nationalgalerie bauen zu lassen; 1985 protestierte er in einem Offenen Brief an Erich Honecker gegen die politische Inhaftierung zweier Ostberliner Architekten. Seine Sympathie galt denen, „die wissen, dass sie der Gesellschaft Entwürfe schuldig sind". Als die TU Cottbus ihm 2001 die Ehrendoktorwürde verlieh, nutzte U. C. (so sein berühmtes Kürzel) das Festkolloquium zu einem denkwürdigen Auftritt. Von seinen dort proklamierten „Sieben Tugenden des Architekturkritikers" hat eine Forderung es rasch zum geflügelten Zunftspruch gebracht: „Dem wahren Kritiker gilt nur ein einziger Maßstab – der Maßstab 1:1." Doch nicht weniger wäre aus den Leitsätzen jenes Menschenbild zu beherzigen, das er auf seine unnachahmliche Weise natürlich zum Gesellschaftsbild erweiterte: „Der Architekturkritiker ist ein Mit-Mensch. Er besitzt die Fähigkeit, sich in die Biografien der neben ihm Lebenden einzufühlen, sich mit den Lebensweisen, Lebensrhythmen, Lebensbedürfnissen der Armen wie der Reichen, der Versklavten und Bedrängten (…) zu identifizieren. Er weiß, dass in naher Zukunft die momentan grassierende Große Beliebigkeit des Bauens ein Ende haben wird, (…) dass die natürlichen Energien nicht länger in Repräsentationsbauten verheizt oder verkühlt werden können. (…) Mit einem Wort: im wahren Architekturkritiker steckt insgeheim ein Pädagoge in Angewandter Politik." Was soll's – keiner konnte sein Lebenswerk trefflicher umschreiben als er selbst.

The editors of 'Bauwelt' chose a wonderful photo for the lead-in to their obituary: it depicts an intoxicatingly spacious work and living landscape, while in the foreground, close to the edge of the frame, the head of the household sits atop three steps. The house, commissioned by Scharoun's pupil Heinz Schudnagies, was programme in action. The man, private and unpretentious in socks and sandals, was in the process of compiling his important texts into a bequest: 'Zeit des Labyrinths' ('Time of the Labyrinth'), his last book.

Ulrich Conrads, who was born in Bielefeld in 1923 and conscripted into the Wehrmacht on finishing his schooling, belonged to the generation that acknowledged its experience of the War with non-negotiable scepticism and morality. Following his studies of art history, archaeology, philosophy, sociology, literature and drama, a prominent debater soon emerged who challenged, stirred up and shaped ideas about architecture in the Federal Republic of Germany like very few others. The list of publications that he founded is longer than the œuvres of many of his famous colleagues: from 1952 to 1957, he propelled the heated debate over the rebuilding of Germany in the magazine 'baukunst und werkform'. Then, beginning in 1957,

the journal 'Bauwelt', published in Berlin under his leadership, became the essential authority in all questions of architecture. Starting in 1964, urban planners received its specially-themed issue 'StadtBauwelt' four times each year. His 'Daidalos' magazine (1981–92) was intended for devotees of architectural flights of fancy. Nevertheless, he saw his audience everywhere: RIAS Berlin broadcast his show 'Neues Bauen in unserer Zeit' ('New Architecture in Our Time') approximately 800 times. In 1963, he published 'Programme und Manifeste' ('Programmes and Manifestoes'), the legendary first volume of the renowned 'Bauwelt Fundamente' book series, which now encompasses 150 volumes. He even entered the field of lobbying and advocacy: in co-operation with the Bank für Gemeinwirtschaft, he founded the 'Deutsche Städtebaupreis' (German Urban Planning Award) in 1980. Discussing architecture from a political standpoint was part of the culture of discourse prevalent in the 1960s and 70s. However, even when 'Bauwelt's' editor-in-chief occasionally indulged in unfashionable terminology, defending utopian viewpoints or stressing such virtues as courage, conscience and staying power – no, these were never the words of a naïve dreamer. His texts regularly dealt with questions of land ownership and social justice, and the idea that 'in issues of residential construction, the term "social" should always be written in capital letters,' so that it doesn't come across like a bureaucratic cliché. He was undaunted in championing his goals: in 1961, he demanded that the West Berlin Senate finally allow Mies van der Rohe to build the New National Gallery. In 1985, in an open letter to Erich Honecker, he protested against the political detention of two East Berlin architects. His sympathies belonged to those 'who know that they owe their designs to society'. When the Brandenburg Technical University in Cottbus awarded him an honorary doctorate

in 2001, U. C. (his famous nickname) used the ceremonial gathering to make a memorable appearance. Out of the 'Seven Virtues of an Architecture Critic' which he proclaimed on that occasion, one of his requirements quickly evolved into a popular dictum: 'For a true critic, only one scale is valid – the scale of 1:1'. Yet from these guidelines, it is just as important to take to heart that image of humanity which, in his inimitable manner, he naturally expanded into an image of society: 'Architecture critics are fellow human beings. They have the ability to empathize with the biography of those living to him – to identify with the manners, rhythms and necessities of life of the poor as well as the rich, the enslaved and the oppressed. (...) They know that in the near future, the currently rampant 'anything goes' in construction will come to an end, (...) that it will no longer be possible to heat or cool natural energies in prestigious buildings. (...) In a word: inside a true architecture critic is a secret educator in applied politics.' What can we say? No one could more accurately sum up his life's work than the man himself.

Wolfgang Kil

Die TU Cottbus hat Ulrich Conrads ein eigenes Archiv gewidmet, und sie hat auch die großartige Rede über die „Sieben Tugenden des Architekturkritikers" als Mitschnitt ins Netz gestellt:
The BTU Cottbus has devoted an archive exclusively to Ulrich Conrads. Through the university, a recording of his outstanding speech on the 'Sieben Tugenden des Architekturkritikers' ('Seven Virtues of an Architecture Critic') is available online:

http://www.tu-cottbus.de/theorieder-architektur/Wolke/deu/Themen/022/Conrads/Conrads_Prolog.htm

CARLO WEBER
(6. 4. 1934 – 15. 5. 2014)
Carlo Weber hat der Architektur Flügel verliehen. Kurz nach seinem 80. Geburtstag ist er verstorben.
„Die Störung, wie im Leben, gehört dazu. Es geht um die Balance von Ordnung und Störung." Daraus entstehe, sagte Carlo Weber im Gespräch

über das Anliegen der Architektur von Auer Weber einmal, im besten Falle so etwas wie Poesie. Vielleicht sogar: Baukunst, die, wenn sie glückt, stets viel mehr ist als Funktion und Form. Eben auch: ein Moment der Poesie. Das aber ist kaum planbar. Denkbar wohl. Die Störung also. Wie im Leben – und also auch wie im Tod. Wobei der Tod dann doch bar aller Poesie sein könnte. Möglicherweise sähe Carlo Weber, den man sehr souverän in Erinnerung hat, gelassen und auf heitere Weise einverstanden mit der Welt, das anders. Jedenfalls aber gilt es für die, die nun zurückbleiben, um einen der Großen in der Architektur in aller Verstörung zu betrauern. Carlo Weber kam als Karlheinz Weber am 6. April 1934 in Saarbrücken zur Welt, doch nahm er sich als Architekt die Freiheit, den ordnungsgemäßen Vornamen Karlheinz durch ein störrisch-spitznamiges Carlo und somit durch eine auch namentlich gekennzeichnete Referenz an die Italianità zu ersetzen. Diese Italianità kennt man aus seinen Bauten: heiter, leichtfüßig, dem Leben und den Menschen zugewandt. Es sind oft lebenskluge und fröhliche, ja unbeschwerte, zugleich relevante, bleibende, prägende Bauten. Und da sie uns bleiben, mag man versöhnt sein mit der Störung, die sein Tod bedeutet. Die großen Feierlichkeiten, Rückschauen und Würdigungen zu seinem 80. Geburtstag hat Carlo Weber, unberechenbar bis zum Schluss, in gewisser Weise doch noch unterlaufen. Für Ehrungen hatte er nicht zu viel übrig, die Arbeit aber war ihm immer wichtig. Bis zuletzt arbeitete er am Umbau des berühmten Kaufhauses Schocken von Erich Mendelsohn zum Staatlichen Museum für Archäologie Chemnitz. Ein anderes Projekt, dessen Vollendung er nun nicht mehr erlebt, ist die Fertigstellung der Orgel in der Konstantin-Basilika zu Trier. Doch war ihm das Unvollendetsein immer ein räumliches

Anliegen. Seine Architekturen schaffen Raum für das Leben darin – daher ist ihnen das Unvollendetsein eingeschrieben. Erst der Mensch vollendet den Raum. „Inkonsequenz" ist daher ein weiterer wichtiger Begriff im Denken Carlo Webers: Es sei die Ausnahme von der Regel, die beides, die Ordnung wie die Störung der Ordnung, erst bewusst mache. Insofern fällt sein Tod in eine Ära, die das Festgefügte, Vorgegebene, Unabänderliche, Absolute wieder als architektonisches Credo aufscheinen lässt. Der Balance in diesem Ringen um das wahre Bauen (manchmal auch: das Bauen als Ware) wird Carlo Weber fehlen. Ohne ihn gäbe es zum Beispiel auch das Areal des Münchner Olympiaparks aus den 1970er-Jahren nicht in der bekannten Form, die man nur als Bauwunder begreifen kann. Der eigentliche Urheber ist natürlich Günter Behnisch, denn sein Büro hatte den entsprechenden Wettbewerb gewonnen. Aber tatsächlich war dies: Teamarbeit. Und eben vor allem auch Carlo Weber und Fritz Auer zu verdanken. Die beiden Freunde, die sich seit ihrem Architekturstudium in Stuttgart kannten, waren erst Mitarbeiter bei Behnisch. Dann Partner. Später, 1980, entstand das Büro Auer Weber, das ganz aus dem Geist der Olympiabauten agierte – und, fortgeführt von Fritz Auers Söhnen, auch weiterhin sich vornehmen dürfte, Bauten zu schaffen, die vollendet nur insofern sind, als sie Möglichkeitsformen des unvollkommenen Lebens darstellen.

Carlo Weber gave architecture wings. He died shortly after his eightieth birthday.
'Just as in life, disturbances are a part of things. It's a matter of finding the balance between order and disturbance.' In the best cases – Carlo Weber once said in a discussion of the goals of Auer Weber's architecture – this balance results in something like poetry. Maybe even this: architecture, when it is

successful, is always much more than function and form. In fact, it is also a moment of poetry. However, this can scarcely be planned. But it can be imagined. Disturbance, then: just as in life – and then also, as in death. Although death might be devoid of all poetry after all. It is possible that Carlo Weber, whom we remember as very confident, relaxed and light-heartedly at ease with the world, would disagree. At any rate, for those who are now left behind, it is time to mourn one of the great men of architecture with all the distress natural in the circumstances. Carlo Weber was born in Saarbrücken on 6 April 1934 as Karlheinz Weber. As an architect, however, he took the liberty of replacing his official given name, Karlheinz, with the obstinate nickname of Carlo – thereby also making a reference, through his name, to Italianità. We recognise this Italianità in his buildings: cheerful, light-footed, focused on life and on people. They are often worldly-wise and joyful, even carefree – but nevertheless relevant, enduring and influential buildings. And since they remain with us, we may be able to reconcile ourselves with the distress that his death has caused. Carlo Weber, unpredictable to the end, was after all able in a sense to avoid the great celebrations, retrospectives and honours marking his eightieth birthday. He did not have much use for tributes and awards, but work was always important to him. Right up to the end of his life, he was working on the conversion of Erich Mendelsohn's famous Schocken Department Store in Chemnitz into the State Museum of Archaeology. Another project whose completion he will no longer see is the organ in the Basilica of Constantine in Trier. Yet for Weber, incompleteness was always a spatial concern. His architectural works create space for the life inside them; therefore, the quality of incompleteness is built into them. It is the people who complete the space. Thus, 'inconsistency' is another impor-

tant concept in Carlo Weber's thinking: it is the exception to the rule which makes both order and the disruption of order perceptible. In this respect, his death comes during an era in which the established, the predetermined, the immutable and the absolute are once again emerging as a credo of architecture. The equilibrium in this struggle over the true art of building (and sometimes, building as a commodity) will miss Carlo Weber. Without him, for example, the site of Munich's Olympic Park from the 1970s would not exist in the form in which we know it – one which can only be understood as a miracle of construction. The actual creator was, of course, Günter Behnisch, since his office was the winner of the relevant competition. But in fact, this project was the result of teamwork, and credit is owed especially to Carlo Weber and Fritz Auer. The two friends, who had known each other since their days as architecture students in Stuttgart, started out as employees of the Behnisch office. They then became partners. Later, in 1980, they founded the office of Auer Weber, which operated very much in the spirit of the Olympia project, and, carried forward by Fritz Auer's sons, continued to take on the task of creating buildings which are completed only insofar as they represent possible forms for an uncompleted life.

Gerhard Matzig

FELIX ZWOCH

(8. 10. 1952 – 10. 2. 2014)
Felix Zwoch war seit 1981 Redakteur der „Bauwelt", von 2002 bis 2010 ihr Chefredakteur. Sein Großprojekt war die „Stadtbauwelt", die er mit viel Leidenschaft deutlich veränderte, vor allem internationalisierte. Die „Stadtbauwelt" entwickelte sich zu einer Reihe großer Stadtporträts aus aller Welt. Er zeigte weniger die Planungen, sondern suchte nach der Seele und Magie der Städte, nach ihren Geschichten. Die Ausgaben zu Lodz, Bukarest, Algier, Saigon, Tiflis, Hongkong,

Magnitogorsk und Marseille sind legendär. Man musste sie als Ganzes lesen. Er verlangte vom Leser ein Hineindenken. Wer den Eingang fand, wurde reich belohnt.
In den 1990er-Jahren hat Felix Zwoch deutlich Stellung bezogen zu den großen Bauprojekten in Berlin nach dem Fall der Mauer. Unvergessen ist das „Bauwelt"-Heft mit dem Titel „Die Herren mit der weißen Weste am Förderband Berlin Mitte". Er zeigte 66 Projekte von Investoren aus aller Welt, die wie Kletten am Senatbaudirektor und an der Berliner Politik hingen. Diese Projekte waren für ihn alle „erbärmlich oder größenwahnsinnig, oft beides zugleich". Das „Bauwelt"-Heft war ein Protest gegen den Ausverkauf der Stadt und rüttelte auf. Was er wollte, ist nachzulesen in seinem mit Klaus Novy herausgegebenen „Bauwelt Fundamente"-Band 93 aus dem gleichen Jahr 1991. Dort schrieb er mit Stephan Reiß-Schmidt den Aufsatz „Städtebau jetzt! Von der Verantwortung für die Schönheit der Stadt". Thematisch war er in den 1990er-Jahren der Zeit voraus. Mit seinen Stadtporträts wollte er sich von der Planungssprache, den spröden, unsinnlichen Gedanken zu Stadtbau-Konzepten der damaligen Zeit lösen. Er wollte sogar ganz weg von den in seinen Augen besserwisserischen Planungstheoretikern mit Konzepten, die überall greifen sollen. Erst Jahre später wurde dies zu einem allgemein anerkannten Forschungsgebiet. Denn die Erkenntnis, dass jede Stadt ihre Eigenlogik hat, war angekommen. In China war er früher als viele andere. Er knüpfte dort enge Kontakte. Mehrere „Stadtbauwelt"- und „Bauwelt"-Hefte hatten chinesische Städte und Architekturbüros zum Thema. Er befreundete sich mit Ai Weiwei. Die Erinnerungen an Felix

Zwoch sind vielfältig. Für mich begannen sie 1988 als Praktikant bei der „Bauwelt". Mir wurde sofort gewahr, dass ich es hier mit einem Menschen der Stärke und Willenskraft zu tun hatte. Er hat mich immer wieder erstaunt mit seinem phänomenalen Gedächtnis. Er erzählte gerne Anekdoten. Diese Geschichten, das Erzählerische bei ihm, auch wenn es manchmal ein wenig kryptisch oder nur zu ausführlich war, fehlen mir. Er hatte immer eine klare Meinung. Vieles war für ihn eine Glaubensfrage. Manche fühlten sich vor den Kopf gestoßen. Es gab persönliche Enttäuschungen, auch Verletzungen.
Felix Zwoch ermutigte und unterstützte diejenigen, die er schätzte. Er besaß die große Gabe zu redigieren, Texten durch sprachliche, manchmal auch inhaltliche Umformungen und Vereinfachungen und manchmal durch gnadenlose Kürzungen eine Struktur und Klarheit zu geben. Es gab wunderbare Reaktionen oder – eher selten – Beschwerden. Er liebte die Ordnung, begeisterte sich für den Film und für Kriminalromane, lebte bescheiden, war uneitel, genoss vor allem beim Redigieren seine Gitanes sans Filtre und bot dem Gast seinen aus der Pfalz gelieferten Wein oder Tiger Bier aus Fernost an. Sein Zuhause stand für Freunde immer offen. Unvergessen bleiben die Stadtbauweltabende der 1990er-Jahre. Es waren rauschende Feste in seiner Wohnung, ein Berliner Ereignis der Architekten- und Planerszene.
Er bleibt als ein Mensch mit Ecken und Kanten in Erinnerung, aber auch als einer mit vielen feinsinnigen Gedanken. Seine Positionen forderten heraus, selbst das Auge zu schärfen und einen Standpunkt einzunehmen. Meinungen gibt es heute viele, die Haltung ist das entscheidende, sie ist unverzichtbar. Felix Zwoch ist am 10. Februar

nach langer Krankheit mit 61 Jahren in Berlin gestorben.

Felix Zwoch was an editor of 'Bauwelt' from 1981; from 2002 to 2010, he was the magazine's editor-in-chief. His major project was the 'StadtBauwelt' edition, to which, thanks to his great passion, he made significant changes – above all, making it an international publication. 'StadtBauwelt' developed into a series of great urban portraits from all over the world. He focused less on urban planning; rather he searched for the spirit and magic of the cities – for their stories. The issues on Łódź, Bucharest, Algiers, Saigon, Tbilisi, Hong Kong, Magnitogorsk and Marseille are legendary. One had to read them as a whole: he demanded that his readers completely immerse themselves. Those who found their way in were richly rewarded.

In the 1990s, Felix Zwoch took a clear position with regard to the major construction projects in Berlin after the fall of the Wall. His 'Bauwelt' issue entitled 'Die Herren mit der weissen Weste am Förderband Berlin Mitte' ('The Gentlemen in White Waistcoats on the Central Berlin Conveyor Belt') is unforgettable. He presented 66 projects by investors from all over the world that hung like burrs on the city's director of urban development and on Berlin's politicians. To him, all of these projects were 'pathetic, megalomaniac, often both at the same time'. The 'Bauwelt' issue was a protest against the selling off of the city, and it shook people up. One can read about what Felix Zwoch wanted in Volume 93 of 'Bauwelt Fundamente', which he published together with Klaus Novy the same year, 1991. Here, along with Stephan Reiss-Schmidt, he wrote an essay entitled 'Städtebau jetzt! Von der Verantwortung für die Schönheit der Stadt' ('Urban design now! On responsibility for the beauty of the city').

Thematically, in the 1990s, he was ahead of his time. With his city portraits, he wanted to break away from planning language – the dry, non-sensuous thinking that characterized urban design concepts at that time. In fact, he wanted to move completely away from those (in his eyes) conceited planning theorists with their concepts which were intended to be applied everywhere. Only many years later did this become a generally recognized area of study. The realization that every city has its own individual logic had finally arrived. He was in China much earlier than many of his colleagues, and he made important contacts there. Numerous issues of 'StadtBauwelt' and 'Bauwelt' focused on Chinese cities and architectural firms. He became friends with Ai Weiwei.

The memories of Felix Zwoch are wide-ranging. For me, they began in 1988, when I was an intern at 'Bauwelt'. I was immediately aware that I was dealing with a powerful and strong-willed person. He repeatedly astonished me with his phenomenal memory. He liked to tell anecdotes. I miss these stories

and this narrative quality of his – even if they were sometimes rather cryptic or simply too detailed. He always had a clear opinion; many things, for him, were a question of belief. Some people felt offended by him. There were personal disappointments, even injuries.

Felix Zwoch encouraged and supported the people he valued. He had a great gift for editing and revising: he could bring structure and clarity to texts by reformulating and simplifying them with regard to both language and content, sometimes even through merciless abridgement. There were wonderful reactions to his work – or, less frequently, complaints.

He was a lover of order, a film and crime novel enthusiast; he lived modestly and with no hint of vanity. Particularly while editing, he enjoyed his Gitanes sans Filtre; he offered his guests wine delivered from the Palatinate, or Tiger Beer from the Far East. His home was always open to friends. The StadtBauwelt evenings of the 1990s were unforgettable: they were lavish celebrations in his flat,

a Berlin event for the architecture and planning scene.

He will be remembered as person with rough edges, with a mind of his own – but also as a person of subtle and complex ideas. His positions challenged others to sharpen their own observations and take standpoints of their own. There are many opinions to be found today; taking a position is what is decisive and essential. Felix Zwoch died on 10 February in Berlin after a long illness. He was 61 years old.

Sebastian Redecke

WEGBEGLEITER DER ARCHITEKTUR IN DEUTSCHLAND
A GUIDE TO ARCHITECTURE IN GERMANY

HANS HOLLEIN
(30. 3. 1934 – 24. 4. 2014)

Geflügelte Worte entwickeln ein Eigenleben, ihre Quellen vernebeln. „Alles ist Architektur" – das ist ganz klar Hans Hollein, der diesen Leitspruch 1967 prägte und ihn bis zu seinem Tod wörtlich nahm. Denn was hat dieser Erfinder, Debattenanstoßer, Grenzüberschreiter, Lehrer, Künstler und ja, natürlich auch Baumeister nicht alles unternommen, um den Architekturbegriff zu weiten und Funktionalität und Sinnlichkeit im Bauen zu vermählen. Der Wiener Architekturavantgarde wurde er zugerechnet und hat das mit frühen Texten untermauert. Sein erster Bau, das winzige Kerzengeschäft Retti (1966) mit Aluminiumfassade, schlüssellochartigem Durchschlupf und schräg eingesetzten Schaufenstern geriet zum gebauten Manifest. Der „Pionier der Postmoderne" hat es nie beim reinen Zitieren von Stilelementen belassen. In Holleins Entwürfen sitzt stets auch Spielerisches und Ironie, in seinen Gebäuden Bühnenbildhaftes und die Inszenierung von Wegen und Raumfolgen. Letzteres entrümpelte 1982 die bisherige Museumsarchitektur: das terrassenartige Museum auf dem Abteiberg in Mönchengladbach. Und ein entfernter

Verwandter des visionären „Flugzeugträgers" aus den 1960er-Jahren ging 30 Jahre später als keilförmiges Museum für Moderne Kunst mitten in Frankfurt am Main vor Anker. Zwei Ausstellungen, auf dem Abteiberg und im Wiener MAK, waren als Geburtstagsgeschenke gedacht – und sind nun zu Nachrufen geworden.

Oft-quoted words take on a life of their own; their sources become obscured. 'Alles is Architektur' ('Everything is architecture'): without a doubt, it was Hans Hollein who coined this phrase in 1967, and to the end of his life he took these words literally. For this inventor, initiator of debate, transcender of boundaries, teacher, artist – and yes, of course, master builder – there was very little he did not undertake in order to expand the definition of architecture and to combine functionality and sensuousness in construction. He was classified among the Viennese architectural avant-garde, and he corroborated this status with his early writings. His first building project, the tiny Retti Candle Shop (1966), with its aluminium façade, keyhole-shaped entranceway and diagonally inserted display windows, became a constructed manifesto. The 'pioneer of the postmodern' never stopped with the simple quotation of stylistic elements. Hollein's designs always contain an element of playfulness and irony; his buildings are reminiscent of theatre scenery, with the staging of paths and spatial sequences. In 1982 the latter action decluttered the concept of museum architecture which had been prevalent up to that time, with the terrace-like Abteiberg Museum in Mönchengladbach. A distant relative of his visionary 'Flugzeugträger' ('Aircraft Carrier') from the 1960s dropped anchor 30 years later in Frankfurt am Main, in the form of the wedge-shaped Museum für Moderne Kunst. Two exhibitions – at the Abteiberg and in Vienna's Museum für angewandte Kunst – were intended as birthday presents; instead, they have become memorial tributes.

Christina Gräwe

Architekten-Register der Jahrbücher
Index of architects in the annuals
1980–2014/15

Die fett gesetzten Jahresangaben verweisen auf Essays und Textbeiträge

The dates in bold refer to essays and other texts

ABBILDUNGSNACHWEISE
ILLUSTRATION CREDITS

Sämtliche hier nicht aufgeführten Abbildungen wurden uns freundlicherweise von den Architekten für die Publikation ihrer Projekte in diesem Buch zur Verfügung gestellt. Sollten unabsichtlich Referenzen nicht erfolgt sein, bitten wir um Entschuldigung und eine entsprechende Mitteilung an das DAM.

All photographs not listed here were either kindly made available to us by the architects for the publication of their projects in this book. Any omissions are entirely unintentional. We apologise to anyone not acknowledged and would request that details be addressed to DAM.

Umschlag | Cover
Florian Holzherr

Umschlaginnenseite
Inside Front Cover
Florian Holzherr

1–3 Florian Holzherr
4 Hess Talhof Kusmierz
5–9 www.pk-odessa.com/
Lanz/Schels
10, 11, 13 Florian Holzherr
16 www.pk-odessa.com/
Lanz/Schels
23 Uwe Dettmar

25, 26 links | left
Stadtarchiv Ulm
26 rechts | right **Achim Bunz**
27 links | left **Stadtarchiv Ulm**
27 rechts | right, **28 links** | left
Achim Bunz
28 rechts | right
Kunstsammlung Weishaupt/
Christoph Seeberger
29 links | left **Achim Bunz**
29 rechts | right
Yohan Zerdoun
30 links | left **Achim Bunz**
30 rechts | right **LRO**
Lederer Ragnarsdóttir Oei/
Aldinger&Wolf
31 links | left
Conné van d´Grachten
31 rechts | right **Achim Bunz**
35–39 AFF architekten
41–45 Roland Halbe
47–51 Werner Huthmacher
53–57 Fernando Alda
59–64 Stefan Müller-Naumann
67–69 links | left, **Mitte rechts** |
centre right **Tomas Riehle**
69 oben rechts | top right
Oliver Elser
71–73 © BRIGIDA GONZÁLEZ
75, 76, 77 links | left **CFH**
Photography, Frank Heinen
77 oben | top, **Mitte** | centre
Yorck Förster
79 Ferdinand Heide/
Michael Wolff
81–85 Stefan Müller-Naumann
87–93 © Christian Gahl
95–97, 99 Andrew Alberts

101 Jörg Hempel
102 links | left **Jens Kirchner**
102 rechts | right,
103 oben | top **Jörg Hempel**
103 Mitte | centre
Jens Kirchner
105 Stefan Müller Fotografie
106 links | left
Thomas Spier, apollovision
106 rechts | right, **108**
Stefan Müller Fotografie
109 links | left
Thomas Spier, apollovision
109 rechts | right
Stefan Müller Fotografie
111–115 Thomas Mayer, Neuss
117–121 © BRIGIDA
GONZÀLEZ
123–127 Jörg Hempel
129 Patricia Parinejad
130 Thomas Spier,
apollovision
131 Roland Halbe
132 Thomas Spier,
apollovision
133 Roland Halbe
135, 136 links | left
Stefan Müller Fotografie
136 rechts | right
Thomas Spier, apollovision
137 oben | top
Stefan Müller Fotografie
137 unten | below
Thomas Spier, apollovision
138 Stefan Müller Fotografie
139 Thomas Spier,
apollovision
141–145 Lisa Farkas,

Frankfurt am Main, Germany
147, 149–151 Thomas Heimann
153 Anton Grassl
154 Behnisch Architekten
155 Tom Arban
156 links | left **David Cook**
156 Mitte, rechts | centre, right
Roland Halbe
157 Stefan Behnisch
158 links | left **Christof Janzen**
158 rechts | right
Stefan Behnisch
159 © Gerber Architekten
163 David Matthiessen
164, 165 Brad Feinknopf
166 links | left
David Matthiessen
166 rechts | right, **167**
Brad Feinknopf
169, 170, 172, 173
Christian Richters
175, 177 oben | top
Erhard An-He Kinzelbach
177 unten | below **Zhou Zewo**
178, 179 Erhard An-He
Kinzelbach
181–183 Uwe Dettmar

IMPRESSUM | IMPRINT

Herausgegeben von | Edited by **Peter Cachola Schmal, Christina Gräwe und** | and **Yorck Förster**
Im Auftrag des | on behalf of **Dezernats für Kultur und Wissenschaft, Kulturamt der Stadt Frankfurt am Main**

© **Prestel Verlag, München · London · New York, 2014**
© **Deutsches Architekturmuseum, Frankfurt am Main, 2014**
© **Für die abgebildeten Werke bei den Architekten und Künstlern, ihren Erben oder Rechtsnachfolgern; Abbildungsnachweis siehe Seite 200**
For the artworks with the architects and artists, their heirs or assigns; picture credits see page 200

**Urhebernennungen stammen von den beteiligten Architekten selbst. Für die Richtigkeit dieser Angaben übernehmen
das Deutsche Architekturmuseum und der Prestel Verlag keine Gewähr.**
Names of copyright holders of the material used have been supplied by the architects themselves.
Neither the Deutsches Architekturmuseum nor Prestel Verlag shall be held responsible for any omissions or inaccuracies.

**Die Deutsche Nationalbibliothek verzeichnet diese Publikation in der deutschen Nationalbibliografie;
detaillierte Bibliografische Daten sind im Internet über http://dnb.ddb.de abrufbar.**
Deutsche Nationalbibliothek holds a record of this publication in the Deutsche Nationalbibliografie;
detailed bibliographical data can be found under: http://dnb.ddb.de

**Library of Congress Control Number is available British Library Cataloguing-in-Publication-Data:
a catalogue record for this book is available from the British Library**

**Prestel Verlag, München
in der Verlagsgruppe Random House GmbH
Neumarkter Str. 28
81673 München
Tel. +49 (0)89 41 36-0
Fax +49 (0)89 41 36-2335
www.prestel.de**

**Prestel Publishing Ltd.
14–17 Wells Street
London W1T 3PD
Tel. +44 (0)20 73 23-50 04
Fax. +44 (0)20 73 23-02 71**

**Prestel Publishing
900 Broadway, Suite 603
New York, N.Y. 10003
Tel. +1 (212) 995-27 20
Fax +1 (212) 995-27 33
www.prestel.com**

**Deutsches Architekturmuseum
Schaumainkai 43
60596 Frankfurt am Main
Tel. +49 (69) 212-38 844
Fax +49 (69) 212-36 31-86
E-Mail: info.DAM@stadt-frankfurt.de
www.dam-online.de**

Koordination und Redaktion DAM | Editorial direction and coordination DAM: **Christina Gräwe, Yorck Förster**
Projektleitung Prestel | Project Management Prestel: **Anja Besserer**
Übersetzung aus dem Deutschen | Translation from the German: **Mary Dobrian**
Lektorat | Copyediting: **Dr. Willfried Baatz (deutsch** | German), **Michael Scuffil (englisch** | English)
Für | for **alpha & bet VERLAGSSERVICE, München**
Gestaltung | Design: **LIQUID | Agentur für Gestaltung, Augsburg**
Herstellung | Production: **Andrea Cobré**
Satz | Typesetting: **LIQUID | Agentur für Gestaltung, Augsburg**
Lithografie | Lithography: **Reproline Mediateam, München**
Druck und Bindung | Printing and Binding: **Passavia, Passau**

Gedruckt in Deutschland auf chlorfrei gebleichtem Papier
Printed in Germany on acid-free paper

ISSN 1865-3545
ISBN 978-3-7913-5393-7 (Buchhandelsausgabe | Trade edition)
ISBN 978-3-7913-6557-2 (Museumsausgabe | Museum edition)

Verlagsgruppe Random House FSC® N001967
Die FSC-zertifizierten Papiere BVS und PlanoPlus liefert Papyrus.
The FSC-certified paper BVS and PlanoPlus has been supplied by Papyrus.

Ein Klassiker bekennt Farbe

LS 990 in den Les Couleurs® Le Corbusier Farben

Weltweit exklusiv bietet JUNG seinen zeitlosen Schalterklassiker LS 990 in den 63 originalen Les Couleurs® Le Corbusier Farben an. Um die beeindruckende Farbtiefe abzubilden, werden die Schalter in einem speziellen Verfahren handlackiert.

Die ganze Vielfalt erleben Sie unter: www.jung.de/les-couleurs

ALBRECHT JUNG GMBH & CO. KG | Volmestraße 1 | 58579 Schalksmühle | www.jung.de

ERCO

Ich bin Architektin.
Ich plane keine Gebäude.
Sondern Orte, an denen Menschen sich wohlfühlen.
Am Anfang eines Auftrages setze ich mich nicht in ein ruhiges Büro.
Ich setze mich in das belebteste Café am belebtesten Platz der Stadt.
Sehe die Menschen.
Höre die Geschichten.
Rieche den Duft.
Fühle das Licht.
Ich sitze da und warte, bis der Funke an meinen Tisch kommt.
Er stupst mich an und sagt „So machen wir es. Genau so."
Ich bin Architektin.
Ich plane keine Gebäude.
Sondern Orte, an denen Menschen sich wohlfühlen.

Inspiration findet den, der sie sucht.
Finden Sie Ihre Lichtlösung unter www.erco.com/inspirations

ERCO, die Lichtfabrik.

Landesarchiv NRW, Duisburg:
Baukunst trifft Griffkultur.

Das Gedächtnis des Landes Nordrhein-Westfalen hat eine neue Heimat: Die Architekten von Ortner & Ortner Baukunst haben einen alten Getreidespeicher zu Europas größtem Archivgebäude transformiert. Vergangenheit und Gegenwart treffen auf 148 Regalkilometern wie auch baulich aufeinander. Dem roten Klinkerbau aus den 1930er Jahren „entwächst" in der Höhe ein kühner Turm-Neubau und schließt sich in der Verlängerung ein wellenförmiges Gebäude mit Lesesälen, Büros und Erweiterungsflächen an. Eine fürwahr radikale Erscheinung, mit der eine klassische Griffgestaltung bestens harmoniert: Das reduzierte Design des Türdrückers FSB 1070 und der schlanke Fenstergriff FSB 1005 vermögen sich in die historische Bestandsarchitektur einzufügen und eine Brücke in die Jetztzeit zu schlagen. www.fsb.de/landesarchiv_nrw

FSB

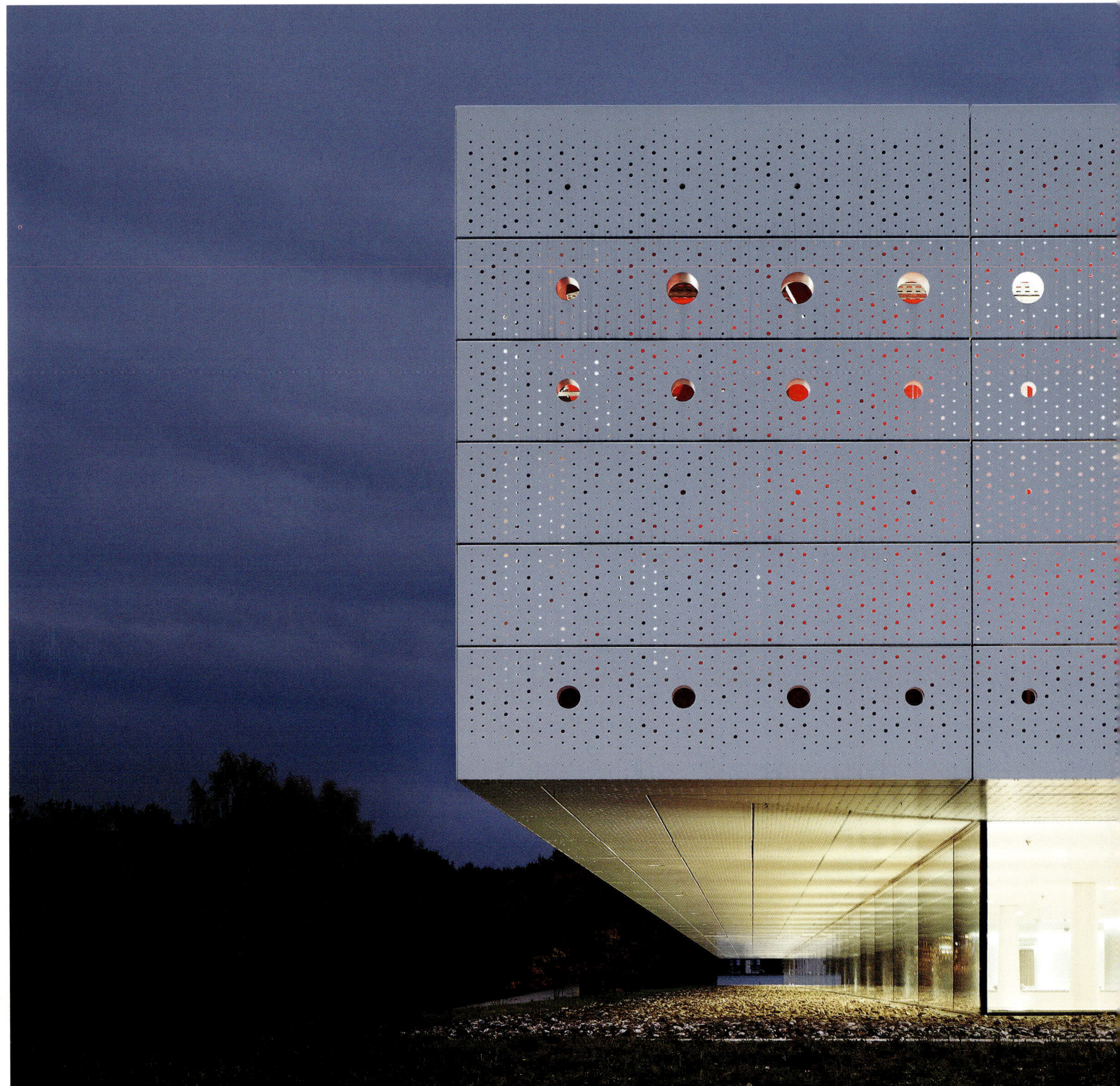

Deutsches Zentrum für Luft- und Raumfahrt, Köln/D

Your light in a world of change.

„Und so sind im Gebäude beide Arten des Lichts präsent: Das natürliche Licht, mit seinem unvorhersehbaren lebendigen Spiel, das durch die ins Dachvolumen eingeschnittenen schmalen Lichthöfe in die öffentlichen Bereiche einfällt und das künstliche Licht, das berechenbar Tages- und Nachtzeiten verändert und die Forschung der Luft- und Raumfahrtmedizin als wesentliches Element von Simulationen unterstützt."

Uta Graff
Prof. Dipl. Ing. Architektin bda

Zumtobel. Das Licht.

ZUMTOBEL

www.zumtobel.com

DIGITALE FLEXIBILITÄT FÜR
IHR GROHE SPA®
ALLURE F-DIGITAL
GROHE
SPA
grohespa.de

Wir setzen auf Premium-Objekte und Sie auf einen starken Partner.

Sie haben interessante Bestandsobjekte in hochwertigen Lagen anzubieten?
Dann sprechen Sie mit einem der führenden europäischen Investoren:

- 24,6 Mrd. Euro verwaltetes Immobilienvermögen.

- 451 Immobilien in weltweit 23 Ländern.

- Transaktionsvolumen 2013 ca. 2,8 Mrd. Euro.

Partner des Internationalen Hochhaus Preises der Stadt Frankfurt am Main.

DekaBank Deutsche Girozentrale

Finanzgruppe

VOLA Runde Kopfbrause.
Einzigartig erfrischend. Konsequent VOLA.

German
Design Award

WINNER 2014

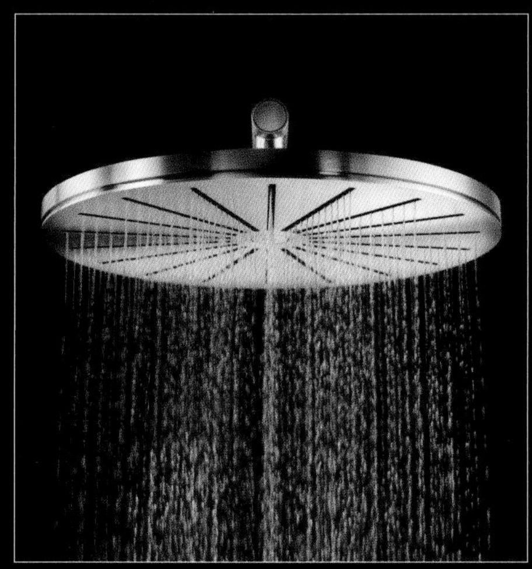

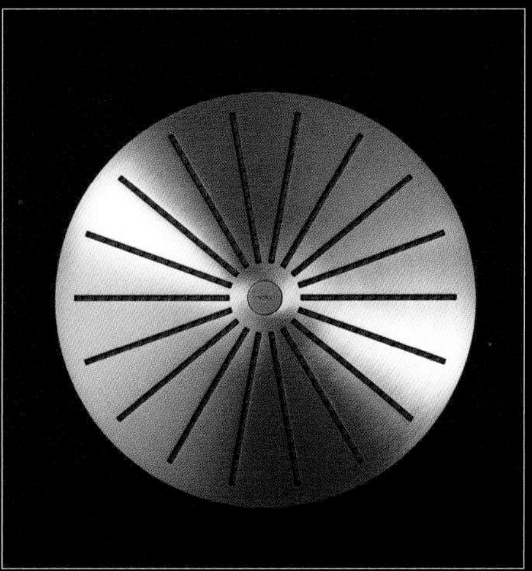

VOLA GmbH
Schwanthalerstraße 75 A
D-80336 München
Tel.: (089) 599959-0

vola@vola.de
www.vola.de

Grontmij – Ihr Partner für Hoch- und Ingenieurbau

Grontmij ist eines der größten Ingenieurbüros in Europa und gehört mit rund 700 Mitarbeitern zu den führenden Planungs- und Ingenieurgesellschaften in Deutschland.

Unsere langjährige Erfahrung mit Hoch- und Ingenieurbauwerken aller Art bildet das Fundament für die kompetente Lösung Ihrer Aufgaben u. a. in den Bereichen:

- Objekt- & Tragwerksplanung
- Nachhaltiges Bauen (DGNB, BREEAM)
- Bauphysik
- Projektsteuerung
- Bauüberwachung
- Verkehrsanlagen

Grontmij GmbH
Hanauer Landstraße 135 - 137
60314 Frankfurt am Main

T 069 95921-0
E frankfurt@grontmij.de
W www.grontmij.de

unabhängig beraten | innovativ planen | nachhaltig gestalten

Wechseln Sie doch mal die Perspektive: Das neue Miele Buch ZWIEGESPRÄCHE stellt Themen unserer Zeit einander gegenüber, zeigt Meinungspole, die inspirieren. Tauchen Sie ein in Spannungsfelder wie Konvention – Vision, Funktion – Emotion, Grenze – Weite. Und entdecken sie die beiden Designlinien unserer neuen Gerätegeneration. Projektentwickler, Architekten, Innenarchitekten und Planer können das Buch kostenlos anfordern unter architekten@miele.de www.miele-project-business.com

IHR ZUVERLÄSSIGER PARTNER FÜR DIE UMSETZUNG HOCHWERTIGER ARCHITEKTUR

GENERALPLANUNG · BAULEITUNG · BAUHANDWERK

RZB
EDO
Sicherheitsbeleuchtung
LED